One Good Word a Day is like a daily trea[sure]
look for the work God is doing in your [life through each]
day's word. As a self-proclaimed word n[erd, I was led]
through so many applicable themes at just the right time. Focusing on one word
a day is a brilliant way to remember the Scriptures provided and truly internalize
their meaning. Julie, Kendra, and Kristin have a unique gift of inviting you into
their lives and pointing back to Jesus through the relatable and refreshing words
on these pages.

LINDSAY MAY, publisher of *Truly* magazine and founder of thetrulyco.com

As though a lovely memoir, this devotional uses events and life lessons from the
authors' lives to guide and soothe like a fragrant balm to the sojourner's soul.
Julie, Kendra, and Kristin offer encouragement to take one good step a day
toward a deeper faith.

SHELLI LITTLETON, author of *A Gift Worth Keeping*

Julie, Kendra, and Kristin touch the hearts of those who, like myself, love words.
One Good Word a Day is more than a devotional. It's a sweet place to go deeper
in, examining who we are in the face of the good and the difficult days, coming
out better able to serve the world around us.

CHRISTINA SUZANN NELSON, award-winning author of *More Than We*
Remember and *If We Make It Home*

Sometimes our circumstances threaten to crowd out our walk with God. But our
daily time with him doesn't have to suffer. If you are looking for a devotional to
go to for that much-needed encouragement in your day, *One Good Word a Day*
will bring perspective and hope to whatever you are facing.

RUTH SCHWENK, co-host of Rootlike Faith podcast and author of *The Better*
Mom Devotional

With so much contending for our attention, women are longing for daily, deep,
and satisfying encounters with Jesus. We crave to be awakened deeper into who
we are and who we are called to be. *One Good Word a Day* delivers transformative,
rich, and thought-provoking invitations infusing fresh perspectives lasting
far beyond one day. The varying backgrounds of this writing trio deepen the
understanding and application of each devotion. Through richly applicable
and focused daily readings, readers will be both encouraged and challenged to
approach each day with fresh beauty and awe.

AMANDA DAVISON, founder of A Wife Like Me

My spiritual journey can feel overwhelming at times. That's why the sweet simplicity of *One Good Word a Day* was exactly what my fatigued heart needed. Each page gave me the spiritual boost I needed, one day, one biblically-infused word at a time!

AMBER LIA, coauthor of the best-selling Triggers book series and *Parenting Scripts*

This incredible resource is more than just a daily devotional. It is a miniature, digestible word study with resonant application. There is not an abundance of books that actually live up to their subtitle promise, but Julie Fisk, Kendra Roehl, and Kristin Demery have truly launched 365 invitations to encourage, deepen, and refine your faith, and you won't want to miss a single one. This is a book I'll be going back to again and again!

TIFFANY EDMONDS, managing editor of *The Joyful Life* magazine

If recent times have taught me anything, it's that the future is way too uncertain for me to choose a single word to drive an entire year. (Anyone else choose the word *gather* for 2020 and then have to backpedal in March?) Even so, I still see the value of allowing words to help me intentionally focus on the things of the Lord. This devotional offers the perfect mix of ambition and practicality. Instead of offering a single word to ring out as the anthem for our entire year, *One Good Word a Day* allows our focus words to serve as a soothing soundtrack instead. The beauty of these morning coffee-sized devotions is that they give the Holy Spirit an opportunity to whisper a just-right word at a just-right time. *Peace* when you need it. *Resolve* when you require it. And yes, even *gather* when you've missed it.

EMILY E. RYAN, author of *Guilt-Free Quiet Times: Exposing the Top Ten Myths about Your Time with God*

One Good Word a Day

One Good Word A Day

365 Invitations to Encourage, Deepen & Refine Your Faith

Julie Fisk | Kendra Roehl | Kristin Demery

TYNDALE
MOMENTUM®

The Tyndale nonfiction imprint

Visit Tyndale online at tyndale.com.

Visit Tyndale Momentum online at tyndalemomentum.com.

Visit the authors' website at theruthexperience.com.

TYNDALE, Tyndale's quill logo, *Tyndale Momentum*, and the Tyndale Momentum logo are registered trademarks of Tyndale House Ministries. Tyndale Momentum is the nonfiction imprint of Tyndale House Publishers, Carol Stream, Illinois.

One Good Word a Day: 365 Invitations to Encourage, Deepen, and Refine Your Faith

Designed by Eva Winters

Edited by Erin Gwynne

Published in association with the literary agency of Books & Such Literary Management, 52 Mission Circle, Suite 122, PMB 170, Santa Rosa, CA 95409.

For information about special discounts for bulk purchases, please contact Tyndale House Publishers at csresponse@tyndale.com, or call 1-855-277-9400.

ISBN 978-1-4964-5261-0

Printed in the United States of America

27   26   25   24   23   22   21
7   6   5   4   3   2   1

To Kendra and Kristin's aunt Delpha, whose storytelling inspired their own and whose wise words have encouraged them to share about the mercy, grace, and love of God through his people's everyday lives. And to Julie's parents for faithfully reading the stories she penned starting in elementary school, for encouraging her sense of adventure, and for showing her what it means to love God and love others.

Introduction

INVITE. Abide. Balance. Simplify. Behold. Sustain. Each January, people claim a word of the year, choosing an inspiring word that helps set a goal or intention for the coming months. Some years, we've even chosen one ourselves. But what we noticed was that—more often than not—no matter how excited we were by the word we chose at the beginning of the year, the words were eventually overlooked or perhaps even forgotten by the time June arrived. Or, sometimes, life threw us a curveball and the word we chose in January wasn't the word we needed the most in September.

As the three of us talked about our failed attempts to hang on to one word for an entire year—and our desire for God to use it to transform, shape, and grow us—we wondered if there was a way to reframe our focus on words and the powerful intention behind each one.

We asked, "What would happen if we focused on one good word—one thought-provoking, encouraging word—each day of the year?" Reframing our days with a single, powerful word can be transformational. Rather than trying to swallow and digest huge hunks of teaching or inspiration, landing on one key word each day gives the mind and heart a place to return to, rest on, consider, and often take action.

> The word of God is alive and powerful. It is sharper than the sharpest two-edged sword, cutting between soul and spirit, between joint and marrow. It exposes our innermost thoughts and desires.
> HEBREWS 4:12

This year, let's choose to be transformed by the Word of God each day. These five-minute meditations will help us focus on one word each day so we can identify and reflect on how the Word influences our lives throughout the course of that day. We can take time to consider words we'd never choose for an entire year, allowing our faith to grow deeper and wider as we step out of our comfort zones, allowing God to refine us, challenge us, and recalibrate us as we strive to live lives that reflect God, always.

Julie, Kristin, and Kendra

January

Begin

Forget all that—it is nothing compared to what I am going to do.
For I am about to do something new. See, I have already begun!
Do you not see it? I will make a pathway through the
wilderness. I will create rivers in the dry wasteland.

ISAIAH 43:18-19

HERE WE ARE at the beginning of a new year. Everything feels so hopeful and fresh. We're at the starting point where the possibilities of what could be are endless. For some of us, this is exciting, and for others it might feel overwhelming. I personally run the gamut of emotions, vacillating between excitement over the thought of something new and dread or even fear over what I might have to change.

I have a love/hate relationship with stepping outside my comfort zone. Often I'd like to just stay where I am. I sometimes need a nudge to push me to do a new thing, and a new year feels like a good time to do that. Many people love resolutions, but I've never been big on coming up with those. I get discouraged and usually quit when I inevitably break them, but I do like to have goals. Goals feel more attainable to me because I can mess up, try again, and still be in pursuit of my goal. Resolutions aren't meant to be broken, while goals can ebb and flow throughout the year.

So whether you are someone who is excited about the possibility of this new beginning or a little trepidatious, I believe that God will start with us right where we're at. God does not change, but he is always doing a new thing. Do we see it? He promises to make pathways through a wilderness and rivers in dry wasteland. These are things I'd love to have in my life. I just have to be willing enough to begin again, try something new, and set some goals.

Lord, thank you that you are always doing a new thing. Thank you that you bring things about for our good. Give us the eyes to see the new things you are doing in and through us and give us the courage to begin again with you. Amen.

-Kendra

One Good Step: Spend some time in prayer asking God what new things he'd like to do in your life this year. Then write them down.

Welcome

On the other side of the lake the crowds welcomed Jesus,
because they had been waiting for him.
LUKE 8:40

"MOM, I LIKE IT WHEN I get home and you already have the music on," my oldest daughter said, shrugging out of her backpack and jacket. She sighed deeply, then inhaled. "And it always smells good too."

A few months earlier, I'd learned about the concept of *hygge*. Pronounced "hoo-gah," it's a Danish word that roughly translates to all things cozy, a feeling of comfort that fosters contentment. As the busy whirlwind of the holidays moved into the deep chill of winter, I found myself gravitating toward things that made me feel this sense of coziness. Candlelight. Soft music. Fuzzy blankets. Chunky mugs. Even the twinkling lights leftover from holiday celebrations that still wound around our banister and lit our otherwise empty tree.

Those small changes were less about the atmosphere in my home and more about the attitude of my heart. I was grateful, and I wanted my life and home to reflect that gratitude. I wanted both to feel welcoming.

The word *welcome* is from the Old English *wilcuma*, meaning "a person whose coming is pleasing." From the beginning, the word was meant positively, expressing pleasure at a person's visit. Welcoming someone reveals our happiness at their arrival in the intimate confines of our home. It shows a level of trust in that person and comfort in their presence.

Similarly, Jesus' followers once welcomed him with gladness. As they waited for him on the opposite side of the lake, preparing for his arrival, a sense of anticipation rippled through the crowd. They were ready to welcome Jesus and the good news he bore, of salvation and mercy and healing. When we think of Jesus, do we bear the same posture the crowd did, of joyful expectation? Do we cultivate a heart that's ready for him, or one that considers our time with him an unwelcome intrusion?

I love the idea of hygge because, though the changes are external, they are meant to foster an environment of contentment and ease. Similarly, when we actively prepare our hearts for Jesus, the work we have done in advance means that our time with him is more likely to be fulfilling.

Lord, help us to welcome you into our hearts and homes with a posture of joyful expectancy. Amen.

-Kristin

One Good Step: What are three ways you can actively
welcome Jesus into your life today?

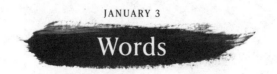

Words

The tongue can bring death or life;
those who love to talk will reap the consequences.
PROVERBS 18:21

WHEN THE MESSAGE CAME THROUGH, my immediate thought was not very kind. Instead of responding with my initial reaction, I stopped, took a deep breath, and prayed. I waited several hours and then talked to my husband, Kyle, before replying. I wanted to be wise and measured in my response.

If I'm honest, I'm someone who would love to—at times—put another person in their place, at least from the way that I see it. My love of words can sometimes get me into trouble when I allow foolish talk to leave my lips unfiltered. I've regretted words that were spoken and sought forgiveness more times than I can count.

I've seen the power the tongue has to bring death or life in relationships. I know how it can be used to tear another down, discourage or bring heartache to those around me. But on the flip side, I've also seen how our words have the potential to bring life, to speak peace, to encourage and build others up. There is power in the way that we talk and the way that we choose to use our words.

In an age where people often seem to say whatever they think and feel haphazardly, spilling reckless words onto others and often causing discord and division, we can be the ones to step in to use our words wisely. We can be the ones to use the way that we talk to bring life to situations and people around us. We can calm a situation or send it into a frenzy, all by the things we let slip from our mouths. And the result will be, for better or worse, that we will reap the consequences of the things that we say.

Lord, help me watch what I say today. Give me wisdom to know when to speak and when to remain silent. Help me to use my words to build others up, not tear them down. Amen.

-Kendra

One Good Step: Be mindful to use your words to bring life to yourself and the people around you.

JANUARY 4

Before

Do not be afraid or discouraged, for the LORD will
personally go ahead of you. He will be with you;
he will neither fail you nor abandon you.

DEUTERONOMY 31:8

AS I WALKED BRISKLY across the polished granite floor, the clickety-clack of my high heels declared my presence, exuding both confidence and purpose to anyone watching. Despite my calm and competent outward appearance, my heart beat faster than normal and my palms were clammy. I knew the importance of today's motion hearing, and I was understandably nervous. As I moved toward the large, ornately carved wooden doors leading into the courtroom, I, as was my custom, was silently praying. *Lord, go before me. May your presence be in this courtroom this morning. Give the judge divine insight and wisdom, whether she knows you or not. May I argue my client's case with excellence and integrity. But, Lord, may your perfect will be done, always. Amen.*

Pausing outside the room to straighten my shoulders, I pulled open the door and entered, ready to defend my client's position to the best of my ability but relying upon God for the outcome based on his perfect understanding of the parties and the situation at hand.

I often ask God to go before me, before loved ones, before perfect strangers who find themselves facing uncertainty or scary situations. I not only invite God into school buildings, hospital rooms, operating theaters, courtrooms, and even into conference rooms where important decisions are about to be made, but I ask him to be the advance guard—to already be present as the person I am praying for steps through the doorway.

There is something immensely comforting in knowing that God's presence is already awaiting us as we step across a threshold. When he goes before us, we are not alone, not even for a millisecond as we move from one space to another. We are not abandoned, even in our worst moments and deepest grief. His presence brings peace and comfort, no matter what we face.

Lord, go before me and those I love today. Be already present in all the places and spaces we enter today. May I perform to the best of my ability, leaving the outcome to you. Amen.

-Julie

One Good Step: As you cross thresholds, pause to ask God
to go before you, meeting you as you enter.

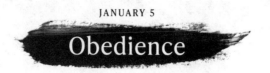

Obedience

Serve only the LORD your God
and fear him alone. Obey his commands,
listen to his voice, and cling to him.

DEUTERONOMY 13:4

MY PARENTS WERE JUST A FEW YEARS into their marriage with two small children in 1980 when they were headed home one evening. As they drove down their country dirt road, they passed a man walking. He looked rough and out of place since the nearest town was several miles away. Feeling compelled to pick him up, they stopped and offered him a ride. As they drove toward town, he told them how he had two kids, no money, and no food for the last two days. They stopped in town at the only gas station and gave the man all the money they had in their checking account, just a little over nineteen dollars, to buy food for his family.

When he asked why they'd helped him, they told him how they'd just become Christians and felt like God had asked them to stop. They left him with their information and told him about the little church community they were a part of, inviting him to join them.

What they would not know until months later was that the man and his family had once been Christians themselves. His dad had even been a pastor. But things had happened in the church his dad pastored that had wounded his family, and they had all drifted away from the Lord. My parents' obedience and sharing the little they had was the catalyst that brought the man back to God. He started bringing his family to the church my parents attended, and over time, his whole family came back into a relationship with Jesus.

We never know the impact our actions may have when we act in obedience to what God asks of us. My parents had no idea that this man's family had been deeply wounded by the church, but God knew and cared enough to want to draw him and his family back. We may not always see the result of our actions, but we can always trust that if God is asking us to do something, he will use it for good. We just have to be willing to obey.

Lord, may we listen and obey what you ask of us today. Amen.

-Kendra

One Good Step: Listen for God's voice and take the step
of obedience when he asks you to.

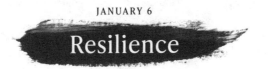

Resilience

We are pressed on every side by troubles, but we
are not crushed. We are perplexed, but not driven to despair.
We are hunted down, but never abandoned by God. We
get knocked down, but we are not destroyed.

2 CORINTHIANS 4:8-9

HUGGING MY ARMS TO MY SIDES, I shivered a bit. It was Saturday morning, and the chill of the ice rink was seeping through my not-as-warm-as-I-thought vest. On the ice, kids spun in dizzying circles or practiced tiny steps as coaches encouraged them or demonstrated skills. I watched as my oldest daughters mostly managed to stay on their feet but caught sight of my five-year-old just as she wobbled and fell down, catching herself on her elbows. Unperturbed, she clambered back to her feet, smiling widely.

Describing it to my friend Lindsay later that week, I couldn't help but marvel at the skaters' resilience. The kids—especially the littlest ones—fell and got back up countless times. An avid figure skater during our childhood, she shrugged and smiled.

"That's what they do," she explained. "That's the first thing the coaches teach the little ones: how to get back up."

As children of God, that kind of resilience should be our default too. Life will topple us at times; it may even knock the breath from our lungs. But instead of thinking badly of ourselves or telling ourselves that God can't use us, those moments can be opportunities to build our resilience muscles. Like a rubber band snapping back into place, resilience is demonstrated by elasticity. It's not a measure of how hard someone falls, but of how they are able to recover and bounce back. In our Christian walk, that flexible response should be our posture as well. Though we will fall, with God's insistently loving coaching we can bounce back to our feet again. He never gives up on us—so we shouldn't, either.

Lord, thank you that our hardships can be lessons in resilience. Help us to always look to you and rise again. Amen.

-Kristin

One Good Step: Work on resilience by listening for negative comments in your head, then replacing them with positive ones *(With God's help, I can do this, I'm a great friend, I'm good at my job).*

Safe

A troublemaker plants seeds of strife;
gossip separates the best of friends.
PROVERBS 16:28

"Hey, Julie, do you have a moment?"

"Sure, what's up?" I noted my place in the brief I was proofreading before setting it aside and cleared a small space in the piles of neatly stacked papers cluttering my desk.

As she slipped inside and closed the door, I suspected this visit was personal rather than professional. She was one of several people who felt safe slipping into my office for a quiet chat about hard things, and I'd learned that the soft snick of my closing door usually preceded tears.

On occasion I'd pray with those seeking respite in my office, but more often than not I listened sympathetically, offering my box of tissues, silently asking God for discernment when I was asked for advice, dispensing biblical wisdom without directly invoking Jesus' name.

In a workplace that loved gossip, thriving on juicy tidbits, the things shared with me in those private moments stayed private, unrepeated unless I had express permission. I was a safe person and quickly became a trusted sounding board for several coworkers.

I don't know who among my friend group first used the word *safe* as shorthand to describe a woman who does not talk about others negatively when they step out of the room, does not make gossip a habit, and does not stir up drama, but we use that label with our daughters as they learn the ins and outs of female friendship.

In a world of oversharing and overexposure, being a safe person is valuable and increasingly rare. It is a habit that can be developed and practiced, rather than an innate characteristic or personality trait. And it is a behavior that will silently speak of our faith, setting us apart culturally, inviting questions about why we choose to live differently than those around us, pointing others toward God, whether they realize it immediately or not. We admit that we are imperfectly on the journey, slipping from time to time, but the intentional focus on being safe women and safe friends has helped tremendously.

Lord, show us where we need to do better, helping us develop strong defenses around gossiping, tearing other women down, and creating unnecessary drama. May we be safe women. Amen.

-Julie

One Good Step: Pick one area—gossip, backbiting, or drama—to focus on this week, asking God to show you where you fall a little short.

Attention

Listen to me; listen, and pay close attention.

ISAIAH 28:23

WHEN I WAS A CHILD, my parents were selective about the movies and TV shows we watched, but classic musicals got a free pass. Judy Garland was born in my hometown, and her films were a favorite. My sisters and I spent hours watching *Meet Me in St. Louis, Easter Parade*, and *The Harvey Girls*. Although I saw *The Wizard of Oz* less frequently—the melting witch was terrifying—I did love the ruby red slippers Judy wore as the character of Dorothy.

One day, we heard those sparkling slippers were going to be displayed locally. I was thrilled. After paying the cost of admission and walking inside the creaky old building in the center of town, we were herded through halls filled with movie memorabilia. But there were so many visitors that we seemed to be on a time limit. By the time we got to the end, I realized I hadn't actually seen the slippers! In my haste to see everything else, I'd overlooked those glittering shoes. I was too distracted to see what mattered most, and too embarrassed to tell my mom that I'd missed them.

Life offers its own kinds of distractions. Work, family, friends, church, entertainment, hobbies—all add up to a noisy, attention-seeking buzz in our ears. It can become so distracting that it's easy to miss the voice of God. I can't help but appreciate Matthew's words to the reader. While in the midst of relating Jesus' important words to his followers about the end of the world, the author adds an astonishing sidenote: "Reader, pay attention!" (Matthew 24:15).

As Christians, how can we discern who and what we should choose to listen and pay close attention to? We can actively and intentionally listen to the Word of God by reading the Bible or utilizing an audio version. And we can weed through our calendar by following the lead of Jesus, choosing opportunities where we can love God and love others well. We don't want to miss what's most important because our calendar is too full to pay attention to the work God is calling us to. Like those ruby slippers, it's too easy to get to the end and wonder where we missed out.

Lord, give us the eyes to see the tasks and people you want us to give our attention to. Amen.

-Kristin

One Good Step: Take stock of your calendar. In what areas of your life can you reclaim space in order to refocus your attention on God?

Comfort

As a mother comforts her child, so will I comfort you;
and you will be comforted over Jerusalem.

ISAIAH 66:13, NIV

SHE COMES INTO OUR ROOM guided by the moonlight shining through our lace curtains. She finds my side of the bed, running her hand over the comforter as she walks. I hear a little whimper. Eyes still closed, I reach my hand instinctually toward her.

"What's wrong, honey?" I ask, wiping my eyes as they slowly open.

"I had another bad dream," she replies.

I pull the covers back and reach my arms out to her as she slides into the warm spot I've just vacated to make room. As I stretch the covers back up over her small body and tuck her in close to me, I whisper a prayer in her ear. Words of comfort and peace, a reminder that God is always near. She lets out a sigh as her eyes slowly close. She's safe and comforted, and she feels it.

Lately my life has felt a little crazy. Between kids being sick with the stomach flu and my teenage son being hospitalized after a snowboarding accident, I've felt stretched thin. But as I finally took the time to sit and pray, I cried out to God and realized once again my need for him. I asked myself, *Do I see him the same way my young children see me? Do I run to him for comfort? Do I believe that he is as gentle with me as I am with my kids?* Sometimes I'm not sure.

And then I read Scriptures about how God is with me, how he is my comforter, just as I often am my children's. It's a reminder that we can always go to God whenever we feel sad, lonely, or depressed. He will comfort us. Of this we can be sure.

Lord, thank you for loving and comforting each one of us. We thank you that you care about all the big and small things that fill our days. Be near to us today. Offer us comfort and encouragement, and may we take the time to receive it. Amen.

-Kendra

One Good Step: Take some time to remember that God is your comforter, bringing to him any fears or worries you have and imagining him loving you just as you love your children or family members.

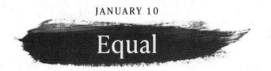

Equal

Peter replied, "I see very clearly that God
shows no favoritism. In every nation he accepts
those who fear him and do what is right."
ACTS 10:34-35

"OH, BOY. I suppose Jake is the favorite child this week." I chucked a piece of roll at my brother Jake as I laughed and ducked around the kitchen corner to avoid his return throw, Mom sputtering from the table as she simultaneously scolded me about not throwing food and about not having favorites.

As adult siblings who live in different states and see each other infrequently, when we do get together, my brothers and I can't resist rascally moments in which we act like our former twelve-year-old selves, and we tease our mom about having a momentary favorite because she has always been staunch in her unconditional love for her children, no favorites allowed.

All teasing aside, I have friends with deep hurts and tense family relationships because of favoritism. I've watched women struggle in friend groups because of the dynamics associated with favoritism. And I've watched as the church—denominations across the spectrum of Christianity—believe themselves to be *just* slightly more loved by God than all the rest, their quiet smugness about being the favorite impossible for others to miss.

I'm not talking about theological differences and whether one denomination is closer to living out what God intends than another, I'm talking about the unconditional, everlasting love of our heavenly Father and our very secret, rarely confessed assurance that he loves our particular faith community the tiniest smidgen more than the faith community down the street. I have been guilty of this particular sin, and I recognize its look and sound as I serve alongside women from different denominations.

In Acts 10, Peter went to visit Cornelius, a Gentile and a Roman soldier, at his home. Although Jewish law prohibited Peter from entering a Gentile home, God used both visions and an angel to arrange the meeting, and when Peter visited Cornelius and his family, he confessed they were just as beloved as any Jewish follower—that God has no favorites.

Lord, show me the ways I've secretly considered myself or my denomination your favorite. Forgive me for failing to see others through the love you have for them. Amen.

-Julie

One Good Step: Ask God to show you the people
you encounter through his eyes today.

Justice

Speak up for those who cannot speak for themselves;
ensure justice for those being crushed.

PROVERBS 31:8

IT WAS TWENTY YEARS AGO that I sat in one of my graduate studies classes and first heard how much human trafficking was prevalent in my home state of Minnesota. As our professor shared with us the numbers of women being trafficked, where traffickers would find victims and how many would use the interstate I drove on almost daily to transport the women from state to state, my heart sank into the pit of my stomach. There was a part of me that wanted to just stop listening, to turn away from the uncomfortable feelings it gave me, but instead I chose to sit with the pain and take it all in.

I left that day with my eyes opened but my heart heavy. I needed to process all that I had seen and heard. Sure, I knew that slavery still existed, but (and this is hard and a bit embarrassing to admit even now) I could easily put it out of my mind when I only thought of it as being somewhere else in the world. Seeing faces of women who had been rescued was shocking, waking me up to an issue I'd ignored for far too long. I determined to do something about it, raising my own awareness and looking for organizations who were already addressing the concern.

Today, my husband and I talk with our children about human trafficking, we donate, and we continue to pray for those who are affected. There is no more excuse to not be aware: my eyes have been opened, and I won't turn away.

So much of God's heart displayed throughout the Old and New Testaments centers on justice for the oppressed and the lowly. If we are to follow his lead, then the pursuit of justice—in all of its many forms—should be not just something we talk about, but act on. To do that, we need to be willing to listen, to learn from those who are being oppressed, and to take steps to come alongside those in need of justice.

Lord, thank you for having a heart bent toward justice. Give us the courage to join you. Amen.

-Kendra

One Good Step: Ponder God's heart for those in need of justice, and search for stories of oppression. Find how often God speaks of justice for the oppressed in Scripture.

Rise

Though the righteous fall seven times, they rise again.
PROVERBS 24:16, NIV

AT FIRST, my friend laughed when she saw the portrait her son had drawn. Hastily scribbled on lined notebook paper, the ink drawing featured a woman with bloodshot eyes and a snarling mouth with rows of jagged teeth inside. "You sometimes" was scrawled at the top of the page.

But as the picture continued to sit on her dresser, propped in plain sight, she found her eyes lingering on it more and more. Did her kids really think she was that angry person?

Parenting brings the highest of highs and the lowest of lows, and big feelings, hormones, and sibling spats contribute to all sorts of challenges. Privately, my friend admitted that it felt like the harder she tried, the harder she failed. That's a secret fear all parents have felt at one point or another.

God's Word doesn't promise that we won't falter. In fact, a lot of heroes of the faith failed in pretty spectacular ways. But Proverbs reminds us that even when we fall, we'll rise again. The word *rise* comes from the Old English *risan*, and it's characterized by action: "to rise, rise from sleep, get out of bed; stand up, rise to one's feet; get up from table; rise together." It's important to notice that no one is going to push us to our feet or lift us up without our cooperation—when we rise, we must make a choice to do so.

On days when we feel like we're failing, the reminder that we can rise again is a comfort we can hold on to. It's a promise that meets us, even in the face of our own imperfections. It's a hope for hard days, quiet despairs, and softly spoken prayers.

Every time I worry about how my kids will remember their childhood, I remember my own mom. She got angry every once in a while, but those moments were offset by her steady presence and quiet love. At the end of the day, that's what I believe our kids will remember. And as I messaged my friend back, still aching over the drawing, that's what I told her, too.

Tomorrow's a new day. We'll rise again.

Lord, thank you that each time we fall, you help us to rise again. Amen.

-Kristin

One Good Step: Encourage someone you know
who is struggling in an area of their life.

Beautiful

You are altogether beautiful, my darling,
beautiful in every way.
SONG OF SONGS 4:7

"HERE YOU GO, BEAUTIFUL," Aaron said as he handed me that morning's first cup of coffee.

"Have you looked at me this morning?" I muttered as I took the cup he offered. Still rumpled from sleep, I was clad in my soft-from-ten-thousand-trips-through-the-washer shirt I'd received for finishing my first 5K race. I love the memory it evokes and its worn softness despite its obnoxious kelly green color and the forty-odd local business names printed on its back. My sleep shirt may be beloved, but it does me no favors in the looks department.

"Beauty is in the eye of the beholder."

With a small snort as my response, I smiled at the man who is my very best friend, before taking a sip of coffee as I closed my eyes and breathed deeply, enjoying the few moments of early morning quiet before our household awakened.

According to our culture's standards, my cesarean scars, stretch marks, laugh lines, and extra weight that I can no longer claim is purely due to childbirth puts me outside traditional definitions of beautiful. Our society tells us that once the first blush of youthful beauty has passed, women lose value. I've watched this reality as women around me reach the age of cultural invisibility, and I stand on its cusp if I haven't crossed over that invisible divide already.

But I've also reached the age where women finally exchange man's definition for God's. I find myself—for the first time—comfortable in my own skin, appreciating my scars and wrinkles because they are visual evidence of my story—hard, miraculous, glorious moments forever etched into my skin—living reminders that this body has served me decently well while I'm away from my heavenly home.

Lord, help me redefine beauty so that it lines up with your Word rather than culture's unsustainable, impossible expectations. Amen.

-Julie

One Good Step: Spend ten minutes with pen and paper
quietly before God. Ask him to tell you what makes you beautiful
in his eyes. Tape your list on your bathroom mirror.

Declare

I have declared to them Your name,
and will declare it, that the love with which
You loved Me may be in them, and I in them.

JOHN 17:26, NKJV

WE WERE IN THE MIDDLE of Sunday dinner with new friends when the question dropped with all the subtlety of a thunderclap.

"How come we only pray when other people come over?"

Conversations died down as adults and kids alike stopped midsentence to focus on the child who had spoken up. He blinked, owl-eyed, and repeated the question.

"Well?" he prodded, looking over at his parents, unaware of their discomfort. They grimaced and laughed nervously, embarrassment apparent. As his mother turned aside to whisper quietly to him, my husband and I politely moved on to a new topic of conversation.

Later, at home, I couldn't help but reflect on the son's question. Our family prays together regularly, but there's any number of embarrassing questions my own children could ask. Which begs a larger conversation: as parents, how do we weave Jesus into the fabric of our lives—the morning routine, homework, dishes, snuggles, laughter, bedtime—so that our home carries his breath at every moment?

Jesus, speaking aloud to the Father, ended his prayer by saying that he had declared the Father's name to his disciples so that the love of God would be in Jesus, and the love of Jesus would be in his disciples (see John 17:26). There's a strength in *declaring* something to be true—the *Cambridge Dictionary* defines *declare* as "to announce something clearly, firmly, publicly, or officially." When we declare the truth of God's love and mercy to the world, it establishes the truth of our belief and reflects the love of the Father into the world. According to *Ellicott's Commentary for English Readers*, the Greek word used for *declared* is from the same root as the verb rendered "known" in John 17:25. It's hard to love something or someone you don't know.

Put that way, Jesus' prayer to the Father becomes a prayer we can pray over our own lives: that we will continue to make his name known. And that the love with which he has loved us may be in us, and in our families.

Lord, help us to declare your name and make your love known. Amen.

-Kristin

One Good Step: Brainstorm a new way
to demonstrate God's love in your household.

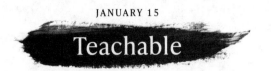

Teachable

Instruct the wise, and they will be even wiser.
Teach the righteous, and they will learn even more.
PROVERBS 9:9

MY HUSBAND AND I had been parents for more than ten years and had taken countless hours of parenting courses. As foster parents, it'd been required of us, and even after we stopped foster care, we would often buy books and attend trainings. But as one of our children entered their junior year of high school, additional concerns began to arise, and we once again found ourselves at a place of not knowing what to do.

About that same time, an email came through offering a new parenting course in our area. It seemed like the perfect fit for the challenges we were facing, so immediately we signed up. The group met weekly for several weeks, and my husband and I both listened and learned a new approach to try with our child. Even though it was going to be challenging to implement something new, we left feeling hopeful that this would help us connect with our child.

There are lessons to be learned in any season of life if we're willing to pay attention to what they might be. Even when we think we have a good understanding of something, there is always more to learn. And as much as I hate to admit it, I have often grown more and gained more wisdom during a challenging season than when everything is going along smoothly. This time was no exception.

Being teachable can be difficult at times. It is hard to remain in a space where we're willing to learn something new, listen to different perspectives, and at times shift or adjust our thinking or actions accordingly. But if the wise are willing to listen to instruction, Scripture says they'll become even wiser. I want to be someone who is wise. And if I'm going to be a person of wisdom, I have to always remain teachable. Wisdom and learning go hand in hand.

Lord, give us hearts and minds that are open and teachable. Thank you for the wisdom we can gain when we are willing to always be learners. Amen.

-Kendra

One Good Step: What is an area of life you need to gain more knowledge in? Today, take some time to learn or gain wisdom in an area you are lacking in.

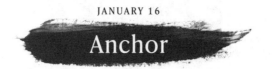

Anchor

This hope is a strong and trustworthy anchor for our souls.

HEBREWS 6:19

"WE'RE DRIFTING! Julie, drop the anchor!" Aaron's voice had that particular edge it only gets when things have gone awry and life is teetering on the edge of dangerous.

The boat wouldn't start, and the unrelenting waves were sweeping us toward the wild, uninhabited shoreline on the opposite end of the lake. I'd been trying not to panic in front of Lizzie and Jonny, but the situation felt precarious. There were no good options if we couldn't get the boat started.

As I maneuvered the anchor from its place and awkwardly pushed it overboard, I wondered whether such a small piece of metal could actually hold against such a blustery wind. It did. We gently tugged to a stop and continued bobbing on the waves, but moved no further toward the rocky shore. It gave Aaron time to problem solve, and twenty minutes later, we were puttering our way back to the dock. When the motor kicked to life and I began slowly, hand over hand pulling up the anchor, my mind turned to Hebrews 6:19 and its imagery of an anchor.

Jesus is our hope, and like that tiny anchor that held my family safe while the wind blew and the waves pounded, he is a strong and trustworthy foundation. He is steady and unchanging in a world that gives us merely the illusion of control. When that illusion is stripped away in the midst of financial woes, health issues, and strained relationships, Jesus remains, offering us a safe place to cling until we can catch our breath and the proverbial waters have calmed. He is our anchor in a chaotic and uncertain world, our certainty when nothing is certain. He is our greatest hope.

Lord, thank you for being our hope and our anchor, holding us steady and secure when we often feel like tiny boats being tossed among enormous, unrelenting waves. Amen.

-Julie

One Good Step: Memorize today's verse. Write it on a Post-it Note and place it where your eyes will see it until you can repeat it without cheating. Meditate on the idea of Jesus as your anchor during those hard moments.

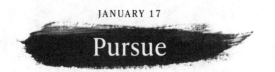

Pursue

Let us pursue what makes for peace
and for mutual upbuilding.
ROMANS 14:19, ESV

As a NEWLYWED, I loved my husband but was less than thrilled with his decor. Although a leather couch fit perfectly in our home, I was not enthusiastic about numerous artificial plants. Though we had joined our lives together, I struggled to cobble together our belongings. The most egregious item—in my opinion—was a faux marble bath set. The cup was chipped, and the soap dish had seen better days. I didn't want to hurt his feelings, but they were ugly.

At the time, Tim would leave for work on Sunday evening and return Thursday night. So on Monday mornings, I'd stash the bath set underneath the sink—out of sight, out of mind. When he returned home later in the week, he'd notice the missing set and good-humoredly replace it on the countertop. It would remain until the following Monday, when I would put it away again.

The cycle continued until I realized my not-so-subtle approach wasn't working. Moreover, the situation was symptomatic of the communication skills I lacked. When I was growing up, my parents had resolved to never fight in front of us, which was well-intentioned but had an unintentional consequence: I didn't know how to fight fair. I didn't know how to fight at all. Instead, I avoided conflict entirely, something much more problematic than a little ugly decor.

The Bible provides guidance on how to deal with conflict: to watch our tongue, be slow to anger, speak the truth in love. More importantly, it tells us to pursue peace. In doing so, we actively seek to accomplish the goal of mutual harmony. Peace doesn't mean avoiding conflict. Instead, pursuing peace asks us to lay down our smaller, individual preferences in order to prioritize the larger, mutual goal. In this way, both parties are honored. This results in a "mutual upbuilding" in which a family, a friendship, or a church body is constructed on the foundation of Christ, our cornerstone.

My husband couldn't have cared less whether we kept the bath set. He just wanted to see how long it would take me to talk to him. When I finally did, we discarded it. It's a lesson I've never forgotten.

Lord, help us to pursue peace with others, resolving conflict in healthy ways. Amen.
-Kristin

One Good Step: In what ways are you actively pursuing peace in your life? What is one thing you can do today to pursue peace for yourself?

Body

I praise you because I am fearfully and wonderfully made.
PSALM 139:14, NIV

AS A YOUNG WOMAN I worked out almost every day. I would love to tell you that I just wanted to be healthy, and that may have been partly true, but the reality was I was much more concerned about the way my body looked. I wanted to fit into a certain size and keep to a particular weight. And I would do just about anything to achieve that goal.

But the truth was that even though on the outside I looked very physically fit, on the inside, I hated my body. I didn't like the way that I looked and was constantly critiquing myself. No one knew these internal thoughts that I was having because I kept them to myself, but I berated myself over what I saw in the mirror and treated my body harshly.

It wasn't until several years had passed and I'd birthed two children that I began to see my body differently. I still continued to work out, but my thoughts and feelings toward my body began to change. Instead of caring only about my external appearance, I began to see how my body carried strength in the way that I could run, play with my kids, and do other physical activities. When my children would comment on my physique, I would tell them how I loved my body for what it could do, not what it looked like. And over time, I began to believe it. I started to talk to God about his creation, including my physical being. And I began to thank him for it. Today, I still exercise and take care of myself physically, but I'm much kinder in the way that I talk and treat my body than I ever used to be.

It is important to take care of our physical bodies, but the way we do it matters. How we talk about ourselves matters to God. In his eyes, we are fearfully and wonderfully (notice Psalm 139 doesn't say "perfectly") made. I believe he loves for us to care for ourselves the way that he does: in a way that builds us up, not tears us down.

Lord, thank you for creating our physical bodies. May we love them the way that you do. Amen.

-Kendra

One Good Step: Take one intentional step to take care of your physical body today.

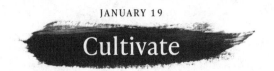

Cultivate

Remember this—a farmer who plants only a few seeds
will get a small crop. But the one who plants
generously will get a generous crop.

2 CORINTHIANS 9:6

MY CHILDHOOD HOMETOWN developed around twin lakes connected by a channel. Once a resort destination during the Roaring Twenties, its large, lakeside park draws visitors all summer long. Its large, sandy beach and swimming area marked by buoys, playground equipment, fishing pier, and a wooded hill filled with picnic tables and charcoal grill sites is the perfect setting for gatherings of family and friends.

As the public works director, my dad had his desk in the industrial shop filled with equipment, located near the rear of the park, and one of his many tasks was to make sure the park was tidy and ready for guests each morning. He and his crew rotated Saturday morning park walk-throughs, and he'd bring one of my brothers or me when it was his turn.

We loved those early Saturday mornings with Dad. We picked up the trash people neglected to put into the bins, gathered up towels and beach toys left behind for the lost and found box, all the while chattering away about whatever was important to us that particular week. We didn't often get time alone with Dad, and we reveled in it, not caring what we were doing but delighting in the time spent. We were too young to realize it, but Dad was intentionally cultivating a relationship with us those early Saturday mornings as we worked alongside one another.

Healthy relationships require the intentional investment of time. And while strong relationships can run on autopilot, being sustained for a season on the strength of past connection, they, too, need cultivation. There is no substitute for time spent doing life alongside one another, intentionally investing in growing and strengthening the bonds tying you together. Cultivating your relationships need not be glamorous, expensive, or at exotic locales. It need only be intentional, filled with listening both for what is said and what is left unsaid.

Lord, what relationships need cultivation, an intentional investment of time and energy? Bring those individuals to my mind today. Amen.

-Julie

One Good Step: Make plans to spend uninterrupted time with a family member or friend whose relationship with you needs an investment of time.

Notice

O LORD, what are human beings that you should notice them,
mere mortals that you should think about them? For they are
like a breath of air; their days are like a passing shadow.

PSALM 144:3-4

THE PARTY WAS in full swing. Our family had the highest bid on the PTA's silent auction for a classroom pizza party, and today was the big day. On one side of the cafeteria, pizza boxes were stacked high on tables while a few lay open, their cheesy smell wafting through the air. A few steps away, long tables full of squirming second and fourth graders sat waiting their turn for a slice.

As I served up hot slices of pepperoni and sausage to polite students, I saw my husband out of the corner of my eye. He was walking toward a custodian sweeping the floor on the edge of the room. As I moved closer, I heard Tim introduce himself, shake the man's hand, and offer to get him some pizza.

Dave, the staff member, seemed surprised by the offer but said yes, he'd like some. As Tim made his way back to the tables, my eight-year-old daughter asked what they had talked about. Hearing that Dave would like some pizza, she got up out of her seat to retrieve the slices and hand-deliver them.

As the event ended and Dave came over to the tables to help stack empty pizza boxes, I thanked him again. He simply smiled broadly and returned to his task.

Sometimes we assume that kindness requires lavish gestures or money, but oftentimes all it really requires is noticing. Noticing someone who isn't in the spotlight. Noticing the person working hard behind the scenes. Noticing the people in our daily life who we walk by, work with, or see in the checkout line. When we choose to notice those around us, we reflect the Father's notice of us. It is miraculous that despite the vastness of God and his creation, he takes the time to count the hairs on our heads. As God, he sees both the big picture and the minutiae of our existence, and he values it all.

Everyone wants to be seen and known. Let's not only notice others, but go out of our way to invite them in.

Lord, thank you that you notice and know us. Help us demonstrate your love to others. Amen.

-Kristin

One Good Step: Notice someone you cross paths with
and thank them for their hard work.

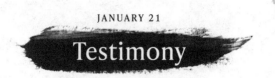

Testimony

Come and listen, all you who fear God,
and I will tell you what he did for me.

PSALM 66:16

THE HARD WOODEN PEW creaked beneath me as I wiggled to get comfortable. Our old church smelled of wood polish and musty hymnals, but it was familiar to me, even comforting. I remember the pastor asking for testimonies and watching parishioners raise their hands and then stand across the aisle to share their story. They'd sit down to nods and smiles and amens as another would chime in, offering an example of something God had done recently in their life.

My own parents love to tell the story of how often my dad would get up to share the testimony about how he came to know Jesus in a very personal way, but his heart was so tender to the experience that he would often break down in tears, unable to finish. My mother, who abhors the spotlight, would have to stand up next to him, finishing their story of how our family became believers. She smiles now as she teases my dad about those days.

I remember, as a child, how I loved those nights. I loved hearing the testimonies of what God had done. It's not that I so much remember the details, but I remember the feeling I got knowing that God was working in people's lives—in the good and the hard things that happened. It brought the things I was being taught in Sunday school, all those old Bible stories of God's faithfulness, to life in the present.

As an adult, I've come to know that there is much power in our testimonies and the telling of them. The Bible is filled with stories of people who were imperfect and weak, ill-equipped and sinful—yet God showed up to do something in their lives that they could have never accomplished on their own. Our stories are no different today. No one can argue your story. When we tell others of what God has done for us, we bear witness to his grace, mercy, and love.

Lord, give me eyes to see all that you have done in my life, the ways you have shown up in the good and hard times. Amen.

-Kendra

One Good Step: Spend time thinking about or writing down the things God has done in your life. Share your testimony with someone else.

Peace

May the Lord of peace himself give you his peace
at all times and in every situation.
2 THESSALONIANS 3:16

SITTING IN THE WAITING ROOM next to my dad, I prayed—for the millionth time—peace. Peace over racing thoughts, peace over hearts beating triple time, peace in that surgical room, peace, peace, peace in the midst of Mom's cancer.

This was our family's second time facing the big "C," and this time it was aggressive and scary, requiring surgery and chemo. This hated disease had already stolen others I loved, and as I sat next to my dad, I was reminded yet again that our lives on earth are fleeting, fragile, and precious.

Mom is the glue of our family, and my thoughts wanted desperately to spiral down the rabbit hole of what-ifs, to start contingency plans for the contingency plans for the contingency plans in case cancer stole her, too.

Don't borrow trouble; tomorrow has enough of its own. My paraphrase of Matthew 6:34 was my mantra, the words I chanted in my head to keep my thoughts from spiraling before I'd turn, once again, to prayer.

When life is uncertain and chaos reigns, oftentimes the only thing we can control is our thoughts. We have a choice: give in to the temptation to panic, allowing our thoughts to spin wildly through all the worst-case scenarios, or keep a firm reign on our inner dialogue, praying God's promise of peace over ourselves and our loved ones every time our thoughts try to spiral into panic mode.

Peace does not mean we live in denial or present a falsely positive front as we stuff emotions deep. Peace means we get off the Tilt-A-Whirl of fear and anxiety and keep getting off that Tilt-A-Whirl, even if we have to get off one hundred times an hour. It means we intentionally still our bodies and our thoughts before the one who created the universe, asking him into the midst of our crisis. He promises that he will not leave nor forsake us, and that he will give us peace, no matter what we are facing.

Lord, nudge us when our thoughts start to spiral into fear and anxiety, reminding us you've promised us peace, no matter how scary, desperate, or uncertain the situation.

-Julie

One Good Step: Develop your own peace mantra. Memorize your favorite Scripture on peace, and practice chanting it in your head when you find yourself on the Tilt-A-Whirl of fear and anxiety.

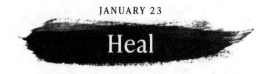

Heal

He heals the brokenhearted
and bandages their wounds.
PSALM 147:3

MY SISTER WAS SICK AGAIN. No one had said anything, but I knew it was true. I'd been studying abroad in England, touring castles and reading Jane Austen, visiting pubs for dinner and living as a carefree twentysomething—but a part of me knew that, at home, something was very wrong.

Katrina's breast cancer was first diagnosed when I was sixteen and she was twenty-two. Over the years, I'd prayed for healing as I watched her fight an on-again, off-again battle with the disease. But though I communicated with my family via letters, emails, and occasional phone calls, they said very little. The lack of information spoke volumes, and as the months passed, I felt fear and dread take root. Not knowing felt worse than knowing possibly could.

When I returned home, my fears were realized: she was sick, worse than she had been in a long time, with lengthy hospital visits that had increased in frequency. Though I knew my family had been trying to protect me and let me enjoy my adventures, inside I felt betrayed. How could I live such a carefree existence when my dear sister was suffering half a world away? How could they not have told me the truth? Though well-meaning in intention, the pain cut deep.

My family withheld the truth because they loved me and wanted to protect me, but as a young adult I interpreted their silence as a judgment on my ability to handle hard news and cope with challenges. Their secret-keeping damaged our relationship, but my allowing my secret hurt to fester didn't help. Once that hurt was laid bare, God had room to heal me. We may often think of healing in the physical sense, but healing does not always arrive as a medical miracle; oftentimes, it's in the quieter recesses of our hearts and minds that God binds our wounds and heals the hurts we've experienced. Though it's inevitable that we'll be bruised by life's unpredictability, his healing touch offers a balm to wounded hearts seeking solace.

Lord, thank you that your love offers hope and healing when we experience loss or betrayal. Help us to seek your comfort when secrets and unexpected knowledge arise. Amen.

-Kristin

One Good Step: What secret hurts are you holding close?
Ask God to heal you with his touch.

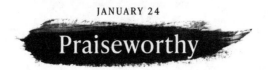

Praiseworthy

I will praise you forever for what you have done. In the presence of your
faithful people, I will put my hope in your name, for it is good.

PSALM 52:9, CSB

"I'M GLAD WE HAVE SCHOOL AGAIN, because then I know I'm going to eat every day," a
young boy simply stated during Sunday school one morning after we'd had a few
days off from school for staff training. I made eye contact with my ten-year-old son,
who immediately recognized the meaning behind this boy's words.

For the past couple of years, my family and I have been attending Sunday
morning services at our local homeless shelter just two blocks from our house. It's
been a good experience for each of us in learning to accept and love others. But
most of all, it's been teaching us what it is to be grateful for the things we have, and
to praise God for all that we have, no matter how small. Every Sunday we see kids
and adults who are homeless, looking for security, jobs, safety, food—all the things
I can easily take for granted in my daily life. It's humbling to see people who are
genuinely grateful and excited for the most basic of things that I easily dismiss on
my own list of gratefulness.

We've had a lot of conversations with our children over this time about the
value and worth each individual person carries, simply because they are made in the
image of God. We talk often about what it looks like to walk with others, without
trying to swoop in and be the hero. How grateful we are for what we have beyond
just the necessities, things like love, security, and supportive people around us—and
how God is worthy of our praise for each of these things.

What I've realized is that gratitude and praise are not something we achieve
in life and move on from. There's a constant coming back to consciously being
grateful for all that we have—in good and hard seasons. We can easily praise God
one day and curse him the next. We can be a fickle people. That is why so often
in Scripture we are reminded to praise God for who he is and all that he has done.
Praise and gratefulness go hand in hand, constantly bringing us back to the goodness of God.

*Lord, may we praise you today, remembering all you've done as we put our hope
in you for the future. Amen.*

-Kendra

One Good Step: Give God praise for something you are grateful for today.

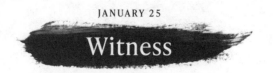

Witness

A truthful witness saves lives,
but a false witness is deceitful.

PROVERBS 14:25, NIV

KENDRA AND ELLE LED THE WAY, hand in hand, taking us toward the intersection of Chicago Avenue and 38th Street in Minneapolis. I was the caboose, making sure we didn't lose anyone. Our field trip that sunny midweek morning consisted of two moms and five kids, and my heart ached as we passed by boarded-up businesses damaged by riots three days before, barricaded streets, and homes with signs in their front yards: *We Can't Breathe.*

Drawing near to the spot where a black man, handcuffed and unresisting, had been unjustifiably killed by a white officer kneeling on his neck, the collective grief was palpable. Those present were silent and contemplative, moving around one another carefully and slowly. It was a wake, but instead of being in a funeral home, it was open air and blocks long. Murals and poetry covered the plywood on windows and the asphalt beneath our feet. The smell of flowers filled the air from hundreds of bouquets laid out and wilting beneath the sun.

We were there to feel the anger and grief, to hear the rallying of a community as citizens cleaned up streets, to see local churches buzzing with activity as people distributed donated supplies to those who needed help. We were there to bear witness.

Being a witness is a sacred task. It requires those who see, hear, smell, taste, and touch to report accurately to those who were not there. Without witnesses, justice is elusive. We are commanded to seek justice, and in order to do that, we must be willing to look unflinchingly into the face of evil and speak up, with no agenda and with nothing in it for ourselves. Police brutality is evil. Systemic racism baked into our legal system is evil. Pretending that everything is okay in this country when an entire people group, many of whom are brothers and sisters in Christ, is telling us otherwise is evil.

Lord, forgive us our obliviousness to injustice in our communities and neighborhoods. Open our eyes and ears, that we might bear witness to injustice—in any form—occurring in our vicinity. Amen.

-Julie

One Good Step: Look for injustice in your community.
Bear witness to the evil underlying the injustice—whether that involves
being physically present at a location, doing research, or something else.
Prayerfully ask God what action he would have you take.

Light

You are the light of the world—
like a city on a hilltop that cannot be hidden.
MATTHEW 5:14

MY GRANDPA HANS was a car guy. For many years, he ran the service station in town and always had beautifully maintained vehicles. In photos from that era, he can be seen smiling proudly next to an old-fashioned gas pump, wearing spotless white coveralls, ready for business.

In many ways, my grandparents were opposites. Grandma Jo was the youngest daughter of well-established farmers and left home to pursue degrees in music and Norse, graduating from college in 1939. My grandpa, on the other hand, left school after eighth grade to help provide for his siblings after his father died unexpectedly in an accident. Both of them were hardworking, but my grandpa was more practical in nature.

Despite their differences, they got along well. Both of them had a good sense of humor, and Grandpa loved to tease Grandma. One time when they were driving together in town in one of his beautiful cars, they had a small disagreement about something. But instead of overlooking it or resolving it quietly, he decided to take a different approach. As they drove down the street of their small town, he turned a spotlight in the car directly on her so that everyone could see her pouting. It was impossible to miss.

Years later, they told that story with smiles on their faces; she hadn't stayed angry for long. Imagine if we had a spotlight shone on our features: What would it reveal about us? Would we look angry, exhausted, worried? Or would we appear to be joyful, gracious, hopeful? As Christians, we are lit from within. The light is not derived from an outside source; it lives within us. Because of this, the love of Christ should radiate from us, spotlighting the grace and mercy we've received and are able to demonstrate through the example of our own lives. Like a spotlight that highlights and reveals the best and worst parts of ourselves, the light within us can't be hidden and shouldn't be overlooked.

Lord, may the light of your love shine in and through us. Help us to reflect your glory to those around us. Amen.

-Kristin

One Good Step: If a spotlight was placed on you, what would it reveal?

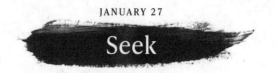

Seek

Look to the LORD and his strength;
seek his face always.
PSALM 105:4, NIV

MY FRIEND LORI recently told me of an experience she had with her four-year-old grandson at a wedding they attended. She said he was so good during the ceremony and then—just as the pastor prayed over the couple, asking that God's presence would be with them—the little boy's head popped up as he exclaimed, "Presents? I want presents!" Everyone chuckled as my friend quieted him down.

Later on she told me that God had whispered to her how that's often how we live our lives. We all want God's presents—all the blessings and good gifts he brings us—but we don't want to take the time to be in his presence. We can often hurry through our days, not taking much time to be with him.

As she relayed her story and the truth God taught her through it, I thought about how that is true in my own life. I love what God can do for me, but I often rush through my time with him or the harder things in life where he may be wanting to teach or refine me because it's easier to focus on the good stuff he can do for me.

It's easy to seek God's hand, to ask for all the things we need or want, but it's harder to seek his face. Because to seek God's face means I need to be willing to spend time in his presence. I have to be intentional to be with God, and this sometimes feels less tangible or purposeful. But when we're willing to just be with God, that is often when his character is revealed to us. That is when we see his heart for us and those around us. It's often in those moments that God begins the work to change our own hearts or grow us. Then as we live our lives, we walk through our days more confident of who God is, not just what he can do, because we've come to know him even better. Because we've sought his face.

Lord, help us to seek your face and not just your hand. Amen.

-Kendra

One Good Step: Spend time seeking God's face today
by being present with him.

Temptation

Temptation comes from our own desires, which entice us
and drag us away. These desires give birth to sinful actions.
And when sin is allowed to grow, it gives birth to death.

JAMES 1:14-15

I GET SNACKY AT NIGHT, and the siren song of salty treats lures me into the kitchen. If I give in, it takes only a couple of bad choices before I undo all the good decisions I've made the entire day with respect to food, calories, and exercise.

It's a frustrating loop because I know what I'm doing even as I do it, and I know I will regret my decision even as I reach for that bag of momentary deliciousness. *And yet I still do it.*

While midnight snacking in and of itself is not sinful, it is my giving in to temptation that I recognize as a serious problem.

I find that I'm the world's very best justifier in moments of temptation. I'll lie to myself about all of the ways in which this particular decision isn't actually *that* bad for me. Depending upon the temptation, I'll tell myself that this isn't actually *that* sinful since others are doing significantly worse things, like murdering innocent people. I'll tap-dance all around the rule, looking for loopholes and ways to techni-cally comply while still getting to do whatever it is I'm hoping to do. I'll tell myself that since God knows my heart, it's okay to do this little thing. I recognize these tactics for what they are: an enticement to give in to what I momentarily desire instead of standing firm on what I know is good for me long-term.

Temptation is a choice, and we often choose short-term delight despite long-term, negative consequences. When the temptation involves sin, the choice is between life and death—perhaps not immediate death, but it is a choice toward turning from God and toward physical and spiritual destruction. When we choose sin, our ability to resist temptation weakens, but as we choose not to sin, our resis-tance to temptation grows stronger and stronger until the desire fades away.

Lord, help me identify my sinful temptations, and grant me the strength to refuse my desires until my resistance grows strong enough to fade away. Amen.

-Julie

One Good Step: Pick something that tempts you and a corresponding
Scripture to memorize. Recite that verse when faced
with the choice toward life or toward death.

Abundance

The thief comes only to steal and kill and destroy.
I came that they may have life and have it abundantly.
JOHN 10:10, ESV

RESTLESSLY, I scrolled through websites on my phone. We'd just finished the bones of renovating the room above the garage, separating it into a bedroom for our daughter on one side and a home office on the other. But the renovations had left me with new spaces to fill, which is why I was up late looking for the perfect literary print to place in our new book nook in the office and dreaming about a desk for Elise's room. Finally deciding I should wait to purchase anything, I set my phone aside and went to bed.

I adore shopping. But it can be a challenge, sometimes, not to use it as a crutch. I've mindlessly looked at websites to escape after a long day. I've reconsidered areas of my house after noticing, with envy, someone else's gorgeous home. It's hard not to fall into the trap of looking longingly at something I don't need, even though I know it will just become one more piece of clutter.

As people who can order items to arrive on our doorstep with the click of a couple buttons, realigning our desires with God's priorities often means shifting our mindset from one of scarcity to abundance. In a scarcity mindset, we don't have enough: enough time, enough talents, enough possessions. Scrambling to grasp what we feel is missing, we fill the empty places in our hearts and homes with temporary treasures. But when we shift to truly believing the second part of Psalm 23:1—"the LORD is my shepherd; I have all that I need"—we can experience the abundant life Jesus promised. Through Christ's death and resurrection, and the new life we have because of it, we have more than enough.

Abundance comes from the word *abound*, traced to the Latin *abundare*, which means "overflow." *Abundare* is formed by *ab*, which means "from" and *undare*, which means "surge" (from *unda*, "a wave"). This word picture illustrates the depths of the abundance God has promised: not a trickle, but a deluge. The abundant life—one focused on God's plan and purpose—fills us to overflowing in a way that the material possessions of this world can never satisfy.

Lord, help us to see that—in you—we can have an abundant life. Amen.

-Kristin

One Good Step: Do you find yourself focusing on gratitude for what you have or longing for more? Does your answer reveal a scarcity mindset or an abundance mindset?

Helper

If you can help your neighbor now, don't say,
"Come back tomorrow, and then I'll help you."

PROVERBS 3:28

It was a Saturday evening, and we were seventy miles from home when the tire on the 1950 Chevy blew. *Thank you, Lord, that I insisted on following Aaron and the kids home. Please, help us figure this out.* I prayed as I watched my husband chug-a-lug his dad's car into the nearest parking lot, the already flat tire shredding to bits in the process.

My prayers turned a bit more desperate as we eyeballed the spare tire nestled in the trunk, rotted through and unusable. As we wrestled the spare off my car, only to find its lug nut alignment was incompatible, we knew we were officially out of options and in trouble.

It was as Aaron and I stood, trunks open, tools scattered, spare tires lying upon the pavement, that three people pulled up in a truck, admiring the Chevy while asking if we needed some help.

One of the men worked at a nearby salvage yard, and they spent hours getting us fixed and back on the road. Our adventure involved two trips to the salvage yard for a free-to-us tire with the right lug nut arrangement before wrestling everything into place.

As we pulled onto the highway, once again headed for home, I could not help the tears that rolled down my cheeks. Complete strangers spent their Saturday night helping us. They set aside their plans and to-do lists to meet us in our moment of need with cheerfulness and funny jokes. They did not make us feel ashamed or belittled, even when it was clear that changing tires and repairing cars was something we knew little about.

I want to be a helper like that—someone who does not delay, who comes alongside cheerfully and without condescension, someone who sees the humanity in the person being helped, who treats others with dignity and gentleness in their moment of need. That's the kind of helper God is looking to deploy into the world.

Lord, may we be compassionate in our helping, lending a hand without arrogance or superiority, coming alongside in ways that preserve dignity and humanity. Amen.

-Julie

One Good Step: Think back to times you received help or watched as others received help. What behaviors preserved dignity and humanity? What behaviors were arrogant or belittling? Take notes on how you can be a compassionate helper.

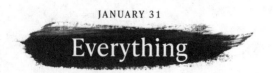

Everything

God has given each of you a gift from his great variety of spiritual gifts.
Use them well to serve one another.... Then everything you do
will bring glory to God through Jesus Christ.

1 PETER 4:10-11

I NEVER IMAGINED MYSELF throwing a birthday party for a stuffed animal. Elise is our quintessential party planner—always looking for a reason to celebrate or bake a sweet treat—and I initially resisted her plan. But by the time she hung sparkly decorations, blew up an array of starry balloons, and wrapped a present for Rainbow the stuffed poodle, I was secretly on board.

While the girls were at school, I picked up cupcakes. When they arrived home, I ordered pizza. By 5:30 p.m., the girls and I had wrapped up a birthday bash for Rainbow, complete with exuberant singing and a candle for each girl to blow out. It was more fun than I had expected.

That evening as I tucked my daughter into bed, she turned to me with a question in her eyes.

"Mom, I thought you wouldn't want to do the party for Rainbow."

Catching her expression, I told her the truth: "You're right, I wasn't really interested at first in throwing a party for Rainbow. But I'm interested in you—and the things that interest you, interest me, too."

The way her face lit up with joy was the best present I could have received that day.

As Christians, everything we do should be for the glory of God. In the Bible, we're reminded that we should always be mindful about our choices—that in welcoming strangers we may actually entertain angels, that the things we choose to spend our money and time on reveal the state of our heart, and that we should look not simply to our own interests but to those of others as well. Each of those reminders point to our role as the hands and feet of Jesus in this world. When we serve one another, we partner with Jesus in the mission of loving God and loving others. Though "everything" may feel like a tall order, we can start by making the choice to show love in small ways—even if it means throwing a party for a stuffed animal.

Lord, thank you for the freedom we have to express your love by serving one another. Give us the courage and enthusiasm to do that daily. Amen.

-Kristin

One Good Step: What simple thing can you do to let someone know that you're interested in the things that interest them?

February

Privilege

When someone has been given much, much will
be required in return; and when someone has been
entrusted with much, even more will be required.

LUKE 12:48

"I'M READY," my son, Jonny, said as I pushed play. The video showed fifty eighteen-year-olds on the starting line of a race as we heard the announcer declare, "Before we get started, I'm going to make several statements. Take two steps forward if the statement is true."

"Take two steps forward if your parents are still married."

"Take two steps forward if you attended private school."

"Take two steps forward if you never had to help your mom or dad with the bills."

"Take two steps forward if you've never wondered where your next meal would come from."

With the final question, the video switched to an overhead shot. Racers were now spread out, with some still standing on the starting line, some fifty feet ahead, and people everywhere in between. It was a sobering image.

"Those questions had nothing to do with the choices those kids made, right? They were all things beyond their control. And some of them have a huge head start," I whispered as Jonny nodded slowly, processing.

Privilege is any advantage you have because of the country or region where you were born, the era in which you were born, the body you received, the family you were born into—the list goes on. There is no shame in where you stand at the beginning of life (in this analogy, at the beginning of the race)—whether it be on the original starting line or with a head start. But today's verse reminds those of us who are somewhere ahead of the original starting line that God requires more of us.

If you have been given a head start, what are you doing about it? How are you using your advantages, your privileges to assist others and bring honor and glory to God? What eternal fruit will your earthly labor produce? These are hard, convicting questions, and I find myself falling short of the mark on a regular basis. It's never too late to reexamine faulty assumptions, make changes, and course correct.

Lord, help us to see clearly the areas in which we've received a head start and help us to be wise in stewarding that investment. Amen.

-Julie

One Good Step: Read the parable of the talents found in Matthew 25:14-30. Ask God to show you one way to use your talents and giftings for his Kingdom.

Listen

Your own ears will hear him. Right behind you
a voice will say, "This is the way you should go,"
whether to the right or to the left.

ISAIAH 30:21

"MOM, SOMETIMES I HEAR a voice in my head, but I don't know if it's God." I looked back at my six-year-old who was staring out the window as we waited to pick up books from the library.

As she noticed my gaze, she turned back to me, brow furrowed. "What if it's just me?" she asked. I slowly nodded; I've often had the same thought: *How do I know if what I'm hearing is from God and not just what I want?*

I started speaking, slowly measuring my words, wanting her to understand. I told her that we can always look at our thoughts and compare them to the Bible and the way that Jesus lived and the things that he taught us.

"But I don't know everything about Jesus," she said as she shrugged her shoulders, looking defeated. I agreed, but then went on to ask her what she knows about God and his character.

"What is something you think God would tell you to do?" I asked.

"Love other people."

"Exactly. You know that comes from God. And what if you heard a voice that told you that God didn't love you or care about you? Would you believe that was from God?"

"No!" she responded.

"Right." I said. "See, you know more about hearing God's voice than you think." She smiled back at me, a relieved look on her face as we went on to talk about how we can begin to recognize God's voice.

Even as adults we can struggle to know if we are hearing God's voice, confidently trusting that we are on the right track. The longer we follow the Lord, the easier I believe it is to know and understand his voice. And anytime we aren't sure, we can hold a thought up to Scripture to see if it rings true. God's voice is still speaking to us; our own ears will hear him. He will tell us the way we should go—all we have to do is listen.

Lord, help us to hear your voice, to listen, and to walk in the way you tell us to go. Amen.

-Kendra

One Good Step: Spend some time listening for the voice of God, and then do what he asks of you.

Fearless

God has not given us a spirit of fear,
but of power and of love and of a sound mind.
2 TIMOTHY 1:7, NKJV

I AWOKE IN THE EARLY HOURS before dawn, heart pounding wildly. As I lay counting the rapid beats, my husband snoozing beside me, I could feel my anxiety rise. Minutes passed, but still my heart raced. Trying to distract myself, I walked into the bathroom to splash water on my face and met my own troubled gaze in the mirror, wondering what to do next.

Returning to bed, I closed my eyes and began to count my breaths. Inhaling on a count of four, holding for a beat of four, exhaling for four, and sustaining no breath for four. Steadily, I visualized those counts as though tracing the outlines of a square in my mind.

As I did, I recalled the verse my father prayed over me when I had nightmares as a child: that our fear doesn't come from God. Instead, he's given us power, love, and a sound mind. Even now, the words Paul spoke to Timothy—reminding him of the rich spiritual heritage he possessed—come to mind whenever I'm afraid. As I pray those words and slow my breaths, counting evenly, peace slips over me and my heart slows enough to send me back to sleep on restless nights.

Fear can be negative or positive. When used judiciously, it can help us respond to or avoid danger, but it can also paralyze us. However, Psalm 112 notes that those who fear God are actually the most fearless because they trust that the Lord will care for them (see verses 1, 7-8). Their confidence is in him. Fearing the Lord makes us wise in that we are better able to recognize that while the world's threats are temporary, our focus is on the eternal. When we know that the power rests with God rather than in our earthly circumstances, we need not fear.

We, too, have a rich spiritual heritage, just as Timothy did. We are God's children, dearly and deeply loved. That's our identity, our hope, and our future. Today, take a moment, a breath (or four), and say a prayer to combat fear and trust God. Peace is on the other side.

Lord, thank you that our confidence rests in your power. With you, we need not fear anything. Amen.

-Kristin

One Good Step: When fears or anxieties arise, try a simple breathing exercise like the one mentioned above.

Interruption

We can make our plans, but the LORD determines our steps.
PROVERBS 16:9

I DON'T HAVE TIME for this right now, I thought as I looked at the list of things I needed to get done for the day. A friend had texted me, asking if I had time to chat, and my initial reaction was, *No, I don't.* I waited for a few minutes before I responded. I felt a nudge that I needed to talk to her, so I set my list aside and called her instead.

She spent the next hour pouring out concerns that were weighing heavy on her heart. I sat at my kitchen counter, listening and offering support. In return, she asked me about some things in my own life that had felt heavy lately, and I was able to share with her some struggles I was having in a close relationship. As we ended the call, she thanked me for taking the time to listen, and in response I thanked her as well.

I once again picked up my list, and instead of worry or dread over what needed to be done, I felt peace. I knew I had made the right choice in making time for my friend and realized afterward that I was the one in need of the break from my daily to-do list. I was the one who was comforted. I whispered a prayer of thanks to the Lord for my friend as I continued on with the plans I had started before I was interrupted.

How often do we make our plans, unwilling to allow for or complaining about interruptions that come our way? What if instead we chose to see these interruptions as possible ways that the Lord is determining our steps? What if his plan for our day is way better than what we have in mind or have planned for ourselves? God knows we have responsibilities, but he also knows what we need. We can trust that he always has our best in mind. Even when he interrupts our plans.

Lord, help me to follow your steps today and not get hung up on my own plans. Amen.

-Kendra

One Good Step: When your plans are interrupted today, look for how God may be determining your steps.

Flesh

Is not this the fast that I choose: . . . to let the oppressed go free, and to break every yoke? Is it not to share your bread with the hungry and bring the homeless poor into your house; when you see the naked, to cover him, and not to hide yourself from your own flesh?

ISAIAH 58:6-7, ESV

I THOUGHT I WAS DOING a forty-day sugar fast for improved health. After eating more than my fair share of Christmas cookies, avoiding sugar sounded good. But the morning I found myself fighting tears and searching "Bible verses when you feel like a bad mom" on my phone, I realized what I'd gotten myself into. It wasn't my child's tantrum, my less-than-patient response, or the mom guilt that ensued. No, what struck me was how, while grabbing something else from the pantry, I caught a glimpse of marshmallows and thought, *You'd feel better if you ate those.*

I wouldn't have said I'm addicted to sugar, but those forty days gave me time to consider how often I fill my mouth with food when my spirit is crying out for the Bread of Life. After the meltdown-and-marshmallow day, I had to reconsider my fast.

A passage from Isaiah illustrates the true fast God desires. Instead of a religious ritual or quick fix to better health, God wants more from us (and for us). True fasts require work: to seek justice for the oppressed, to give aid to the poor, hungry, and homeless. They require us to face uncomfortable truths in our lives. Rather than turning a blind eye, we must look—or, as Isaiah says, "not to hide yourself from your own flesh." The recognition of the frailty of our own flesh is paramount. Our flesh isn't bad, but it is weak. I wasn't fasting from sugar—I was fasting from the privilege of my own comfort. How often do I see a news story on TV about a tragedy and change the channel, or quit reading a story about abuse partway through because it feels hard and lingers? It's easier to grab our phone or dive into a novel or clothing store to escape our discomfort than to confront it.

Let's not be so quick to choose temporary satiety over the eternal wellspring Jesus offers. Though the truth of our weak flesh can be uncomfortable, with God's strength we can confront it.

Lord, help us fast in the way you desire. Nudge us to confront the parts of us we avoid. Amen.

-Kristin

One Good Step: Who or what do you turn to when life feels hard?

Allow

Don't look out only for your own interests,
but take an interest in others, too.
PHILIPPIANS 2:4

IT STARTED SMALL in our congregation. Little whispers about how loud the music was, how much one person wished we would sing more hymns, be more traditional. Then another person chimed in with their opinion that we should only use contemporary music, because that was what they liked best.

The situation escalated until some harsh words had been spoken, causing hurt feelings all the way around. Everyone became preoccupied with sharing their own personal preferences, unwilling to make allowances for the preferences of others. They wanted the worship team and pastor to choose a side. Some people left, indignant. Others stayed.

Looking back, what I am most struck by is not who was more right or wrong in the situation, but by the desire for one's personal preference to be seen as more worthy than another. There was a complete resistance to see and respond to someone else's interests. On both sides, an individual's own desires and what that person preferred became paramount, without any consideration of another's thoughts or feelings.

I would love to say that this is an unusual occurrence, but I know that it is not. I would also love to say that I have never been someone to put my own desires for what I want above another person's, but I know that isn't true as well.

Although the world may say we should look out for ourselves and our own desires first, as followers of Christ, this shouldn't be. We are asked to be counter-cultural, keeping in mind the interests of others and not just our own interests, likes, or preferences. It takes maturity and wisdom to know the difference between the things worthwhile to take a stand for, and what is worth letting go of our own personal interests for someone else's preference. We should be the first ones in a group willing to make allowances for the desires of someone else, graciously putting aside our own preferences to allow another to feel welcomed, heard, and even loved.

Lord, help me to see and consider the interests of others, graciously making allowances for another's preferences and not just my own. Amen.

-Kendra

One Good Step: Make allowances to accommodate someone else and their preferences over your own today.

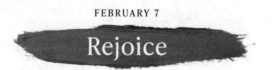

Rejoice

We can rejoice, too, when we run into problems and trials,
for we know that they help us develop endurance.
ROMANS 5:3

"WHEN YOU WAVED AT ME for the third time, I figured you might be in trouble instead of just being friendly," he called, his boat pulling near enough to ours to talk without shouting.

"Yeah, we're dead in the water. The motor made a loud popping noise, and now . . . nothing," Aaron called back, as I silently thanked God for another boat on the lake, for this man's decision to draw near, just in case, for help to arrive within minutes instead of hours.

We were first-time boat owners, and this was our first weekend on the water. Our small, circa 1993 ski boat was great for pulling the kids on a tube, when we could keep it running. It'd been a rough two days of trial and error with a touchy motor, and I was ready to sell it and be a landlubber for life.

As the Good Samaritan towed us back to shore with his ski rope, Jonny whispered, "Mom, were you praying?"

"I was. Were you?" I asked, a bit teary eyed as relief and humiliation washed over me in equal parts.

"Yes. As soon as it popped, I started praying. I knew God would help us." Jonny's utter confidence in God sending someone to our aid had me rethinking the terrible-no-good-boating-day long after we'd safely been delivered back to dry ground and the boat had gone to the repair shop.

Truth be told, I crave a life filled with predictability and comfort, for smooth sailing and an absence of hardships. But Jonny's words had me rejoicing in our boating mishap because his faith grew when he prayed and God sent someone to our rescue. It is when we have nothing left but prayer that our faith learns to endure and not give up. And we need a strong, enduring faith on this earth because we will face hard times, and we need to know that God is God, unchanging and good, no matter what we face.

Lord, help us rejoice in the face of trials and problems, knowing that you will ride to our rescue and that our faith is being developed. Amen.

-Julie

One Good Step: Make a list of the times God has rescued you (or someone you know). Recite this list to yourself the next time you face a difficult situation.

Create

The LORD merely spoke, and the heavens were created.
He breathed the word, and all the stars were born.
PSALM 33:6

WE PLAY WITH a lot of LEGOs. And by *a lot*, I mean buckets of them tipped over in the living room, primary-colored blocks scattered across the floor—which often leads to me extracting them from our shag carpet or rescuing them from our over-zealous vacuum.

Despite the way those tiny blocks hurt like crazy to step on, I like them. I enjoy the fantastical houses, vehicles, and schools my daughters create. I relish seeing them absorbed in the minutiae of finding the perfect tiny part or immersed in playing a game whose rules only they understand.

And each time I watch my daughters play with LEGOs, their enjoyment serves as a reminder of how God, the Creator, has called us to create.

God created the heavens. He breathed a word, and the stars were born. The vastness of the universe demonstrates God's power and his ingenuity. But the same God who sketched out the heavens also designed the tiny ant. And he used the same care to build planets as he did in ensuring our hearts would pump life-giving oxygen through our bodies.

God didn't just create our world and abandon it. No, he continues to create. He makes paths through the wilderness of dashed hopes and unexpected illness and financial woes, forges streams of life-giving water in the parched seasons of our lives. He is always and already at work, even when we don't recognize his plan.

Our generous God endowed us with the same impulse to create. Unless we are architects or artists, it's hard to see ourselves in the role of creator—making something out of nothing, or making something new out of what already exists. But we participate in creation when we make meals and create welcoming homes. We foster creation by digging our hands into the sun-drenched soil of a garden or revitalizing battered furniture with fresh paint.

Our lives display the masterpiece of God's glory. And the work of our hands is a reflection of his work in our lives.

Lord, thank you that you are a God of creation. Help us to recognize it in our own lives. Amen.

-Kristin

One Good Step: In what ways do you see God continuing to create in your life, neighborhood or community, or world?

Love

God showed his great love for us by sending Christ to die
for us while we were still sinners.

ROMANS 5:8

RECENTLY MY CHILDREN AND I were having family devotionals as a start to our day. Once we'd read the passage of Scripture, I shared with them a story of a person of color who was killed in our country for no other apparent reason than the color of his skin. We talked about the travesty of the situation, how a history tainted by racism and privilege has brought us to the place we are today. And in response, my kids felt passion for justice to be served against the people who had harmed this man.

We then began to speak of God's heart and love for all people. How God weeps with those who weep and how sad these kinds of crimes must make him. We talked about the men who had committed this heinous crime and how they had since been arrested and would await trial, as they justifiably should.

I then looked at my children and whispered, "But what about these men who killed another? Does God love them, too? Are they worthy of his love?"

My children stared at me blankly for a moment, taken aback by my question. They hesitated to answer, struggling to think that God's love reached these men too. And there is a part of me that cringes as well. Because although in theory it's easy to dismissively say that God loves everyone, when faced with a hard situation, the validity of that statement rolls less easily off our tongues.

Love does not mean that people should not be held responsible for their actions. They should be. We can always advocate for justice. But the fact that God's love is available to everyone is still true. He died for us while we were sinners. While we committed crimes. While we were steeped in our own evil ways. That's the great love of God for us—all of us.

Lord, thank you for your great love. Help us to see that it is available to those who we think deserve it and even those we do not. Amen.

-Kendra

One Good Step: Who is someone you find difficult to love?
Spend time today praying for that person.

Salt

You are the salt of the earth. But what good is salt
if it has lost its flavor? Can you make it salty again? It will
be thrown out and trampled underfoot as worthless.

MATTHEW 5:13

KAREN, our elementary school's music teacher, loves every child, knows every family, and is the best example of a "salty" woman (the biblical kind) I know.

When schools unexpectedly shut down for the last part of the school year, my community responded with generosity, setting up locations to pick up prepackaged meals for children who would normally eat a free breakfast and lunch at school. Karen, aware that many families in her school had difficulty getting to the collection sites, jumped into her car for several hours each afternoon to run a lunch route, dropping off more than one hundred meals at doors with a kind word and a wave, working late into the evenings to make up for the time lost during the midday.

Parents of her students confessed heartbreaking circumstances as they tearily thanked her for going out of her way to show care and compassion, for seeing them, for making sure they had healthy food.

While this is a beautiful story of going above and beyond in a time of crisis, those of us who know Karen were not the least bit surprised. Crisis or not, she remains the same. She nurtures our children with a loving, firm hand in her class and alongside her on her piano bench in ways that go beyond mere music lessons. We've been part of the troops she has rallied again and again when a need was too big for one person to meet, dropping bags of groceries, school supplies, and winter gear in her entryway.

Karen is salt, and she invites us to be salty with her. She meets needs without shaming, and she leads by example, mentoring the rest of us in how it's done with compassion and dignity. She is the best example I know of a woman who is the hands and feet of Jesus.

Lord, help us to see and respond to needs around us with compassion and dignity. May we be salty. Amen.

-Julie

One Good Step: Make it a habit to quietly meet a need each week.

But God is so rich in mercy, and he loved us so much,
that even though we were dead because of our sins,
he gave us life when he raised Christ from the dead.
EPHESIANS 2:4-5

THERE IS A PLAQUE that sits in my mother's house, easy for anyone who enters to notice. There are just two small words etched into the stone that simply reads, "But God." I asked my mother about it one day, and she smiled a little as her eyes fell on the sign. She told me those are really the only two words that need to be on her gravestone. Those are the two words that define her life.

Those words signify to her what it was like to live for years without a very clear understanding or knowledge of God, and then the shift that happened the day she surrendered to Jesus, accepting his offering of grace. She fully believes that but for God, her life would look completely different than it does today, and she shudders at the thought of what that could be. She is secure in nothing more than who he is and his sovereignty in her life. She clings to him, like no one or no thing she had known before or since. He is her everything. She knows these two words to be true to the core of her being.

And although I grew up very different from my mom (my earliest memories have everything to do with God and the church), this understanding of how much God means to my own life also resonates with me. I, too, can see where his grace has met me, where his conviction has changed my heart, where fear has been replaced by his love. But for God, my life would look nothing like it does now.

Whether we've known God our whole lives or just started a relationship with him recently, we can all appreciate his mercy and love that meet us every day. The truth is we were all dead because of our sins, but because of Jesus, we now have life. And hope. Each of us has had turning points where God changed us, and grew us, bringing us from death to life.

Lord, thank you for your mercy and love that change our lives. Amen.

-Kendra

One Good Step: Take some time today thinking about how God has changed your life, and then give him thanks that you are where you are.

With

Teach these new disciples to obey all the commands I have given you.
And be sure of this: I am with you always, even to the end of the age.

MATTHEW 28:20

THE TEXT FROM MY FRIEND ANDREA dropped, out of the blue, into my messaging app on a Tuesday morning. She told me she was thinking and praying for me that day, but then the text shifted, ending with these words: "I was also thinking about your sister, and even though I never had the chance to meet her, I have to assume she had all of your amazing qualities. I miss her with you."

Immediately, tears crept into my eyes, dropping unashamedly on my cheeks. I've known my friend for a decade, but my sister died from breast cancer a few years before we met. Even more than the sweet sentiment was the phrase *I miss her with you.*

Her phrase reminds me of how Matthew, echoing the words of the prophet Isaiah, described Jesus as Immanuel, *God with us* (see Matthew 1:23). When Isaiah mentioned Immanuel, he meant that the birth of the child would signify God's presence with the Jews in their deliverance. But Matthew, after describing the miraculous conception of Jesus in his narrative, gives it a different meaning: fully divine and fully human, Jesus is truly God with us. Immanuel makes the presence of the divine something that is direct, immediate, and personal. The word *with* moves us from sympathy to empathy, and it signals to someone, *I'm on your side. Together, we've got this.*

Jesus—who walked dusty roads with disciples, washed the dirt off their feet, healed those on the margins of society, spent time at the tables of tax collectors and in the company of fishermen, taught crowds who feasted on his message and filled their bellies with bread and fish, wept at the death of his friend Lazarus, calmed storms and loved well—our Jesus was and is a personal and immediate God who has always been and will always be *with* us. The promise was fulfilled through his life and ministry and even beyond—at the end of his ministry on earth, he told his followers that he would always be with them. Oh, what a friend we have in Jesus.

Lord, thank you for your constant presence. We are so grateful you are with us. Amen.

-Kristin

One Good Step: Send a friend a note to tell her you are "with" her.

Draft

Do not withhold good from those who deserve it
when it's in your power to help them.
PROVERBS 3:27

"DO YOU SEE HOW those geese are drafting off one another? When the leader gets tired, it moves to the end of the formation and allows another goose to take its place."

Hands shading our eyes, we watched as a flock of Canada geese flapped in V formation. Justin, goose hunter extraordinaire and beloved uncle, continued, "They fly faster together than they would as individuals because the lead goose does the hard work of breaking the wind while the others rest as they fly in its wind stream."

"That's why I run just behind other runners at cross-country," Lizzie chimed in. "It's easier to run behind them and then pass them at the very end."

"Exactly! You're drafting—allowing someone else to pull you along so you conserve energy for the end of the race." Turning to look at his audience of nieces and nephews, Justin asked, "What other ways do you draft?"

My mind wandered in a slightly different direction with a slightly different question, *Do I invite others to draft off me?*

Those questions have stayed with me, in large part because they are countercultural. I'm far more likely to hear people commenting about maintaining or erecting barriers for others rather than breaking ground, making the way forward easier for those a month or a year or a decade behind. Admission exams that everyone knows unjustly weed out high-potential candidates, draconian work requirements for the newest member on the job as they "do their time"—these and more tend to stem from the "I sweated it out, toughed it out, survived the gauntlet, so they should, too" mentality rather than any notion of drafting, of offering a helping hand.

God is the God of infinite resources, and his economy is one of generosity, not scarcity. When we are operating in God's Kingdom, someone else's gain is not at our expense. As Jesus-followers, we are called to be windbreakers, barrier smashers, and drafters for those coming a step behind us.

Lord, who might draft behind us? Whose journey can we make easier because of what we've experienced already? Help us to see and respond. Amen.

-Julie

One Good Step: Mentor someone at work, in their spiritual life, or in a new life season, helping them avoid a pitfall or quagmire you've encountered.

Changed

All of us who have had that veil removed can see and reflect the glory
of the Lord. And the Lord—who is the Spirit—makes us more and
more like him as we are changed into his glorious image.

2 CORINTHIANS 3:18

FOR THE PAST FEW YEARS, I have been writing letters to women who are incarcerated. I joined a nonprofit organization that sends out names and addresses of women all over the country who I can correspond with. Some women reply, but many do not. I've made connections with several women whom I have gotten to know quite well.

We write back and forth about everything from our extended families to the children we have, professions we've held, and hopes and dreams for the future. Many have the same struggles and joys that we all do. Several are grateful for all that God's saved them from, while others wonder how God could love them. I often send them Scriptures based on the truth of who I believe God is and what he says about them. They in turn send me prayers for my kids and encouragement for things in my own life.

I've sometimes been asked if I know what the women are in prison for, and most often I do not. Sometimes the women tell me, and other times they don't. Although it's public information, I don't go searching to find out. I care only that they know God's love for them.

One common theme that comes through our conversations is how their lives have changed since entering prison and how they hope to do and be different when they leave. They want to be changed. And that I fully understand: I want to be changed too.

Most of us will not go to prison in our lives, but we can all live with regrets over decisions we've made, relationships we wish would've turned out differently, or life circumstances we'd hoped would've had a different outcome. The good news is that no matter what we've done, God is always in the process of making us more and more like him. We are all being changed into his glorious image.

Lord, thank you for loving me and constantly being in the process of changing me into your image. Amen.

-Kendra

One Good Step: Ponder how God has changed you over the years, and thank him for the work he is continuing to do in your life.

Encourage

Encourage each other and build each other up,
just as you are already doing.
1 THESSALONIANS 5:11

IT WAS ONLY FEBRUARY, but my joyful expectation of what the new year had in store was already fizzling out. The first six weeks of the year had been full of loved ones in the hospital, sick kids, grieving friends and neighbors, accidents, and dismal weather. Driving to a women's small group, I wondered if there was a lesson I was supposed to learn in the midst of so much suffering. How could I possibly find joy in these circumstances?

Bracing against the cold, I entered the echoing foyer and greeted friends as my attention was drawn by a woman motioning from the coffee bar.

"I have something for you," Erin said, rummaging through her purse. Pulling out a gift card for a local gas station, she pushed it toward me. "I know you've been doing a lot of driving back and forth to the hospital to see your dad lately. I thought this might help."

Caught off guard, I recovered enough to smile and thank her warmly. But afterward, heading home, I found myself gripping my steering wheel as my eyes welled up with tears. It wasn't the gift—it was that someone took the time to notice I was struggling and found a way to help.

The word *encourage* comes from the Greek verb *parakaleo*. The related noun form of this word, *parakletos*, means "advocate" or "helper."

According to Strong's Concordance, *parakaleo* comes from *para* ("near") and *kaleo* ("to call"): to call near, invite, invoke. Jesus, who intercedes on our behalf with the Father, is our ultimate advocate. But we can follow his lead by encouraging others, advocating for hope and joy in the midst of challenging circumstances. There's a beautiful intimacy in inviting someone to be near when they are in distress.

Each of us face silent heartaches and discouragements. Let's be people who recognize that the small things we do are never wasted. Let's assume a hug, an out-of-the-blue text, a coffee, a gift card, or the loan of a favorite book may have repercussions far beyond what we've considered. We can be the hands and feet of Jesus in this world, and the encouragement we offer has the power to remind others that we have a God who sees and cares for each of us.

Lord, give us eyes to see and ears to hear opportunities to encourage others. Amen.

-Kristin

One Good Step: Encourage someone with a small gift or a thoughtful message.

Heritage

Let me share in the prosperity of your chosen ones.
Let me rejoice in the joy of your people; let me
praise you with those who are your heritage.

PSALM 106:5

"THIS WAS YOUR GRANDMOTHER'S favorite brooch, and I'd like you to have it." Hugging my aunt Claire tight, I whispered my thanks, trying not to get her with my wet tears as I clutched the small box with an antique brooch nestled safely inside. Not valuable by earthly standards, it is beautiful and precious to me.

My grandmother, Clara, died when I was very young, but the stories of her make me wish I could have had the opportunity to meet her as an adult so that I could sit with her in quiet conversation. She was a woman who persevered with grace, faith, and humor. She is a part of who I am, and her stories, her struggles are part of my heritage, the tangible and intangible things passed from one generation to the next.

But I am also the beneficiary of a spiritual heritage. The woman who poured out prayers over me and my young family while I sat bawling in a parking lot, giving me godly wisdom during a rough parenting phase, is a part of my spiritual heritage. The pastor of a tiny church who tucked me under her wing when I was a country girl living and attending school in a huge city for the first time is a part of my spiritual heritage. The friends who challenge me when I start to get a bit wriggly in my faith are a part of my spiritual heritage. My spiritual family has shaped me in ways as important as my bloodlines, and they are an equal part of my heritage, one that stands with me, for me, and around me. There is support, love, discipline, and accountability found in spiritual community, and it is part of our heritage.

Lord, may we recognize our spiritual heritage with a new appreciation, seeing those who have paved the way for us spiritually, who have helped us grow deeper in our relationship with you and with our outward expression of faith. Amen.

-Julie

One Good Step: How are you laying the spiritual groundwork
for those who are coming up behind you? Take one concrete step
toward building a spiritual heritage for someone else this week.

Kindness

Your kindness will reward you,
but your cruelty will destroy you.

PROVERBS 11:17

SEVERAL YEARS AGO, Kristin, Julie, and I did a year of kindness where we and our families performed one small or large act of kindness every day. At first it felt overwhelming. *What could we possibly find to do every day?* But as we got into the habit, our minds became trained to start to notice ways to be kind in the ordinary places we found ourselves. It became second nature to be kind. Our children began to see it as well and would regularly come up with ideas for some small way to show kindness to another.

That year changed us in many ways. On the surface, kindness sounds sort of weak or insignificant, but over the course of that year, we found out that kindness took much more grit and determination, much more laying down of our pride or our own desires, than we could have ever realized. Our hearts softened. We began to see God in a new way, and our love for him and his people grew. We began to listen to stories of people who were oppressed, and our own biases began to surface. But as we dealt with our own faults, God began to change us.

We certainly received a reward for our kindness, but it wasn't what we'd expected. Instead of gaining a good reputation or financial reward, we saw God shape our hearts toward things and people that mattered to him. We were faced with our own uncomfortableness and asked to leave our preconceived notions behind. It changed our lives for the better because we now see God so much better.

When God speaks of kindness, it is often in the context of how we treat other people. Our kindness will reward us. How? By softening our hearts toward God and others. Our cruelty destroys us because when we harden our hearts toward God and others, we miss out on the joy, peace, and love that only following God affords us. Kindness has a way of rewarding us by making us more like Jesus, if we'll let it.

Lord, thank you for the kindness that you extend toward me. Help me to turn and offer kindness to those around me. Amen.

-Kendra

One Good Step: Think about the kindness of God toward you, and then ask him to bring someone to mind that you can offer a small act of kindness to today.

Story

Tell your children about it in the years to come, and let your children tell
their children. Pass the story down from generation to generation.

JOEL 1:3

WHEN I WAS A CHILD, my uncle Jimmy had a larger-than-life presence. His big, booming voice was countered by his tenderness with little kids. He spent long hours working at the paper mill, then came home and worked on his farm in northern Minnesota. He raised Belgian draft horses, and I grew up loving the jingling harnesses that signaled hayrides in the summer and sleigh rides in the winter.

He also told great stories—usually ones poking gentle fun at a family member—that made us laugh. Though he died several years ago, our memories of Uncle Jimmy and the stories he told remain alive and well.

Recently, my aunt stopped into the local feed store to purchase chicken feed.

"What's your last name?" the owner asked, fingers poised to look it up on the computer.

When my aunt responded, the man paused. "I never met your husband, but he was a legend around here."

Telling me about it later, my aunt Delpha said, "That sure made me smile, thinking I was married to a legend. Jim would've gotten a smile out of that. Probably an attitude, too."

If my uncle is a legend, it's because of the man he was and the stories we tell about him. Stories matter. The stories we tell ourselves about who we are, the ones we tell our family members that turn into family lore, the stories we tell the world about what matters to us—all of those define and demonstrate what matters most.

Even more important are the stories we tell about Jesus—how he's been faithful, how we can trust him, how his love and mercy have defined the way we treat others. It's easy for people to argue a fine point about theology, but it's harder to dispute the testimony of our story: *I was lost, but now I'm found.* We are the hands and feet of Jesus in the world. We are the church—but we are also witnesses to the miraculous work of our Savior, Jesus.

Lord, thank you for the opportunity to tell the Good News of your story. Help me to faithfully pass it on. Amen.

-Kristin

One Good Step: What stories do you tell others about Jesus?
Does your depiction make him seem like someone worth following?

Confess

Confess your sins to each other and pray for each other
so that you may be healed.

JAMES 5:16

"I'M STRUGGLING," I began. "I'm not sure what to do, but we need help. I just need to tell someone else what is going on," I said as I poured out my heart on the screen. I then took a deep breath as I hit send to two close friends in an email early one morning.

My husband and I were walking through a challenging season in our marriage, and we needed prayer and accountability. We needed others who loved us to come alongside us to pray for and encourage us. And as my friends' responses came back, ones of prayer, of support, and of being completely for both of us and our marriage, I breathed a sigh of relief. I no longer felt alone. The heaviness of the situation lifted as I saw my friends now carrying my burden with me. I felt lighter than I had in a long time. It took several months, but healing began to come, and it started by allowing others into our pain.

Admitting to things in our lives that we have kept hidden can be hard. Sometimes we're afraid of being ashamed or embarrassed. Maybe we've struggled with sin for years and aren't sure how to confess it to someone else. The enemy would love nothing more than for us to keep our sins hidden, because that is where they retain control over us. Confession is much more than just admitting to someone else something we've been struggling with; confession sets us free. Confession opens the door for healing to occur. When we confess our shortcomings to one another, God uses that process to bring about healing and freedom for what we are struggling to overcome. We're no longer alone in our pain. God is there. Trusted friends are there to pray with and for us. And then our healing comes.

Lord, give me the courage to confess my sin to you and to a trusted friend. Amen.

-Kendra

One Good Step: Pray and ask God to give you wisdom to know what trusted friend you can confess your sin to, and then reach out to them, acknowledge your struggle, and ask them to pray with you.

Linger

We're in no hurry, GOD. We're content to linger in the path sign-posted with your decisions. Who you are and what you've done are all we'll ever want.

ISAIAH 26:8, MSG

"PROF, CAN WE TALK?" Those words come most often as I erase the old-fashioned chalkboard, intentionally lingering a few moments at the end of each class, giving my students the opportunity to seek me out for conversation or questions.

I teach a business law class to juniors and seniors at a nearby university, and despite how awful and boring the topic sounds, it is one of my favorite things. Our American legal system is fascinating—filled with intellectual nuance that invites wrestling with hard questions concerning justice, equity, and ethics, and my students are delightful. Their curiosity, dreams, and enthusiasm for life fills me with hope for the next generation and for the future.

While I have established office hours with the promise of a chocolate stash consisting of the "really good" stuff, it's lingering those few moments after class that invites approach. And when the conversation requires more time or a bit more privacy, I'm then able to say, "Let's walk upstairs to my office and chat." And we do. We talk about missing assignments, about that hard thing they are navigating, possibilities around future careers. As much as I love teaching, it's the lingering I love the most, the opportunity to listen to a young person's thoughts with a few probing questions from me nudging them forward.

The benefits of lingering are lost in our cultural obsession with hustling. We race from task to task, activity to activity, catching dinner and one another in frantic, fleeting moments in which we barely make eye contact. We no longer linger, allowing quiet moments to stretch, giving one another space to ponder and process. We were made to linger—before God, with our spouses, with our faith communities. Lingering is not wasted time. It is an invitation to trade mundane, day-to-day topics for real life, heart-to-heart conversations with God and with others.

Lord, may we find renewed contentment in lingering before you and with those around us. Amen.

-Julie

One Good Step: Build time into your schedule for lingering—in the mornings with Jesus, at the coffee machine at work during breaks, around the dinner table.

Do

Whatever you do or say, do it as a representative of the Lord Jesus,
giving thanks through him to God the Father.

COLOSSIANS 3:17

READING THROUGH the local message boards one day, my friend Eli noticed that a woman from church had posted an idea. As the mother of a child with medical challenges, she thought it would be great if the community hosted an Easter event her son could participate in. Because it was more difficult for her son and other children in wheelchairs to reach eggs hidden on the ground, she suggested tying balloons to the eggs so they'd be easier to pick up.

Eli didn't comment on the post. Instead, the following Sunday, he waited until he saw the family arrive at church. Then he drove to the store, purchased candy, balloons, and eggs, and assembled the items. Though it was a challenge to fit ten bobbing, multicolored helium balloons in the back of his car, he managed to squeeze them in and drive over to the family's home. Once there, he left the items on their doorstep with a card signed by church staff. The family was so touched when they arrived home.

So often as Christians, it can be difficult to know what to say. Let's go beyond words and choose to do the work of loving well. Love is quietly showing up when it matters: dropping off a hot meal for new parents, picking up groceries for a sick relative, mowing the lawn for a neighbor, sending an encouraging message to a friend. Many of our most loving actions cost very little, but the return on investment for a life well-lived is exponential.

After all, it was through the things he did that Jesus demonstrated his love for us during his earthly ministry—healing the sick, eating dinner with sinners, washing the feet of his disciples, even raising the dead. What we do matters. Though Jesus' words had impact, it was the things he did that sparked belief in the hearts of his followers. It was through his servant leadership that he offered a way for each of us to love one another with humility and care. And though our actions do not prove our love for him, they are the best proof we ourselves have of demonstrating a loving God in the face of an unbelieving world.

Lord, help us honor you in all that we do. May we demonstrate your love in each action we take. Amen.

-Kristin

One Good Step: Do something kind for someone today.

Neighborly

If you really fulfill the royal law according to the Scripture,
"You shall love your neighbor as yourself," you are doing well.

JAMES 2:8, ESV

ROGER HEARD THAT one of his neighbors had taken ill. A dairy farmer himself, he knew the precarious situation his friend was in if he couldn't take care of his herd of cattle. Two other neighbors along with Roger decided to split up the man's herd amongst their three farms and care for the animals until the man got well. It took six weeks for him to recover before Roger and the other neighbors were able to return his herd to him.

Roger told me that if they hadn't taken the neighbor's herd, he would have had to send them all to slaughter. He would have lost not only his cattle but his livelihood. When I told him that it was pretty amazing that he would do that for a neighbor, Roger just smiled and shook his head. "That's just what you do for one another," he explained.

Roger and his wife, Staci, are the epitome of what it looks like to be a good neighbor. They are the first to offer you help when you need it. You never leave their farm without taking something with you, even if it's just fresh eggs or meat from their freezer. They may not be wealthy, but they share everything they have with others.

Loving your neighbor is one of the core tenets of our faith. The only way to fully love God is to also love others. These two commands go hand in hand; you can't have one without the other. It sounds simple enough, loving your neighbor, until you reach a place where loving someone else is inconvenient, sacrificial, or just plain hard.

But to fully love others, we need to know our neighbors and see their needs. Roger was able to help his neighbor because he already had a relationship with him—so when a need arose, he was one of the first to hear. We have to first ask ourselves, *Do I even know my neighbors enough to love them?*

Lord, help me to love my neighbors as I love myself. Give me the wisdom and courage to step in, even when it's hard, and to love others well. Amen.

-Kendra

One Good Step: Be on the lookout for how you can
step in and show love to a neighbor today.

Image

God created human beings in his own image. In the image of God
he created them; male and female he created them.
GENESIS 1:27

"BUT, MOM, I've already picked out my outfit for picture day." Jonny's heaving sobs made his words barely distinguishable.

Eyeing my preschool-age son sprawled across the living room floor, an object of utter despair, I carefully weighed my strategy. "What outfit would make you feel the most handsome today, Jonny?" I asked, kneeling so I could ruffle his hair and rub his back.

In between hiccupping breaths, I heard the whispered words that made me cringe: "My pocketless pants and my sleeveless shirt."

My son wanted to wear his beloved but slightly ratty black muscle shirt and a pair of black athletic pants sporting a red racing stripe and a strange metallic shimmer.

Swallowing my objection, I told him that he could wear whatever he wanted and watched as his face lit up. He scampered upstairs and returned shortly after with a megawatt smile and an extra spring in his step.

After years of school pictures, that year's photo remains my favorite. His dapper pose juxtaposed with his 1980s miscreant look is absolute perfection. He is unabashedly Jon at Age Almost 5 wearing what delights him most, and it is obvious. I love him so much, and I love that picture because it is an authentic record of who he was at that age.

As I first gazed at that photo, I felt the Holy Spirit whisper, *That's how God feels about you.* Those words are as true for me as they are for you.

We are created in the very image of God, and we are beloved, just as we are. He sees the girl we bury beneath the polished veneer we present to the world, beneath the pretense of makeup, coordinated accessories, and the latest trendy outfit. God sees the barefaced girl who stares back at us each morning in the mirror, and he loves her. I don't know about you, but I sometimes need that gentle reminder.

Lord, meet me in this moment, reminding me of your deep love—not for what I do or can do, but simply because I am your image bearer. Amen.

-Julie

One Good Step: Write "Made in the Image of God" on several note cards and place them where you will see them.

Space

There is another serious problem I have seen under the sun.
Hoarding riches harms the saver.

ECCLESIASTES 5:13

ONE YEAR, we decided to renovate the space above our garage. It had built-in cabinets, two useful desks, exercise equipment—and a whole lot of junk. Like a scene from a reality TV episode, the room was stacked high with reams of paper, piles of clothes in the wrong size, forlorn office equipment, childhood memorabilia, boxes of photos, odds and ends, and various other things that didn't fit anywhere else. Honestly, it looked like a wasteland of forgotten items. Whenever friends would visit, I would hurriedly toss the extra stuff lying around my house into the room and close the door firmly behind me.

For many years, it remained in a perpetual cycle of cleanup and mess. When we finally decided it was time to clean up and split the space, putting up a wall and turning it into two separate rooms, I dreaded it. Overhauling the space felt overwhelming. But after hours of cleaning, countless trips to local charities and the garbage, we finally had two beautiful, usable rooms. What a relief!

Not all of us have messy spaces—at least, externally. But how often do our internal lives resemble that overcrowded room? We clutter up our hearts and minds with an overfull schedule or tasks we hope to get to "when we have time," trying desperately to feel safe or worthy by clinging to things that take up space without adding value. We box ourselves in with bad decisions and shelve regrets we don't want to face. Perhaps we leave only a small walkway for Jesus, asking him to step over our messes or ignore parts of ourselves. Unfortunately, all of those things only serve to block our way to experiencing true freedom.

The Bible cautions that hoarding harms the person who does it. I can't think of a more apt description of the harm that befalls us when we fail to let Jesus work in each and every space within our lives, bringing life and fresh air and freedom to the things we've been captive to or felt weighted down by. He longs to clear our clutter and—through him—help us experience new life.

Lord, thank you that you free us from the things that clutter up our lives. Help us trust you with the cleanup process. Amen.

-Kristin

One Good Step: Take an inventory of yourself. What areas of your life do you need to create more space in?

Unoffendable

An offended friend is harder to win back than a fortified city.
Arguments separate friends like a gate locked with bars.
PROVERBS 18:19

"I'M UNOFFENDABLE."

Even as those words crossed my lips, I was desperately wishing I could rewind three seconds and say something, *anything* else.

God has a tendency to use whatever I declare in strident, self-assured tones to refine me, and it turns out that I am quite easily offended, much to my dismay. I've repented of my offense more times than I care to admit over this past year, and because offense is something I'm actively working on, I've noticed our culture is similarly vexed with this particular vice. Outrage equals attention, and offended outrage seems to be our specialty. We pay attention to those who are the most offended and will scream it loudest on cable news, late night talk shows, and social media for all to hear. We adopt their offense and pass it on.

It's true that offended people are like a fortified city—withdrawn and impenetrable. This is no way to live. Offense taking and grudge holding are not the way of Jesus. Mercy, grace, and redemption are his themes, and there is no room for those things in the midst of offense. And, worse yet, clinging to offended unforgiveness toward others will result in our own sins not being washed clean.

How then do we live unoffendable lives? When in doubt, we assume the best of another's intentions. We remember that we are not the center of the universe and presume "it" (whatever situation you are tempted to take offense over) is not about us, unless we are specifically told otherwise. We pause to consider what else is happening in that person's circumstance that might be impacting her behavior. We practice listening to hear rather than listening to respond. And, when we are hurt, we turn to Jesus first, asking him to keep our hearts tender and compassionate rather than turning into a fortified city.

Lord, may we be women who assume the best, listen to hear, stay tender, and take our hurts to you, the Great Physician. Amen.

-Julie

One Good Step: Track the number of times you are invited to take offense on social media, by the news, or by others today. Practice taking a deep breath and saying, "No thank you, in Jesus' name" as you reject the invitation.

Delight

The LORD your God . . . will take delight in you with gladness. With his love,
he will calm all your fears. He will rejoice over you with joyful songs.

ZEPHANIAH 3:17

MY DAUGHTER WALKED into the kitchen and sat down at the center island, a defeated look on her face. She had just had dance tryouts and she was nervous. She wondered if she could have done better and was assessing all of her actions, correcting herself on things she thought she should have done differently.

I listened to her for a few minutes before I placed my hand over hers and said, "Honey, please stop. You need to know that I am so proud of you." She rolled her eyes. "I'm serious. Whether you did well or not, I could never be more proud of the person that you are than I already am. You bring me great joy." She gave me a sheepish grin as I hugged her close and told her I loved her before smothering her in kisses as she giggled.

Later that day I was thinking about how the way God must feel about us is similar to the way that I feel about my daughter. He delights in us. Just as we are. There is no need to perform or have a long list of presumed accomplishments. He values us, simply because we are human. Made in his image.

I sat down at my kitchen counter and took a moment to imagine how, just as I did with my daughter, he would cup my face in his hands, a smile on his own face, and tell me how much he loves me with a love that calms all my fears. How proud he is of me. And even rejoices over me in song. But this truth isn't just for me. This is how he feels about each one of us. God's heart is one of a delighted Father toward all of his children. Not one of us is left out or overlooked.

Lord, help us today to experience and accept your love for us. Help us to see how much you delight in us as your children. Thank you for being such a good Father. Amen.

-Kendra

One Good Step: Take time to just sit and imagine God as your loving Father. What would he say to you? What things would he be delighted by in you? What fears would his love calm?

Comfort

May our Lord Jesus Christ himself and God our Father, who loved us
and by his grace gave us eternal comfort and a wonderful hope, comfort
you and strengthen you in every good thing you do and say.

2 THESSALONIANS 2:16-17

MY SEVEN-YEAR-OLD DAUGHTER kept stealing my pillows. It didn't bother me in the evening, when unmaking my bed was something I hoped to soon do myself. No, it was in the morning when I'd feel mildly annoyed—my bed unmade, my room less than tidy.

"What's going on with the pillows?" I finally asked, exasperated.

"I don't know." She shrugged. For a few days, the pattern continued: the pillows would disappear at night, and I'd ask for them back the following morning.

One night, as I was poised to enter my daughter's room, I overheard my oldest daughter asking her sister the same question.

"I like them because they smell like Mom," she said. "And because they're next to me, I feel like she's giving me a hug."

The next week I was gone overnight. My husband texted to say my daughter had gotten a little teary and missed me. "Give her my pillows," I said. "Tell her it's me giving her a hug."

"She liked that," he responded. "She got a huge smile on her face."

In that moment, her smile matched mine.

Like the downy pillows my daughter sought, we seek comfort in a cozy blanket or a warm hug from a friend. Seeking comfort sounds like something that, while helpful, is ultimately weak. But according to *Meyer's New Testament Commentary*, our eternal comfort is not so much from our hope of heaven as it is from the "indestructible confidence" we can claim, knowing that nothing can ever separate us from God's love. Rather than being weak or ineffective, God as our Comforter provides each of us with an extra measure of strength to face any circumstance in our lives. And the comfort we receive doesn't just cushion us against life's uncertainties; it strengthens and bolsters us with the knowledge that we are loved, always and unconditionally, by our Father God.

Lord, thank you for the confidence we can have and comfort we can receive from your unconditional love. Amen.

-Kristin

One Good Step: What is one way you can comfort someone today?

Protect

There is no greater love than to lay down one's life for one's friends.

JOHN 15:13

"TELL MOM TO STOP!" I shouted to my younger brothers as all three of us scrambled through the front door, racing along the porch stretching the full length of our farmhouse. Waving our arms frantically, the fire alarm screeching in the background, we watched Mom wave back cheerfully as she drove away in our family's beige Pontiac Caprice.

With no such thing as a cell phone and about thirty minutes before Mom would return, I went back into the house on shaky legs, alarm still shrieking, to call our neighbor Gwynn. Gwynn's girls had been our babysitters for years, and Mom had already connected with Gwynn, letting her know we were staying home alone for the first time in case we needed help.

Five minutes later, Gwynn's car pulled into our farm driveway, and she got out, marching with calm determination toward the three of us huddled on the porch, clutching her giant fire extinguisher. Her presence brought an immediate peace, a sense of protection as she headed into the house to check things out. Returning three minutes later, she declared it all clear, guessing correctly that Mom's car had set off the fire alarm as she left the garage, and that she'd be staying with us until Mom came home.

We've laughed over that memory so many times. We give Mom a hard time for misinterpreting our frantic waving as an enthusiastic, first-time-by-ourselves good-bye, and recount Gwynn's march as she came to our rescue. But what I remember most is how I felt when Gwynn arrived and then stayed, setting aside whatever it was she had been doing. I'm certain she could see that our confidence had been shaken, and what had initially seemed like a grand adventure in staying home alone was now, in this moment, terrifying. And so she stayed, protecting us from the fear of being home alone.

We are the hands and feet of Jesus, and he deploys us on rescue missions. Sometimes we protect physically, but more frequently we protect emotionally, inviting others to belong, to draw comfort and peace in a space carved out just for them without fear or rejection or diminishing their concerns with clichés or pat answers.

Heavenly Father, may we be women who protect those around us physically and emotionally. Amen.

-Julie

One Good Step: Ask God who around you needs protecting today. Reach out.

March

Fill

He satisfies the thirsty and fills the hungry with good things.
PSALM 107:9

THE MESSAGE WAS SHORT AND SWEET: "Let me fill your cup this Saturday! Message me your address, put your cup on your front step, and I'll come by and fill it up with Dunn Brothers coffee! You mamas are all amazing and deserve a cup of good coffee."

It had been a tough couple of months, and the small MOPS community I was a part of had been unable to see one another. So when my friend Erin snapped a photo of her own coffee mug on the porch and offered to make the trip to homes around the area to do the same for others, her idea was met with excitement.

When Saturday arrived, she spent more than two hours driving from one house to the next. Some simply waved. Others left thank-you notes or small gifts next to their mugs. One woman opened her door for a heartfelt conversation. Across porches and on front steps, Erin faithfully filled each mug. As the morning wore on, she found her own joy increase, knowing she was able to bring hope to others in a hard season.

Psalm 107 describes weary travelers longing for their hunger and thirst to be satisfied. God responds with an abundance of "good things" (verse 9). As travelers in this world ourselves, we don't receive a miserly few drops of water or a small slice of bread from our faithful God. Instead, this outpouring is akin to a cup full to overflowing, a banquet in our honor.

The physical filling is important, but our spiritual filling is even more so. As one translation frames it, "He satisfies the longing soul, and the hungry soul he fills with good things." (Psalm 107:9, ESV). Our longing soul hungers for the presence of God. We thirst for the living water Jesus later tells a Samaritan woman only he can provide, a spring of water that will never run out or dry up (see John 4:7-15).

Yet Jesus invites us to not just witness his goodness, but to participate. In the upside-down nature of God's Kingdom, the last are first, the humbled are lifted up, the poured out become filled. And the physical act of filling someone else's cup often results in the spiritual nourishment of our own soul. When we refresh others, we're refreshed ourselves.

Lord, help us notice the longing of our souls. Fill us with your presence. Amen.

-Kristin

One Good Step: Fill someone's mug by dropping off a drink, inviting them over for coffee, or sending a small gift card.

Place

If you keep quiet at a time like this, deliverance and relief for the Jews will arise from some other place, but you and your relatives will die. Who knows if perhaps you were made queen for just such a time as this?

ESTHER 4:14

"LORD, WHAT WOULD YOU HAVE ME DO?" Trish prayed. "Who am I here for? Help me to see people as you see them. Help me to bring salt and light to a hard place."

When my friend accepted the offer to be a long-term substitute teacher, she thought God was sending her to a classroom of children, and he was. But she soon realized that he was also sending her to her colleagues—a collection of delightful individuals who had trouble functioning as a cohesive second-grade team because of mistrust and deep hurts.

She found herself in the strange role of temporary insider, an objective third party who was part of the team and yet, not. She knew she couldn't fix the relational dysfunction developed over years of misunderstandings and power struggles, but she also knew that God deploys us into workplaces and onto youth sports sidelines, into neighborhoods and onto community committees to intersect lives. And so she did what she does whenever she enters a new place—she prayed God would reveal who he was sending her to.

Trish was intentional in relationship building. She gently deflected conversations inviting gossip and quietly offered (often uncited) biblical wisdom when asked for advice. By the time her temporary contract had ended, Trish had become a mentor to two younger women, helping them navigate situations around marriage, parenthood, work, and faith.

Esther did not seek a spot in the king's court, but once there, she recognized that her placement was not accidental. She was positioned in that place, in that time, to accomplish God's will—saving his people from genocide by thwarting Haman's plans. In response, she prayed, fasted, and then obeyed God. Just like Esther, followers of Jesus are God's emissaries. Our placement in communities, neighborhoods, school districts, workplaces, youth softball field sidelines, and volunteer positions is not a surprise to God. And, if we listen, he will use us in those spaces to accomplish his will.

Lord, help us to see our coworkers, neighbors, PTA parents, and others who surround us through your eyes, and give us a heartbeat for the hurting.

-Julie

One Good Step: Fast (a meal, sugar, social media) this week, asking God to show you who he is sending you to in the places you already inhabit.

True

Fix your thoughts on what is true, and honorable, and right,
and pure, and lovely, and admirable.

PHILIPPIANS 4:8

"I FEEL LIKE nothing ever goes right." The text came in on my phone late one night. One of my five children was having a hard time.

"What do you mean?" I asked, looking for more information.

She went on to explain a current problem she was facing that had suddenly come up without warning. I listened, offered comfort for what she was facing, and then tried to rebut her claim. I reminded her of all the good that was happening in her life at the time—how she had just completed a college course and gotten an A, how she had a good job that she enjoyed, and how many people she had around her who loved her. Even with the reminder, I knew it was still hard for her to believe it, so I ended by telling her I'd be praying for her.

That night, my daughter was struggling to take her thoughts and feelings captive to what was true (see 2 Corinthians 10:5). All of us, at times, can allow our thoughts and then feelings to lead us to a place where nothing seems right. And although it can be good and even healthy to pay attention to our feelings, they are not always an indicator of what is true.

As Christians, we are encouraged to fix our thoughts on what is true. Scripture doesn't say to focus on what makes us happy or what only feels good. Because sometimes even what is true is a hard thing. As followers of Jesus, we don't avoid reality—just as we don't avoid our feelings—but we can always put it in the perspective of what is true and right and pure. One way we can do this is by turning our worries, our fears, and our doubts over to God, praising him for what is true and clinging to him no matter what our circumstances may be.

Lord, help me today to take all my worries, fears, and doubts to you in prayer and focus on what is true. Amen.

-Kendra

One Good Step: Today if your thoughts and feelings begin to spiral negatively out of control, stop, pray, and ask God to help you focus on what is true.

Feast

The LORD of Heaven's Armies will spread a wonderful feast
for all the people of the world.

ISAIAH 25:6

"HOW CAN I HELP?" I asked Amna, drying my hands on a dish towel. She smiled and paused from making dolma to hand me a jar, demonstrating how to carefully extract the grape leaves and rinse them to remove acidity. As we spooned a rice-and-meat mixture onto the rinsed leaves, her daughters flitted through the kitchen before rushing back to play with friends.

A few months earlier, my friend Samantha had the idea to create a multicultural community cookbook. She and her husband, Andrew, worked with the community's refugee and immigrant population, and they planned to sell the cookbooks as a charitable endeavor. After some initial planning, Sam had invited a group of ladies to her home for a feast in order to try out the recipes.

The main floor was a flurry of activity, and conversations hummed as spices from around the world wafted through the air. Delicious dishes lay spread across the kitchen island, waiting to be sampled as women from Somalia, China, Iraq, Mexico, and the United States mingled with one another.

For that night's gathering, we worked together to create a few dishes while others had been prepared in advance. And while we feasted on pozole rojo, eggplant kofta, sambusa, and klecha cookies, we discussed recipes and children, husbands and jobs. Even though the experiences and recipes of each woman were unique, the variety was what made the evening so memorable.

The diversity this world has to offer is what makes life a beautiful feast. After all, Jesus is the Bread of Life, and the physical representation of hunger and satisfaction that bread represents is mirrored in the spiritual hunger and satisfaction that can be found in him. Valuing the vast experience this life offers is akin to being seated at a perpetual banquet of ever-changing flavors, and recognizing the beauty that can be found through our diverse world leads to joy and satisfaction.

Lord, help us to see the diversity of this world as a feast to be celebrated. Amen.

-Kristin

One Good Step: Make or order something to eat that you've never tried before.

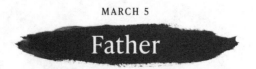

Father

Whatever is good and perfect is a gift coming down to us
from God our Father, who created all the lights in the heavens.
He never changes or casts a shifting shadow.

JAMES 1:17

WHILE I WAS READING in my Bible one morning, it struck me how often God refers to himself as our Father. As a therapist, I've met many people over the years with complicated family histories. Some clients had wonderful earthly fathers, but many had awful, even abusive fathers. Oftentimes I found that a person's view of God was based, at least in part, on the perception they had of their earthly father. Many who had a hard time with their earthly father would also see their heavenly Father as mean and unapproachable, someone to be feared. But those who had a good relationship with their father saw God as loving and kind.

I began to see how important our earthly family relationships are in the views that we have of God. For those clients who had a difficult childhood and now a healthy view of God as their Father, I noticed they most often had done a lot of work to proactively see God for who he really is, as a loving Father. Through these interactions, I realized that it's possible for us, no matter what kind of earthly father we had, to see God as the kind and loving Father he wants to be to all of us.

The truth is we can believe that God is a loving Father because we know that he does not change. His character stays the same. And this is such good news no matter what our early memories or experiences have been, because we can trust that God is good. That he is loving and kind. That he offers us good gifts, always.

Lord, thank you that you do not change and for being such a good Father to us. Help us to cling to what we know is true about you and your character and to release anything that does not line up with who we know you to be. Amen.

-Kendra

One Good Step: Think about what kind of early family relationships shaped your view of God, and then spend time today in prayer, either thanking him for those examples, or asking God to show you who he is as your Father who loves you.

Hide

Even in darkness I cannot hide from you. To you the night shines as bright as day.
Darkness and light are the same to you.

PSALM 139:12

IT WAS SOMETIME IN FIFTH GRADE that my daughter stopped wearing color. I found her formerly beloved sequined, rainbow-hued Unikitty shirts shoved into the recesses of her drawer, the few plain T-shirts I had for her on continuous rotation.

When I gently broached the subject on her wardrobe shift and her penchant for grays, dark blues, and blacks, her words struck me—"Mom, I want to blend in, not stick out."

Mom friends of similarly aged girls confirmed the experience. Our girls, in different schools, different states, and from a variety of backgrounds, were choosing clothes designed to hide after spending years in childhood wardrobes designed to loudly proclaim their presence.

As I told a girlfriend about Lizzie's wardrobe shift, her thoughtful response was that her own love for dark, muted colors was likely a similar attempt at hiding. We both paused at that confession, allowing her words to hang in the air for several heartbeats. Her words have stayed with me. Starting somewhere around middle school, we start to hide the truest version of ourselves. Dark clothes, makeup and a perfectly coiffed appearance, a jokey, fun-loving demeanor, a competent, take-charge attitude—all of it is clever camouflage meant to protect the core of who we are.

But we can't hide from God. He sees the vulnerable girl who stares back at us in the mirror, freshly scrubbed and clean, devoid of layers and pretense. And he loves her. He is not distracted by our attempts at camouflage, and he sees past our attempts at deflection. With him, we get to be the young girl who proudly wears every color and every pattern, all at once. We are invited to be the truest, rawest, most honest version of ourselves. Instead of hiding, we are invited to lay our broken, most vulnerable pieces before him, and he will heal us, welcoming us into his Kingdom, his family, his arms.

Lord, we cannot hide from you, for you see everything, with no regard for day or night. Help us practice bringing our broken pieces to you instead of trying to hide them away. Amen.

-Julie

One Good Step: How do you hide? Start watching for behavior patterns
when you feel insecure and uncertain, taking those insecurities
to God in prayer instead of continuing to hide.

Vulnerable

Each time he said, "My grace is all you need. My power works best in weakness." So now I am glad to boast about my weaknesses, so that the power of Christ can work through me.

2 CORINTHIANS 12:9

IT WAS AFTER A LONG DAY that a new group of friends and I sat down to dinner. As we ordered our food and the discussion turned to our families, our conversation circled around my sister who had passed away from cancer several years earlier. I looked around for a moment at my friends who were waiting for my response to their question of what those years had been like.

Like many other times before, I was at a crossroads. I could offer them surface answers about that time, or I could go deeper, sharing more of the hard moments that very few people actually knew about. I decided this was a time to be vulnerable, and with a little sigh I began to share with them how hard that season was in my life. They listened intently, nodding in understanding and wiping their eyes as tears left unchecked fell from my own. I felt heard and seen and was so glad that I had taken the time to share honestly.

As I finished, the women around the table were silent for a few moments before another friend began to tell us about her brother and his death. Again, our little group listened, asked questions, and shed tears together. I left that evening feeling glad that I had opened up to my new friends and not just dismissed their questions with surface answers.

Sometimes it's scary to be vulnerable with others. We can worry whether we'll be accepted or judged by our honesty. So often our choosing to go first tells others that it's safe for them to be vulnerable too. God and his power are seen more fully when we are vulnerable, because it's no longer about us, but what Christ can do in and through us.

Lord, thank you for your grace that works in and through us. Thank you that we do not have to pretend to be strong and that your power works best in our weaknesses. Amen.

-Kendra

One Good Step: Take the lead in sharing vulnerably with someone today.

Life

Turn my eyes from worthless things,
and give me life through your word.

PSALM 119:37

"WHO NEEDS TO BE LOGGED IN?" I called, looking for the Zoom link code buried in the text thread. It was a mad-dash scramble as Aaron and I logged three separate devices into the Zoom call, and the kids scampered off to their respective rooms with a device in hand.

"Good morning, Family!" Aaron's sister Amy called out as Jonny and Lizzie each entered the virtual meeting, with Aaron and I joining a few moments later from the kitchen. Aaron's mom, Connie, was already there, as were our nieces and Chad, Amy's husband.

"I've got a new game to try this week, and Aunt Marigrace sent Grandma Connie another joke to tell," Amy said.

It was Sunday morning, and we were experimenting with a new way to gather when schedules and activities make trips to see one another in person difficult. Amy suggested a Sunday morning family Zoom call a few weeks back, and it had become an easy, fun way to gather. We played games, told jokes, and enjoyed seeing one another's faces more frequently than we would if driving was required.

We live just far enough apart to require intentional effort to gather in person, and with four cousins involved in activities it can get tricky to match up schedules. As they say, life happens. And unfortunately, we too often let it.

As we hung up, I considered what a gift technology can be, providing creative ways to stay connected to those we love when the busyness of life feels overwhelming.

And while technology helps, it is more a Band-Aid than a solution, and I find myself asking what things I can release—even for a season—to create margin, to create space and time for living between the rushing. Pausing to sift our lives from time to time is important, learning to separate the important from mere distractions—releasing the things we've fallen into because of cultural expectations or boredom.

Asking periodically how and where we are spending our one, precious life, is healthy and wise. And regular reflection before God will reveal the answers, asking him to redirect us when we start seeking too many distractions, too many time wasters, too much we'll deem worthless when we stand before his throne.

Lord, align our hearts with yours, and help us rebalance how we spend our days, setting aside the worthless for life through you. Amen.

-Julie

One Good Step: Keep track of how you spend your time for one week.
Prayerfully consider what worthless things you could stop doing.

And

In the day of prosperity be joyful, and in the day of adversity consider:
God has made the one as well as the other, so that man
may not find out anything that will be after him.
ECCLESIASTES 7:14, ESV

MY HUSBAND WASN'T SLEEPING. Over the past several months, a slipped disk had led to increasing numbness in his arm and constant pain. When he did manage to fall asleep, it was in brief snatches that never lasted long. Although I was pregnant and had my own aches and pains to navigate, I watched him with increasing concern as time went on.

Finally, six weeks after our daughter was born, he had surgery to replace the disk. The relief was immediate, and so was his return to sleep. As a family, we rejoiced.

But his experience was a reminder of how much of our life is lived in the "and." Even in the midst of our joyful expectation over the impending birth of our daughter, he struggled with debilitating, sometimes overwhelming pain. A moment that should have been only good was also terribly hard.

Many things in life aren't an either-or question. God, in creating the world, referenced the "and" as both complementary and necessary. Heavens and earth. Evening and morning. "And God saw everything that he had made, and behold, it was very good" (Genesis 1:31, ESV).

In life, *and* represents the tensions that surface in our lives, the ones that present the greatest joys and sorrows. Hard and good. Bitter and sweet. Long days and short years. Opposing forces that can both, nonetheless, be true.

And, sometimes, it represents the choices we have available to us in our response. As Proverbs 18:21 notes, "Death and life are in the power of the tongue" (ESV). Death and life—both available, both true, but governed by our choices.

It's a reminder that it's often how we choose to see the "and" moments in life that influence our perspective, propelling us forward or getting us stuck. Whether we face joyful prosperity or painful adversity, may we choose to be people who see possibilities, rather than challenges, in the "and."

Lord, help us to see the "and" moments in our lives with new eyes. Help us recognize that there is beauty, even in the tension between two seemingly incompatible forces or circumstances. Amen.

-Kristin

One Good Step: Write down some "and" moments in your life.

Rooted

Now, just as you accepted Christ Jesus as your Lord, you must
continue to follow him. Let your roots grow down into him, and let your
lives be built on him. Then your faith will grow strong in the truth you
were taught, and you will overflow with thankfulness.

COLOSSIANS 2:6-7

"MY BASIL IS DAMPING OFF!" I wailed to no one in particular as I turned to examine my tray of heirloom tomato seedlings, hoping to avoid having to start over with planting because of this nasty pathogen.

I'd become something of a reluctant expert when it comes to damping-off and knew that fungi were the problem. Spores attack newly emerged seedlings, rotting the stem at the soil line. Established seedlings with strong roots and thicker stems are not nearly as susceptible, so I wage my battle against damping-off in the few weeks of my seedlings' lives, but not beyond.

There are so many farming metaphors in Scripture, and the command to "let your roots grow down" (Colossians 2:6) reverberates through my soul in this season of emerging seedlings and new growth. Sprouting seedlings are not much different from those of us with new faith—tender and weak.

Unrooted faith is vulnerable to attack by our enemy, the devil. He is real, and he is treacherous. The longer we linger with a surface-dwelling faith, the more susceptible we are to his whispered doubts, unable to push back against his flawed but convincing arguments because we don't have the foundation and understanding to do so. It's only as we put down roots that are deep and wide in our knowledge and understanding of who Jesus is (and is not) and who he calls us to be (or does not), that we can recognize and push back on our greatest enemy's tricks and traps. Committing our hearts to Jesus is not the end. It is the beginning of an amazing new adventure—one that requires a firm, strongly rooted foundation built on knowing Jesus.

Lord, no matter how long it has been since we first gave our hearts to you, help us to grow deeper, healthier roots—whether that's in our digging up wrong or twisted theology and replacing it with truth or in your revealing new knowledge and truth to us. Amen.

-Julie

One Good Step: Buy a study Bible or a Bible commentary so you can dig deeper into the cultural context and history of the Scriptures you are reading. I recommend the *NLT Study Bible*.

Belong

There is no longer Jew or Gentile, slave or free, male and female.
For you are all one in Christ Jesus.
GALATIANS 3:28

WE WERE TAKING a short vacation over spring break close to home and decided to invite several friends to join us. As I prayed about who to invite, one family in particular came to my mind. We didn't know them well, but I decided to ask them anyway. They responded back almost immediately and booked a place close to ours for the week. I was surprised, but also happy that they would want to join us.

The week of our trip, they, along with several other families, headed up to the resort. One evening during a shared meal with our group, my new friend leaned over and said, "Thank you for inviting us. Everyone is so welcoming." I smiled back at her and told her how grateful I was that they could come.

Just an hour earlier one of our friends had asked her what it was like to move to our area and how their family had been received. "Terrible," she'd replied honestly. "It took us a long time to make any friends." My friend acknowledged her honesty, stating that he'd asked because he'd heard the same thing from many others who'd moved to our area. It wasn't easy for new people to find a place to belong.

I shook my head in shame, because I knew that her words were true. I admit that I am not always the one looking to invite someone new. My circles can be closed off, as I stay comfortable being with people I already know. It takes intention for me to step outside of that and welcome others in, offering them a place of belonging.

The early church struggled with this too. There were people who belonged and those who didn't. Their circles were closed off. But Jesus changed all of that. He admonished the walls that divided people and invited everyone into his family, giving everyone a place to truly belong. As followers of him, we should be the most welcoming of all people, seeing the value that is in everyone around us. People are desperate to belong, so let's be the ones to offer them the invitation to join us.

Lord, help me to keep my relationship circles open and be willing to invite others in, offering them a place to belong.

-Kendra

One Good Step: Take time to ask God to show you who around you needs a friend and a place to belong and then invite them to dinner, coffee, or some other outing.

Hidden

How can I know all the sins lurking in my heart?
Cleanse me from these hidden faults.

PSALM 19:12

A FEW YEARS AGO, we celebrated my husband's fortieth birthday. Our ten-year anniversary was just two weeks later, so we decided to combine the occasions by taking a trip to the warm shores of Riviera Maya, Mexico. The resort was ideal: a not-very-busy beach and pool, several great dining options, free spa services that only required a generous tip, and pristine accommodations.

The only problem we ran into was that the electricity would turn off at random times. Sometimes it would be off for just a few minutes, while other times the outage would last hours. One random shutoff turned dinner into a candlelit affair, which felt like a fun adventure. But another time it went off in the midst of a massage, and the sudden silence and lack of air conditioning made the remainder of the experience awkward and stiflingly hot. Though the staff remained optimistic and helpful, the sudden outages were disorienting.

If our understanding of the resort had only been through the lens of what was visible—a shining new lobby, well-appointed rooms, shimmering pools—we would have assumed it was perfect. The power outages didn't lessen our overall enjoyment, but they did spark a question: What else was lurking under the "perfect" surface?

The analogy can offer insight into our own lives. Often, it's not the obvious, outside sins that are most insidious, but the hidden ones—ones we may have a hard time fully recognizing—that trip us up the most. Our internal biases and judgments, our pride, our envy, our habits—those hidden parts of ourselves can easily be glossed over or camouflaged by a smile or politeness.

When the light disappeared at the resort, its absence revealed the flaws. Similarly, when we choose to allow the hidden parts of ourselves to remain in darkness, we often miss the very sins that entangle us. But when we actively seek the hidden parts of our hearts and choose to shed light on those dark places, the Word of God illuminates every corner of our lives, bringing life and light to those things that would remain hidden.

Lord, help us to seek the life-giving light of your truth. Reveal the parts of ourselves that we've hidden, even from ourselves. Amen.

-Kristin

One Good Step: Prayerfully consider whether there's an area of sin in your life that you've ignored or kept hidden. If something comes to mind, ask God to forgive you and help you to bring it out into the light.

Ask

Keep on asking, and you will receive what you ask for.
Keep on seeking, and you will find. Keep on knocking,
and the door will be opened to you.

MATTHEW 7:7

I AMBLED ALONG THE BEACH, my eyes scanning the undulating waves for shells as my family frolicked in the surf fifty yards ahead. I was too late, and I knew it. I had always wanted to find a big, perfect shell—the spiral kind—but we'd missed low tide and fellow beachcombers were out in droves.

This is pointless. Finding a shell today would be a miracle. My internal dialogue snagged momentarily on the word *miracle* before continuing. *Lord, this is silly, but could I please find a shell, the spiral kind?*

God has far more important things to do than sending me a seashell. But I'm practicing asking God, to keep a running dialogue with him throughout the day—in the big and the small.

The overwhelming theme in Scripture about prayer is summed up in two words: ask God (see Matthew 7:7). And when we ask, we should be consistent and persistent. Prayer is our most powerful spiritual tool, despite our not fully understanding the why or how behind it. And yet we hesitate to ask because we are afraid God will be offended or bothered or because we don't want to waste God's time, or we're afraid to ask because God might not answer, at least not in the way we want.

I've prayed heart wrenchingly desperate prayers that weren't answered in the way that I hoped. Asking doesn't mean God will respond with exactly what we've requested. But Scripture is clear: God hears us when we ask, he tells us to ask, and something happens in the spiritual realm when we dialogue with God.

As my thoughts swirled on the mysteries of prayer, my eyes snagged on a small depression carved in the sand already submerged by the incoming tide. And in that trench lay a perfect, beautiful, spiral shell waiting for me to pick it up.

Lord, may we set aside our excuses and approach you with our requests as small children ask their parents—knowing you are loving, good, and generous. Amen.

-Julie

One Good Step: Practice dialoguing with God while in the shower, while driving to the grocery store, or during other quiet, small snatches of time. Practice asking for small delights amid more serious requests.

Imitate

Imitate God, therefore, in everything you do,
because you are his dear children.
EPHESIANS 5:1

"WHERE ARE YOUR GLASSES?" my friend Molly asked her four-year-old daughter on a recent visit to our home. The little girl shrugged and kept walking past our seats on the deck, turning to follow my daughter Ashlyn down the stairs toward the swing set in the backyard.

"Watch your step," she called out.

"There's a railing to hang on to," I added.

From the bottom of the stairs, the girls' voices drifted up toward us. Molly could still hear them, and she narrated the scene: "Your daughter is so sweet. Ashlyn just said, 'There's a step here,' and then, 'Watch out for that big weed.'"

My daughter had overheard the concern Molly and I had for her friend and, without being asked, had stepped in to demonstrate the same care.

Even though I'm a few decades older than my five-year-old, her sweetness toward her friend is a good reminder of the power of imitation. Children are natural imitators. It's how they discover language and learn social skills, decipher facial expressions and develop gross motor skills. Imitation isn't just helpful; it's essential.

Just as parents desire their children to imitate them in the best of ways—how they treat others and interact with the world around them—so God desires for us, his children, to imitate him. We can't imitate his power or glory and we can't fathom his knowledge, but we can show his love. As his beloved children, reflecting God's love should be our aim—not just in the words we say but in the actions we take. We can demonstrate mercy, we can freely forgive, and we can help those in need.

Imitation reflects the relationship the child has with their caregiver, as the child seeks positive feedback, attention, and a one-on-one connection. In the same way, when our words and actions reflect the Father's love, our relationship with him grows. As we model the love of God, we become more and more like him.

Lord, thank you for loving us. Help us to imitate you by showing love to those around us. Amen.

-Kristin

One Good Step: Through your words or actions, intentionally demonstrate God's love to someone around you.

Wait patiently for the LORD. Be brave and courageous.
Yes, wait patiently for the LORD.

PSALM 27:14

"I LOOKED AT the job posting you sent. You'd hate it." My heart ached for my friend Abby as I sent the early morning text.

"Ugh. You're right. I would hate it. It's just so hard to wait. I'm unhappy."

"I know, and I'm sorry. Stop jumping ahead of God. Wait for him. His resolution is worth waiting for."

Abby and I tend to take charge and problem solve any task set before us. We've both worked in the legal system, and any natural tendency to problem solve has been magnified by years in careers that value finding creative solutions to tough situations. It's a great trait to have unless God is asking me to stand still and rely upon him; then it becomes a power struggle over who is in control, me or God.

We know this about ourselves, and we support one another's faith journey in ceding control back to God. We've had some version of the above conversation for years: half the time I'm waiting while Abby is reminding me to stay put and stay still, and the other half I'm telling her to do the same. We've encouraged one another to wait patiently for God's move with respect to so many situations—jobs, moves, remodels, children, marriages, health—there is no part of life exempted from waiting. We make situations worse when we leap without God. God's timing oftentimes comes with a blessing beyond our wildest dreams when compared to what we might have achieved on our own.

It can be tricky to distinguish between when God is saying wait and when he is telling us to jump. The best I can tell you is that God's voice—that small nudging somewhere deep inside you—will never deviate from Scripture. Drawing near to God through prayer and reading Scripture is vital, and seeking divine counsel from faith mentors can help you hone the ability to hear God's voice. While God may send confirmation through others, he will speak directly to you.

Lord, give us peace in our hearts, minds, and bodies as we wait on you. Amen.

-Julie

One Good Step: Set aside time this week to be still and quiet before God, practicing hearing his voice over your circumstances.

Mercy

Be merciful, just as your Father is merciful.

LUKE 6:36, NIV

WHEN A RELATIVE OF OURS needed a car, a dear friend heard about the need and insisted on giving us a car that he was no longer using. It was an older car with a lot of miles, but it still ran well. At first, Kyle and I resisted. *How could we take a car without giving our friend anything in return?*

We offered to pay him something for it, but he refused, telling us he just wanted to bless our family. After a while, my husband and I humbly and gratefully accepted his gift.

But even as I was so thankful for my friend, I struggled to pass the car on to our relative. This person has prejudice against the race of our friend who gave us the car, and I know that if the tables were turned, our relative would not return the favor.

I sat in angry indignation toward this family member, begrudging them the car. It's not that I didn't think they deserved a vehicle; I just didn't think they deserved one from our friend.

As I struggled to know what to do, I listened to a message about the Good Samaritan. Although I've read the story many times, one comment the speaker made struck me. She said, "The Good Samaritan helped the man who'd been beaten on the side of the road, knowing full well, if the roles were reversed, the beaten man most likely would not have stopped to help him." I sat stunned. I knew these words were for me. I asked for God's forgiveness and for a heart to love my relative the way the Samaritan showed love to the beaten man.

Mercy is often defined as compassion or unmerited grace toward another person. Mercy sounds wonderful, until you are in a situation where someone needs mercy who doesn't seem to deserve it. As Christians, we have to remember that this is also us. I didn't deserve God's mercy, and yet he offered it to me, freely. In turn, we are to be merciful to others, just as God is to us.

Lord, showing mercy to others is not always easy. Help us to see the mercy you've given to us first and then change our hearts so that we can show mercy to others. Amen.

-Kendra

One Good Step: Show mercy to someone who doesn't seem to deserve it.

Strangers

So now you Gentiles are no longer strangers and foreigners.
You are citizens along with all of God's holy people.
You are members of God's family.

EPHESIANS 2:19

THE SEMESTER I STUDIED ABROAD in England, I spent my spring break in Austria. One of my friends had a friend in Vienna, and she agreed to show us around. After a flight to Linz, a train ride to Vienna, and a mix-up about where we were staying that led to an exhausting evening bumping our luggage around the streets of Vienna, we settled in for the week.

Once there, we had a wonderful visit. We went to the opera, sat in the cheap seats, and marveled at the performance. We visited St. Stephen's Cathedral, went to an art museum, and spent an afternoon at a Kandinsky art exhibition. We did a bit of shopping, ate schnitzel, and spent a day exploring Schloss Schönbrunn, the biggest castle in Austria.

But even with friends at my side, I remember feeling a bit lost. Though many people spoke English and no one was unkind, I wished desperately that I knew even the tiniest fraction of German. My high school Spanish and college French were of no use to me there. By the time we returned to England, it felt like a sweet relief to be understood by those around me.

The experience gave me a small sense of what it must feel like when others move to my community, knowing no one, perhaps struggling to feel understood. It's isolating and lonely. Now, when I encounter folks who are new to my area, I try to be welcoming, remembering that lonely isolation of being in an unfamiliar place.

As citizens of heaven, we ourselves are strangers in a foreign land—yet while we are here, we must be united in our love. When we recognize that those around us are part of our family—regardless of background or culture—we honor the grace and mercy extended to us through Christ's sacrifice. Let's honor the spirit of that promise by treating each person we meet with love and respect.

Lord, thank you that we are family, not strangers, to you. Help us to treat others in the same way you've treated us. Amen.

-Kristin

One Good Step: Who can you befriend that may feel lonely or out of place?

Gentle

Always be humble and gentle. Be patient with each other,
making allowance for each other's faults because of your love.

EPHESIANS 4:2

"I'm NEVER GOING TO BE that sweet, soft-spoken grandma who bakes cookies, am I?" Asking the question with a sigh, I reached around Aaron to tuck a glass away as we unloaded the dishwasher. I had been a bit *too* honest when asked my opinion in a phone call that afternoon, and I regretted my lack of tact.

"No." A slight smirk tugged at his lips as he agreed with my assessment. "But I love my Mack Truck wife."

My mom teasingly calls me a Mack Truck because, like those heavy-duty vehicles, I tend to plow directly forward when faced with a situation that needs solving, rather than delicately dancing around the topic and allowing others to arrive to the same conclusion at their own pace.

God created us with a unique blend of traits, but he calls us to gentleness regardless of whether it's a natural inclination of ours or not. I am learning that my strengths are also my weaknesses if taken in too big a dose or applied with too heavy a hand. If I am not careful, I can run right over those who are quieter than me, those who need more time to process information, those who communicate in less direct methods. If I'm not careful, I miss out on the excellent offerings of others when I am not gentle.

Being gentle is not about denying our God-breathed giftings, but we might need to slow down and sit still, encouraging others to speak up and share their opinions. It requires us to see others, to listen carefully to what they have to say without jumping in with a response. It often means laying down our rights. We are commanded to exercise gentleness precisely because it is countercultural and hard, but we create opportunity and space for those around us to flourish when we walk in gentleness.

Lord, reveal what gentle means for each one of us today and this week. Help us decrease so those around us are heard and seen. Amen.

-Julie

One Good Step: Practice listening more than you talk today. Start by using questions to keep the conversation going rather than sharing your thoughts or your stories.

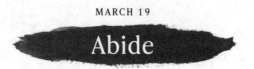
Abide

As the Father has loved me, so have I loved you.
Abide in my love.
JOHN 15:9, ESV

EVERY MORNING since my college days, I have had the habit of getting up and spending a few moments reading the Bible and a simple devotional before work. A morning person by nature, it became an easy habit for me to make a cup of coffee and sit down for a few minutes with my Bible and journal before leaving for class or work.

As social media and smartphones became more prevalent, I found that although I was still getting up and reading my Bible for a few moments every morning, it wasn't the first thing that I would do. I would often shut the alarm off on my phone and then spend a little time scrolling social media before getting up for the day.

At first I didn't notice any change to my attitude, but over time—and especially during seasons of hard things happening in our world—I found my peace slowly leaving. I found myself disgruntled and restless as I would go through my day. As I tried to pinpoint exactly why this was, I realized it had much to do with my mind being held captive to the things I'd seen and read on social media. It was filling my thoughts to the detriment of my own peace of mind.

I started to limit my social media use and stopped scrolling first thing in the morning. I returned to my habit of spending the first moments of my day with God, and as I did, my peace returned.

Setting healthy limits affects so many areas of our lives, and maybe nowhere as much as our thought life. That is why abiding in God and his love is so important. It's not that we stop paying attention to what is going on in the world—we certainly can and should know what is happening—but filling our minds and hearts with God's Word first and abiding in his love sets us up to handle the rest of the day well.

Lord, help me to come to you first. Thank you for your love and the invitation to abide in it today. Amen.

-Kendra

One Good Step: Take the first few moments of your day and spend them with God, abiding in him and his love for you.

His

The heavens are yours, and the earth is yours;
everything in the world is yours—you created it all.

PSALM 89:11

"I FOUND AN ABANDONED QUARTZ MINE with lots of good-sized quartz chunks. It was at the end of a dirt trail I decided to follow." Smiling, I listened as my dad told me about his latest adventure on public land in a western state, wondering how many hundreds of people had passed by that trail.

Dad once told me that he feels close to God when he is outside, immersed in creation. In that way, I am most definitely my father's daughter. I am reminded of God's sovereignty over even the hardest things I face in the shadow of mountains, the stillness of forests, and on the edges of oceans, and I find peace as I compare my puny, fleeting existence to the immense timelessness of his earth.

But it's his tender care revealed in the tiniest details of creation that serves as a tangible reminder that the same God who created and named the stars also counts the strands of hair on our heads. When the storms of life rage, we are not abandoned. I hear God's love when a robin trills for the first time each spring. I feel God's love as I bask in those first warm rays of the sun in March, knowing spring is just around the corner. I see God's love when I find an agate half buried in the mud, the beautiful red and white swirls revealed with a swipe of my thumb against the dirt. I smell God's love on the warm days when the melting snow reveals the scent of fresh, wet earth. I taste God's love in the raspberries that never quite make it to the house because the neighborhood children delight in my invitation to eat their fill straight from the brambles.

Everything is God's. He created it, and he reveals himself in all of it—from the sweeping panoramas to fragile butterfly wings. And as much as he loves his creation, he loves and cares for us more. We are his beloved.

Lord, we are yours. Remind us of your sovereignty, your love, your provision for those who seek first your Kingdom (see Matthew 6:33). Amen.

-Julie

One Good Step: Find a quiet place outside. What do you feel, smell, taste, hear, and see that reminds you of God's sovereignty and his love?

Blessing

Whoever brings blessing will be enriched,
and one who waters will himself be watered.

PROVERBS 11:25, ESV

ONE YEAR I HEARD ABOUT a single moms' retreat that was being held in our state. Even though I wasn't a single mom and didn't know very many single moms personally, I knew I wanted to get involved. The retreat met both physical and spiritual needs of the women by providing car care, a boutique where they could shop for free, a spa, and speakers who would encourage and speak the truth of God's love and grace.

I thought that I would go to help and offer support by working as a volunteer, but what I did not know was how it would change me and my heart. And how I would see, firsthand, how truly courageous, hardworking, and selfless these single moms are.

At the retreat, I heard stories of mothers who put their needs second to those of their children. They fed their children before themselves. They dressed and bought necessities for their children before themselves. They scrimped and saved to get the things their children needed. They put aside their own desires to meet the needs of the young ones in their charge. And I was moved. More than moved, I was challenged and humbled.

The very heart of Father God was modeled and mirrored in these beautiful women who came from different places, different backgrounds, and different experiences. All weekend as women expressed gratitude to us for helping with the retreat, I simply responded by thanking them for being with us. It was an honor to be serving, a privilege to hear stories, and a blessing to get to know the women.

Oftentimes when we contemplate a blessing, we think of the people we'll be serving as the ones being blessed. But Scripture says that those who bring a blessing are enriched themselves. And anyone who waters, will himself be watered. Why? Because when we give to others, when we offer kindness, love, or a listening ear, we find those same things in return. There's no power differential in true blessing toward each other; we give and receive to one another, mutually supportive. And in so doing, we're all blessed.

Lord, may we all be willing to give and receive blessing. Amen.

-Kendra

One Good Step: Today either bless someone or be willing to accept a blessing yourself, knowing that either way, your life will be enriched.

Resurrection

Now, as to whether there will be a resurrection of the dead—haven't you ever read about this in the Scriptures? Long after Abraham, Isaac, and Jacob had died, God said, "I am the God of Abraham, the God of Isaac, and the God of Jacob." So he is the God of the living, not the dead.

MATTHEW 22:31-32

THE EMAIL DROPPED unexpectedly into my inbox. Opening it, I began to read a letter detailing how a friend had betrayed my trust. As I scrolled the message, I felt like I was underwater, struggling to resurface, cold chills running through my body as though I were in shock.

Feverishly recalling our interactions, I thought about details I'd missed, actions I'd overlooked, and warning signs I hadn't heeded. The words on the page were the first sign of trouble, but when I asked my friend and the truth was confirmed, it felt like a death knell for the friendship. I wondered how I could possibly forgive and move on.

Listening to a podcast a few weeks later, I was struck by the speaker's words in the context of my flailing friendship. She said that when it feels like we are walking through some kind of death in our life, we need to remember that death isn't the end of the story: there is resurrection at the end. God himself reminded us that he can bring life again, even to that which seems lost (see Isaiah 43:19). Not only is he about to do something new; he has already begun.

Even when we walk through what feels like dry wastelands, God can forge rivers of mercy and hope that reach even the most parched land. He is the God of the living, not the dead. Though we may experience the death of a friendship, a relationship, a career, or a dream, those experiences can remind us that there's always the hope of more. Though circumstances may not look the way we expected or once hoped they would, his resurrection power is available to us in healing old wounds and in fostering hope and wholeness moving forward.

Lord, thank you that your resurrection power can bring life and healing, even when life is uncertain or circumstances feel immovable. Amen.

-Kristin

One Good Step: Are you struggling with the death of something in your life? How might trusting in God's resurrection power help you move forward?

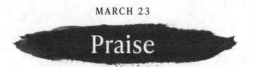

Praise

I will bless the LORD at all times;
his praise shall continually be in my mouth.

PSALM 34:1, ESV

"WHAT ATMOSPHERE are you creating? Is it one of praise, in which people around you are pointed toward God, or is it something else?"

I winced, reaching for the church bulletin to take notes because I knew these questions were directed at me as much as anyone else that Sunday morning. My impatient and slightly snappish attitude with my kids before church and my recent general grouchiness toward a never-ending to-do list as mom, wife, volunteer, and small business owner filled my thoughts as I scribbled frantically.

We've been conditioned to think of praising God as one-dimensional, something we do in church. And while worshiping God in community with other believers is a form of praise, it is only one small part, not the fulfillment of it. We bless God when we adopt a lifestyle of praise, an atmosphere cultivated with our words, our attitudes, and our actions patterned after the words and teachings of Jesus.

And, truth be told, it's easier for me to create an atmosphere of praise for coworkers and acquaintances than it is for my own family. I can exemplify the fruits of the Spirit—love, joy, peace, patience, kindness, goodness, faithfulness, gentleness, and self-control—toward those I interact with for short periods of time, intentionally using my words and actions to point them toward our Savior while I push the ugly stuff down, leaving all the frustration, insecurity, anxiety, and anger to bubble over when I am with my family.

Praising God is a lifestyle, not a temporary mask we wear when we are in public or have invited others into our home. Living a life that continually blesses God requires intentionality, repentance, and trying again when we fall short. But, when we get it right, we create a space that others long to linger in, an atmosphere that invites the presence of God.

Lord, show us one way to bring praise into our everyday lives and into our homes. Amen.

-Julie

One Good Step: Pick one fruit of the Spirit to practice this week as you cultivate a lifestyle of praising God. Pick a new fruit each week for the next eight weeks, and then start over.

Presence

You make known to me the path of life; in your presence there is fullness of joy; at your right hand are pleasures forevermore.

PSALM 16:11, ESV

MY HUSBAND AND I got married at 10 a.m. on a Saturday. Our brunchtime wedding on a brisk March day is the only wedding at which I've eaten bacon and French toast. Not long ago while cleaning our home office, I stumbled on our wedding video. As Tim and I watched it, I again witnessed my walk down the aisle, my husband's tears, our vows, and our joy. But as special as those moments were, it was the glimpse of everyone who attended that resonated the most.

I saw my now-grown nephew as our patient ring bearer, shuffling his feet and scratching his face as he squirmed through the event. I saw my now twenty-year-old niece, hair curled, directing her little brother.

And as the guests filed out at the end of the ceremony, I saw Uncle Jimmy, Uncle Michael, and Uncle Fritz—all now deceased—make their way out of their rows. Those few, fleeting moments of watching them brought to life again made my eyes blur with tears.

It was their presence, and that of the rest of our family and friends, that made the occasion memorable.

Whether we are in the company of someone else or fully present as a state of being, there is an immediacy in the word *presence*. Our choice to be fully present helps others to feel seen, known, and cared for like few other actions do.

Similarly, Jesus serves as a steady, never-absent presence in our lives. He wants us to see each moment we pass through—the good and the hard—as moments where we glimpse visions of him, are held tightly to him, and feel a greater joy in knowing he is there now, has been, and will be—no matter what the future holds. Like a good friend, his unwavering presence has the power to make us feel seen and heard.

At a wedding or other family gathering, we invite our closest friends and relatives. It's an honor to be invited. And in our lives, it's an even greater honor for us to invite Jesus in. He doesn't push his way in. Like a wedding guest, he waits for an invitation.

Lord, thank you for the gift of your presence. Amen.

-Kristin

One Good Step: What moments of your life stand out as times where you felt the presence of God? How can experiencing his presence bring you greater joy?

Grieve

I will never forget this awful time, as I grieve over my loss.
LAMENTATIONS 3:20

"IN THE MIDST OF KATE'S CANCER, she told me stories of visits in which she comforted another's grief over her cancer, assuring her visitor that it would be okay. It was emotionally exhausting." Kendra's voice held a note of wistfulness, missing her older sister as we talked about the strange ways people respond to those grieving.

Grief is a tricky beast, and our clumsy attempts to provide comfort sometimes make things worse, not better. I've learned, often the hard way, several helpful ways to support someone's grief:

> **Don't share your own story of loss in an attempt to provide comfort.** While the intent is to express a shared experience, the impact shifts the focus of the conversation, and the grieving person now comforts your grief. Instead, allow the grieving person to control the topic of conversation and follow her lead.
> **Understand that there are circles of grief.** Seek comfort from those further away from the grief epicenter and provide comfort to those closer to the epicenter. For example, when someone dies, grieving friends comfort the spouse, children, siblings, and parents. Those friends should seek comfort from one another and from their own circles of support, but not from those closer in relationship to the person grieving.
> **Avoid offering clichés, which are meant to soothe but often cause a new hurt.** Phrases such as "God doesn't give us more than we can handle," "God has a plan," "God must have needed another angel," "she's better off now," and "everything happens for a reason" are meant to comfort but—in the midst of fresh, raw grief—can feel like sandpaper scraping against the wound. Instead, try acknowledging grief without trying to answer why it happened. Saying something like, "I am so sorry this is happening/happened" is a great way to express love and empathy without resorting to clichés.

I'm guilty of comforting with a cliché or sharing my own story of loss, and my past self deserves grace even as I learn to respond to the grieving in better ways.

Lord, may I acknowledge those grieving with gentle, compassionate words and actions that provide comfort rather than unintentional, additional pain.

-Julie

One Good Step: Ask a friend who has walked through grief what she most appreciated hearing when grief was raw. Determine ahead of time a comforting sentence you can say to someone in the midst of fresh grief.

Control

I know that you can do all things;
no purpose of yours can be thwarted.

JOB 42:2, NIV

I WAS WISHING HER ill will, and I hated it. She had wronged us (at least that's how I felt), and I wanted nothing more than to retaliate. I knew it wasn't right to have these thoughts, but I just couldn't shake them.

"I'm angry," I whispered to my husband later that evening, "and I hate it. But I especially hate that I feel so helpless and out of control to do anything about the situation." And there was the heart of my anger. I hate when things are beyond my ability to control and that, most often, expresses itself as anger.

Kyle, who is often much more even keeled and levelheaded than I, looked at me with love and sympathy in his eyes.

"Honey," he stated, "what good will it do to hold on to your anger? You can't control it; you need to let it go."

I knew that he was right. And yet, it was still hard to actually do. To stop the cycle of negative thoughts that swirled in my head and replace them with something else, but even still I tried by telling myself the following things:

I don't need to be in control of everything because God already is. And he is a good God. Who loves me. Cares for me. Protects me. Who believes the best about me and offers me grace every time I respond in anger instead of forgiveness. Who understands my own propensity for error and still welcomes me to walk with him.

And as I allowed myself to marinate on these things, I realized these were the same things that God offered to the woman who hurt me, and I felt a slight shift in my feelings and thoughts. Maybe not a complete letting go, but a moving away from anger, toward letting go.

There are days when we all need the reminder to trust and to forgive. To remember God's deep, abiding love and care of us. And even to those around us. We all need the reminder that God is in control, and therefore, we do not need to be. We can let go.

Lord, help us to give to you the things that we cannot control and to remember that you are ultimately in control. Amen.

-Kendra

One Good Step: Release to God in prayer something you've been trying to control.

Need

The LORD is my shepherd; I have all that I need.

PSALM 23:1

THE PRAYER REQUEST popped up in a small, online community group: a mom on a fixed income with mounting legal expenses from a pending divorce, significant health challenges, children whose clothes were too small, and no incoming money for food or gas in the week ahead. She was asking for prayer, but it was obvious she had tangible needs too.

Immediately I thought about extra funds stashed away from selling some things online that I didn't use anymore. *What do I really need?* I thought. The answer came quickly: *Nothing. I need nothing. I have a home, food, clothes, my health.*

The desire for less has been a slow shift and an ongoing struggle. But in the last couple of years, I've been meditating on Psalm 23. In a world that feeds us the lie of scarcity—that we can always use more, consume more, enjoy more—the psalm reminds us that if we have God, we have all that we need. It's fitting that it was written by David, a king who was once a shepherd and had experience with both roles, who chose to envision God in the beginning of the psalm as a guardian and caregiving shepherd rather than a powerful, privileged king.

The words he speaks echo those that were spoken to the Israelites about their forty years of wandering in the desert, describing their past—"you have lacked nothing" (Deuteronomy 2:7)—as well as their future in the Promised Land where "nothing is lacking" (Deuteronomy 8:9). The Israelites' past experience not only influenced the present; it gave them a confident hope for the future. David's echo is a reminder—for him and for us—that with God, we have all that we need.

With a quick prayer, I dashed off a note and some funds to the stranger, who responded with gratitude. But I waved off her thanks—generosity was a gift from the Father long before it was a gift from me.

Lord, thank you for supplying all our needs. Help us to recognize that, in you, we already have all that we need.

-Kristin

One Good Step: Share something—a coffee, a favorite recipe, your time—with someone in need.

Release

Give all your worries and cares to God, for he cares about you.

1 PETER 5:7

OUR SON MOVED OUT of our home just two months prior to his high school gradua-tion. As an eighteen-year-old young man with friends already leasing an apartment, he decided he wanted the freedom that living on his own and out from under his parents' roof afforded him. The past year had been challenging for all of us as he struggled to follow the rules set up in our home. My husband and I cautiously let him leave, understanding that at his age, the choice to stay at home with us or not was ultimately his.

We remained in close contact, calling and texting every few days. At first I wor-ried a lot. I worried for his safety and wondered if he'd have everything he needed. I felt shame, worried that other parents and friends would question our ability to parent our kids well. I lay awake at night, praying for him, wishing things had gone differently. Ultimately wishing for control of the situation that I knew I did not have.

Through my prayers in the days and weeks after our son left, God slowly brought me to a place of seeing myself releasing my son into his loving hands. Worrying incessantly was not helpful. I needed rest, and I needed to trust that God was in control and that I was not. I still pray for my son, but anytime I feel worried, I give him back to God, releasing him once again to our heavenly Father's care.

There are so many things in life that can cause us to worry. So many things that, if we are completely honest with ourselves, are beyond our ability to control. And much of this life of faith is releasing back to God that which we cannot control. It is not always easy, and often we will have to release the same thing over and over again. Life and relationships are messy, and not everything will always wrap up with a neat little bow, but we can be confident that God will continue to take our worries from us, because he cares so much for us.

Lord, help us to release to you the people and circumstances that we cannot con-trol. Give us your peace in place of worry. Amen.

-Kendra

One Good Step: What worries do you need to release to God today? How can you give them to God and then trust his care for you?

Look

Why do you look the other way? Why do you
ignore our suffering and oppression?

PSALM 44:24

AS WE WALKED into the theater, I swallowed nervously. The kids and I were there to
see *Just Mercy*, a movie based on the book of the same name by Bryan Stevenson.
An attorney, professor, and founder of the Equal Justice Initiative, Stevenson makes
a compelling argument that within our American legal system, the opposite of
poverty is not wealth, but justice. And as an attorney who has stood in courtrooms
on behalf of clients, I know this to be true. If you do not have money, you face
a significant disadvantage in the courtroom, no matter the reason you are there.

Popcorn in hand, we watched the story unfold about real people on death row
in the 1980s Deep South as a young attorney appealed their convictions. They each
had compelling facts suggesting they were innocent as execution loomed, and as
the tension mounted during one particularly uncomfortable but not inappropriate
scene, one of my children declared a sudden need to use the restroom.

"Stay. You need to watch this part. You need to look. It is truth, and it is important." I whispered gently, refusing the attempt to escape discomfort.

As we slowly walked back to the car after the movie, we talked about poverty
and justice. We talked about young black men and their incarceration rates. We
talked about how expensive it is to hire a criminal defense attorney and how completely overwhelmed the "free" public defenders are with unimaginable caseloads.
We talked about the tension between victims of terrible crimes and the percentage
of innocent people on death row.

Suffering and oppression are not new to the human condition, and we are not
asked to have a simple solution or clichéd answer for complex, deeply entrenched
injustice. But we are asked to bear witness, to look, to see, to hear, and not turn
away.

Lord, confront our tendency to look away from uncomfortable situations. Convict
us when we choose comfort over justice for our neighbors, our community members,
our brothers and sisters in Christ. Amen.

-Julie

One Good Step: Practice not looking away from things that make you uncomfortable.
Start with watching *Just Mercy* or reading the book by Bryan Stevenson with a friend
and discuss this statement: "The opposite of poverty is not wealth, it is justice."

Today

Jesus replied, "I assure you, today you will be with me in paradise."

LUKE 23:43

HOW MUCH TIME do you spend truly living in the present? A study in *Science* found that people spent almost 47 percent of their waking hours thinking about what wasn't going on, something researchers call "wandering."[1] Our brains wander into the past, into what may happen in the future, and even into what may never happen at all. Yet people in the study reported that brain wandering generally made them feel unhappy. How, then, can we stay firmly focused on today?

Luke 23 powerfully demonstrates just how important *today* is in the scheme of our lives. The narrative begins by telling us of Jesus' trial before Pilate, his sentencing, and ultimately his crucifixion. As Jesus is nailed to the cross, a criminal is placed on each side of him. While one prisoner mocks and scoffs at Jesus, the other protests.

"We deserve to die for our crimes, but this man has done nothing wrong," he says. He then turns to Jesus and asks him to remember him in his Kingdom (see Luke 23:41-42).

Jesus, in his response, reveals both the power of a single day and his kindness: "Today," he says, "you'll be with me in paradise." What a powerful testament to both the immediacy and the far-reaching nature of forgiveness. Jesus didn't waste a breath or take the time to berate the man, remind him of how great his sins were, or leave him unsure of whether or not he was truly forgiven. Instead, his sins were immediately wiped clean, the promise of paradise guaranteed.

We, too, can access immediate forgiveness—today. Too often I find that I am berating myself for an action or for something I've said, even after I've asked God to forgive me. Yet Jesus doesn't do that—instead, if we humbly confess our sins, he is faithful to forgive us. He does not hold our sins over our head, making us wait until some future time before reluctantly pardoning us. He does not keep a record of all our past wrongs to use as ammunition against us later on. No, his forgiveness is all-encompassing. What a gracious God! Let's focus on living today with him.

Lord, thank you for today. Amen.

-Kristin

One Good Step: What words or actions have you failed to forgive yourself for? Spend time considering how Jesus is ready to forgive you today. There's no need to wait.

---

[1] Matthew A. Killingsworth and Daniel T. Gilbert, "A Wandering Mind Is an Unhappy Mind," *Science* 330, no. 6006 (November 12, 2010): 932, https://science.sciencemag.org/content/330/6006/932.

Assurance

As surely as the sun rises, he will appear; he will come to us like the winter rains, like the spring rains that water the earth.

HOSEA 6:3, NIV

I LOVE SPRINGTIME. It is not necessarily my favorite season, but it is the one I am most grateful to see arrive. I live in Minnesota, where winters can be bitterly cold, dragging on much longer than they are welcome and often sending the last remnants of snow and cold into April.

But as the weather slowly warms and we emerge outside for walks and hikes in the woods around our city, I am always struck by the buds on the trees and the green that begins to once again appear across fields of grass, assuring me that spring will come. I love stopping to listen to the now warmer wind rustle through the branches, the birds chirp, and the bullfrogs call across the pond. It calms my mind and allows me to breathe deeply of the fresh, spring air.

As I watch spring arrive with my physical eyes, it offers me the assurance once again that God is in control, even in the things that I cannot see. No matter how much uncertainty we experience, the sun rising is a reminder that God will surely appear.

There's not always a lot in life that we can be sure of, but just as the rains come to water the earth, we have this promise that the Lord will come. We must ask ourselves, *Do we have eyes to see it? Do we acknowledge his presence? Do we rest in the assurance that he will appear?* Or do we spend too much of our time worrying and wondering where God is, even doubting that he will show up when we need him? If so, take heart, friends; we have the confident assurance that God is nearer than we realize.

Lord, thank you for the assurance that you are in control and that you will appear here on the earth. We give all of our worry and uncertainty to you and cling to the promise of your steadfast presence and love. Amen.

-Kendra

One Good Step: Take a walk outside in nature and look for the ways that God shows up through his creation and assures us that he will appear.

April

Fast

He must increase, but I must decrease.
JOHN 3:30, ESV

I DIDN'T GROW UP with a Lenten tradition. In fact, it wasn't until I completed a forty-day sugar fast a few years ago that I truly appreciated the practice and symbolism of fasting.

Up until then, I largely viewed fasting as a form of self-discipline. As a teenager, I watched friends give up drinking pop or eating chocolate during Lent, and it seemed like a test of their will. There was a part of me that resonated with that idea, because whenever circumstances in my life have been beyond my control, I have clung to things I could control: decluttering my belongings, purging my schedule, creating rhythms to help manage my household. Those are useful actions, but they were all about me—my need for control. And so, when I made the decision to fast, I thought it was one more area of self-improvement, another kind of decluttering. But as I pivoted from the sugar fast to Lent and found myself experiencing the presence of God in new ways, I was forced to rethink that perspective.

Reading through the gospel of John, I was struck by the story of John the Baptist. Though he had a vibrant ministry, he recognized that his true mission was preparing the way for Jesus. When John's followers complained to him that Jesus was baptizing people—a role they considered to be John's—he didn't respond with the outrage they expected. Instead, he simply said he was glad to hear it. Comparing himself to a groomsman rather than the bridegroom, he said that Jesus must increase, while he must decrease.

I was struck by the humility of John's posture. Despite possessing influence and his own ministry, John offered his life's work to the living Christ. Similarly, fasting is a physical representation of the spiritual humbling of our hearts, removing the focus from ourselves and placing it squarely on Christ. When we fast from our reliance on the comforts of this world, doing so increases our desire for more of Jesus: more time with him, more time in his Word, and more friendship with one who loves us deeply.

Lord, thank you that when we focus less on ourselves, we're able to focus more on you. Give us the courage to do so. Amen.

-Kristin

One Good Step: If you are able to, fast from one meal.
Spend that time praying and reading God's Word.

Invest

Before he left, he called together ten of his servants and divided among them ten pounds of silver, saying, "Invest this for me while I am gone."

LUKE 19:13

"MOM, IT WAS Fun Free Friday today. Marcus and I couldn't find any free things, so we decided to go to Ms. Kruse's house and ask her. We knew she'd help; she gave us freezies and donuts!"

An annual tradition, Fun Free Friday is where the cross-country team breaks into small groups and follows garage sale signs during their run. The goal is to bring the most interesting items from the garage sale "free" pile back to the coach. I smiled when I saw Lizzie and Marcus in the photos later posted in the Facebook group, holding up ten freezies and two packs of mini donuts. These two had clearly hit the jackpot by going to Ms. Kruse.

Karen is the music teacher at my daughter's elementary school, and she loves her students with a firm hand and a generous heart. She invests in her students, in their families, and in our small community school in ways that blow me away. She offers piano lessons at a price her students can pay, she uses her personal resources to quietly meet needs, and she loves us all, issuing hugs to anyone who comes within hugging range. In the parable of the ten servants given silver and told to invest it, she is the servant who gets the gold star—the one who received a tenfold increase on the original investment.

When we think of investing, it doesn't just mean in our finances. We have other resources available to invest as well. We have time, skill sets, talents, connections, experience, possessions. . . . All of these and more are tools we can use to invest in God's Kingdom—the place for the best possible return on any of our investments.

Let us not fall into the comparison trap, measuring our resources against those of our siblings, neighbors, friends, or work colleagues. God asks us to take what we have and use it, invest it in others, share it generously with those around us. If we do that, we'll be like the faithful servant in the parable who pleases his master by bringing in a tenfold increase on the original amount.

Lord, may we be wise stewards of our resources, investing in your Kingdom. Amen.

-Julie

One Good Step: Make a list of your resources—financial and otherwise. How can you make an investment today?

Worthy

The very hairs of your head are all numbered. Don't be afraid;
you are worth more than many sparrows.

LUKE 12:7, NIV

ONE SPRING a few years back I spent the weekend at a women's conference with friends where I'd been encouraged and uplifted. But by the following Monday, I felt tired.

I decided to spend a few moments in prayer, and as I did, God began to show me a vulnerability in my heart, something I've dealt with for years, that got rubbed over the weekend. Part of my responsibility during the conference was to collect clothing for a single moms' retreat. The year before, they had collected a lot at this conference, so I was prepared to do the same. I had lined up friends with vehicles to carry boxes and even enlisted the help of my husband to come down on Saturday with his work van to bring back an extra load. I was prepared and excited for what would happen.

Friday night came and went with just two bags. I thought, *That's okay. I'm sure we'll get plenty tomorrow.* And then Saturday came and went—with less than the first day, just a couple of small bags. We filled only three boxes between the two days. And it hit a chord deep in my heart.

It's the little voice that says, *You're not good enough. You can't do a good enough job.* And off I retreat to this place in my heart that quietly whispers, *You don't measure up.*

I have dealt with the untruth of this lie before and combated it with the truth of God's Word. But this perfect storm of weariness created a place for these thoughts and feelings to rise again. And so I went back to the truth of what I already know. I am loved. I am wanted. Called. Equipped. I am worthy. Because of my own abilities? No. Because of Christ in me.

Maybe you've been there too? Maybe you've experienced the low valleys, fighting against thoughts and words that were meant to defeat you, but this reminder is for all of us. Let's allow the truth of God's Word to be our guide, our strength, and our reminder of our worth against that which would mean to defeat us.

Lord, thank you that we do not have to fear or worry about our worth. We can trust and believe that we are valuable to you. Amen.

-Kendra

One Good Step: Spend time thinking about the truths of who God says that you are. Then write them down as a reminder.

Affirm

The word of God is alive and powerful. It is sharper than the sharpest
two-edged sword, cutting between soul and spirit, between joint and marrow.
It exposes our innermost thoughts and desires.

HEBREWS 4:12

My DAD IS a words-of-affirmation person. He's good with hugs and helping around the house, too, but he's particularly intentional with his words.

Just the other day, he was telling me how much he likes to read my writing; how it sometimes brings him to tears. For as long as I can remember, he's been saying words to the same effect: "You're a great writer." When I was a child, he'd follow it up with the question, "When am I going to read your first book?"

What's always struck me—more than the words themselves—is the intent behind them. I've always loved writing, but what I really heard when he spoke was, *You can do whatever God has called you to do.*

Words have the power to create worlds. They have life. My dad's words were powerful to me because they dared to speak into existence a secret dream I'd always held. They took my doubts and transformed them into the confidence I needed to pursue my dreams. On my best days, his words were affirming. But on my worst days, they were a lifeline.

Just like my dad's words, the Bible is a life-giving, affirming message from another Father. It's often referred to as *logos*, the Word of God, and that seems appropriate considering its ability to transform our lives. The Word of God can convict us, yes—removing the harmful growths of sin and death that can grow in our lives if left unchecked—but it also encourages us. Throughout Scripture, God promises us that he loves us, that he desires to be in relationship with us, that he's just and good and merciful. And like my dad's encouraging words, those are lifelines we can hold on to when hard days come.

The Word of God has the power to transform our hearts, our minds, and our actions. Like any true conversation between a father and his child, it isn't a lecture or a monologue—it's interactive. Let's recognize the affirming power of the Word of God to teach, encourage, and change us for the better.

Lord, thank you for the gift of your Word. May we join the conversation. Amen.

-Kristin

One Good Step: First, spend time thanking God for the ways in which
his Word has affirmed you. Next, choose to affirm someone else
today by speaking words of life and hope to them.

Discernment

Look beneath the surface so you can judge correctly.
JOHN 7:24

"DO YOU WANT TO KNOW why you feel uneasy telling her personal things?" I asked a friend who was telling me about a mutual acquaintance we had who she was working with as part of a nonprofit.

"Because she's not safe." I continued. "And I don't mean not safe like she won't challenge you when you need to be, we need friends who'll do that. I mean she wouldn't think twice about publicly shaming you or outing something you told her if you did or said something she didn't like. That's what makes her an unsafe person."

My friend nodded in agreement. "That's exactly what makes me so unsure about her."

"Be kind to her," I responded, "but don't feel like you have to bring her into your inner circle of people you share the most intimate parts of yourself with."

Discernment can be a touchy subject. Sometimes people use the idea of discernment to keep their circles closed off from certain people or to separate themselves from others in a way that judges or shuns them. But there is a godly discernment that comes from listening to the Holy Spirit and creating healthy boundaries around people who could potentially be harmful to us, either emotionally or spiritually.

This does not mean we have to completely cut people out of our lives, but we can be discerning in how much we share with them, how far we let them into our inner circle. We all need people close to us who we are free to open up to, sharing the hardest parts of ourselves with them. But discerning who those people are and who they are not is important. Whenever we are unsure, we can pray and ask God to give us discernment about our relationships. He can help us judge who is "safe" and who is not.

Lord, may we be people who are able to see below the surface, discerning who is healthy for us to be close to and who is not. Bring us people who are true and safe friends. Amen.

-Kendra

One Good Step: Think about the people you spend the most time with. Are you able to discern who is safe and who is not? Spend some time asking God for wisdom as you navigate your relationships.

Hopeful

We are pressed on every side by troubles, but we are not crushed.
We are perplexed, but not driven to despair.
2 CORINTHIANS 4:8

"HOW WAS YOUR CONVERSATION?" Aaron asked, knowing my friend and I had indulged in a luxurious, two-hour phone call while her toddler napped the day before.

I paused, searching for the words to adequately describe our wide-ranging conversation around whether the deep divisions in our country and in our faith community could ever be healed. We'd hung up feeling overwhelmingly sad, which was an anomaly for us and for our normal conversations.

"I don't know. It was really good to catch up, but life feels so heavy right now, and we are both struggling," I admitted, my shoulders sagging in defeat.

Despair. The word came to me hours later as I folded socks. The hopeless, no-way-forward, unnavigable, unfixable, in-over-my-head feeling threatening to pull me under and swallow me whole was despair. *Jesus, what do I do with this?* I prayed, gathering together and setting aside the unmatched solos, hoping their match was in the next load. *I can't change what is happening in my country and the church, so how do I navigate this?*

Despair does not come from God. Ever. And if I allow it, despair will infect me, spreading through my thoughts and ratcheting up stress, fear, and anxiety, dictating my actions from a place of fear instead of hope. Despair wants to consume us, rendering us ineffective members of God's Kingdom at best, and, at our worst, people who inflict damage on the reputation of Jesus-followers.

We fight despair with hope, reminding ourselves to fix our minds on heaven rather than focusing on circumstances around us (see Colossians 3:2). Replacing doomscrolling social media posts with prayer is a great first step toward being hopeful rather than despairing.

God is not surprised when the world is topsy-turvy, and some of his best work takes place in the midst of chaos. When confronted with seemingly overwhelming odds, I'm learning to fight against despair by whispering to God, *What good things are you doing during this hard time? In what new ways are you building your Kingdom? Use me!*

Lord, help us keep our eyes on you, and deploy us as hope-bringers when circumstances are hard and despair looms. Amen.

-Julie

One Good Step: Pick three Scriptures that fill you with hope, and meditate on those Scriptures when you feel despair looming. Then ask God for an assignment as a hope-bringer.

Display

The heavens proclaim the glory of God.
The skies display his craftsmanship.

PSALM 19:1

CLIMBING ON THE COACH BUS that would transport us from the hotel to the church, I surveyed the group of guests in wedding finery chatting in the seats. All were strangers, although a few of Tim's old classmates were present. When we took our seats and the line of buses rolled forward, I watched in astonishment as our little parade was accompanied by the keening sirens and rumbling motorcycles of a police escort.

It was April in New Orleans, and each moment of our trip had been a display of the city's history and charm. We'd spent the past couple of days wandering the French Quarter, eating crawfish étouffée and po'boys, soaking in music and art. By the time we attended the wedding of a childhood friend of Tim's, we understood why he and his fiancée had met at Tulane and fallen in love with each other—and with the city.

As the day unfolded, each part of the wedding was not only a celebration of marriage, it was a display of the best of New Orleans. The reception was held at a historic location across from Jackson Square, and we all indulged in both the traditional wedding cake and the city's tradition of a groom's cake. Though the three forms of musical entertainment—including a Grammy Award–winning singer—were impressive, the brass band that led us around the square for a "second line" captured the spirit of the city. By the time fireworks exploded as we stood in the street, I was thoroughly amazed.

Each experience celebrated the couple, but it also displayed their love for the city. When we love something or someone, we want to boast about our object of affection. We want others to see the person or place the way we do, highlighted in the best of ways. Just as creation displays the glory of God, as his children, we are witnesses and participants in displaying and demonstrating the greatness of our God. Our words and actions are the best opportunities we have to display the grace and mercy of Jesus to a watching world.

Lord, you are worthy of praise. May we display your power and love in all that we do. Amen.

-Kristin

One Good Step: Intentionally display Jesus today by talking about him to those you love or demonstrating his work in the world through your actions.

Connect

If one part suffers, all the parts suffer with it,
and if one part is honored, all the parts are glad.

1 CORINTHIANS 12:26

STAYING CONNECTED with one another became even more necessary one spring as we, like much of the country, spent months in isolation. After our initial shock and then settling into a new routine at home, my family and I started to once again look around us and see who needed help. *Who was lonely? Who needed encouragement or a friend?*

We saw many people that we could reach out to and spent time writing letters and making phone calls to our former neighbor, now living in an elderly apartment complex and unable to have visitors. We made little gifts for friends and neighbors and left them at their front doors. We had video calls with grandparents and game nights online. We wrote words of encouragement up and down our neighborhood sidewalks, all in order to intentionally stay connected with those around us.

It was a difficult season, there is no doubt, but it also was a time of slowing down and connecting with others in ways we wouldn't have normally when life was so busy. I began to really see and value the way that we need one another and how interconnected our lives really are. When a friend would call and feel overwhelmed, we would listen and lament with them. When someone cried tears of loneliness, we would cry too. We joined in one another's pain, connected even while being apart physically.

We are all connected in more ways than we realize. God made us this way. We were never meant to go through life alone. We are to suffer with those who suffer and rejoice with those who are rejoicing, just as we hope they would do for us. We were created for community.

Lord, help us to reach out when we are lonely and to look for others who may be in need of encouragement or a friend. Help us to see how connected we are and how we need one another. Amen.

-Kendra

One Good Step: If you are lonely, reach out to a friend, or look for someone around you who may need encouragement and connect with them today.

Nothing

I am convinced that nothing can ever separate us from God's love. Neither death nor life, neither angels nor demons, neither our fears for today nor our worries about tomorrow—not even the powers of hell can separate us from God's love.

ROMANS 8:38

"I BROUGHT YOU BACK A GIFT," Li said, handing me a tightly rolled scroll. It was our reunion BBQ, celebrating her return to the US for her second year of teaching. Li was part of an exchange program in which teachers come to the States to teach middle schoolers.

As I unfurled the scroll, I gasped in delight at the hand-painted Chinese calligraphy with the roughly translated phrase, "I'll love you until the rock rots and the oceans dry up."

With misty eyes, I hugged my dear friend, laughing as we remembered one of our dinner conversations about expressions of love in our respective cultures. She'd asked me about our phrase "I love you to the moon and back," and I'd fallen in love with the Chinese equivalent she'd had commissioned for my scroll.

But my very favorite expression of love is Romans 8:38. Nothing separates us from the love of God. Not our actions, not the things done to us, not even the powers of hell. In a culture made up of shades of gray in which absolutes like always and never come with caveats and loopholes, situations in which someone, somewhere finds the one time it doesn't apply, today's word brings a breath of reassurance.

When God tells us that *nothing* will separate us from his love, that is a promise we can take to the bank. And when we grasp that promise with both hands, absorbing it fully, it brings healing to our deepest wounds, and to all the secret shame we carry. It makes me wonder what this world would look like if we believed, wholeheartedly, this promise.

Lord, reveal to us the ways we have hedged our bets, not fully believing that nothing separates us from your love. Amen.

-Julie

One Good Step: What things have you imagined separated you from God's love? Make a list of those lies you've believed. Rip up the list, and write the word *nothing* on the palm of your hand to remind yourself of God's promise.

Masterpiece

We are God's masterpiece. He has created us anew in Christ Jesus,
so we can do the good things he planned for us long ago.
EPHESIANS 2:10

FRANKLY, I THOUGHT the Botticelli paintings would be smaller. After all, I'd once spent a day touring the Louvre in Paris and—while it was amazing overall—I was underwhelmed by the *Mona Lisa*. In books, it felt larger-than-life, but in reality it seemed dwarfed by the echoing hall and gaggle of onlookers.

Now in Florence, I walked into the Botticelli room at the Uffizi Gallery and felt completely overwhelmed. Sliding onto a bench in the center of the room, I sat in silent astonishment at the scale of the paintings. *The Birth of Venus* was more than 5½ feet tall and 9 feet wide, while *Primavera* ("Spring") was more than 6 feet tall and 10 feet wide. Each took up a large part of the wall.

For about an hour, I took in the expressions on the characters' faces, the curves of windswept gowns, and the exquisite details of flowers and figures. I stared for so long that my friend, sitting next to me, fell asleep. I just couldn't seem to comprehend the obvious deliberation in each painted stroke. I was awed at the mastery displayed.

Originally, the word *masterpiece* was used in the European guild system to refer to a piece of work created by an apprentice, someone who aspired to become a master craftsman and submitted the masterpiece in order to qualify for membership. Their livelihood depended on the piece's quality, and they took great care in producing their work.

That afternoon in an Italian art museum gave me a new appreciation for how God views us as masterpieces. Other translations of Ephesians 2:10 use words like *handiwork* (NIV) and *workmanship* (ESV), but all give the same impression of God as a master craftsman, carefully creating us as *imago Dei*, the image of God in the world. Too often we see the flaws in our humanity and overlook the miracle of our beating heart, unconscious breath, and ability to reason. But a masterpiece is exceptional: a visible representation of the invisible hand of God in the world. We are works of art, created with intention, meant to have a purpose in the world.

Lord, help us to see ourselves and one another the way you do. Amen.

-Kristin

One Good Step: Consciously choose to see a friend or family member as a masterpiece. Name three qualities that make them exceptional.

Resolve

If another believer sins against you, go privately and point out
the offense. If the other person listens and confesses it,
you have won that person back.

MATTHEW 18:15

A DEAR FRIEND OF MINE was heartbroken. A few families in her church were having a dispute over words that had allegedly been spoken. Instead of handling the concerns with the person involved, they chose to go behind their back, involving several other families, until it was unclear any more what had actually been said and what had not.

My friend had many interactions with people from the church who wanted to pull her into the middle of it all, but she chose to stay out of it, encouraging the people involved to speak with the person who'd offended them, along with their pastor. They refused, instead choosing to leave the church and creating animosity in their wake while never resolving the situation with the other party or seeking to find a solution.

My friend was frustrated over the lack of resolution, especially since everyone involved was a Christian and had been a part of their church for many years. She was heartbroken to see the rift in relationships this offense had caused. I prayed with her, asking God to give her peace and wisdom in a way to move forward, with or without any resolution.

There are times when conflict comes and a solution between the parties involved follows, but what do you do when people are unwilling to try to resolve an offense? We do not have control over others' thoughts or actions, only our own, which can make resolving an issue difficult at times. As Christians, we are to go to one another with our grievances and attempt to be reconciled. Even if it wouldn't be healthy to continue a relationship with another person, we can still work to resolve any offenses between us. That will show our maturity as believers and our love for one another.

Lord, give us the courage to honestly and lovingly confront offenses when they occur. May we have ears to listen and wisdom to know what to say. Amen.

-Kendra

One Good Step: Do you have an offense against someone?
Today, pray and ask God to show you one way you can move toward
addressing the concern and toward a resolution.

Tranquility

Better one handful with tranquility than two handfuls
with toil and chasing after the wind.

ECCLESIASTES 4:6, NIV

I LEFT THE PRACTICE OF LAW after fifteen years of clients, courtrooms, and conference rooms. Aaron and I each had intense careers, and as our children grew, we were being tugged in increasingly divergent directions. There were not enough hours in the day for me to be the attorney I wanted to be, the wife I needed to be, and the mom I longed to be.

We budgeted for life on one income a year in advance, reducing expenses and making plans, and then, one day, God told me it was time to be done. I wish I could tell you that it was a smooth ride, with no regrets, no tears, no questions about what might come next. But I found myself plunged into grief, despite knowing it was the right decision for our family. I struggled with identity and with feelings of failure for having stepped away from the American dream, the feminist goal, the calling of an independent woman.

As months passed and a new normal settled in, my grief lifted, and I found tranquility. Now, instead of competing with Aaron over early mornings and late nights at the office, I'm usually able to support whatever he needs. We rarely struggle to juggle school pick up times, practice schedules, or various appointments. And while I fully admit that I am no Domestic Goddess, I put every one of my mediation and courtroom skills to good use navigating the emotional roller coaster of tweenagers, ferreting out trouble before it sets roots and grows.

By releasing what I'd toiled and strived for my entire life (well, since becoming doggedly determined to be a lawyer in sixth grade), our marriage has found a bit of margin and peace, tranquility in a world telling us we must run the rat race as hard and as fast as possible.

Our house is older. Our cars are not new. We cannot keep up with the Joneses, but we don't mind. If two handfuls require us to chase after the wind, we will always choose tranquility and just one.

Lord, show us where we might choose tranquility over toil and chasing. Show us where we might find that one handful is more than enough. Amen.

-Julie

One Good Step: Intentionally begin living with one handful instead of two in an area of your life that has been causing stress. Watch what God can do with less.

Dwell

I love your sanctuary, LORD, the place where your glorious presence dwells.

PSALM 26:8

MY HUSBAND AND I moved to our current home a decade ago, on our oldest daughter's first birthday. Though we loved our original home, its location an hour from my husband's work made the commute long in the summer and intolerable in the winter and spurred our decision to move to a smaller town that cut his driving distance in half.

Our first home was located on a corner lot across from a pond, which we loved. But it had too many bedrooms for couples looking to downsize, and the lack of a backyard made it a tough sell for young families. As a result, it sat on the market for a couple of years.

One day, we decided to check on the house, which was still for sale. As we pulled into the driveway, I spotted our former neighbors outside and walked across the lawn to chat with them. Returning to the car, I was astonished to hear our now-two-year-old daughter cry out, "My home! My home!"

We'd moved to our current house when she was just twelve months old, young enough that we had assumed she wouldn't know or care about our previous house. No one had told her we were heading there; my husband and I hadn't discussed our visit in her presence. Yet she remembered—without being told—that we had lived there. She knew it had been her home.

On the surface, the word *dwell* references a living space. But it's also often a mark of something that holds a place in our minds and thoughts—we dwell on a situation or problem, thinking it through, lingering on its repercussions. Whether we mentally dwell on circumstances or physically dwell in a house, we live within them. Perhaps, when Ecclesiastes 3:11 says that God "has planted eternity in the human heart," that is what is meant. That, like my two-year-old daughter, there is an essential part of us that recognizes and longs to dwell in heaven, our eternal home. We see the work of our Father God in each sunrise, on every mountaintop, and in the praises of his people, but when we have a relationship with Jesus, his presence dwells within us, a steady hope of home.

Lord, thank you for your presence in our lives. Amen.

-Kristin

One Good Step: Reflect on what it means to dwell with God.

Hope

I am certain that God, who began the good work within you,
will continue his work until it is finally finished
on the day when Christ Jesus returns.

PHILIPPIANS 1:6

"I THINK THE GREATEST THING we can do to show our adopted kids love and that we believe in them is to just get up every morning and consistently show up. We're not perfect, but we're here," my husband stated, as he looked at me across the island in our kitchen after everyone had finally made their way to bed at the end of a harder day with one of our kids. Sometimes parenting feels a bit like a roller coaster of emotion and behavior that I often find myself resisting the urge to ride. Being a steady force in a person's life when they are emotionally coming undone is harder than I ever thought it could be.

Each morning, I pick up my Bible, looking for hope. A confirmation about who God is and what his character is like, and every day I walk away more determined to claim what I know about God: he is strong, faithful, forgiving, loving, kind, compassionate . . . and on and on the list goes.

This is where my hope lies. God's mercies are new every day. He is relentless in his love and pursuit of me. He never gives up on any of us. And my husband and I consistently showing up for our adopted kids, on good days and hard days, is a reflection to them of God's character. We don't mirror it perfectly, but the hope still remains in our trying.

Every day we have the opportunity to get up and start new. And when we do, we show others around us that they have the opportunity to get up every day and start fresh. They observe hope through our words, but more importantly through our actions. Don't be discouraged by what you see only with your eyes; God's not done yet. We can cling to the hope that he will finish the work that he's started, in us and in those around us.

Lord, thank you for the way that you consistently show up for each one of us. Thank you for your promise and the hope we have that you will be faithful to complete the work you've started in us.

-Kendra

One Good Step: What is one area of your life where you are holding out hope that God will intervene or act on your behalf? Ask God to show you how he is working, even in the smallest of ways.

Treasure

Don't store up treasures here on earth, where moths eat them and rust destroys them, and where thieves break in and steal. Store your treasures in heaven, where moths and rust cannot destroy, and thieves do not break in and steal.

MATTHEW 6:19-20

ONE OF MY VERY FIRST COWORKERS at one of my very first jobs collected Beanie Babies—the original ones subject to public hysteria as limited-edition varieties released, only to be immediately snatched up by people queued in long lines wrapping outside stores. Even as a teenager munching peanut butter and jelly next to her in the break room as she told me all about her Beanie Baby retirement plan, I remember pondering the wisdom of that investment.

I've thought of her and those Beanie Babies repeatedly over the years as I've seen piles of them at thrift shops and as I've watched friends navigate downsizing or liquidating their parents' households, struggling with collections of all kinds that, despite all the promises of future wealth, hold little more than sentimental value.

Collecting can be fun. I love the thrill of the hunt as much as the woman sifting through fine china next to me at Goodwill, looking for that elusive pattern to add to my grandmother's dishes, now passed to me. But I'm careful not to mix up the fun of collecting with treasure.

Our treasure is not gold and silver. It is not the equity in our home or our 401(k) plans. Our treasure is eternal in nature. It is intangible and impossible to quantify on our net worth statement. Our treasure is the relationships we've built with spiritual family as well as those far from Jesus. It is the sacrifices we've quietly made to help loved ones, neighbors, those we've never met, and our enemies. It is the times in which we've chosen the good of someone else over our comfort. It is the unnoticed, unappreciated gaps we've filled. It is toilet scrubbing, the nursery duty, the pacing all night long with a sick child while utterly exhausted. It is when we store up these treasures, that we'll find a heart beating in tune with God.

Lord, help us exchange what our culture defines as treasure for your definition. Amen.

-Julie

One Good Step: Do one thing that builds your heavenly 401(k) plan today.

Prepare

He who has prepared us for this very thing is God,
who has given us the Spirit as a guarantee.
2 CORINTHIANS 5:5, ESV

MY FRIEND MELISSA'S FAMILY had been farming for decades. One year, they asked if I'd like to help prepare for planting by picking rock. Curious, I agreed, and soon found myself walking the fields with Melissa and her cousins. Dust tickled our noses as we walked behind a truck, searching for rocks. Whenever we'd spot one of the many rocks in the field, we'd toss it onto the trailer attached to the truck.

Sometimes a rock would be a bit too big, and one of Melissa's cousins would step in and grab it, heaving it over the edge. It was hot, dirty work, but with a group of us together it was fun. At the end of the day, I wiped a sweaty arm across my forehead and surveyed the rocks, amazed at how many we'd accumulated.

In colder climates like ours, farmers have to remove rocks that rise to the surface from their fields every year. It's a necessary part of preparing the ground for planting. The rocks are from glacial deposits and migrate upwards over time due to the effects of freezing and thawing. The effect is most obvious in tilled soil—like a farmer's field or a gardener's vegetable bed—because the rocks are able to move upward unimpeded by things like trees. Farmers pick rock so that their equipment won't be damaged. Their ability to plant and harvest is directly tied to how they prepare the soil.

Like those dusty fields, our hearts are often compared to soil, the seeds of God's love and his message of our salvation a truth that is scattered and waiting to take root. Yet it's also true that our hearts can resemble the rocky soil of a spring field, with smaller hurts and larger pains emerging over time to interrupt the ability of God's love to grow in our hearts. As Christians, we must prepare our hearts to receive God's truths by removing impediments. Let's sift through the soil of our own hearts to prepare room for Jesus and his light to shine within.

Lord, help us to address the rocks that rise in our own hearts. May we foster the truth of your love and mercy in our hearts instead. Amen.

-Kristin

One Good Step: What rocks need to be removed from your heart
so you can prepare room for Jesus' light to shine?

Sure

I know that nothing can keep us from the love of God.
Death cannot! Life cannot! Angels cannot! Leaders cannot! Any other
power cannot! Hard things now or in the future cannot! The world above or the
world below cannot! Any other living thing cannot keep us away from
the love of God which is ours through Christ Jesus our Lord.

ROMANS 8:38-39, NLV

RECENTLY, events around the world have caused an upheaval of our routines and threatened our sense of security. I've seen people clinging to any and every piece of information, looking for things that they can believe are sure. I understand why they would do this. It makes us feel safe when we think we fully understand what is happening to us.

As we've walked through this season, I've tried to resist this pressing urge to find out answers to everything. I've thought a lot about my sister who passed away at twenty-eight from breast cancer, leaving two small children and a husband behind. In the fifteen years since her death, I've often tried to figure out the *why* behind how it could happen, and if I'm honest, I've yet to find an answer. So instead, I started asking myself about God and what I knew to be true about him.

In the present situation, I began to ask myself the same thing: What do I know about God that is sure, even when life is not? Because no matter what I'm facing in life, this answer never changes. God is love. He is kind. He is near. And maybe most important: nothing, in all of eternity, will separate us from his love.

There are many things in life that will remain without answers, but who God is and his love for us remains sure, always. This I will cling to when life gets hard, when circumstances come along that are out of my control, or when the answers I've been hoping for simply aren't there. This life is full of uncertainty, but God's love for us is always certain.

Lord, when I don't find the answers to the questions I have in life, help me to instead lean into the promises of who you are. Help me remember that, in all things, your love for me is constant. Amen.

-Kendra

One Good Step: What questions do you have that just
don't seem to have answers? How can knowing who God is
help you as you walk through those unknowns?

Fortress

The nations are in chaos, and their kingdoms crumble! God's voice thunders,
and the earth melts! The LORD of Heaven's Armies is here among us;
the God of Israel is our fortress.

PSALM 46:6-7

"WELL, I'VE STARTED WATCHING the clouds for Jesus. I expect his return any day," I say with a rueful chuckle, clearly teasing but often with a decent dollop of wishful thinking.

That's my pitiful attempt at apocalypse humor when asked what I think about the churning, never-ending chaos in current events. And, in truth, I follow it up with a sincere discussion because I know anxiety and fear often lurk just beyond the question.

What *do* we do when faced with an increasingly chaotic, mixed-up world?

We pray, certainly. But categorizing the chaos helps me determine my next steps as I pray. A person far smarter than me suggested we separate chaotic events into one of two categories: predicaments and problems. Predicaments are issues over which we have little to no control. Problems are issues in which we have control. We manage predicaments; we solve problems.

Once I label something a predicament, I waste no additional energy trying to solve it. It is something that belongs solely and wholly to God, our defender and our fortress. It's a relief, honestly, to release it in its entirety to prayer. I still have to live with it or through it, and I have to manage it—but I trust God to be with me in the midst of it, my foundation and shelter.

If something is a problem, I have prayerful choices to make. I have a role to play in the resolution, and I can focus my attention on making discerning, scripturally sound decisions. I have a way forward, action steps, even if it's distasteful and something I'd rather not do.

Chaos in the world is nothing new. Our spiritual ancestors experienced as much and more chaos as we have at the hands of governments, natural disasters, and disease. God is not surprised, and we are not alone. Jesus is our great hope and firm foundation, a solid rock, a secure anchor in the midst of chaotic events.

Lord, reframe our perspectives in the midst of chaos. Keep our eyes on you and give us wisdom over which things are predicaments to be managed and which are problems to be solved. Amen.

-Julie

One Good Step: Prayerfully categorize the chaotic events causing you unease. Ask God to give you an action step for the things you've labeled a problem.

Tradition

Be imitators of me, as I am of Christ. Now I commend you because you remember
me in everything and maintain the traditions even as I delivered them to you.

1 CORINTHIANS 11:1-2, ESV

WHEN I WAS GROWING UP, my mom cooked dinner throughout the week, but Sunday
was typically the day we'd fend for ourselves. As an avid fan of leftovers and cold
cereal, I didn't mind those options—unless Dad offered to make Norwegian
pancakes.

Originally from North Dakota, my dad is the son of Norwegian immigrants
who arrived on the prairie more than a century ago. As a child, I grew up eating
lefse, rutabaga, and other Scandinavian foods, but my favorite item was Norwegian
pancakes. They were thin and fried fast, and they reminded me of crepes. We'd
slather them in butter, sprinkle them with brown sugar, then roll them up and eat
them. They were sweet and delicious, and to this day I'm confused on how they
qualified as dinner rather than dessert.

Norwegian pancakes were one of the many traditions my family cherished. As
a mother now myself, I've tried to cultivate our own traditions—like movie nights
with "fancy" chocolate-sprinkled popcorn, our annual visit to Madeline Island,
Sunday sundaes with all the toppings, a summer bucket list, and daily acts of
kindness during December. All of those are special to me, not just because of the
activities themselves but because they remind me of happy memories of times past.

Throughout the Bible, traditions were seen both positively and negatively. They
governed everything from sacrifices to festivals to behavior on the Sabbath. While
some were helpful, others caused clashes between Jesus and his followers and the
religious leaders of the day. Paul, in his letter to the Corinthians, reminds them to
follow the traditions he has laid out for them—but only after reminding them that
he himself is imitating Christ.

We lead by example. Our traditions, too, can be positive or negative, depending
on how they affect others. Are they inclusive or exclusive? Do they honor Christ's
example? Do they invite us into deeper relationships with God and one another or
are they just a set of rules? As Christians, let's consider whether or not our traditions
reflect the love of Christ.

*Lord, help us to cultivate traditions that honor you and the way you love each
and every person. Amen.*

-Kristin

One Good Step: Consider your traditions through the lens of Christ's love.

Lavish

How great is the goodness you have stored up for those
who fear you. You lavish it on those who come to you for protection,
blessing them before the watching world.

PSALM 31:19

"DID YOU KNOW your daddy ate shrimp every day before afternoon kindergarten with his grandma Grace?" Grandma Connie asked Jonny as she took his plate, handing it to Aaron for a dollop of cheesy potatoes from the far side of the table before giving it back. We were at my mother-in-law's house for dinner when she shared this beloved memory, which has been retold countless times, yet we never tire of hearing it.

"Every day? He got shrimp every day?" Jonny asked, glancing at Aaron with a mischievous grin, knowing the story and yet loving to hear about his dad's childhood.

"Just about every day," Connie confirmed. "Grandma Grace stayed with us that winter, and she'd take him out for lunch before she dropped him off at kindergarten. Your dad loved the shrimp basket, and as they ate, they'd chat all about the things he wanted to talk about."

There is the tiniest whiff of scandal around the word *shrimp*, an extravagance for an otherwise financially conservative woman. Grandma Grace so loved her grandson that she not only took him out for lunch every day, but she let him get the *popcorn shrimp basket*.

I love this story. I never tire of hearing it. Grandma Grace lavished love upon her grandson in the form of his favorite food and her undivided attention. It delighted him, and I'm sure it delighted her as well.

As much as Grandma Grace loved her grandchildren, God's love is infinitely deeper. He lavishes love upon his children: freely poured out and everlasting. His gift of peace always, even in the midst of hardships and difficult circumstances, is an unconditional promise, ours for the asking (see Philippians 4:7). God's peace gifted to us is but one example of the blessings he promises to lavish upon us, gifts with eternal value, things that will not rot, be stolen, or fade away.

Lord, thank you for your lavish love, for gifts with eternal value as we press onward, following you. Amen.

-Julie

One Good Step: Who can you lavish love upon this week? Make a list
of three people and surprise them with a coffee, an old-fashioned note
in the mail, or some homemade cookies left on their doorstep.

Perspective

We don't look at the troubles we can see now;
rather, we fix our gaze on things that cannot be seen.

2 CORINTHIANS 4:18

NOT LONG AGO our garage door up and died—on the morning my husband left on a weeklong business trip. And as I was standing in my garage looking at my door that was completely ajar—listening to the garage door repair man talk about door differences, tracks, springs, and such—I threw a little pity party in my head.

But then I talked with a friend who had water in their basement. For the third time. In a house that had never flooded before. This all happened the same week another dear friend's house burned in a fire that started in the attic. It was the worst place for a fire to begin, as it seemingly smoldered for hours before it was discovered. Her family emerged safe and sound, but they would have to spend the next several months living in a rental as their house was gutted, cleaned, and fixed.

So how do you overcome a poor attitude over a minor (or even major) fiasco? I thought about my friend with water in the basement and how much worse that was for her to deal with, and suddenly, my garage door didn't seem like that big of a deal.

And when I talked with my friend about her water troubles, she said she reminded herself of our other friend who had just had the fire, and suddenly, the water didn't seem too bad.

And when I talked with my friend who'd just had the fire, she shared about others whose life situations were far worse than hers.

Remembering who in this world may have it just a little bit worse than I do can do wonders for my perspective. Whether they're big or small, we all face situations every day meant to steal our joy, our drive, or our dreams. Shaking our heads in response, grumbling under our breath, or becoming annoyed with life can be common responses. But we always have a choice. We can choose to focus on the trouble we see now, or we can shift our gaze to what is eternal. Changing our perspective can make all the difference.

Lord, help me to shift my perspective from what is fleeting to what is eternal. Amen.

-Kendra

One Good Step: What is one area in your life that you need to change your perspective on? How can thinking about and praying for the struggles of someone else or looking at it from an eternal perspective help you to do that?

Reign

Then God said, "Let us make human beings in our image, to be like us. They will reign over the fish in the sea, the birds in the sky, the livestock, all the wild animals on the earth, and the small animals that scurry along the ground."

GENESIS 1:26

"WE DON'T RECYCLE," she said, tossing the aluminum cans into the trash. "God gave us the earth, and since this is temporary, we can do what we want."

"Don't we have a responsibility to take care of what God has entrusted us with?" I asked.

"We won't be around long enough for it to matter. Jesus will return before it's a problem."

Her words, spoken to a far younger version of myself when I wasn't entirely sure what I believed about God, left me puzzled. While we have hints about the timing of Christ's return, Scripture is clear that God alone knows the day and time. In fact, everyone who has predicted Christ's imminent return over the last roughly two thousand years has been wrong. Already struggling in my faith, I wondered why Christians would be so blasé in refusing to recycle, so certain Christ's return was within their lifetime or their children's lifetime.

As the years have passed, I've returned to that conversation periodically, replaying it and the inherent arguments underlying her position as my own faith has grown and matured.

Everything belongs to God—all of creation, every possession we consider ours, even our bodies (see 1 Corinthians 6:19). As Creator, he granted us the authority to reign over all of the earth, entrusting it to us, allowing us the freedom to use its resources, to enjoy its beauty, to oversee it as we see fit. The earth is his creation, but we reign. We control the earth's resources, but we also have responsibility for its care.

We can be both followers of Christ *and* good stewards of the earth, regardless of what political parties or extreme views from the right or the left might try to tell us. To reign is to have responsibility, and to reign over the earth is to be entrusted with a precious, beautiful resource not only for us, but for our children's children's children, for as long as we wait for Jesus' return.

Lord, may we be good stewards of all the resources you have entrusted to us, including the fish of the sea, the birds of the air, and over all of the earth. Amen.

-Julie

One Good Step: Choose one new habit to make you a better steward of the earth and do it.

Team

Don't team up with those who are unbelievers. How can righteousness
be a partner with wickedness? How can light live with darkness?

2 CORINTHIANS 6:14

ONE SUNDAY, a few of my fellow students and I decided to venture over to the Oxford vs. Cambridge fencing match. None of us knew anything about fencing, but it seemed quintessentially British, and our interest was piqued. It was held in a large room at Oxford's Examination Schools. Dark paneling covered the bottom half of the walls, while the top half was painted a muted yellow. Large windows spanned from window seats upwards to the arched ceiling that was divided into sizable white squares featuring mythical animals.

Initially, we sat in the chairs provided. But after realizing that most spectators were standing, we climbed onto one of the window seats for a bird's eye view. The fencers were split into teams of three each, rotating so that each person would fence against all three opponents. Each player's sword and areas of their body were hooked up to electronic equipment that helped discern when someone scored a hit. How long they fenced varied: it either lasted three minutes, or ended after the competitors exchanged a certain number of hits.

One of the things I found the most interesting was that all the hits in fencing are added throughout the entire round-robin—that way if some are stronger than others, they can "make up" hits. Though fencing itself isn't usually a team sport—each person must face their opponent individually—over those three hours, I was struck by the idea that the stronger members can make up for those who aren't as strong.

We, too, must face our own battles as individuals, yet as members of the body of Christ, we can support one another in our weaknesses and team up to accomplish the work of Christ in the world. When we know we are part of a team, we work differently, leaning into our strengths and noticing where we can come alongside others to support them. And, being part of a team helps us consider the good of others, not just ourselves, as we work to the mutual benefit of all.

Lord, thank you that we're not alone. Help us remember that we're part of a team, working together. Amen.

-Kristin

One Good Step: Imagine yourself as part of a team, working toward accomplishing God's work in the world. What are some of your strengths? What are some of your weaknesses?

Authentic

Every good and perfect gift is from above,
coming down from the Father of the heavenly lights,
who does not change like shifting shadows.

JAMES 1:17, NIV

NOT LONG AGO, my husband and I discussed pornography with our children. We talked about the harmful effects it can have on our minds, bodies, and relationships, and how it is a counterfeit experience to the authentic love, comfort, and closeness God designed us to have with another human being. Pornography gives us the impression of closeness while—in reality—creating walls and distance between us and those we love. It's a lie, disguised as a way to satisfy us, but never really authentically fulfilling our desire for closeness with another person.

Since our conversation, I've been thinking about other ways I allow counterfeit comforts or securities into my own life. I may not struggle with pornography, but how often have I turned to food for comfort? How often have I watched Netflix to soothe my pain? What counterfeits have I substituted as a way to fill a void in my life when, really, what I need is God's healing and maybe another person's compassion?

This, to me, is the lie of sin. Cheapening what God intended, offering fulfillment, but always coming up short. Counterfeits may seem good for a season, but left unchecked, will soon gain momentum and easily end up beyond our ability to control.

As children whom God deeply loves, we have access to good, authentic things that he wants to give us. And he promises that every good gift, every authentic gift, is from above. He desires for us to be able to live out our days in healthy and loving ways, free from the bondage of sin and immune to cheap replacements that alter our relationship with him and one another. He longs to offer us authentic and lasting love and joy that no cheap replacement will ever be able to fill.

Lord, thank you for the authentic things you offer us in life that will satisfy all of our desires. Help us to notice counterfeits and to turn away from things that won't last. Amen.

-Kendra

One Good Step: Are you filling your life with counterfeit things that don't really satisfy? Bring them to God today and ask him to fill you with that which will last.

Invite

I was hungry, and you fed me. I was thirsty, and you gave me a drink.
I was a stranger, and you invited me into your home.

MATTHEW 25:35

I ONCE HEARD someone say that in order to invite people into your home, all you really need are fifteen minutes and three items: bacon, a laundry basket, and baby wipes. Fifteen minutes before someone is due to arrive, throw bacon on the stove to make your guests feel welcome, grab a laundry basket to pick up stray items from around the house, and finish up by using wipes to get rid of any sticky messes lingering on tables and floors.

Not only do I love that "necessities" include bacon—that seems like a delicious piece of advice—I appreciate the idea that welcoming others requires very little preparation. Instead, it requires only a willingness to invite others into your home, regardless of its imperfections.

I used to feel differently. A friend once told me that inviting people into my home is a gift of mine, but inside I scoffed. She didn't know that I had nagged my husband until he moved his pile of papers from the kitchen counter and hollered at my kids to get dressed just before she arrived. But then she continued, "I always feel at home here. I love how the girls hug me and you assume I'll stay for dinner. I like knowing where your water glasses are and that you don't worry about washing your floor before I visit." Put that way, her words made more sense: while I was worried about the tidiness of my home, she was focused on the welcoming warmth of our response to her visit.

It's freeing to realize that our less-than-perfect invitation is often more than enough. When we set an extra place at our table or pour a glass of water for someone who stops by, when we invite someone who needs a hand to stay in our spare bedroom until they're on their feet, when we live openhanded and openhearted lives that simply share what we have—our lives become an invitation. If you're made in the image of God, you're invited to the table. After all, this open-door living echoes the heart of God, who is always ready with an invitation.

Lord, thank you that the invitation began with you. Help us to invite others into our lives and into community. Amen.

-Kristin

One Good Step: Invite someone to your home.

Why

Cry out for insight, and ask for understanding. Search for them as you would
for silver; seek them like hidden treasures. Then you will understand what
it means to fear the Lord, and you will gain knowledge of God.

PROVERBS 2:3-5

"WHY?"

There was a season in which that word was constantly on my toddler son's lips,
his quest for knowledge nearly insatiable. I loved his unending curiosity, and I tried
to answer his questions accurately, even if it meant I, in turn, was constantly asking
Google.

His whys had me viewing the world through fresh eyes, reawakening my own
curiosity about things I had taken for granted, allowing them to simply be in the
background of my life. I learned more during the season of Jonny's incessant questioning than I'd learned in years as I looked up answers to all the things I did not know.

Jonny's curiosity got me thinking about what other things I've simply accepted
at face value, including Scripture. I've started reading the Word of God with "why"
on my lips. Why did the heavenly host appear to shepherds that night Jesus was
born? Why was Mary the first person Jesus encountered upon arising from his
grave—a woman tasked with carrying arguably the most important message in the
history of the world back to the men? Why did Jesus make the parable of the Good
Samaritan about a Samaritan, rather than another people group? As I dug for the
answers to these questions, I marveled afresh at the goodness, the love of God for
the underdogs of society.

Scripture has layers of cultural context woven throughout its stories and word
choices immediately understood by those who saw Jesus and heard his words that
add depth, clarity, and nuance mostly lost to us unless we go digging. Unfortunately
for us, those nuances are lost unless we read with "why" in mind, with our curiosity
piqued and primed to understand more. When we seek out contextual clues, we
find a deeper understanding of God embedded in the verses and stories we've heard
or read at surface value a multitude of times, additional insights into his character,
a new perspective on how we should be living our lives as followers of Christ.

*Lord, restore our curiosity. Help us to ask why, to dig deeper into your parables
and analogies, to look for the cultural context in Scripture. Give us fresh insight on
who you are. Amen.*

-Julie

One Good Step: Start reading Scripture with "why" on your lips. Seek out
answers in trusted commentaries and from trusted sources.

 Lean

The LORD is my strength and shield. I trust him with all my heart.

PSALM 28:7

MY DAD ALWAYS owned his own business. When I was a child, he was a farrier, traveling from farm to farm, putting in long days, coming home smelling like animals and outside and barnyards.

When I was in middle school we moved. Horseshoeing had become just too physically taxing for my dad to continue doing, so he needed a change. As he worked to grow his new business in another community, I distinctly remember how lean the first few years were financially. Not that my parents complained or worried in front of us kids, but we could sense that we needed to cut back on spending.

And so as my husband walked through a similar lean season in his own business over the past few years, I found myself mostly trusting but somewhat vacillating between trying to figure out what I could do to help, to security in trusting that God has it all under control.

We all experience lean seasons of insecurity in a variety of ways. Maybe for you it's not financial but relational. Perhaps you and your spouse just aren't communicating the way you'd like, or you have a child who's angry with you. Maybe there are rifts with extended family members, and you wonder how they'll ever be repaired. Or you could be experiencing leanness in your own work or in finding purpose for your life. I don't know where life feels lean for you; I just know you are not alone.

There are two things I've held on to in a lean season. The first is that we are meant to live life in the community and support of others. And second, that God sees us, he knows us, and he loves us. These two things are always secure.

Because although we may not have answers to all our questions or know all the reasons why we are facing this lean situation, we can know and trust that God will show himself faithful. It may not be a way to escape our lean space, but it is enough to know that we have God and others to stay with us in the midst of life's lean times.

Lord, thank you that we can trust you to be with us during the good times and the lean times of life. We are always secure in you. Amen.

-Kendra

One Good Step: What season of leanness are you experiencing today? Who can you ask to support you, even if only through prayer?

Washed

He saved us, not because of the righteous things we had done,
but because of his mercy. He washed away our sins, giving us
a new birth and new life through the Holy Spirit.

TITUS 3:5

I HEARD THE SCREAMING FIRST. Racing into the bathroom, I saw my three-year-old sitting in the shower stall. I'd left her with the water turned off while I went to snag a clean towel. As she stood up, wet and hysterical, I noticed that even though I had rinsed her off, her legs were once again coated. Slicked up with bubbles and a slimy coat of shampoo, she looked like nothing so much as a greased-up pig. As she skidded across the slippery tile floor toward me, I simultaneously grabbed for her and scooped the shampoo bottle out of her hand.

It was then that I realized that in my momentary absence, she had squeezed out the contents of the bottle. A full two-thirds of my newly opened shampoo was now on the shower floor. And since she'd been sitting in the mess, her skin felt like it was on fire. Thank goodness a good dose of water could wash away the sting.

I can sympathize with my daughter's pain in not recognizing how her small choice—dumping the shampoo—could turn into a problem much larger than she'd anticipated. All too often, our seemingly harmless choices have far-reaching consequences. The friendships we maintain, the careers we choose, the communities we live in—all of those begin with small choices that can spiral into situations and circumstances with much larger ramifications for our lives.

Thankfully, though our choices do have consequences, our salvation doesn't come and go based on our daily choices. It's not the measure of our own righteousness that leads to salvation; it's only through the mercy of Jesus that we can experience new life—our sins washed away, our poor choices forgiven. It's the washing—pouring out, regenerating, cleansing, making whole—that matters in the end, not the deed.

And so, when days come when I feel like I'm on fire from the choices I've made, I try to remember that when we ask for forgiveness it's often received like a good dose of water, meant to take away the sting. Cleansing. Regenerating. Making whole.

Lord, thank you for the cleansing power of your forgiveness. Amen.

-Kristin

One Good Step: Each time you wash your hands today, let it be a reminder of how Jesus has washed away your sins. Use those twenty seconds to pray and thank him for his mercy and forgiveness.

Pleased

The LORD's delight is in those who fear him,
those who put their hope in his unfailing love.

PSALM 147:11

SEVERAL YEARS AGO I began speaking around the same time I started writing regularly. Terrified of public speaking for as long as I could remember, I dreaded the idea of standing in front of others.

So when the first inquiry for speaking came my way, my initial response was *Nooo!!* But even as my head said no way, I knew in my heart I was supposed to do it, and so I did. I prayed and prepared, and stood with shaky knees in front of that crowd, praying I wouldn't mess it up too badly. For the next few years as I would get asked to speak, it got easier, but I always had the sense that I had to do a good enough job so God would be proud of me, that it was a test I needed to pass to please him.

Then one day I read in my Bible how God delights in us. And I thought about my own children, how I love them and am proud of them, even when they try and fail. And the realization that God might already be pleased with me—simply because I was obedient to speak when he asked me to—hit deep in my heart. The understanding that I had nothing to prove, that he was proud of me just for being obedient, no matter the outcome, freed me from feeling like I always had to be perfect and settled in my soul the truth that he is already pleased with my efforts and not only delights in me, but rejoices over me.

When we understand that God is pleased with us, even delights in us, things change. We have courage to take steps of faith we maybe otherwise wouldn't because we know that God's unfailing love will be there whether we fail or succeed. We don't have to try to impress God by what we accomplish, he's pleased simply that we would try.

Lord, may we stop striving for your approval and rest in the fact that you are pleased with us, not because of our successes or in spite of our failures, but just because we're willing to try. Amen.

-Kendra

One Good Step: How can knowing that God is pleased
with you help you step out in faith?

Trust

Trust in the LORD with all your heart; do not depend on your own understanding.
Seek his will in all you do, and he will show you which path to take.

PROVERBS 3:5-6

"MY DAD LEARNED to trust God by watching his parents, and I'm learning to trust God, in part because of my dad's stories of how God provided for my grandparents."

Ceena's grandfather Yohannan and grandmother Kunjamma Idicula trusted God to provide in ways many of us cannot fathom. Life in Kerala, India, was hard. On more than a few occasions, there were stretches of weeks in which food was scarce, and their family of twelve knew what it meant to be hungry. And yet her grandfather, a pastor, brought home strangers to share whatever meager fare Kunjamma put on the table.

"Somehow, they always made it," Ceena said. "God always provided. And my dad learned to be generous, to rely on God, to trust him when things looked impossible because he watched his mom and dad trust God. I think of my grandparents when I'm trusting God. It's encouraging."

I claim to trust God, but how often do I trust God only out of my abundance? As I listened to Ceena talk, I wondered whether I had Grandfather Yohannan's trust, the assurance that as I generously shared whatever last small amount I had, God would provide the rest. Do I trust God in my lack?

Ouch. That question makes me wince as I consider the times I've had a backup plan, you know, just in case. If we say we trust God, then we have to trust him in our lack, not out of our abundance. How do we do that? We seek his will, asking him to direct our path rather than setting off and asking him to bless what we've already done. We share generously with others rather than hoarding the last little bit, knowing that God can and will provide more. We collect the stories of those who have trusted God in their lack, clinging to that knowledge and understanding while we wait.

Lord, may we be women who trust in our lack rather than who only trust out of our abundance. Amen.

-Julie

One Good Step: Where might you need to trust God in your lack instead of out of your own abundance? Remind yourself of Grandfather Yohannan as you wait.

May

Content

Yet true godliness with contentment is itself great wealth.
1 TIMOTHY 6:6

WE HAD RENTED A CABIN on a lake near our home for a weekend to plan, write, and dream together. Next door, there was an older couple along with their kids and grand-kids. The days were warm and beautiful, and as we'd sit out on the screened-in porch to write, we could hear the comings and goings of the family next door.

Near lunchtime one day, I heard the dad tell his young son that they were going to eat lunch and then go for a boat ride around the lake. The son asked what was for lunch, and the dad told him that he could have a hot dog, brat, or chicken. The boy then exclaimed, "But I really wanted a hamburger!"

I chuckled to myself as I heard the father patiently again tell his son the choices for lunch, explaining that they did not have hamburgers, but he should pick from the other three choices offered. Still disgruntled, the son followed his dad inside for lunch.

I sat for a few moments, pondering similar conversations I've had with my own children.

But then I began to think of how often discontentment happens for all of us in life. It can come in large or small ways and often starts when we are young. No one has to teach us to be discontent. And left unchecked, little things can grow and fester. How often are there many options in front of us that are God given, but all we can see is the one thing that we can't have right in the moment? Discontentment comes when things don't work out like we'd hoped or wanted. But as I thought about how contentment is itself great wealth and what that could mean, in the big and small things of life, I realized there is no price or dollar amount that can be put on peace of mind. Or joy. Or patience or love. All things that come with content-ment. And that is priceless.

Lord, allow me to see all that you have given me. Help me to be content with where I am, even as I look to the future. Amen.

-Kendra

One Good Step: Spend time today thinking about the things God has done for you in the past. How can you be content with where you are now, even as you wait on God for other things?

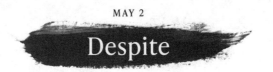

Despite

Instead, God chose things the world considers foolish in order to shame those who think they are wise. And he chose things that are powerless to shame those who are powerful.... As a result, no one can ever boast in the presence of God.

1 CORINTHIANS 1:27, 29

"Oh, God doesn't use me . . ."

I found myself leaning in, trying to catch the rest of her statement as her companion shifted and the conversation at the table next to me resumed from its momentary lull. I hadn't meant to eavesdrop, but her statement was so startling that I'd automatically tuned in to that particular conversation as I waited for my own coffee companion to return from ordering a flat white.

I've often wished I'd tapped that woman gently on the shoulder, assuring her that God uses us, sometimes, oftentimes despite ourselves. We sometimes forget that God uses anyone and everyone to accomplish his will, including the bad guys— Scripture states that God intentionally used both Pharaoh and Nebuchadnezzar, among other baddies (see Romans 9:17 and Ezekiel 29:19-20).

When we believe there is a holiness threshold requirement to being used by God, we get fooled into thinking that as God uses a particular person or church, then it must be that they have arrived, with no flawed theology, no skeletons in their closet. That belief, when it is applied to us and our church, comes perilously close to boasting and is certainly false.

God uses people, institutions, us, *despite* ourselves. To be sure, it is an honor to serve as his hands and feet, to be used to further the Kingdom of God; however, let us not confuse being used by God as a faithfulness litmus test establishing who has "arrived" and who has not. Despite our imperfections and our flaws, we are used by God. In fact, God often chooses the foolish, the weak—so that none of us can boast. God is God, and he gets the glory.

Lord, thank you that you use us, despite ourselves. Help us to remain humble, giving the glory always back to you, as you accomplish your work through us. Amen.

-Julie

One Good Step: In what ways have you declared yourself unable to be used by God? Start praying God would use you, despite yourself.

Brevity

Teach us to realize the brevity of life, so that we may grow in wisdom.
PSALM 90:12

THE SHIFT HAPPENED SUDDENLY. One day I was in a familiar groove—getting the older kids off to elementary school, dropping my youngest daughter at preschool, working at home for a few quiet hours before returning for preschool pickup—and then, suddenly, the routine was gone.

My kids were home from school unexpectedly, but I still needed to get work done. Normally a night owl, I found myself going to bed earlier so I could wake earlier each morning. In the quiet dawn hours while my children slept, I would sit with my coffee and laptop, moving quickly through my to-do list. Those early, uninterrupted hours were my best opportunity to get work accomplished before children stumbled down the stairs to snuggle up beside me on the chair or tell me about their dreams.

As I realigned my schedule, I found myself reorganizing how I spent my time. Admittedly, it was challenging to get all my work done in those early morning hours. But, strangely, I had more time than I thought I would throughout the rest of the day. As I reevaluated my schedule, I realized that I had time for more important items if I streamlined some of the activities that had sucked away my attention. More time for art projects with my kids; less time for scrolling social media. More time valuing the quiet and solitude of the morning; less time trying to squeeze in the TV shows or books on my phone that kept me up late at night. In the busyness of life, I'd lost sight of what mattered to me and forgotten how brief and precious this life truly is.

Those pockets of time I'd previously overlooked were now essential. And reevaluating how I chose to spend each hour of my day made me realize how precious a commodity it was. It's true that life is brief and precious—but it's equally true that it's easy to take it for granted. Unexpected challenges are often the greatest catalyst for recognizing and realigning our lives, if we take the time to let them change us.

Lord, help us recognize the value of each moment of our lives. Amen.

-Kristin

One Good Step: How can rethinking your schedule in the context
of the brevity of life help realign how you allot each day's hours? Today,
write down your daily schedule to see if there are pockets of time
you would be better served utilizing in a new or different way.

Zeal

Never be lacking in zeal, but keep your spiritual fervor, serving the Lord.
ROMANS 12:11, NIV

OUR FRIENDS JASON AND CHRISTA recently told us of their desire to adopt from Haiti. Over the past several years, they would visit Haiti multiple times, partnering with a school there and building relationships with a local Christian organization that was meeting the needs of the people.

As we sat around our dinner table and they passionately told us of their plans, Kyle and I couldn't hold back our excitement for them. This was such an amazing thing they were doing, and we could not be more proud or happy for them!

One evening, as we were discussing adoption, they told us that although most people were excited when they told them the news, they'd also had several comments from other well-meaning friends about their age and the fact that their three biological children were so much older. *They were almost done parenting, so why would they want to start over? Didn't they want to be free to travel? Enjoy their life?*

Kyle and I listened as they shared, and then I told them of my aunt and uncle who adopted the last of their children when they were well into their fifties. We encouraged them that they were pursuing what God had for them, even if people questioned it.

A little while later I was listening to a podcast where the host commented to his guest who happened to be in his sixties, regarding his passion for Christ, calling it a "youthful zeal." I knew it was meant as a compliment, but I immediately thought of my friends. And I was struck by the incorrectness of the statement.

Zeal or passion is not meant just for the young. There is no age limit on who can have an impact for the Kingdom of God. We don't reach a certain age and suddenly lose our effectiveness for his Kingdom. At least not from God's perspective. No matter what stage of life we are in, listening and obeying God's leading, with zeal, is what we as Christians are called to do.

Lord, thank you that you have plans for each one of us to fulfill, no matter our age or stage of life. Give us the courage to do what you are asking of us today. Amen.

-Kendra

One Good Step: Choose to serve the Lord with zeal today.

Restored

The LORD will redeem those who serve him. No one
who takes refuge in him will be condemned.

PSALM 34:22

RUSS AND SHARON were in their forties when their business partner betrayed them, taking everything: the business, their mutual friends, the blessing of the church they all attended, the perceived "good" side of a business relationship gone bad.

Wiped out financially in the midst of raising a family, Sharon cried out to God for justice, even as her husband steadfastly refused to litigate and did nothing to defend himself against the rumors as their small community supported his former partner. She wept and prayed, begging God for redemption.

Stunned, my friend Sarah and I found ourselves leaning over the small table we were sharing at a favorite coffee shop, listening to our beloved mentor recount a piece of her journey we'd never heard and would never have guessed at these many years later.

God restored everything Russ and Sharon lost. They started a new business that flourished and was eventually passed down to their sons. Sharon was moved into a position that eventually gave her international spiritual influence. They are ordinary people who love God, who clung to him during the darkest parts, leaving redemption in his hands rather than seeking it themselves. And he was faithful in his redemption.

God knows betrayal. It was Judas's kiss that led to Jesus' arrest after years of being doubted, shouted down, and chased out of town. He knows the deep hurt when someone is besmirching our character, when they are telling only the parts that make them look good, when they are lying.

Oftentimes, the best thing we can do is to cling to God when we've been betrayed, resisting the temptation to point fingers back and letting go of the desire to defend ourselves against lies. Time has a way of exposing the truth, and God assures us of redemption as we take refuge in him.

Lord, give us refuge in the midst of character smears and lies. Be our defender. We know that you expose the truth in your timing, and that you will redeem what has been stolen. Amen.

-Julie

One Good Step: Can you stop defending yourself, trusting God to do that on your behalf? Start keeping a list of the times God has been your redemption, reminding yourself of his promise the next time you want to rise to your own defense.

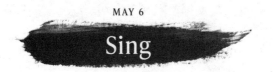

Sing

I hear the tumult of the raging seas as your waves and surging tides sweep over me. But each day the LORD pours his unfailing love upon me, and through each night I sing his songs, praying to God who gives me life.

PSALM 42:7-8

DRIVING DOWN THE FREEWAY, I can hear my daughter singing in the back of the car. Small face dwarfed by the car seat she's buckled into, she stares out the window as she sings her heart out. First humming along, then crescendoing on the chorus, she mumbles the lyrics she's forgotten and sings loudest on the words she remembers best.

"It is well with my soul," she sings. "It is well, it is well with my soul!"

Each time I hear her warbling little voice sing praises to Jesus and peek back to see the earnestness written large across her small face, my heart lifts.

Physically, singing is good for us. It releases endorphins, the brain's feel-good chemicals that boost our mood. It gets more oxygen into the blood for better circulation, another mood-boosting activity. And the deep breathing we do when singing reduces anxiety.

But on a spiritual level, choosing to sing praise to God is a deliberate choice. It's an act of worship. It's a cry for help, a promise, an admission that we trust him. It's contemplative, joyful, triumphant, mournful. Singing expresses the deepest part of ourselves in ways we can't always verbalize. On days when we are glad, singing is a confirmation of the beauty and promise life holds. But on days when we are afraid or worried, it's a lifeline—because it's impossible to sing praises to God and be fearful at the same time. Too often, we can default to fear when we should instead turn to praise. As author Lisa Whittle has said, because God inhabits the praises of his people, he's never further than a breath away. When we choose to sing praise to God, our fears will lift, and our spirits will rise.

Lord, thank you that there is power in singing. Help us to lift our eyes from our circumstances and choose to sing in the face of our joys and our sorrows. Amen.

-Kristin

One Good Step: Put together a playlist of ten worship songs you can listen to when life feels especially hard. If you don't have ten songs, explore stations on your favorite music streaming app until you find ten songs that resonate with you.

New

Anyone who belongs to Christ has become a new person.
The old life is gone; a new life has begun!

2 CORINTHIANS 5:17

A FRIEND CAME HOME from her vacation with family discouraged. When I asked her what was wrong, she told me that her parents and siblings had made cutting remarks about her and her past. When she appeared hurt, they told her it was all in jest, but she knew their words still held some of their underlying beliefs about her and her character.

For years my friend has struggled with addiction and made some pretty poor choices in her life. She has been sober now for eighteen months, but her family, often without even realizing it, still brings up her past. Unwilling or unable to see that she has changed many things about her life, including going to see a therapist, attending support groups regularly, and mentoring younger girls through an after-school program, they still only remember the person she was and don't have eyes to see who she is becoming. They don't see the compassion, love, and generosity she now displays through work and volunteering that could have only come through Christ. And although my friend realizes she spent a lot of years making unhealthy decisions, she has apologized for her past damaging actions and only hopes that her family will one day see the person she is, with God's help, becoming.

Family roles can often be challenging to break out of, especially when a pattern has been set for many years. But what good news we have that we do not have to stay stuck in our unhealthy ways. In Christ, we can become a new person. If we are willing to do the work of seeing what needs to change and asking God and others to help us, we are not beholden to continue to repeat history. We can change and grow. The old life can be gone and a new life will begin!

Lord, thank you for the new life in Christ that you offer us that frees us from the destructive habits of our pasts. Give us the courage to walk in your ways and not return to the unhealthy habits of our former selves. Amen.

-Kendra

One Good Step: Spend some time today thinking of how God has grown you as a person, and thank him for the new life in Christ you now have.

Refuge

You are my refuge and my shield; your word is my source of hope.

PSALM 119:114

"WHAT CAN I DO but take refuge in God? How else do I handle the hurt?" she asked as she finished the story. My friend's pain was palpable. Her vulnerably shared thoughts in a video chat message to two girlfriends had been met with silence. As the days stretched and other conversations on other mediums continued with no mention of what she shared, she agonized. Did she misread the social cues? Was her vulnerability shared inappropriately? Were they uncomfortable and hoping to simply allow the issue to go away?

She felt exposed, raw, and foolish. Hurt, anger, and frustration threatened to swamp her even as she looked for reasonable justifications for their silence: maybe they hadn't had time to watch the string of video messages, maybe they weren't sure how to respond and were struggling, maybe they had temporarily forgotten in the chaos of young families and Mom Brain. Maybe, maybe, maybe—her thoughts swirled through all of the possibilities as she tried to find a path forward.

What do we do when good-hearted people let us down? How do we respond when our friend unintentionally hurts our feelings? Do we succumb to the voice in our head spinning the worst-case scenarios, assigning bad intent and hurtful motives behind silence or forgetfulness? Do we stuff the hurt down, pretending like it never happened and just move on?

While some situations might call for gentle confrontation while others call for allowing the hurt to pass without comment, we can always turn to God both for solace and wisdom. Being in relationships means we will be let down, disappointed, and hurt on occasion. Our loved ones fail us, even unintentionally, from time to time. But God never does. He is a safe place, always. He provides refuge in the midst of hurt. His wisdom revealed in Scripture helps us see the situation with a broader perspective and allows us to navigate with grace, knowing when to speak up and when to simply let something pass. He brings us hope and peace.

Lord, thank you for providing us a safe place when we are hurting. Give us wisdom as we navigate relationships with those around us—especially the hard ones. Amen.

-Julie

One Good Step: Practice finding refuge in God, taking your hurts to him in out loud prayer or in a prayer journal. Memorize a favorite verse about God as our shelter, perhaps Psalm 18:2 or Psalm 119:114.

Habit

Physical training is good, but training for godliness is much better,
promising benefits in this life and in the life to come.
1 TIMOTHY 4:8

MY HUSBAND ROUTINELY WAKES at 4:20 a.m. in order to participate in a 5 a.m. CrossFit class in a neighboring town. While his routine works well for him, I struggled for years to find my own fitness routine. With small children underfoot, exercise seemed like a luxury my limited time couldn't afford. Time and again, I'd motivate myself with goals, only to drift back into old habits. It was so discouraging.

Part of the struggle was that I've never been an athlete; I got smacked in the face with a kickball in elementary school and hated phys ed afterward, and I spent a few years playing mediocre volleyball in junior high before moving on to other pursuits. Since then, I've always been the person who wants to enjoy exercise but doesn't. The problem was that I was trying to create a habit by focusing on what I wanted to achieve (an outcome-based habit), when what I really needed to do was focus on who I wished to become (an identity-based habit).

Things changed when I shifted my mindset. Instead of trying to work out every other day and losing count, I began to tell myself, "I work out every day." I then proved it to myself in small ways by exercising daily, even for just a few minutes at a time. It's now an authentic part of my identity.

Similarly, spiritual habits require the same shift. Many of us want a closer walk with Jesus but try doing so by setting and accomplishing goals rather than focusing on an identity-based habit. For instance, we resolve to get up early to read the Bible, then are discouraged after we hit the snooze button too many times. Let's shift our approach. Rather than focusing on the end result, let's focus more on our identity in Christ. When we tell ourselves, "I'm someone who loves to spend time with God" and prove it in small ways each day, our identity will shape our habits. There is freedom to be found in recognizing the truth of our identity in Christ, and the ripple effect is a stronger relationship with him.

Lord, help us find our identity in you. May it foster healthy spiritual habits. Amen.

-Kristin

One Good Step: Brainstorm one spiritual habit you'd like to cultivate. How can tying it to your identity make it achievable?

Sow

Do not be deceived: God is not mocked, for whatever one sows, that will he also reap. For the one who sows to his own flesh will from the flesh reap corruption, but the one who sows to the Spirit will from the Spirit reap eternal life.

GALATIANS 6:7-8, ESV

"GAH!" My frustrated exclamation carried on the early morning breeze as I stood, hands on hips, glaring at the volunteer flax cheerfully choking out my carrot seedlings.

How many years ago did I spread that chicken manure, too eager in my gardening novice ways to properly compost it, killing any weed seeds before adding it to my soil? Sighing, I bent to the task of hand plucking the flax from among my carrots. *I wish I'd known that I'd be stuck pulling hundreds of weeds every year because of that choice.*

Will I forever have flax invading my vegetable beds? No. But my careless actions have resulted in a painful, years' long process I could have easily avoided if I'd followed the recommendations for applying compost to my raised beds. I've been reaping what my careless actions sowed.

As I pulled weeds, I pondered the scriptural application of sowing and reaping. At its most basic, what we do (or don't do) today impacts what happens tomorrow and tomorrow's tomorrow. We can sow intentionally, doing the hard work up front, knowing the results (what we reap) will be worth it. Or we can sow carelessly, choosing momentary convenience, comfort, or pleasure without fully considering or caring what result we might reap later (like dumping compost with active weed seeds in your garden because you didn't want to wait).

This is hard stuff, and we've all fallen short, having sowed seeds we desperately don't want to reap harvests from. Thankfully, God intersects the principle of sowing and reaping with the concepts of grace, mercy, and forgiveness. He frequently mitigates our crop, protecting us from ourselves.

But, God's protective interference does not change how we should be striving to live our lives. We spend our days sowing and reaping, choosing moment by moment the types and quantities of seeds we will sow. Let us choose wisely.

Lord, give us wisdom as we choose our words, our attitudes, our actions today. Remind us that what we sow today impacts tomorrow. Amen.

-Julie

One Good Step: What seeds do you need to stop sowing? What might you sow instead? Call a friend or loved one to be your accountability partner.

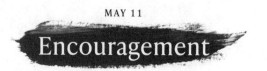

Encouragement

Let us think of ways to motivate one another to acts of love and good works.
And let us not neglect our meeting together, as some people do,
but encourage one another.

HEBREWS 10:24-25

MY HUSBAND INVITED some friends for dinner, and honestly, I was annoyed. I'd spent the week home with our kids and would have liked nothing better than a quiet night out with my husband. Ever the host, when an old friend called, my husband quickly invited him and his family over to our house that Saturday night. I was a bit disgruntled as I helped my husband prepare food and our house for company.

As soon as they entered our home, much of my bad mood lifted, replacing my angst with a feeling of peace and a sense that they were meant to come and be with us that evening.

As dinner was shared and we caught up on life and family, conversation moved to faith and believing God for big things, changes of heart and desiring nothing more than being obedient to God's call.

As we talked about our plans to move out of our neighborhood and more to the heart of our city, something we believed and had peace God was asking us to do, our friends nodded agreement, a shared understanding as they explained much of the same conversations they'd been having with God, very much mirroring our own.

As the hours seemed to move by a little too quickly and dinner ended, tears were shed as we spoke honestly to one another about things that were on our hearts that we had yet to share with anyone else. We ended the night by praying for one another, encouraging each other, and agreeing to get together again soon.

I am often struck by how God knows our need, even before we realize it. How he often brings people to us at just the right time when we need encouragement and understanding that can spur us on toward the good things he has for us to do. Even on the nights we think we don't want to host.

Lord, thank you for the communities of people you place us in so that we can be an encouragement to one another. Amen.

-Kendra

One Good Step: Invite someone for dinner or coffee, share with them what God is doing in your life, and encourage them as they pursue what God has for them as well.

Together

Two people are better off than one, for they can help each other succeed.
If one person falls, the other can reach out and help. But someone who falls alone
is in real trouble. Likewise, two people lying close together can keep
each other warm. But how can one be warm alone?

ECCLESIASTES 4:9-11

I WATCH IN SLOW MOTION as the Tupperware container of large, child-sized buttons topples off the table. They scatter, rolling haphazardly to rest next to crumbs and chair legs. Bright, shiny drops of primary colors gleam in the light spilling over from the kitchen.

"Oh, no!" my three-year-old shouts. "Look at this mess!"

I pause, wincing at the way she sounds *exactly* like me, repeating words I've heard myself say when a tube of dropped yogurt splattered across the floor or the baby pushed the remains of her dinner off her high chair for what felt like the millionth time.

"It's okay," I assure her. "I can help."

"No," she says suddenly, stubbornly. "I do it!"

"Honey, it's easier with help," I protest.

"No!" she insists, dumping out the buttons that we just put back, gripping them possessively. Inwardly, I sigh. But I can't help thinking her behavior reflects my own struggle to do things my own way, by myself.

It's an easy trap to fall into. Jaded from one-too-many projects where a team member didn't pull their weight. Disillusioned by the way someone said they'd help, then reneged. Somewhere along the way, it seems easier to do things ourselves.

Self-reliance says, *I can do it myself.*

But God says, *We were meant to work together.*

And once we recognize that truth—that it's better to work with others or ask for help, even when it needles our pride—we gain much more than we lose. A family who cheers us on in each new chapter of our lives. Friends who rejoice when we rejoice and mourn when we mourn. A church community of love and faith and acceptance. We were made for more. Because together we're stronger, and better, and less alone. The church—together—as one. One body, one spirit, one glorious hope for the future.

Lord, thank you that you created us for togetherness. Help us to strengthen the bonds we have with those around us rather than trying to rely solely on ourselves. Amen.

-Kristin

One Good Step: Thank a friend for helping you when you needed it.

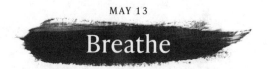

Breathe

Control your temper, for anger labels you a fool.
ECCLESIASTES 7:9

SHUTTING MY BEDROOM DOOR did nothing to lessen the saw's high-pitched whine nor stop the wafting sweet-sour stench of cut wood from filling my nostrils. The carpenters were back, and I was *ticked*.

Dust as fine and light as talcum powder was airborne, settling upon every surface, nook, and cranny I'd spent all weekend deep cleaning. I hadn't realized that this one last, small construction task would fill my house—once again—with a dust so floaty and insidious that I despaired ever conquering it.

We were nearing the end of a renovation project that had consumed our primary living spaces for over four months. Until recently, I'd been a good sport about living with a bathtub as a sink and my fridge in the garage. But we were *almost* done, and so was my patience.

My jaw clenched, I took several deep breaths as I silently began praying, *Lord, you know how grateful I am for this new space. We are so excited to welcome friends, family, and others into our home and lives. Please, help me handle these last few days with grace. Help me end well.* And with that, I forced myself to let my irritation go, returning to deep breathing as I surveyed my dusty house when the work crew left. I chose gratitude, thanking God as I—again—wiped wood dust off the island, countertops, and coffee maker, making a conscious decision to refuse anger's invitation.

Our American culture invites us to fan the flames of small irritations and annoyances into a roaring inferno of outrage. Spewing "how dare he/she/they/it" type posts garners attention on social media like few other things, and we are encouraged to take up offenses. We become foolish in our anger, saying words and acting in ways we regret afterward.

What if, instead, we paused to breathe deeply, stepping back from anger's invitation and turning to God, asking him to shift our perspective? Refusing an angry response is countercultural and unexpected, and our deliberate choice quietly speaks of our faith, a silent testimony of God's presence in our life.

Lord, help us to recognize today's invitations to be offended, irritated, and angry. May we decline those invitations with a deep breath. Amen.

-Julie

One Good Step: Practice mentally labeling situations and people who invite you into anger and irritation and, instead, take a deep breath and tell God three things for which you are grateful.

Affection

Love each other with genuine affection,
and take delight in honoring each other.
ROMANS 12:10

MY OLDEST DAUGHTER was born six weeks early. At just over five pounds, her tiny body needed a little extra time in the hospital. For three weeks after her birth, I quickly got into the routine of visiting her each day in the NICU, going home to sleep, then returning the next day.

As a new mom, those three weeks felt like three years. Though the staffers were kind, I chafed at the lack of privacy. Monitors beeped constantly, and curtains were all that separated one Isolette from the next. But as days turned into weeks, the close confines meant increasing familiarity with the rhythms of the unit—who was able to go home, who would remain after we left, which families were there frequently and which ones weren't able to visit as often.

One bright spot was an older woman who was often present. A faithful volunteer who had been there for years, she would hum and soothe and hold the tiny infants for hours. The nurses referred to her as "Grandma," and I'd often find myself smiling or saying hello to her open, kind face. In the absence of a parent, Grandma Jeanne was a soothing hand and a comforting touch to the infants she snuggled each day. To an outsider looking in, the love and affection she displayed made her appear more like a family member than a volunteer.

Even though the newborns were, in effect, strangers to Grandma Jeanne, her affection and delight in caring for them was evident in every move she made. As Christians, we're also called to love those around us—our neighbors, our friends, even our enemies—with genuine affection. To me, that means caring for others the same way we would our own family. That's because, in Christ, we *are* one family. In fact, the Greek origin for the word "affection" in Romans 12:10 is *philadelphia*, meaning "brotherly love," from the word *philadelphos* ("fraternal affection"). As children of God, we have the distinct privilege of showing affection and care for others in the same way Grandma Jeanne did, freely and openly.

Lord, thank you that we are part of your family. Help us to do our part to love others well by showing true delight and affection for one another. Amen.

-Kristin

One Good Step: How can you demonstrate your love
for someone else through your words or actions?

One

If a man has a hundred sheep and one of them wanders away,
what will he do? Won't he leave the ninety-nine others
on the hills and go out to search for the one that is lost?

MATTHEW 18:12

AS LIZZIE AND I walked the path around our local park, her meandering recollecting stopped me short: "I got into ALA by one point. I still remember having to sit in the hallway last year to take the test. It was so noisy with classes walking by and people talking. I prayed I could do well enough to get in."

My daughter is in Advanced Language Arts at her middle school, and it is her *favorite* class. Her teacher grades hard, expects a lot, and is adored. I hear more stories about that class than all of the rest combined.

One. Measly. Point. Many of her favorite memories this year, some of her best school experiences to date, and access to an incredible teacher who knows when to push and how—all of it because of one point. I'd forgotten how stressful those few weeks had been as we waited to hear if she would be accepted. How I'd prayed, knowing she needed a win after a really rough school year.

How often do we forget the power of one, assuming that we are too small, too weak, too little equipped to make a difference and, so believing, don't? We quit before we've tried, convinced that our contribution could not possibly matter.

But God knows the power of one. One decision, one action, one conversation, one point on a test makes all the difference in a life. He left the ninety-nine for one. Do not be fooled into thinking that world changing requires grand gestures and gobs of resources. God will use grand gestures and unlimited resources, certainly, but he also uses ordinary girls living in Nowheresville, if we let him.

Lord, use us as world changers! May we see others through your eyes, meeting a need, giving an encouraging word, smiling as we hold open a door. Help us to see the one you send our way today. Amen.

-Julie

One Good Step: Ask God for one daily assignment. Keep track of your assignments on a calendar, watching how powerfully God works through one small thing.

Afraid

Do not be afraid.... For the Lᴏʀᴅ your God will personally go ahead of you.
He will neither fail you nor abandon you.
DEUTERONOMY 31:6

Several years back my daughter had dance tryouts for the competition teams at the studio she attends. As I watched her get into line with other little girls her age, all dressed in black leotards with their hair pulled tight into buns, then scurry into a closed room to be judged, I couldn't help but feel a little nervous and excited for her.

Jasmine already had a lot of dreams and things she was passionate about, and as her parent, I wanted to support her. But even with all her personality, she confided in me that she was nervous: What if she didn't make the team?

I know that feeling. Fear has always played a big part in my life and often—too often—my decisions. I looked her in the eyes and told her I am often afraid too. And then she asked, "What do you do?" My answer to her was the same one I tell myself often: Do it afraid.

I went on to explain that fear is a normal part of life and sometimes doing new things makes us nervous, but we don't have to let fear dictate what we do. Often we chase our dreams, even while fear is there alongside us. Fear doesn't dissipate just because we want it to. Sometimes we close our eyes, take a deep breath, say a little prayer, and *do it afraid.*

I reminded her that I believed she was capable. That even if she failed, she was *not* a failure. That there was no shame in trying. And she seemed to soak up these truths.

These reminders aren't just for her, but for all of us. We can all do scary things. We were meant to dream big and live life to the fullest. Fear is mentioned often in the Bible, but only in the context that we do not need to allow it to control us. Our lives do not have to be defined by our fears, not if we're willing to take God at his word, trusting that he goes with us. And deciding to just simply do it afraid.

Lord, thank you that with you, we can be brave, even when we are afraid. Amen.
-Kendra

One Good Step: Where has fear been holding you back?
Today, simply choose to do it afraid.

Wisdom

The wisdom from above is first of all pure. It is also peace loving,
gentle at all times, and willing to yield to others.
JAMES 3:17

WHEN CAROL FIRST CONFIDED that God was telling her to move the women's conference to St. Cloud, my eyes bulged just a bit. I'd long ago learned that Carol's wisdom—gleaned through prayer—often does not match what conventional business gurus would suggest. I could think of several places better suited to holding the conference, but Carol is more finely attuned to hear from God than most, and I'd learned to hold my tongue and watch God and Carol work.

Over the next three years, Carol gently, humbly, prayerfully established relationships, took risks, soothed naysayers, and moved Thrive to St. Cloud. It sells out every year, and, in hindsight, it was a brilliant move.

God's wisdom is often upside down and inside out from what the "experts" would say, at least initially. He knows what is coming, and he often places his people in position for Kingdom work before the time arrives. Remember poor Noah!

How do we know we're hearing from God? God is consistent and unchanging. His wisdom will not conflict with Scripture. And our enemy embeds a kernel of truth in his most devastating lies. Read Scripture. Know the Bible. It is your best way to know whether you are hearing from God or believing a lie.

Secondly, God may use someone else to confirm what he has already told you, but be wary when someone claims to have heard from God on your behalf. God promises wisdom to anyone who asks. He will not tell your friend, neighbor, or fellow church member something he hasn't also told you.

Finally, remember that God might be asking you to wait rather than to leap. We often want to wriggle our way out of an uncomfortable situation ahead of God's timing. God's timing, God's way, God's wisdom is always worth waiting for.

Lord, you promise wisdom to any who ask. We lay our circumstances at your feet. Give us wisdom in how to proceed. Amen.

-Julie

One Good Word: Pray James 1:5 over a situation. ("If you need wisdom, ask our generous God, and he will give it to you. He will not rebuke you for asking.") Then pause, allowing God an opportunity to respond.

Brother

A friend is always loyal, and a brother is born to help in time of need.

PROVERBS 17:17

MY SISTER-IN-LAW Marlene's father, Maury, was born in the San Fernando valley in 1926, where he lived until his retirement. During the decades he spent in his predominantly white community, he had very little exposure to people who didn't look like him.

But in his final years, Maury moved in with Marlene and his son-in-law Phil in Northern California. Although he was independent at the beginning, over time, he gradually needed more care. In the last four months of his life, the family hired a man named Denis to stay overnight every other night so Marlene could rest. Denis was from Uganda, and though he had taught high school chemistry and physics in his home country, he'd moved to the United States in the hope of finding more opportunities.

Maury and Denis quickly struck up a friendship. As their time together transitioned to days, as well, Denis's stories and Maury's gregarious laugh could often be heard through the house.

But in the final weeks of his life, Maury wrestled with what felt like an injustice to him. Though Denis had started the green card process, it had stalled. The idea that his friend had a wife he was separated from, a daughter growing up without his physical presence, and a son he had never met in person was intolerable. As their conversations deepened, Maury saw Denis not through the lens of his own upbringing, but as a husband and father, just as he himself was a husband and father. Privately, he told Marlene that he would like to help support Denis in his efforts to reunite with his family.

One evening, Denis reported to Marlene that Maury had stopped breathing in his sleep; they both cried. One of Maury's final wishes was that his family use his remaining funds to buy Denis a plane ticket to meet his son. Later that week, Denis got the long-awaited notification that his green card interview was scheduled.

When we see those around us as brothers and sisters—children of God alongside us—perspectives shift. The bonds we have together as children of our Father are stronger than the tethers of our upbringing.

Lord, thank you that your love overcomes all barriers to unity with brothers and sisters in Christ. Amen.

-Kristin

One Good Step: The next time you're tempted to categorize someone else—because of heritage, socioeconomic factors, gender, or something else—instead think, *He is my brother* or *She is my sister.*

Handle

The name of the LORD is a strong tower; the righteous run to it and are safe.
PROVERBS 18:10, NKJV

WHY CAN'T LIFE just go along smoothly like I planned?! I thought as I sat down on a Monday morning after a weekend of unexpected mishaps. Willing myself to open my Bible, I instead sat for a few moments, pondering how often life takes twists and turns I have no control of.

Being able to keep things within my ability to handle them is something I wrestle with too often. It's a topic that regularly comes up in Scripture, but not in the way that it'd suit me as a means to hang on to my nice little life, wrapped up with a pretty red bow slapped across the front.

No, my trying to handle everything is often asked to be laid down—willingly—trusting in God who has promised to take care of me and all the little bits and pieces of my life.

But all too often I find myself clinging to my desire to want to handle everything and everyone around me—including my husband, my kids, my circumstances, myself, and anyone else within arm's reach of me (whether they like it or not). But what I've realized is that trying to manage everything often has the reverse effect. Instead of freeing me from worry or dread or fear, handling everything often just leaves me exhausted, stifling myself and everyone around me.

I begin to read how the Lord is a strong tower. *My* strong tower. All I have to do is run to it. I visualize myself running to that tower. Giving my control and my desire to want to handle everything on my own over to a force much greater than I, telling myself that I don't need to handle everything in my life, I just need to remember to always turn to the one who does.

Our lives may never be perfectly wrapped up and far worse things may come our way than the trials we face today, but joy and peace can still be found when we turn and run to God. When we choose to cling to the truth of these words, we can choose to let go of our desire to handle everything and let our control rest with him.

Lord, give us the courage to bring to you all the things we are trying to handle ourselves. Amen.

-Kendra

One Good Step: What have you been trying to handle that you should give to God? How can you give that to him?

Reveal

Don't make judgments about anyone ahead of time—before the Lord returns.
For he will bring our darkest secrets to light and will reveal our private
motives. Then God will give to each one whatever praise is due.

1 CORINTHIANS 4:5

"I THOUGHT LINDA was a friend. I guess we aren't friends, at least not in the way I thought we were." Sheila's shoulders slumped in resignation as she fiddled with the paper wrapping from her frappé's straw.

"What? I thought you and Linda were relatively close, as far as coworkers go. What happened?" I asked as I slid into my side of the booth at our favorite coffee shop.

Sheila and Linda are coworkers at a local government agency. When a temporary position became available at a higher pay grade, most of their department applied, despite its temporary nature. An email announcement had gone out late Friday afternoon announcing Sheila had received the position.

"When Linda got to work on Monday, she mumbled a terse greeting instead of our normal few moments of chatting as our computers turned on. That was days ago. She barely looks at me, despite us sitting next to each other. She even went to our supervisor and accused him of rigging the process! I know she loves Jesus as much as I do, at least I thought she did. . . . I don't know what to do in the face of her hostility."

There is nothing quite like disappointment to put our faith to the test, revealing what we actually believe. It's easy to quote Scripture, to profess an undying faith when life is relatively smooth sailing. But it is in the midst of deep disappointment that our actions reveal the strength of our faith to those around us, often louder than any words of faith we've professed. And, like Sheila, people take note when our professed faith is not revealed by our actions. While it is natural to be disappointed, what we reveal in the midst of our disappointment is a silent witness to the depth of our faith. We don't have to lie or pretend that we aren't disappointed, but we can abide by the rules of good sportsmanship, and not hold someone else's good fortune against them.

Lord, help us to be women whose faith is revealed consistently in the ups and downs of life. Amen.

-Julie

One Good Step: Ask two faith mentors how they handle disappointment in ways that reveal their faith. What tangible actions can you adopt for future disappointments? How can you practice revealing a consistent faith to those around you?

Drawn

I have loved you, my people, with an everlasting love.
With unfailing love I have drawn you to myself.

JEREMIAH 31:3

"ALL REBELLION is ultimately rebellion against God."

The words cut through my thoughts as I sat back from cleaning the tub to listen to the wise counsel spoken by a parenting expert on a podcast I frequently turned on while cleaning.

I immediately thought of the child who had been lying to my husband and me as of late. It's a sickening feeling, to know your child is not being honest with you. And as I continued to listen, the expert reminded the listeners—and me—that although my child's disobedience can feel very personal, I cannot take it personally. That ultimately, all of us have rebelled against God in some way, at some point in our lives.

The truth of his words landed on my battered heart and began to give me hope in addressing my child's rebellious heart—because haven't I, too, rebelled against God's plan? And don't I still at times, if I'm very honest?

Yet God continues to draw me to himself. And I need to approach my child with a heart of understanding my own propensity to err, even as I work to help them correct theirs, making sure to not be offended personally by their rebellious behavior. Humble correction—that is my goal.

We can all look back over our lives and see times where we intentionally, or even unintentionally, rebelled against God. It happens more often than we'd care to admit. Our anger, frustration, unanswered questions, fear, or doubt can lead us down a path of rebellion if we allow it to. And yet, through it all, we can also see instances where God's love drew us back to himself. God's love is everlasting, never giving up on us, even in our rebellion. How comforting to know that no matter what we've done, God continues to draw us back to himself and into a right relationship with him.

Lord, how awesome you are that you love us unconditionally. Time and time again you draw us back to yourself, even as we rebel against you. Thank you for your everlasting love. Amen.

-Kendra

One Good Step: Spend some time thinking of all the instances where God has drawn you and then thank him for it.

Memory

We will use these stones to build a memorial. In the future your children will ask
you, "What do these stones mean?" Then you can tell them, "They remind us that
the Jordan River stopped flowing when the Ark of the LORD's Covenant went across."
These stones will stand as a memorial among the people of Israel forever.

JOSHUA 4:6-7

MY FATHER-IN-LAW, AL, started making an annual trek to Maroon Bells in the 1960s.
Now, it's a tourist area that can only really be reached by bus. But back then, you
could drive a dusty dirt road to get to the beautiful location high in the mountains
of Colorado and camp on the lakeshore.

By the time my husband, Tim, came along, his dad knew all the best places to
fish—by his telling, you'd have to wade through the river, walk a mile, and almost
fall in the lake—and once you arrived, the fishing was plentiful.

"We almost had a fish hatchery, the fish were so thick," my father-in-law says
now, reflecting on those early years.

One year, Al and Tim caught so many fish that they were well over the limit.
They wanted to keep fishing, so they knocked on other campers' doors and offered
to share their fish. They gave many away. But if no one answered, they simply
opened the camper's cooler and stashed a fish inside.

"I hope they appreciated it," Tim's dad says, chuckling. "But if we hadn't done
that, we would have had to stop fishing."

For my husband and his father, there is joy in reliving the memory. It's the kind
of tale that makes Tim grin every time he tells it. I've often thought that the Bible
is similar: it's a collection of memories, a family history of God and his children.
It's the story of God's great love for his people and his unwavering pursuit in the
face of their fickle, wayward hearts. Like a cherished family memory we retell time
and again, the stories the Bible contains remind us of truths of love, mercy, kindness, and justice. It reflects the heart of a father for his children, and it reminds us
of what matters most.

*Lord, thank you that your words are like memories we can hold close and retell
time and again. Help them to always resonate with us. Amen.*

-Kristin

One Good Step: Write out your favorite verse. Think of it as a family memory,
and consider why it holds meaning for you and what it says about God.

Try

I'm not trying to get my way in the world's way. I'm trying to get your *way,
your Word's way. I'm staying on your trail; I'm putting one foot
in front of the other. I'm not giving up.*

PSALM 17:4-5, MSG

WHAT HAPPENED, LORD? *Where did I misstep?* My thoughts swirled as I stood in the middle of my kitchen, blinking at the food prepared and waiting, trying without success to hold back a tear or three from leaking down my cheeks. My living room was filled with exactly half of the guests we'd been expecting, the half I'd invited. The other half of the guest list were individuals from our refugee community, invited by a community connection in a mutual attempt to share space and conversation in a community beset by misunderstanding and hate and to, hopefully, spark new friendships.

It was my first foray into intercultural bridge building, and it was a failure of gigantic proportions. After several deep breaths and a pause to wipe the tear streaks, I walked into my living room with a smile and invited my guests to eat. I explained that there had been a miscommunication on my end and that our other guests would not be coming, but that we'd try this again.

As Aaron gently shut the front door, having cheerfully sent off our last guest, he walked into the kitchen, intercepting me with a giant hug as I dried my hands on a towel, squeezing me tight as I gave in to my tears.

Several of my friends and I have embraced the life motto "Girls Who Try" as a way to live our lives. Following God's trail isn't easy, and it oftentimes involves stumbling, falling, and failing. We have the choice of getting up, dusting off, praying, and trying again, or quitting. Trying again requires us to examine where we fell short and what went wrong so we can make adjustments before giving it another go. Trying is growth. We become stronger, more resilient, braver people for failing and then trying again. Journeying with God means he is often going to invite us to try something that stretches our faith and makes us uncomfortable. Will you accept his invitations?

Lord, help us be Girls Who Try, who count success by the effort given rather than the initial outcome. Help us to dust off and do it again when we fall short. Amen.

-Julie

One Good Step: What do you need to try again this week? Do it.

Explore

They said to all the people of Israel, "The land we traveled through
and explored is a wonderful land!"

NUMBERS 14:7

"WHAT SHOULD WE PUT ON THE LIST?" I asked, tapping my pen on the paper in front of me. The answers came quickly: the giant candy store. Breakfast in bed. Ice cream for dinner. A treasure hunt. Nodding in response, I filled the lines, adding my own ideas as well.

Every summer, we make a summer bucket list. My kids are old enough that everyone sleeps through the night but young enough to not have too many activities, so summers are flexible. We love to explore, especially if the day ends with ice cream. But there's always a risk to exploring. Sometimes the location doesn't turn out like we expected, the car ride gets long, or the kids are cranky from too much sugar or not enough sleep. Our misadventures are usually outweighed by the fun of spending time together.

Exploring happened in the Bible, as well, most notably when the Israelites escaped from slavery in Egypt. Having successfully made it through the desert, they were on the cusp of entering the land the Lord had promised when they balked. After scouts returned with a report that the land was good but occupied (with giants!), the people responded by weeping and complaining. Surely they would die in battle, they argued. Maybe they should return to Egypt. Joshua and Caleb disagreed: they shouldn't worry about entering because God was with them. Regrettably, the people responded by threatening to stone them, and God responded to the whole mess by sending the Israelites into the desert for forty years, with only Caleb and Joshua allowed to live long enough to enter Canaan (see Numbers 14:1-30).

The Israelites allowed their fears to get the better of them and, as a result, missed out on the Promised Land. New experiences are always a risk, but what the Israelites failed to see was that God was with them. They had nothing to fear. It's a lesson we should remind ourselves of every time we step into something new, whether it's a bucket list item, a friendship, or a ministry opportunity. When God is with us, we need not fear exploring new things. He is faithful to remain with us always, in all the ups and downs we experience.

Lord, thank you that your presence gives us freedom from fear in exploring all this life has to offer. Amen.

-Kristin

One Good Step: Explore a new place.

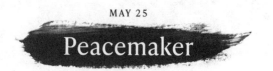

Peacemaker

Blessed are the peacemakers, for they will be called children of God.
MATTHEW 5:9, NIV

I ADAMANTLY DISAGREED with the conversation I unwittingly had become a part of. Struggling for what to do, I glanced around the room, looking for a way out before my face gave away my internal emotions.

Part of me wanted to speak up, but I also knew anger was welling up inside of me, and I was sure what would come out of my mouth in the moment would not be very kind. Instead, I got up from the table and left the room wondering how I could have been a peacemaker in the midst of a challenging conversation.

After several days had passed, I could not stop thinking about how good it felt to know that I had kept my mouth shut when I wanted to say something (potentially) hurtful. How sometimes choosing to keep my relationships intact and being a peacemaker is more important than sharing my opinions or even being right.

This doesn't mean there haven't been times I've needed to go back and have discussions with people about conversations I've quietly left. I'm certainly not an advocate for avoiding issues that need to be brought up or hashed out, but I'm learning that speaking in anger all too often accomplishes little more than hurt feelings and resentment. Usually I just end up saying things I later regret and then have to go back and apologize for anyway.

Being a peacemaker often means watching our tongue. Caring more for another person's heart and well-being than our ability to be free to say whatever we want, whenever we want.

Our mouth is a powerful tool, and we choose if we'll use it for good or bad.

Jesus said that peacemakers would be called children of God, and that is what we should want to be called, more than anything else. More than I want to be able to share my opinions. More than lashing out in anger. More than even getting my own way. This way of Jesus may garner friction when crossing what our flesh desires in the moment, but it's the way of a peacemaker. It's his Spirit that guides and reminds us that speaking peacefully and not harshly is right.

Lord, help us to be peacemakers. Give us wisdom to know what to say and the courage to know when to say it. Amen.

-Kendra

One Good Step: What is one way you can be a peacemaker
in a challenging relationship?

Genuine

Examine yourselves to see if your faith is genuine. Test yourselves.

2 CORINTHIANS 13:5

MY FRIEND AND I were there by appointment. Wide-eyed with excitement, I followed a staffer into the Ashmolean Museum's Print Room, an average-sized space filled with wooden tables and surrounded by built-in cabinets. Leading us toward a table, the staffer donned white gloves to place the drawings upright for us to view: sketches by Michelangelo, now at my fingertips.

Studying abroad in England, I'd only recently discovered a love for art. My small-town upbringing hadn't led to many museum visits, but I was surrounded by it here. History and art felt like they were around every corner, waiting to be discovered. And when I heard that the Ashmolean Museum—just a few short blocks from the building I lived in—possessed some of Michelangelo's drawings, several of which were available for viewing, I jumped at the chance.

Now, as I watched the staffer ceremoniously place the drawings on the table, time felt unhurried and silence reigned. Some were raw sketches in bold slashes of black, others more finely nuanced drawings in red chalk, but all were awe-inspiring visions of architectural designs, studies for the ceiling of the Sistine Chapel and Medici Tombs, and religious subjects such as the Pietà.

They were beautiful, but more than that, they were genuine. In the art world, value is tied to authenticity. Experts used to determine a painting's legitimacy through a surface-level assessment of whether the artistic style fit the artist's usual technique. Nowadays, the test is more challenging—a study of the painter's signature alongside dating and scientific analysis to determine whether or not something is truly genuine.

In this case, art mimics life. It's only through testing that the genuineness of our commitment to Jesus becomes clear. Like the close examination of a priceless piece of art, testing brings the truth to light and determines the depth of who and whose we are. It establishes how genuine something or someone truly is. After all, it takes more than a surface examination to see the heart of someone. When we consider that truth—that testing reveals our genuine, authentic character—it's possible to see the troubles we face in a more positive light. Rather than a trial to endure, it reveals our inner heart. And that genuineness is always something to celebrate.

Lord, thank you that you see beyond the surface of our lives. Help us to be true to you. Amen.

-Kristin

One Good Step: Reflect on times you've been tested and what it revealed about your genuine character.

Surround

Let your unfailing love surround us, LORD, for our hope is in you alone.
PSALM 33:22

I KNOW IT WAS GRADUAL, something that had been quietly sneaking up on me for months, but when I pulled my daughter close last week, wrapping her up in a Momma Bear hug, squeezing her tight for a long moment, I suddenly realized that her head no longer fit under my chin. Surprised, I reared back just far enough to stare into a pair of pretty eyes that are no more than a couple of inches shorter than mine.

"Stop growing!" I teased as I tucked her back in, trying to find a new way to pull her close, a better position from which to physically wrap her up in my arms and in my love, to shield her from the world the way I could when she was little, even as she laughingly protested and squirmed and declared she will soon be taller than me.

Up until now, I've always easily surrounded my kids with love in the form of a bear hug—their smaller forms able to easily fit under my chin as my arms closed around them tight, encircling them in safety as I pressed a kiss to their head. And that's how I imagine God's love for us—an *almost* tangible wrapping us up in a squeezed-tight, never-let-go, nothing-can-break-it bear hug. A child completely and utterly surrounded by the arms of a *good* Father hugging her tightly, loving her unconditionally.

Isn't that beautiful imagery? When I text prayers to hurting friends and loved ones, I almost always ask God to surround them, to hold them close in the midst of pain, loss, and uncertainty because he tells us that this is what he does, that he will comfort us as we place our hope solely, fully in him.

Lord, wrap us in your love today. Surround us with your Holy Spirit, that we can draw comfort from your nearness as we keep our hope in you alone. Amen.

-Julie

One Good Step: Visualize what it looks like to be surrounded by God's unfailing love. Pull that visual to mind whenever you begin to feel anxious or uncertain, pausing to breathe deeply and to remember that you do not walk alone.

Awe

Let the whole world fear the LORD, and let everyone stand in awe of him.

PSALM 33:8

MY SISTER BATTLED breast cancer for five years. During that time, she would have seasons of good health and then bouts of cancer that would come back for her to fight once more. During one particular round of cancer and treatment, she was so sick she had to spend several days in the hospital as they tried to manage her pain and come up with a plan for what to do next. The doctor came in after several different tests had been run to see if and where the cancer had spread.

The news wasn't good. He carefully explained how the cancer had once again spread and treatment would be necessary. She listened to his words, taking them all in and nodding at his explanation of what would need to happen next.

When the doctor finished, the room fell silent for a moment as my family members sat quietly, stunned. And then in response my sister closed her eyes, raised her hands slightly, and began to tell Jesus how much she loved him. She praised him for who he was and for how he had showed up in her life. She was simply in awe of him, and it overwhelmed her at the moment when she was surrounded by nothing but discouraging news.

And although my sister certainly had moments and valleys of doubt and sadness during her journey with cancer, I now remember just as often the moments of joy and of faith that she displayed during those years. And I'm challenged by her ability to praise him, even in the bad news.

It's easy to praise God when the news is good, but how about when the news is not so good, even bad? Can we still praise him? Stand in awe of him? It's not always easy, but no matter what we are going through, we can be sure that God is still sovereign, still good, and still in control. And when we remember that, we can stand in awe of who he is, even when the future is unsure.

Lord, you know what we are struggling through right now. Please help us to remember your sovereignty no matter what we're facing and give us the ability to still stand in awe of you today. Amen.

-Kendra

One Good Step: Think of three ways you are in awe of God today.

Rescue

In all their suffering he also suffered, and he personally rescued them.
In his love and mercy he redeemed them. He lifted them up
and carried them through all the years.

ISAIAH 63:9

LYING IN THE BOTTOM of the car, I listened to the whine of mosquitoes and waited anxiously for help to arrive. My three friends and I had been driving, carefree and young, on Memorial Day weekend, the lowering sun our only accompaniment on the dusty gravel roads. But when the car hit loose gravel and skidded into the ditch, landing on its side, I knew something inside my body had broken. As my friends climbed out of the steaming car and waited for help to arrive, time felt agonizingly slow.

The sound of sirens was the sweetest music I'd ever heard. Through the haze of pain, I felt immense relief when a fireman climbed in with me, his sweat dripping as he covered me with a blanket to protect me from the glass they'd need to shatter to get me out of the vehicle. Voice tight with emotion, he asked me if I knew a certain girl, about my age. We were close to a neighboring town, and I didn't recognize the name, so I shook my head no. I must have reminded him of someone he loved.

In that moment of pain and confusion, as the jaws of life pulled back the roof of the car and they transferred me to the ambulance, I felt overwhelming gratitude for the emergency responders who had shown up when I needed them. They had rescued me from a situation I had no way of escaping on my own.

We don't often need the kind of literal rescuing I did as a seventeen-year-old. But we often experience pain, suffering, circumstances beyond our control, uncertainty, anxiety, and other troubles—and wonder if we'll ever escape. Thankfully, we are beloved children of a God who knows and sees us in our distress and—what's more—sympathizes. He enters into our suffering and walks alongside us, as Jesus himself did in his death and resurrection. And in doing so, he rescues us from the weight of sin. Though we will experience hardship in this life, we are never alone. Our rescuer and redeemer is always at our side.

Lord, thank you for rescuing us. Amen.

-Kristin

One Good Step: Do you see Jesus as your rescuer? Why or why not?
Spend time examining your response.

Rapport

Above all, love each other deeply,
because love covers over a multitude of sins.

1 PETER 4:8, NIV

A YOUNGER FAMILY MEMBER had been having a hard time. She was at the age of wanting to be free from the rules of her parents' house, so she chose to move out of their house to make her own decisions. At the same time, she found herself with a group of friends that weren't very healthy and had started making choices that weren't in her (or their) best interest.

My husband and I were not that close to her. We had not been a part of her life in any significant way for the past several years, only interacting with her on holidays and large family gatherings. We wondered what we could do. *How could we help or encourage her?*

Frustrated, my husband finally stated, "If you want to speak into someone's life, you must have some rapport with them. You have to have a relationship to be able to have permission to speak truth to them." And I agreed, although there are always exceptions to this rule, it is most often true. I value wisdom most from the people who I know, who I trust, and who love me well. We began to work at having a relationship and building rapport with our family member so we could be there to support her as she needed it.

No one wants to be someone's project. We all want genuine relationships with those who truly care for us and our well-being. Building rapport happens over time and as we walk in close proximity with others. And it can only happen when we are willing to, not just say that we love one another, but show it by our actions and the way that we are available to support them. In good times and hard. Rapport takes time and effort, but when we've done it, we'll have the permission to speak into another's life when they may really need it.

Lord, thank you for the love you model and give to us. Help us to do the hard work of building rapport with those around us so that we can love others well. Amen.

-Kendra

One Good Step: Think of someone that you would like to build rapport with and reach out to them in a note, text, or phone call.

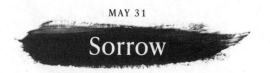

Sorrow

You keep track of all my sorrows. You have collected all my tears in your bottle.
You have recorded each one in your book.
PSALM 56:8

KNOCKING LIGHTLY, I waited on the doorstep. As the creaking screen door opened and my friend waved me in, I could feel a tide of empathy rising in me. I met her eyes, handed her a coffee, and tried to smile. Tears sprang to my eyes, and I noticed them in hers.

"We're not crying," I said wryly, defusing the moment. She smiled—because, of course we were crying—as we headed into the kitchen.

My friend's dad had died unexpectedly. Though she hadn't lived with him growing up, they maintained a good relationship. I had been scrolling social media when I saw a sweet picture of them together, matching smiles on their faces. Reading about her loss, I immediately messaged.

"Can I drop you off a meal or even a coffee?" I asked.

"I'd love a coffee," she said. "I've been up since three thirty because I couldn't sleep."

As I sat at her kitchen table, walked to the park with our collective kids, sat on the grass while she took phone calls from officials, and later settled into a chair in her living room, I didn't try to find the right words. Instead, I listened.

It's okay to sit in the weight of grief with someone, holding space for them in their sorrow. My dad once told me there's a thread of sorrow that binds us all together, weaving through the story of our lives. Perhaps when Jesus is described as fully man and fully God, that's what is meant—that he experienced the heights of joy and the deepest of sorrows, just as we do.

After all, Jesus—on hearing that his friend Lazarus had died—wept. Despite knowing he could (and did) have the power to raise him, Jesus spent time feeling the soul-deep sorrow we feel when we lose someone. He could have skipped the weight of that pain entirely. He could have simply raised Lazarus from the dead. But he didn't. Instead, he embraced that moment of sadness. Scripture says that God keeps track of our tears. Those tiny hallmarks of sorrow matter to us—and they matter to him.

Lord, thank you that you come alongside us in each moment of our lives, including the times when we feel sorrow. We are never alone. Amen.

-Kristin

One Good Step: Let someone who is experiencing sorrow
know you're thinking of them.

June

Aroma

Thanks be to God, who always leads us as captives in Christ's triumphal procession
and uses us to spread the aroma of the knowledge of him everywhere.
For we are to God the pleasing aroma of Christ.
2 CORINTHIANS 2:14-15, NIV

MY HUSBAND LOVES to garden and cook. It's a skill he's developed over time and several years after we were first married. He's spent hours learning how to grow and cook food. He skillfully and naturally puts together flavors and ingredients that I would not even think of, sending aromas throughout the house that naturally draw you to the kitchen. Anytime we go out to a restaurant, he will taste the food, remembering the aroma and flavors, often developing his own take on dishes at home, sometimes even improving on things we've had while out to eat.

But the part my husband loves more than anything is making food and sharing it with others. For him, the greatest joy is found when he can watch others enjoying his food. He loves to host large and small gatherings, carefully planning a menu with ease. Where cooking causes slight anxiety for me, to him, it's therapeutic. I love walking into the kitchen while he cooks, because the aroma alone is enough to make anyone hungry and happy. It creates a welcoming ambience in our home that invites guests in easily. His love of people and creating something that others will savor is what brings him joy.

Just as the scent of my husband's cooking is a lovely aroma for anyone who enters our home before they ever even see his cooking, so we are a pleasing aroma before God because of Christ. When we love others and invite them in, showing hospitality to friends, neighbors, and even strangers, we spread the aroma of the knowledge of Jesus everywhere. Even before people may know we are Christians, the aroma of his love, joy, and peace can be sensed through our lives, often when we do not even realize it.

Lord, let my life be a sweet aroma before you and to those around me. Amen.

-Kendra

One Good Step: Have you ever thought that the aroma of your life is
pleasing to God? Think of one way you can share the knowledge,
the aroma of Christ, as you love those who cross your path today.

Quiet

Let all that I am wait quietly before God, for my hope is in him.

PSALM 62:5

"WHEN I SPEND TIME WITH GOD, I have a tendency to race from topic to topic, mentally telling him all the things I have planned. I have a hard time quieting myself to wait and listen." Kristen confessed, as if she were telling me something only she struggles with, something that everyone but her figured out long ago.

"Oh, friend." I caught her eye as I leaned close to stage-whisper my own confession, "I'm as wriggly as a sugared-up six-year-old if you put me in a chair and tell me to be quiet and listen for God to speak. It's *hard*."

Her eyes crinkled as she chuckled, "Oh, well then. I don't feel so alone. *Gah*. I wish it weren't so difficult to turn my brain off! Every time I try to wait quietly, my brain starts thinking about a million different distracting things."

Kristen is right. Ask me to sit quietly before God, and I become like a squirrel spying multiple shiny objects all at once. My attention ping-pongs between unrelated thoughts and ideas, with the occasional random errand coming to mind as I try desperately to wrangle my attention back to God. Honestly, my inability to sit quietly for more than a few minutes at a time makes me feel like a failure.

But, I've learned the trick, at least for me. If I combine a simple physical task with my prayerful quietude, I can putter and wait, my brain willing to idle along quietly and on task as my hands do something mundane. For me, this is how I hear best from God. Depending upon the season and my to-do list, going for a solo walk, gardening, driving, even taking a shower are all times in which I find myself busy but not engaged mentally, allowing my mind to quiet, ready to hear what the Holy Spirit might reveal, content in my mental stillness even as my body moves.

Lord, thank you for speaking to us when we are willing to slow our racing thoughts and quiet our voices. Show each of us how best to quiet ourselves before you—whether that be sitting still or finding simple tasks to keep our bodies busy even as we quiet our minds. Amen.

-Julie

One Good Step: Take some time to be mentally still before God today, even if that means moving your body.

Beauty

Charm is deceptive, and beauty does not last; but a woman
who fears the LORD will be greatly praised.
PROVERBS 31:30

I PUT MY SWIMSUIT ON, headed out to the pool, and decided to show my kids how a cannonball is truly done. Over the next hour we played tag, saw who could swim the farthest without touching bottom, and took turns on the floaties. As I threw my son in the air for what felt like the hundredth time, something that never gets old to him, he giggled with laughter and then exclaimed, "Mom, you're so cute!"

My immediate response was to deny his compliment, but I caught myself and just smiled, pushing my wet hair off my face, any remnant of makeup long gone. I thought about what I must look like at that moment. What I thought I looked like, anyway, realizing what he sees is much different than what I see.

The next day as I pondered our pool time, I was reminded of a picture of my mom taken years ago on the banks of Lake Superior. In the photo, she's emerging from the frigid water, head back, laughing. A peculiar sight since my mom rarely went more than wading. And I remember thinking at the time how striking my mother looked. To my young eyes she glowed, big hair and all.

My children may never remember my sense of style. But they will remember the times I laughed with them, rode bikes, and cannonballed in the pool. They may not care what size my jeans were, but it'll matter that I listened to them, comforted them when they cried, and cheered them on in their successes.

Beauty is not just an outward look or style; it is an attitude we express. And what others "see" is the beauty expressed through our kindness, love, and sometimes even our silliness. It is our ability to be comfortable with who we are that is so attractive to those around us. Which in turn, allows them to be comfortable in who they are. Our external beauty or charm may fade, but when we follow the ways of Jesus by loving others, our inner beauty will always shine through.

Lord, help us to remember the beauty that lasts and let go of what does not. Amen.
-Kendra

One Good Step: Send a note or text to someone
whose inner beauty has been a blessing to you.

Prideful

Don't be selfish; don't try to impress others. Be humble,
thinking of others as better than yourselves.

PHILIPPIANS 2:3

LISA IS ONE OF the most compassionate people I know. So much so, in fact, that sometimes she gets stuck in a thought vortex—stuck on wondering whether she did or said the wrong thing, certain that another person's upset is because of her.

When we automatically, always assume that our words or our actions are the reason why another is upset, we put ourselves at the center of their story, at the center of their universe, uninvited and often unfairly. We all do or say things that, at times, hurt or anger another, but my tenderhearted, compassionate friend Lisa (and people, like her, who are deeply empathic and compassionate) works from the default that anytime anyone is hurt or upset around her, it is because of her. And that is both presumptuous and prideful.

That sounds harsh, but it is true. Lisa doesn't have a prideful bone in her body, not in the ways we generally define it. But her tendency to get stuck in the mental vortex insisting that she *must* be the cause of another's pain is a different kind of pride, and Satan uses it to tie her up in knots, us in knots. If we're tied, we're less effective for the Kingdom of God. It's that simple, and Satan is that tricky.

How do we escape the vortex, the knot tying? When we can, we ask the upset person what is wrong. I'm surprised how many times I've secretly assumed I'd done something, when the upset had literally zero to do with me. When we can't ask them, we ask God to show us if we did or said something that warrants an apology, and apologize when there is a possibility we're at fault. And then we let it go, remembering that it is prideful to put ourselves in the center of someone else's universe, refusing to give Satan a foothold in our thoughts, not allowing him to tie us into knots.

Lord, help us not to pridefully assume we are the cause of everyone's upset. Help us to distinguish between the hurts we've caused and the ones we haven't.

-Julie

One Good Step: When someone is upset, approach them with loving compassion and ask them why before assuming the blame.

Sustain

Cast your burden on the LORD, and he will sustain you.
PSALM 55:22, ESV

MY FRIEND PASTOR CAROL'S favorite verse is Psalm 55:22, where we are told that God will sustain us when we give him our burdens. Carol has played the piano for decades, and one of the reasons she loves the verse is because, as a pianist, she is familiar with the pedal to the far right that is called the "sustain pedal" and helps hold a note as long as you want. Over the years, Carol has held on to the promise of God's sustaining power through the financial crises she's experienced.

When Carol and her husband, Geary, became Christians, their faith was immediately tested. Within four months of uprooting everything to move to a new town, Geary lost his job. With three kids and no money coming in, it was a bad situation. But Geary insisted that God would provide.

One day, the Lord told Carol to make a grocery list and place it on her windowsill.

"I put the list on the window, and we just prayed," she said. A day later, a woman Carol had never met—someone who had heard about them from a mutual acquaintance—showed up with a carload of groceries.

"I was blown away. I'd never experienced anything like that," she said. "She left, and as I began to unload them, I got to the two cans of Chicken of the Sea tuna and I *knew*. I went and got my list, and *everything* that was on there was in the bags. We didn't even know what we were doing, and God was faithful to us."

Those early years were a training ground for Carol's challenges today. Carol and Geary founded Place of Hope Ministries, which helps provide both immediate shelter and permanent housing to those experiencing homelessness, meals for the hungry, kid-focused outreach, a discipleship program, jail and prison outreach, and church services.

"Because of what we experienced, we can run Place of Hope. Because every day, it's the same. Every day, I'm making my list. *Okay, Lord, is this what I need today?* And he routinely comes through, usually at the last minute," she said. "I would love it if we could pull from a big fund. But we don't; we have to pull from the Lord. He's our Provider."

Lord, thank you that we can trust your promise to sustain us in all circumstances. Amen.

-Kristin

One Good Step: Think of circumstances in your life in which you've had to trust the Lord to sustain your faith. What did that experience teach you?

Thankful

Be thankful in all circumstances, for this is God's will for you
who belong to Christ Jesus.
1 THESSALONIANS 5:18

WE'D HAD A BUSIER SCHEDULE than I had cared to admit when one spring things beyond our control brought all outside activities to a screeching halt. At first it was jarring. *What would we do? How would we fill our time?* Events and outings we'd been planning were all canceled. We weren't able to see our friends. Life felt a little sad and lonely. But as the days turned to weeks and then months, we began to find time for things we hadn't previously had time for. We put together puzzles as a family, watched movies, and taught our kids cooking skills. We ordered out at least once a week, allowing the kids to choose their favorite places to purchase from for dinner.

But one of the biggest blessings during that season was our family's ability to have daily devotions together. Each morning before the regular routine of the day would begin, we would sit in the living room and read a chapter of Scripture together. During those months we read many of the letters in the New Testament and all learned and grew in our faith and understanding of Scripture. Our kids asked deep, thought-provoking questions and we searched out answers as we all learned together. It was time that I had always hoped for but was never quite able to achieve on a consistent basis while our family's schedule had been so busy. Now, it's become routine. We move other activities around to make time for devotions.

It's not always easy to be thankful in all circumstances. Often it takes our being intentional to notice what we can be thankful for in this season of life. We can miss the good things that are happening when we only focus on the hard. When we shift our thoughts to God and all that he has done (and believe he will do), we will find even small things to be thankful for in the middle of life's hard times.

Lord, even in the midst of what is hard, give us eyes to see what we can still be thankful for, no matter how small. Amen.

-Kendra

One Good Step: Take time today to bring any concerns that have been weighing heavy on your heart and mind, and then look for what you are still thankful to God for in this season.

Ablaze

There the angel of the LORD appeared to him in a blazing fire from
the middle of a bush. Moses stared in amazement. Though
the bush was engulfed in flames, it didn't burn up.

EXODUS 3:2

MY HUSBAND HAS ACCIDENTALLY started two grills on fire. Luckily, we had fire extinguishers on hand to stop the blaze each time, but we were both a little shaken. There's something about flames sweeping out of control that tends to make you nervous. Tim is actually an excellent grillmaster. But in those moments, I didn't consider my husband's expertise. Instead, my response was immediately fear and alarm.

I'm struck by the story of Moses and his own encounter with something set ablaze. In his case, it was a burning bush that hosted an angel of the Lord. Though I've often wished God would use a skywriting airplane or giant blimp to get my attention, a burning bush feels dangerous. It's natural to feel fear. But Moses was also curious.

The Lord told Moses about the oppression he'd witnessed in Egypt, the abuse the Israelites endured. Then he called him to action. When Moses protested his ability to lead the people, God asked him to lay down his rod. As a shepherd, Moses' rod represented his work, his finances, and who he was in that moment. And so, even more terrifying than a bush in flames was the call to action: *Lay it down.*

I have to believe that—despite his reservations—the blaze Moses experienced lit an answering fire in his heart. His encounter with the burning bush changed him. It's one thing for us to hear the voice of God and another thing entirely for us to let it alter our future. Too often, we try to tamp the fire down, control it, or extinguish it entirely. Keeping the fire ablaze—and heeding the call within it to lay something of ourselves down—is difficult for most of us to fathom. Yet it's only when we lay down our own proverbial rod that we're ready to see what God holds in store for us. When we do, we may find an answering blaze lit in our own hearts.

Lord, may our hearts be ablaze for you. Amen.

-Kristin

One Good Step: Do you feel like God has tried to get your attention in some way? What do you need to lay down in order to accomplish something for Jesus?

Wise

The wise woman builds her house, but with her own hands
the foolish one tears hers down.

PROVERBS 14:1, NIV

THERE IS OFTEN LITTLE ROOM for my words when I am with my children. Their words, songs, and constant chatter never quit. Sunup to sundown, I am surrounded by noise and laughter, banter and sometimes fights. The days can blur together, and I have to be intentional at times to stop and listen. To take in the small moments and successes as they come.

Like when I sit in the evening and listen to my oldest son share about his recent sporting adventures and plans for taking driver's education this summer, thoughts swirl through my mind, ready to tumble out, but instead I just sit and listen.

When it comes to communication, I've learned that being a wise mom means I'm always walking a fine line between having something and nothing to say. Carefully trying to measure my words, to speak truth, but not dominate my kids, and allowing room for them to be and share all of who they are with me.

I've been reminded lately that a wise woman builds her house (including her loved ones), but a foolish woman tears it down with her own hands. And if I'm honest, I have been a foolish woman at times, tearing down my own household with the things I've said. But even though I may have torn down my house foolishly in the past, today is a new day, and I can choose to build it back up, one brick, one conversation at a time.

It is so important that we guard our thoughts and our tongues wisely. This is most challenging when it comes to our own families. Many times we can want to come in with an answer or instruction—and although there is certainly space for that—there is also something to be said for being quiet and just listening. To hear our loved ones and respond only after we've allowed them to finish. Learning to be wise with our words and not foolish.

Lord, give us wisdom to know when to speak and when to remain silent. Help us to be wise and not foolish with our words. Amen.

-Kendra

One Good Step: Be intentional today to just listen to someone else without always thinking of what you are going to say next.

Weak

Each time [the Lord] said, "My grace is all you need. My power works best in weakness." So now I am glad to boast about my weaknesses, so that the power of Christ can work through me. . . . For when I am weak, then I am strong.

2 CORINTHIANS 12:9-10

OUR FRIEND ELI gave his then-fiancée, Ashley, an adorable boxer puppy, Jax, as a birthday present while they were engaged. Through the first several years of their marriage and birth of two of their children, Jax was a steady presence in their lives.

One day, Jax started limping. Concerned, they took him in to the veterinarian for a checkup. Sadly, he was diagnosed with osteosarcoma, a fast-moving, bone-eating tumor that was untreatable.

Our friends were devastated. "He's only been limping for a few days," they protested. "How could this have happened?"

The veterinarian explained that dogs are, by nature, pack animals. Whenever possible, they avoid showing signs of weakness until they can't avoid doing so. By then, it's often too late.

Although people don't have the same pack tendencies that dogs do, we often have the same unwillingness to show our weaknesses to others. After all, social media feeds typically only showcase the highlight reels of our friends and acquaintances, rarely revealing those who are struggling with hidden pain, navigating tough financial or personal circumstances, or grieving secret losses.

Yet as Christians, we are reminded that revealing our weaknesses only serves to make us stronger. Admitting to areas of vulnerability gives us the chance to recognize how Christ is working in us. Humbled by our weaknesses, we know we could not do it alone—it's only through the power of Jesus that we can carry on. Revealing our weaknesses to those we trust has an added benefit: when our struggles and sins are hidden, we wrestle with them alone—but when we allow them to see the light of day, they lose their power. As friends, we are stronger together.

Lord, thank you that we don't need to be strong on our own—that your power is great enough to carry us. Help us to be willing to reveal our weaknesses to others and get the support we need. Amen.

-Kristin

One Good Step: Who among your friends do you show your limp to? If you haven't already done so, consider confiding a current challenge to a trusted friend.

Close

Even when I walk through the darkest valley, I will not be afraid, for you are
close beside me. Your rod and your staff protect and comfort me.

PSALM 23:4

"MOM!"

"Mom!"

My eyes blurry with sleep, blink open, and I am momentarily confused before
realizing why I'd awoken and what was happening.

"Yes, Jonny?" I call back across the small landing that separates our bedrooms,
rising up on an elbow to peer into the night-light's dim glow to see whether his
little body is hurtling in my direction.

"I love you!" he yells. No hurtling then, I realize as I lie back down, pulling my
share of the covers back to equal as Aaron grunts at my tug.

"We love you, too!" Aaron and I call back sleepily in unison as we all snuggle
back in, with Aaron adding a wry, "Now get some sleep!" We both know that we'll
probably do this little ritual once more before the sun rises.

Our family chuckles over that phase in our collective lives—the year that Jonny
would wake up and holler that he loved us and then wait for our response, sometimes multiple times a night. He was seeking reassurance that we remained close
by, needing only to hear our voices before, comforted, he snuggled under his covers
and settled back to sleep.

I was telling a friend about the year of the "I love you" call and response, when
it occurred to me that I do that with Jesus—I call out to him when the car skids on
ice, when my child crashes his bike in front of me, when danger suddenly looms—
not because I doubt he is there and I'm looking for him, but precisely because I
know he is there, and I find comfort and draw strength and courage from his closeness even as I watch a situation spiral out of control.

We are promised the closeness of God when life unexpectedly goes off the
rails, when we are walking through the darkest valleys of our lives. Before we
call, he is close by, both Comforter and Protector. And when we call out to him,
he responds.

Lord, thank you for being close to us, especially during our darkest moments. Amen.

-Julie

One Good Step: Collect stories of how God has come through for those
around you—and then meditate on those stories when life is hard and you
need to remember that he is our close Comforter and Protector.

JUNE 11

Treasured

The very hairs on your head are all numbered. So don't be afraid;
you are more valuable to God than a whole flock of sparrows.

LUKE 12:7

"So—what are you going to do next?"

The question was posed innocently enough by a friend. I'd just finished describing my work volunteering with a women's conference and meeting a challenging work deadline. I really wanted to say, "I just need to catch my breath." But I didn't. Instead, I rattled off yet another list of things that needed to be done.

I am a to-do list kind of person. I love the satisfaction of checking items off a list. And although there may be nothing wrong with valuing productivity—at least not on the surface—there can be a deeper need driving me. Too often, I can feel that in order to be valuable or make a mark on this world, to be seen and noticed or even sometimes loved, I must perform. Being is simply not enough.

This morning, I sat and listened to my daughter tell me about her weekend. She recounted a tumble she took yesterday, the food she ate last night, the fun she had with friends. As I listened to her talk, I thought about how much I love her. I love hearing her voice, her thoughts, her heart. There is nothing that she does that increases my love. There is nothing she does that diminishes my love. Simply hearing her voice and spending time with her is enough. I treasure her just as she is.

And isn't that just how God thinks about us? Lovely, chosen, treasured, loved—just as we are. Not because of what we do. Our value to God does not diminish or increase based on what we accomplish. His love is always constant. He cares about the largest and smallest details of our lives, down to knowing the very hairs on our heads. He treasures us.

Lord, thank you for being such a good God. Thank you that you treasure us because of who we are and not because of what we can do for you. Amen.

-Kendra

One Good Step: Spend some time thinking of how God has shown his love to you lately, not because of what you've done, but simply because he treasures you and loves to be with you.

Attune

I am always aware of your unfailing love,
and I have lived according to your truth.

PSALM 26:3

A FAMILY FROM CHURCH has a daughter who was born with a congenitally deformed heart. As an infant, she endured several surgeries and lengthy hospital stays. Her family was grateful to bring her home, but the fragile nature of the now-toddler-aged child's condition means that they have to be very careful.

On a recent summer day, the little girl's mother brought her and her big sister, along with their dog Marty, outside to enjoy the sun. Despite fighting some cold symptoms, the child was happy and walked constantly around the yard.

But after a while, the mother started to notice something odd happening with Marty, a collie. He came over to the child and sniffed her, ran away a few feet, then turned back around and cut her off, standing sideways so that she was forced to stop. Then he would turn, sniff her chest gently, and come back around to block her again so she couldn't keep walking.

The mom could tell he was upset, so she brought her daughter inside and found that she had a slightly elevated temperature. Later that night, the mom was amazed to find that even in her now-relaxed state, the child's heart rate was much too high and her oxygen was low. The mom was so grateful to their dog for noticing her daughter's symptoms that she gave him a reward.

Marty was attuned to the little girl's needs, so much so that he noticed a problem before anyone else was aware. His attentiveness was what helped spur the little girl's mom to action.

Similarly, our loving father God is always attuned to us. He not only created us in his image and knows us well enough to number the hairs on our head, he shows his love in myriad ways. He rejoices over us, calls us his children, and quietly loves us. The Bible even says that he bends down to listen when we pray (see Psalm 116:2). As our heavenly Father, God cares deeply about the big and small details of our lives.

Lord, thank you for always being attuned to our needs. Thank you for your loving care. Amen.

-Kristin

One Good Step: Spend today attuned to the idea that you matter to God. What does that mean to you? How does it influence how you perceive God?

Small

Do not despise these small beginnings,
for the LORD rejoices to see the work begin.
ZECHARIAH 4:10

"OKAY, GO," I said, my eyes locked on Jonny stretched out on the tube. Aaron engaged the throttle, adding just enough gas to get the boat on a plane but no more. With Jonny's tube skimming across the water and inside the boat wake, we motored around the lake for a minute before Jonny gave me the signal to stop.

"Honey, cut the motor," I said, and Aaron immediately throttled to a stop.

"What's wrong? Is he okay?" he asked as I hauled in the towrope, pulling Jonny and the tube back to the boat.

"He's just nervous. It's new and hard," I said. I sent Jonny a smile as I called, "It's okay, buddy. Do you want to try again, or are you done?"

By midsummer, Jonny was jumping the wake, riding the waves, and laughing uproariously as the tube caught "good air" and he went flying, asking as he bobbed in the water if he could ride again.

Do not despise your small beginning; God doesn't. Small beginnings count. It is a practice field, a place to fail and flail and figure things out. It is forward movement, and as long as you keep going and keep trying, you'll soon find yourself further along than you'd imagined.

I suspect that we forget that everyone starts small. We see an accomplished worship leader or a skilled speaker at our favorite conference and wish we could be there, at that level, forgetting or not realizing the small beginning and the thousands of hours of hard work behind that moment in the spotlight.

While God certainly has the ability to catapult someone directly into the big leagues, I've never seen it. If you listen closely, you'll hear famous speakers and authors talk about small beginnings, about early failures, about writing words only their moms read, or speaking to a room filled with five people, three of whom organized the event.

God is with us in our small beginnings, and he loves to see us start.

Lord, thank you for small beginnings, for a safe place to practice. Amen.

-Julie

One Good Step: Write down, "Do not despise these small beginnings," and post it where you can easily see it as you work on your small beginning.

JUNE 14

Devoted

Do not be afraid or discouraged, for the LORD will personally go ahead of you.
He will be with you; he will neither fail you nor abandon you.
DEUTERONOMY 31:8

MY MOM CAME INTO a relationship with God as a young married woman. She started attending the Bible study my dad had been a part of the year prior and got to know other Christians very quickly. During one of the first weeks, the young man leading the study told everyone to close their eyes and ask God to bring to their minds a time when they felt alone. As my mom closed her eyes and prayed, immediately God brought to her memory a time when she was a young girl, sitting by her front window, waiting for her mom to come home. My mom's home life was harder than most young girls her age. As her dad would be gone every week traveling for work, her mom would also sometimes leave her alone.

She said she knew that it was God who'd brought it to mind because she hadn't thought about that particular memory in years. The leader then said, "Now, I want you to imagine that Jesus is there with you. What would he say to you?"

My mom immediately was able to picture in her mind Jesus there with her as a young girl, showing her compassion and love. My mom said that had such a profound impact, to realize that Jesus was there with her, devoted to her, even when she did not yet know him. Her understanding of God's faithfulness and devotion was settled right then, and even when she walked through some really hard things later on, she never worried about God's faithfulness. Because she dealt with the lies of her past that said she was alone.

God's promises aren't for just some. They are for all of us, but we've got to be in a place where we can receive them. We need to believe God's devotion to us, even when we do not see.

Lord, thank you that you are near. Thank you that we don't have to rely on our feelings to know that your promises are true. Thank you for being devoted to us and never leaving us alone. Amen.

-Kendra

One Good Step: Take time today to ask God to bring to mind a time you felt alone. And then imagine Jesus is there with you. What would he say to you? How would he comfort you?

Honesty

May integrity and honesty protect me, for I put my hope in you.
PSALM 25:21

EACH TIME I VISITED Tom's small farm, I'd pull into the gravel driveway and step out into the humid heat of summer, the whine of mosquitoes loud in the quiet lane of the country farm. Next, I'd grip a plastic basket with gallon-sized glass jars tucked inside, carefully walking around the barn cat that wound around my feet and ignoring its insistent purring as I'd enter the shed. After snagging a small stool, I'd place it next to the tank and fill my jars. Once I was finished, I would close the spigot and rinse the floor, hefting now-full jars of fresh milk into my arms. On the way out the door, I'd pause to place six worn dollar bills under the hammer placed at eye level.

For years, I stopped at Tom's farm. Sometimes I'd run into him, and he'd pause from his work to chat. But other than learning the process the first time, it was up to me to follow through with his protocol. And as far as payment goes, I was on the honor system.

The expectation of honesty felt a little jarring, at first. Nice, but jarring. What kind of person trusted people enough to let them walk into their barn unsupervised? Didn't he know people could leave without paying for a product that he relied on to pay his bills?

It's true that some people probably did leave without paying. There will always be people who try to take advantage of others; the incidence of evil is very real in our broken world.

Tom's reliance on the honesty of others didn't reflect his assessment of other people's character, but of his own. There's a quote from the Disney movie *Pollyanna* that I love: "When you look for the bad in mankind, expecting to find it, you surely will." If we focus exclusively on terrible things in the world around us, every negative circumstance will confirm our belief that the world is an awful place. The opposite is also true—if we choose to look for the good in people, we'll find it. As citizens of heaven, our hope is not in people but in the Lord. The content of our character isn't a magical elixir that protects us, but rather evidence of the confident hope that we place in Jesus.

Lord, help us to choose to be honest even when it feels hard. Amen.

-Kristin

One Good Step: Is there an area in your life that you have been dishonest about? How can you remedy the situation?

Father

Father to the fatherless, defender of widows—
this is God, whose dwelling is holy.

PSALM 68:5

"TIME TO GET UP, SLEEPYHEAD," I call up the stairs as I scoop up Peanut the poodle for a quick pat before I put him outside. "Don't forget today is Coffee with Dad," I call again as Peanut ambles back in, headed for the food dish.

"Donuts! Dad!" A young voice yells, and I smile as my words produce scurrying sounds with no moaning or groaning over the earlier than normal morning.

Tuesday mornings are extra special in our house. Aaron takes one of the kids out for "coffee" and donuts before dropping them off at the school's front door. Over the years, they've perfected the routine, searching out the *best* donuts and sampling various non-caffeinated drinks from coffee shops all around town. With their chats ranging from inane to deeply spiritual, the time spent together has become what is important, a beloved tradition.

Fatherhood—whether by blood or by love—brings stability and security in ways motherhood doesn't. We know this—the statistics regarding the impact fathering (even very imperfect fathering) has on the lives of children is staggering when it comes to delaying or preventing risky behaviors.

God knows the importance of fathering. And he invites us into a father/child relationship—one that is healthy and *good*, with all of the benefits and none of the sorrows we might associate from imperfect, earthly dads. He offers what many people desperately need—a Father who does not hurt, does not fall short, does not leave us wishing for more.

The question is, do we believe that God is our Father? Do our actions reveal his fathering in our lives? Or do we act fatherless, insecure and unstable, choosing risky behaviors and living out the earthly statistics? For those with hard stories around earthly fatherhood, God is the redeemer of that title and role, able and willing to fill in the holes and gaps in our hearts, and be our defender, if we let him.

Lord, fill in the sorrows and hurts we have around fathering. Remind us that we are not fatherless. Amen.

-Julie

One Good Step: Write God a Father's Day letter, confessing your feelings concerning fatherhood and what gaps you might need filled in.

Leap

Behold, the former things have come to pass, and new things I now declare;
before they spring forth I tell you of them.

ISAIAH 42:9, ESV

STANDING ON THE PRECIPICE of something new, wondering if I should take the risk and leap.

Waiting for clarity of what could be next. Seeing so clearly the next step right in front of me, but little else. Much of what my future holds is a mystery at this point.

I don't have all the answers for my why questions, at least not now. And yet, I've found myself in this place of faith before, knowing I needed to step out before I truly understood all that God would have planned. I know that he is faithful to me. I've seen it. Experienced it.

I can also remember times I lingered too long, allowing my own fear, doubt, or just plain apathy to stop me from leaping into some new thing or space. It usually did not turn out well. Anger and frustration would begin to grow, not because I couldn't choose to stay, no, but because I knew it was time to move and, like a child, decided I'd rather dig my heels in and stay put. But staying put has never boded well for anyone when God has said, "Move on."

And as I've realized how God created us, knowing us in the deepest parts of who we are, I've begun to understand that he knows the best times to move us on. To let go of some things, even while we begin to fumble for new. Even when we're afraid or uncertain.

God is a fearless God. Calling us, beckoning us, inviting us, into a great wide-open space with him. And if we'll have courage and take a leap of faith, we'll find ourselves in a new place. It may not be perfect, we may still struggle, and sometimes it may not even seem to make sense to our earthly eyes. At least not in the moment. But we may never know all that God has for us unless we're willing to sometimes take a chance and leap.

Lord, help us to be willing to let go of the things you tell us to let go of, to see the new thing you are doing. Afford us the courage to leap when you ask us to. Amen.

-Kendra

One Good Step: What is one thing you can do today to take a leap into something new that God is calling you into?

Rest

God gives rest to his loved ones.

PSALM 127:2

As LITTLE FEET pounded up the stairs, I heard my husband gently corral the kids into brushing their teeth and getting ready for bed. Bending down, I picked up the final toy cluttering the living room floor and tossed it into the toy box, stretching backward with a groan. *Uffda.* I was exhausted. But as I surveyed the crumbs on the dining room floor and sticky globs on the counter, I knew I wouldn't head upstairs until the kitchen was spotless too.

As a kid, I never realized how much time adults spend cleaning. Though I kept my own room relatively clean and helped with dishes, I rarely thought twice about laundry or floors. And except for mowing the lawn once a week, I never once considered yard maintenance.

Oh, the rude awakening. As an adult, I spend countless hours cleaning. Add in three kids who seem blithely unaware of their trail of toys, and it's a recipe for constant cleaning. Between that and the mental and emotional real estate being sucked up by our family of five, my exhaustion felt soul deep. I knew I needed rest, but I didn't know how to achieve it.

Seeking that rest, I bought novels to dive into and bath salts to soak in. I had my own secret stash of dark chocolate and splurged on a new shirt. But everything that the world would categorize as self-care fell flat. Though I had enjoyed those experiences, I still didn't feel rested. Instead, I felt unsatisfied and a little guilty. I couldn't understand why what I was doing wasn't working.

Reading my Bible one morning, I ran across Psalm 127:2 and had a light bulb moment: *God gives rest to his loved ones.* Rest isn't a luxury; it's a gift from God. It's not something we earn by crossing enough items off our to-do list or clearing enough clutter; it's a gift we already have access to. Though there's nothing wrong with bath salts or a chocolate stash, the greatest act of self-care you can give yourself is simply permission to rest. With that in mind, I began to be more purposeful in my rest, finding pockets of time each day where I refused to feel guilty. Instead, I accepted the gift of God's marvelous rest, and reveled in it.

Lord, thank you for the gift of rest. Help us to give ourselves permission to truly rest. Amen.

-Kristin

One Good Step: Find a time today when you will purposely choose to rest.

Learn

Intelligent people are always ready to learn.

PROVERBS 18:15

ON TODAY'S DATE IN 1865, US General Gordon Granger stood on Texas soil and read General Order No. 3: "The people of Texas are informed that, in accordance with a proclamation from the Executive of the United States, all slaves are free."

In other words, it was a full two and a half years after the Emancipation Proclamation formally ended slavery in the United States that roughly 250,000 men, women, and children enslaved in Texas finally learned that they were free. That day is celebrated as Juneteenth and is also known as Freedom Day, Liberation Day, Jubilee Day, and Emancipation Day.

Until recently, I. Did. Not. Know. This.

How did I not know about this until I was a forty-something-year-old? I've asked this question of myself more than once as I've confronted uncomfortable truths these past months about race, racism, and our country's complicated history that was ignored in my glossy school textbooks.

I've confessed my regret before God, seemingly continually convicted in new ways of my obliviousness to the deep hurts inflicted on fellow brothers and sisters in Christ, on fellow countrymen, on people I call friends. My response to the gentle conviction of the Holy Spirit around this particularly large blind spot in my life has been to learn and then honor, in every way I can, the voices of those who are teaching me.

I cannot undo my past ignorance, but I can learn. I can read and watch and listen as I prayerfully consider what needs to change about my interactions with BIPOCs (Black, Indigenous, Persons of Color) when they are in the room and, perhaps most importantly, when they are not. I can listen to another's experience and not diminish it when it doesn't match my own. I can admit that I got it terribly wrong, vow to do better, and then do it better. I can make mistakes, ask for forgiveness, and then try again. I can seek truth, even when it is uncomfortable and hard and then ask God what he would have me do with it.

Lord, thank you for Juneteenth. Thank you for true freedom. Thank you for the ability to learn, no matter our background. Amen.

-Julie

One Good Step: Spend time reflecting on the legacy of Juneteenth and celebrating the voices who are engaged in the work of anti-racism. *Be the Bridge* by Latasha Morrison and *I'm Still Here: Black Dignity in a World Made for Whiteness* by Austin Channing Brown are two books to get you started.

Legacy

How joyful are those who fear the LORD and delight in obeying his commands.
Their children will be successful everywhere; an entire generation
of godly people will be blessed.

PSALM 112:1-2

THERE ARE TWO PHOTOS that stay tucked in the front of my journal. One is of my sister Katrina who passed away and the other is of my uncle Jim. The photo of my uncle is worn around the edges, but in it he's sitting on the couch with me perched on his lap. He'd probably just come in from working in the barn. I smile anytime I see it. I loved him and the farm he lived on. But it was more than that. My uncle Jim and aunt Delpha modeled the ways of Jesus before I even really knew what they were.

They welcomed strangers by taking in foster kids for twenty years. They adopted several of the kids brought to their home. They stood up to neighbors when not all their children were invited to play. My uncle would spend hours with us kids, even though I'm sure he had better things to do. He loved us well. That time had a profound effect on my life.

The truth is, no one really knows my uncle Jim and aunt Delpha outside of their small community, but to me, they are modern-day heroes of the faith. My uncle wasn't a saint by any means—he was an imperfect, flawed human being. But he paved a way of love with his life that has sent ripples well beyond his passing. His legacy lives on, woven into the fabric of my life and the many others whose lives have been impacted for the good by him.

Our legacy isn't something we usually give a lot of thought to in the moment. I'm sure my uncle never thought about his legacy as he was spending time with us kids; he was just doing what he believed was important. But our legacy is being created every day of our lives. Does this mean we can never mess up or have a bad day? Certainly not. But it does mean that as we seek to make obeying God's commands a habit in our lives, we will reap the benefits, and so will our children.

Lord, thank you for the legacy of those who have gone before us. Give us wisdom to be intentional about the legacy we want to leave. Amen.

-Kendra

One Good Step: Thank someone whose legacy made a difference in your life.

Go

Don't just listen to God's word. You must do what it says.
Otherwise, you are only fooling yourselves.

JAMES 1:22

"LET'S GO!" I reached for the front door while smiling at Jonny as he finished tying his shoes. "We've got fifteen coffee makers to buy, and I'm going to need your help."

The plea for coffee makers and prayers for our community's homeless shelter had stopped my social media scrolling in its tracks. *Oh, Lord, why didn't I think of Pastor Carol and Geary sooner? I should have known they'd need help. Please help me to be better, do better.* My prayer turned my mind to action, and after gathering a few more bits of information, it was time for me and Jonny to go. We swooped into the nearest big box store, buying them out of their simplest coffee makers, clearing their shelf of filters, and loading our cart with enough small bags of coffee to supply an office for a year. As curious comments over our unusual purchase followed us through the checkout line and out the doors, we grinned. Adventuring with God is so delightfully fun.

Go. Such a simple word. And yet so challenging. If we allow it, there are a million reasons to resist, stuck in inertia. I'm guilty of all of them: assuming that what little bit we have to give is not valuable; distractions that make us good intentioned but terrible at following through; and living at maximum capacity with our time and our money—stretched so thin that there is nothing left over to be used by God. When we pray to be goers, we actively seek opportunities; we live with margin in both our time and finances for when God calls; and we trust God will multiply our smallest contribution exponentially, knowing that God's math doesn't follow earthly rules. Trust me, you won't ever regret telling God you're ready to go.

Lord, may we be active in our faith, doers of your Word, willing to go. Show us what is stopping us from being sent. Amen.

-Julie

One Good Step: Where is God sending you today, this week, this month? Go.

Gratitude

Let the message of Christ dwell among you richly as you teach
and admonish one another with all wisdom through psalms, hymns,
and songs from the Spirit, singing to God with gratitude in your hearts.
COLOSSIANS 3:16, NIV

DESPITE A COMFORTABLE HOME and food in the cupboards, I was feeling a little ungrateful. With my husband working from home and kids doing distance learning, the house felt overly noisy and constantly messy. I chafed at a lack of time and solitude, even as I recognized how minor those concerns were compared to financial and health hardships others were facing.

Brewing coffee one morning, I opened the cupboard and paused. In the front row, facing outward, was one of my favorite cups: a simple cream mug with the word *Grateful*. Snagging it from the shelf, I was reminded of my friend Andrea and our gratitude challenge. For fourteen days, we texted each other every evening with three things we were grateful for that day. Studies have shown that doing so can boost your happiness level for up to six months afterward.

During the challenge, I was struck by how the smallest of details were reasons to be grateful: brisket on the grill, a chat with a friend, going for a walk, a nice family dinner, work finished on time, kids playing well together, a sunny day, new books from the library, donuts, a campfire, and more. None of those items was particularly earth-shattering, but added up over the course of the day, they mattered. The very act of naming so many things that made us grateful increased our joy.

By the end, we were both glad we'd committed to the exercise. Days later, the mug from Andrea showed up on my doorstep. Now, each time I see it, I'm reminded of our experiment and how grateful I am for all that I have.

Lord, help us to see the beauty in the small details of life and appreciate them each day. Amen.

-Kristin

One Good Step: Try a Gratitude Challenge. Find an accountability partner and spend the next fourteen days sending each other three things you're grateful for each day. Discuss it afterward to see how your attitude and perceptions changed.

Discipline

Joyful are those you discipline, LORD, those you teach with your instructions.
You give them relief from troubled times.

PSALM 94:12-13

As A YOUNG CHILD, I remember my parents telling me not to do certain behaviors. When I would ask why, the answer was often simply "Because it's wrong" or "Because it's a sin." That may have been true, but those answers didn't give me much of a reason not to do something I knew I shouldn't. Truth be told, I was the kind of kid who was filled with a burning desire to do whatever I was told *not* to do. With little to no explanation as to the exact reason or consequences for a specific choice, I gave into my own desires, unintentionally creating some unhealthy habits in my life that were not easily undone as an adult.

When I became a young adult and started studying Scripture for myself, I began to understand many of the reasons behind God's boundaries—all stemming from his great love for us. Once I knew God's heart, I wanted to walk in his truth. After several years of having to relearn what was healthy and good for me, especially in relationships, I realized how much conflict and shame and disconnect could have been avoided if I'd simply understood *why* God's law was good for me, right from the start.

God's discipline and instruction always leads us to a place where we are in close connection with him and with one another. God isn't a judge waiting to punish us when we misstep or hold our guilt over us so we'll be shamed into trying to do better. His discipline and law are meant to give us relief from troubled times. They are meant to bring us to the best that this life has to offer—peace, joy, love, and comfort. Does this mean we'll never experience hardships? No, not at all. But it does mean that no matter what we face, we know that God is with us. And we can find comfort in him like we will never find anywhere else.

Lord, help us to follow your instructions, knowing that your discipline comes from a place of love and protection. Amen.

-Kendra

One Good Step: Spend some time thinking about how God's discipline has shown his love and protection for you.

Grow

Dear brothers and sisters, I close my letter with these last words: Be joyful.
Grow to maturity. Encourage each other. Live in harmony and peace.
Then the God of love and peace will be with you.
2 CORINTHIANS 13:11

WHAT SHOULD HAVE BEEN a fun reunion became an evening Laura simply endured. Stacy, her former college roommate, and Stacy's husband were unexpectedly in town, and Laura had invited them to join their previously planned backyard BBQ. It was an eclectic guest list of neighbors, friends, and the life group Laura and her husband led through church, and Laura knew Stacy would fit right in.

While in college, Stacy had been actively involved in Bible studies while Laura struggled with her faith. Stacy had been an encouraging bystander to Laura's earliest steps back to God, and after years of being connected only on social media, Laura was looking forward to Stacy seeing that she'd developed a deep and abiding faith.

During the course of the evening, Stacy's patronizing tone, presumptive comments, and stories shared about Laura caught Laura off guard. Puzzling silently, Laura realized that Stacy's view of her had remained frozen in time, stuck on the girl Laura was a decade ago. Stacy hadn't paused to notice the woman Laura had become.

As Laura wiped down tables, the party long over and the guests gone, she processed the frustration she felt being "stuck" in that long ago moment of time, forever frozen in Stacy's mind as someone Laura now barely recognized.

She paused to ask Jesus to help her recognize the growth, the journey in people around her rather than mentally flash freezing them, keeping them always as they were. Siblings, cousins, childhood friends, classmates, former coworkers—faces from these categories and more came to mind as she sifted through memories, asking God to forgive her for categorizing people with no opportunity for them to change, to grow.

Walking with Jesus is a journey, not an event. We'll never get "there," and we do our fellow travelers a grave injustice when we freeze them as we once knew them, allowing them no room to grow.

Lord, who have we flash frozen, making assumptions about who they are now based on the past? Help us to see those around us with fresh eyes and a current perspective. Amen.

-Julie

One Good Step: Determine to give others the opportunity to grow, mature, and become different people than the individuals you knew or know.

Perceive

Our lives are a Christ-like fragrance rising up to God. But this fragrance is perceived differently by those who are being saved and by those who are perishing.

2 CORINTHIANS 2:15

MY MOM LOST her sense of smell years ago for reasons unknown. Occasionally, she'll catch a whiff of something, but it's rare.

One day as we were driving down the road, she happened to notice a scent. "What's that sweet smell?" she asked.

My sisters and I exchanged amused looks in the backseat. "Mom, it's a skunk!"

"Oh," she shrugged, laughing a bit. "Well, I didn't know. That's what it smelled like to me."

I'm thankful that my own sense of smell is intact, but the story is a good reminder that the way we experience the world around us does not always accurately reflect what is true about God's Kingdom. How God perceives the world and its inhabitants is often different from our human understanding. Paul, in his second letter to the Corinthians, reminds the church that believers' lives give off a fragrance that rises to God. *Meyer's New Testament Commentary* describes the fragrance of our lives as something positive, akin to "the odours of incense that accompanied the triumphal procession; these are to God a fragrance, redolent to Him of Christ." It's interesting that something welcoming to God—incense in the triumphal procession—is likely perceived with indifference by some or perhaps even negatively by others.

Yet the upside-down nature of God's economy often seems counterintuitive to our human understanding. The last are first, the first last. The poor are blessed. Loving our enemies, giving away our wealth, and putting others first are the opposite of what this world values. Humility, meekness, weakness—all are positive characteristics. No wonder the "fragrance" of our lives is perceived differently. Rather than something worrisome, what a relief this should be! Instead of worrying so much about what other people around us think of our lives, let's focus on pleasing God. His is the only opinion that matters.

Lord, may our lives please you. Help us to perceive the world around us with your eyes and ears, open to experiencing this life with your perspective firmly fixed in our minds. Amen.

-Kristin

One Good Step: Read Luke 6:20-49. What do these verses reveal about how Jesus sees the world versus how man sees it?

Shine

Because of God's tender mercy, the morning light from heaven is about
to break upon us, to give light to those who sit in darkness and in
the shadow of death, and to guide us to the path of peace.

LUKE 1:78-79

"I'LL TELL YOU," she whispered more to herself than to me, her voice rough with unshed tears. We were sitting on the back patio, coffee in hand, enjoying a quiet moment. The story that tumbled out was heart wrenching, a deep, hidden hurt that had impacted her life for many years. No one else knew other than her husband and, now, me.

I texted her later, remembering our implicit agreement that nothing we talk about is off limits from our husbands, telling her that her story was hers and that I wasn't planning to share it with Aaron.

"It's okay. I knew when I told you that I was telling Aaron, too. I trust him implicitly." Her response caused me to pause, and after some prayerful thought, I realized she needed a small, trusted circle to know, and she was trusting me to bring Aaron into that circle. Her story needed exposure to the morning light—Jesus—and loving people standing alongside her.

There is a reason light is an analogy for Jesus and darkness is an analogy for Satan throughout Scripture. Our enemy often uses hidden, secret things to destroy us. He convinces us that no one will believe us, that we are the only one, and then he sends boogeymen in the form of dark thoughts and bad dreams to keep us chained up, afraid, alone. He thrives in the dark, hidden spaces, whispering lies with just a kernel of truth to keep us separated from those who love us, unable to see a way forward.

Jesus is and always has been the antidote to the darkness. He exposes the lies we believe in the dark, revealing the inconsistencies and flaws in our twisted-up beliefs we could not see for ourselves. He brings healing, redemption, and new life.

Lord, what lies have I believed in the dark? Which stories need your morning light shining upon them?

-Julie

One Good Step: What needs the healing exposure of Jesus' light in your life? Make a plan to talk to a pastor, a therapist, a trustworthy friend.

Encompass

How often I have wanted to gather your children together
as a hen protects her chicks beneath her wings.
LUKE 13:34

MY HUSBAND AND I were having dinner at the home of some new friends. As we were getting ready to leave, Kyle commented on Rembrandt's painting of the Prodigal Son they had hanging on their wall. Kyle asked if we knew that the artist had intentionally painted the Father's hands differently. I leaned in close to get a better look. He was correct. He explained that many people believe Rembrandt painted one hand more masculine and the other feminine to portray a more holistic, encompassing picture of God and his character. Our host knew that as well and told us that was one of several reasons why he loved the painting.

As we drove home, Kyle and I talked about the characteristics of God and how he encompasses all that is good of both a father and a mother. He is kind, caring, compassionate, as well as strong, protective, and fierce. I looked up the painting of the Prodigal Son and pondered all the ways that God has welcomed me home. All the ways his hands have guided and disciplined, comforted and loved me. And then I thanked him for being the perfect parent. The one who always welcomes us home.

Oftentimes God is portrayed as strong and mighty, and he certainly is those things, but he is also gentle and kind, loving and compassionate. Jesus explained that God longed to gather his children as a hen gathers her chicks beneath her wings. What a beautiful and yet humble picture God portrays of himself and his people.

God is so much more than we could fully understand or know. He perfectly encompasses all that we need, all that we desire, and he lovingly welcomes us home with all the masculine and feminine characteristics that make for a good parent.

Lord, thank you that you aren't defined or limited by masculine or feminine qualities, but that you encompass all the qualities of a good parent. Thank you for who you are and for welcoming us home. Amen.

-Kendra

One Good Step: If you haven't seen the painting of the Prodigal Son by Rembrandt, find a picture of it and then spend some time thinking about and thanking God for all the ways that he has been a good parent to you.

Anxiety

Anxiety in a man's heart weighs him down,
but a good word makes him glad.
PROVERBS 12:25, ESV

A FEW YEARS AGO, I went through a season where I'd wake each morning with my body tight in the grip of anxiety. Though I slept well at night, the anxiety returned with a vengeance each new day.

It reminded me of a college friend who went to see his doctor because he thought he had a throat problem. Each time he would try to eat, his throat would close up, and swallowing was difficult. But when he went to the doctor, he was told that his physical symptoms were a manifestation of the inner anxiety he felt.

Now, more than a decade later, the erratic beat of my heart reflected my own inner turmoil. Seeking peace, I tucked Bible verses into the edges of my mirror to remind me of God's love. I also began to notice the lyrics of the songs I listened to. My dad always said that if you're not singing the gospel, you're singing the blues. I love the blues, but I understood. As I listened, the words in the songs felt like a healing balm, a reminder of God's goodness that I desperately needed.

One of the cassettes I listened to as a child featured upbeat 90s music with lyrics based on Scriptures. So many years later, I can still recall a tune set to the words of Philippians 4:6-7. As my anxiety pushed my stress level higher, I found myself humming the song on repeat, a litany of praise, a request for peace. *Do not be anxious about anything. . . . And the peace of God, which transcends all understanding, will guard your heart and your mind in Christ Jesus.* The Word of God is good news, and it can soothe our worries, calm our tempers, teach us mercy, and remind us of love. A good word is powerful. Though my anxiety didn't diminish overnight, I took comfort in the good words and in the reminder that God cares for us even—and especially—when life is hard.

Lord, may the words on our lips praise you in times of joy and times of pain. Make us aware of your presence; guide us as we seek peace and healing. Let us find comfort in your great love for us and encouragement in the words we hear. Amen.

-Kristin

One Good Step: Send a friend "a good word" to encourage them.

Empathy

They sat on the ground with him for seven days and nights. No one said a word
to Job, for they saw that his suffering was too great for words.

JOB 2:13

"I HAVE SOMETHING TO TELL YOU," I said as a lump rose in my throat. Julie and I had been visiting for over an hour when the conversation turned to a part of my past I'd shared with only a few other people. I brushed my hair from my face as the wind blew by and my eyes spanned the water lapping the shore just beyond the porch where we sat. Julie sat in silence and waited. The words tumbled out before I could think too much about them or take them back.

She listened empathetically as I wiped tears from my eyes, not interrupting or rushing past the moment. She waited until I was done speaking and then after a few moments she whispered, "I'm so sorry, friend." I nodded as we both fell silent. As I explained further, she acknowledged my pain, validated my feelings, and most importantly believed and was witness to my experience. She was the perfect picture of empathy. The next day, she texted me, affirming once again her love and care of me and what I had shared. I breathed a sigh of relief, grateful for her friendship.

Sitting with others in their pain can sometimes be uncomfortable because we don't always know what to say or do. Most often, those who are hurting don't need our words, they just need our presence and our empathy. Job's friends came and sat with him for a whole week and said nothing because they saw that his suffering was too great for words. It's okay if we don't know what to say to someone, just being willing to bear witness to their pain and suffering is often enough to start.

Lord, thank you for giving us the support of friends as we walk through pain. Help us to be brave to share our own with them and help us to be willing to empathetically sit with others in their own suffering. Amen.

-Kendra

One Good Step: Listen to someone as they share a hard part of their story. Don't worry about what to say, just be empathetic by being present, listening, and acknowledging their suffering.

Flourish

The godly will flourish like palm trees and grow strong like the cedars of Lebanon. . . .
Even in old age they will still produce fruit; they will remain vital and green.
PSALM 92:12, 14

WE WERE ONLY GONE FOR A WEEK, but it had been hot and muggy, the kind of weather better suited for late July than late June in my part of the country. As I stepped out the back door and turned the corner on my path through the flower bed, my eyes grew momentarily wide and round.

"Whoa!" I exclaimed to no one in particular. "What happened?" Quickening my pace, I opened the garden gate to investigate.

What had only a week ago been my tidy and sedate vegetable plot had turned into a jungle. Cucumber tendrils had wiggled several feet over into my tomatoes, twining up and around the tomato trellis instead of their own. The pumpkin was a monster, its huge leaves and vining stems threatening to consume the entire garden. The lettuce varieties had gone rogue—bolting several feet into the air as they flowered and started to seed.

As I poked and prodded, nibbling on pea pods that dangled enticingly from their vines, I marveled at the sudden verdant growth. And then I remembered, it was approximately two weeks since I'd brought home a new fertilizer, spreading it liberally among my tiny plants, wondering if it would give them a boost since I'd been a weekend late in getting everything planted.

I think-talk to God as I garden, and as I gently tamed the cukes and redirected the pumpkin, I pondered the idea of spiritual food. How often do we nourish our spirit, feeding it high quality nutrients, giving it a little boost of fertilizer, helping it flourish?

We are what we consume, and when we consistently fill our minds and hearts with the things of God, it will impact every area of our life, growing us, maturing us, allowing us to flourish, despite where we are currently rooted or what we are currently facing. Flourishing requires intentionality and investment, but the rewards we reap are well worth the discipline.

Lord, may we consume those things that are good for us, body, mind, and spirit. And as we do, help us to flourish. Amen.

-Julie

One Good Step: Intentionally feed your spirit this week through Christian music and teaching in the car, in your office, and in your home.

July

Plant

Blessed are those who trust in the LORD and have made the LORD their hope and confidence. They are like trees planted along a riverbank, with roots that reach deep into the water. Such trees are not bothered by the heat or worried by long months of drought. Their leaves stay green, and they never stop producing fruit.

JEREMIAH 17:7-8

FROM ACROSS THE YARD, my neighbor beckoned. I ambled over with a smile as he paused his lawn mower, pulled out his earbuds, and offered a smile of his own.

"I can take care of that for you," he offered, as though it were settled. Together, the two of us turned a critical eye to look at the plants that normally lined my driveway, now interspersed with weeds waving high in the breeze. One towered over the others.

"That would be great. Thank you!" I said, smile in place, although I couldn't help but cringe a little. The weeds out front, though unsightly, weren't half as bad as the ones behind our home. I'd need a hatchet and shovel to get those backyard behemoths out of the ground.

I love seeing things grow—lilacs and hydrangeas are particular favorites—but I'm less fond of the weeds that grow alongside them. In many cases, the weeds seem even more stubborn to survive than any of my plants. Hardier. Immovable. Persistent.

The frustrating effort I spend trying to eradicate them gives me ample time to consider how often the state of my yard resembles the condition of my heart. A friend gave this analogy: God's truths are planted in our hearts. And though the enemy of our souls cannot uproot them, he can plant weeds of doubt or lies right next to them. Too often, we allow the lie to grow alongside the truth, until it casts doubts in our hearts. We must be vigilant to get rid of the lies that try to take root, because they are hardy. Immovable. Persistent. Instead, let's plant things that are true, lovely, noble, excellent, and worthy of praise in our hearts, and water them with the truths of God's Word. Only then will our faith grow.

Lord, help us uproot lies we believe and replace them with your promises. Amen.

-Kristin

One Good Step: Identify some of the doubts that have taken root in your heart. Look up Scriptures to help you replace them with the truth of God's word.

United

Let us not neglect our meeting together, as some people do, but encourage
one another, especially now that the day of his return is drawing near.

HEBREWS 10:25

WE MET WITH ANOTHER COUPLE for coffee for the first time, just getting to know one another. We had a lot of things in common, many of the same dreams and hopes for our family and community. We felt united with them in many ways. As the conversation neared the end, they were adamant they wanted to get to know us better and continue to meet regularly. My husband and I nodded that we would like this too as we got up to leave.

Over the next several months, we tried to find times to get together, with limited success. Their schedule was packed full, with little room for any actual face-to-face time together. It was confusing, especially because we'd felt such unity when we met with them. Even so, they were insistent on their desire to be close friends with us.

After several failed attempts to meet and cancellations, I looked at my husband and said, "I don't think they really want to be close friends with us. They say they do, but how can you get to know someone well if you don't spend any time with them?" He nodded in agreement, politely responding back to their inability to meet once again.

Being united with others is so important. No matter what stage of life we are in, having those we know we can rely on is invaluable. But to build these kind of relationships, we have to be willing to spend time with one another. We can't just say we want to be friends with someone else, and then not put forth the energy to invest in a relationship with them. We need to be willing to take the time to get to know them and be intentional to create opportunities to meet together, recognizing that being united to one another will take our time, as well as our words.

Lord, thank you for the people you bring to our lives. Help us to be united with those around us, inviting others in who may need community.

-Kendra

One Good Step: Who in your life do you feel united with in friendship? Take some time this week to continue to grow that relationship.

Step

We can make our plans, but the LORD determines our steps.

PROVERBS 16:9

"YOU DID WHAT?"

Jonny's grin was enormous as he squatted to untie his shoes, repeating what he'd yelled to me as he burst through the door, "I did the fifty-foot fall. Twice!"

"It was safe," Aaron inserted, walking over to wrap me in a hug of greeting and comfort, realizing some damage control might be necessary.

"Don't worry, Mom. We were told not to look down before we stepped off the platform, so I didn't. I just stepped. And then I fell fifty feet! But I was attached to the zip line the whole time, so I was safe."

"Um . . ." My response was interrupted by Aaron's interjection.

"Don't worry, I went first. And it was a lot of fun, wasn't it?" Aaron's grin caught Jonny's across the room. "The first step was a doozy, but the kids did great."

I trust Aaron implicitly as he takes our kids on adventures that leave my safety-loving, adrenaline-avoiding self wincing. And, honestly, I want my kids to be familiar with overcoming that doozy of a first step, whether it be on a zip line platform high in the trees or standing at the top of a double black diamond ski run. Physically overcoming fear of the first step is good practice for when God calls them outside of their comfort zones spiritually, emotionally, and physically.

God, at least in my experience, requires me to take that doozy of a first step in trust. I almost never know the full extent of the plan when he asks me to step; I step in faith and then watch as the plan unfolds.

Stepping first builds my faith and trust, and God knows that. I step faster now than I did years ago, tamping down my fear more quickly, my trust in God having grown as I've practiced stepping and being caught, stepping and being caught. I can't say that those first steps aren't still a doozy, but they are so, so worth it.

Lord, help us be brave over that doozy of a first step, that we would not miss out on a single adventure along your side. Amen.

-Julie

One Good Step: Make a list of the first steps you (or those you know) have made in faith, trusting in God. Remind yourself of those other instances when you face your next doozy of a first step.

Care

Give all your worries and cares to God, for he cares about you.

1 PETER 5:7

YEARS AGO, I worked for the Veterans Affairs Medical Center in my community. As a clinical social worker, I was part of the inpatient recovery program, meeting with veterans who struggled with addiction and their mental health. As part of my orientation I met with several other staff members to learn about their roles. One older gentleman, a chemical dependency counselor who'd been at the VA for close to thirty years, told me about the different treatment programs they'd used over the years. His least favorite was one that had been utilized when he started where the veteran would sit in the middle of a circle and their family members would sit around them, telling them all the ways they'd messed up or hurt them through their addiction. The intention was to shame the person into different behavior. But it often had the opposite effect.

He said, "These guys are already down. You don't need to tell them how bad they are; they know they've messed up." He explained it wasn't long before they realized the error of this method and implemented a program that was based more on understanding and encouragement. They realized that genuine care for another person had better results than shame or put-downs ever could.

As I listened to the history of the treatment program I was now working in, it reminded me of our relationship with the Lord. God never called out people who were already discouraged. We never saw him kick those who were already down. He always first showed his care and concern for the person. Did God put people in their place? Absolutely. But often it was those who were prideful or arrogant, never those who were already deeply wounded.

The tenderness and care of God meets us right where we are, in the middle of our mess, and then lovingly draws us out, encouraging us to wholeness and healthiness.

Lord, thank you for inviting us to bring all of our cares to you. And for caring so deeply for us. Amen.

-Kendra

One Good Step: Think about how God has cared for you. How can you extend God's care for you to someone in your life who is in a hard place?

Patience

Dear brothers and sisters, be patient as you wait for the Lord's return.
Consider the farmers who patiently wait for the rains in the fall and in the spring.
They eagerly look for the valuable harvest to ripen. You, too, must be patient.
Take courage, for the coming of the Lord is near.
JAMES 5:7-8

BEES BUZZED AROUND US as we fanned ourselves in the sweltering heat. We'd driven winding roads along the Sonoma Coast in California to arrive at our destination high in the hills. From our perch on the outside patio, we were surrounded by trees.

As we perused the menu, the person helping us launched into a description of our location, but as I glanced over the printed page, my eye was caught by the word *Pinotage*. It's my sister Kendra's favorite grape varietal, and though it's well known in South Africa, it's uncommon in the US.

When asked, the woman seemed happy to explain.

"The owners here are originally from South Africa," she said. "They brought grapevines over with them from South Africa. Grapevines from other countries are required to quarantine for a period of time before they can be planted in our soil, and these ones spent five years at UC Davis." She went on to explain that the university's Foundation Plant Services quarantine process itself is lengthy and requires patience: if grapevines develop any kind of disease while in quarantine, the process is extended as the plants must undergo therapy and retesting before they are considered healthy and whole. And there's always the risk that some plants may die completely.

We marveled at the thought of how much time, expense, and patience were required before the grapes in the vineyards below us were even planted, much less producing. There are times in our lives when we feel the same: that we've been uprooted and are experiencing a lengthy refining process. It's tempting to become impatient with our circumstances, but sometimes, those rocky times are what's required before we can move ahead. Patience requires diligence and steady perseverance, but for those whose hope rests in the Lord, it's not impossible. If we have the courage to be patient in the midst of the challenges that arise, we'll eventually reap a harvest—if we don't give up.

Lord, give us your patience, especially on hard days when we want to give up. Remind us that you're overseeing everything with your loving care. Amen.

-Kristin

One Good Step: What circumstances in your life require patience? Write down one way you can redefine a situation in a positive way.

Loyal

Many will say they are loyal friends,
but who can find one who is truly reliable?
PROVERBS 20:6

"HANNAH NEEDS SOMEONE unconditionally and unapologetically in her corner right now, and that's me." I paused to take a deep breath. "Sorry, that was perhaps too blunt. Let me try again. I realize Hannah isn't perfect and she has a part to play in all of this, but in this moment, she desperately needs a person to stand with her. She needs loyalty in the midst of betrayal. I'm that person. I chose Hannah. Steph has plenty of people siding with her."

"Hannah is blessed to have you as a friend. And I agree, right now she needs loyalty." Pam stepped around a small pothole and then lengthened her stride to catch back up to my slightly faster pace down the wooded path. "Business breakups are hard enough, but adding a destroyed friendship into that volatile mix can be an enormous betrayal, especially the way Steph handled it. For what it's worth, I think you are making the right choice."

"I don't know if it's right or not, but I love Hannah like a sister. And in this moment, I feel like she needs unwavering loyalty."

Loyalty, like love, does not require blindly supporting someone, staunchly denying their role in a hard situation. In fact, real love—of family, friends, or spouse—includes an understanding of someone's shortcomings and loving them anyway. We love the whole person. Our loyalty is the same—we are loyal to the whole person.

Friendship sometimes requires us to be the gentle voice of accountability, a person who helps serve as a bridge, a mediator, a mender of rifts. And sometimes friendship means we stand firmly and unwaveringly in our friend's corner, loyal and wholly on her side, fierce in her defense. It can be tricky to know which role to take—gentle peacemaker or staunch defender—but there is a time and a place for each.

Lord, give us the wisdom to know when you are calling us to be loyal and when you are calling us to hold our friends gently accountable. Amen.

-Julie

One Good Step: Think of a time you needed loyalty from a friend and a time you needed a friend to hold you accountable. What was similar and different in those situations? Are you seeing a similar need for gentle accountability or staunch defender in your own friendships?

Refresh

The generous will prosper; those who refresh
others will themselves be refreshed.

PROVERBS 11:25

PEERING OUT THE FRONT WINDOW, my kids waited anxiously for someone to arrive on the doorstep.

"What time will the mail come?" they asked impatiently. "Have you ordered anything lately?"

We weren't expecting anything at all, actually. But that morning, we'd filled a small cooler with ice packs, a few bottles of water, and some snacks. A decorated sign, taped above it on the propped-open lid, read, "USPS, FedEx, UPS: Please take some goodies to enjoy on your route!" The weather had been hot and sunny lately, the humidity almost unbearable, and we hoped that our little gift would be a refreshing surprise.

Finally, the girls heard a truck pull up outside. Scampering for their perch by the window, they peered out, watching as the delivery man arrived. He paused to read the sign. Not content with sitting by the window, they raced over to hover just inside the storm door.

"Those are for you!" they said loudly, through the glass.

"Thanks!" He grinned, grabbing a water and a couple of snacks. As he left the steps and his truck shifted back into gear, they came looking for me in the kitchen.

"Mom, he took the chips and the candy bar—those are totally the best ones," they said, smiling happily. "We would have taken those too. Let's put some more in!"

Like the cooling refreshment provided by the icy water we placed in a cooler on a hot summer day, our kind words and actions can provide much-needed refreshment to the parched hearts of those around us. When we choose to do something kind for another person, we show love to others and we honor God through our decision to selflessly serve another. Yet as my children found out, in the miraculous, upside-down economy of God, when we set out to refresh others through our words or actions, doing so brings us just as much joy in return.

Lord, thank you for the opportunities we have to refresh others. Help us to obey the nudge to do so each day. Amen.

-Kristin

One Good Step: Find a way to refresh someone through your words or actions.

Pamper

This is the day the LORD has made. We will rejoice and be glad in it.
PSALM 118:24

"HEY, KRISTIN AND KENDRA, you guys have to try my slippers. They are amazing!" Laughing, I gently kicked my slippers off, launching one softly toward Kendra in the kitchen and one toward Kristin in the adjacent living room. "Feel that arch support? They don't look like much, but my feet are in pampered bliss when I wear them!"

My enthusiasm over fuzzy footwear started a conversation about the other comfort objects we'd packed for the long weekend. We'd rented a nearby lake cabin for the three of us, giving us time and a beautiful space away from our day-to-day routines to focus on business strategy and planning for the upcoming year. Without intentionally talking about it, we'd each packed a few simple pleasures—slippers, well-worn loungewear, favorite snacks, a scented candle—small items that invoked a sense of cozy security to make our borrowed space feel like ours.

Once upon a time, I scoffed at the notion of pampering, perhaps because it seemed froufrou and extravagant, a wasteful overindulgence, but I've been rethinking that stance since hearing a sermon explaining that earth is a little taste of heaven and a little taste of hell, all wrapped together.

If life's good things are a tiny foretaste of heaven, then why am I dismissing beautiful moments and comforting things as wasteful or unworthy? Instead, I've started embracing them, even calling them out as I encounter them, declaring Lizzie's warm-from-the-oven cookies "a little taste of heaven" as chocolatey goodness explodes in my mouth, asking Jon which scented candle we should buy based on which has the most "heavenly" scent, or pausing a long moment to take in the fiery red and orange leaves on the maple just down the block.

Calling out glimpses of heaven on earth has given me permission to indulge in small and big moments of self-care, enjoying pampering (however you might define it for yourself) and returning refreshed, acknowledging God in the good things and rejoicing in the parts of life that are tastes of heaven.

Lord, thank you for glimpses of heaven on earth. May we embrace moments of pampering, comfort, and beauty for what they are, little pieces of heaven. Amen.

-Julie

One Good Step: Pick one way to pamper yourself today.

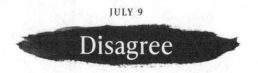

Disagree

By this everyone will know that you are my disciples,
if you love one another.

JOHN 13:35, NIV

A FRIEND RECENTLY POSTED a link on social media with a stance that I totally disagreed with, and the rest of the morning I found myself arguing in my mind against her post. Over and over it continued to roll around in my brain while I tried to rebut what had been said.

Finally I asked myself, *Why am I so angry about this? And why do I feel I need to defend my position so vehemently? Do I really need them to see my point of view? Agree with me?*

And maybe this was why I was truly upset: I want others to agree with me. Validate what I believe. But as Christians, there are many areas where we can disagree about what exactly Scripture means or how it applies to our lives. We can also differ in our opinions on politics, on raising children, and on health care, just to name a few. And we can even argue about seemingly trivial things.

In the end, I stopped the argument that I was having in my mind and instead spent a few moments praying for my friend, asking God to bless her and reminding myself of all the things I appreciated about her.

I came to the conclusion that, sometimes, it's okay if we agree to disagree. I don't need to defend myself all the time. It takes up too much space in my head. And I don't want to give it that much room in my life—room I'd rather spend thinking about how I could bless someone else, love someone, or give away what we have.

We all need to leave room in our lives to disagree with someone and still love them.

To listen without anger. And respond (or not) without resentment. To still care for the person, even as we have differing opinions. The Bible is clear that the world will know that we are Christians, not because we agree on every issue or topic, but because of our love for one another.

Lord, help us to show others love, especially those we disagree with. Amen.

-Kendra

One Good Step: How can you show love to someone today
that you disagree with on a certain issue?

Race

Since we are surrounded by such a huge crowd of witnesses to the life of faith,
let us strip off every weight that slows us down, especially the sin that so easily
trips us up. And let us run with endurance the race God has set before us.

HEBREWS 12:1

I SAT QUIETLY at the giant conference table, soaking in the colorful chaos as my friends and fellow teammates talked, laughed, and caught up on life. We'd packed over twenty women into the night's meeting, some of whom had driven multiple hours to get there. Young, old, married, single, widowed, different races, opposite political views, even different denominations were gathered around the table, bringing such a vast array of skill sets and experiences that oftentimes our differences outweigh our similarities.

Jesus is the glue to our sisterhood, and we cheerlead one another in our individual and collective faith races—no competition, no jealousy, no division allowed. And we watch as Jesus uses all of our individual strengths and skill sets to accomplish his work in ways that are far greater than the sum of our individual parts.

It is this team of talented, dedicated, faithful doers-of-good that I think of when I start to feel discouraged, overwhelmed, or defeated. Because they are each actively serving God in official and unofficial capacities. In quiet, unassuming tasks and on bold, loud platforms, I witness how God uses each of us, perfectly.

My faith race is just that: mine. I run and stumble, falling and getting back up to run again at my own pace and on my own course, without worry about where I fall in the pack of other runners. This is not a competition. It is a collaborative, collective effort among women who love God with all of their hearts, souls, and minds and love their neighbors as themselves. We are unified in mission, even as the tasks God sets before us are different. God is the master weaver, and he weaves all of our efforts together in ways we may never see this side of heaven.

Do not be discouraged in your faith race. Keep moving forward. Keep showing up. And find a group of women who will race alongside you, cheering you on with wild abandon.

Lord, give us other faith racers to run alongside, that we might be encouraged and strengthened by running separately, together. Amen.

-Julie

One Good Step: Encourage a woman you know who is stepping up
for God in some way—big or small.

Companionship

Enjoy the companionship of those
who call on the Lord with pure hearts.
2 TIMOTHY 2:22

MY FRIEND SUE grew up in a household that had company dinners on Sundays. After church was over, her mom would hustle the children out to the car in order to prepare their home for the individual or family she'd just invited over for lunch. While the visitor offered to help get the meal ready and Sue and her siblings placed the pink rose china on the table, her dad would set up their Ping-Pong table in the hope of drawing someone into a friendly game afterward. Extending invitations to newcomers was ingrained, and the companionship provided by the friendships they began during Sunday dinners was a source of warmth and community.

Years later, when Sue moved to a new area, she wondered why other people didn't seem as keen to offer Sunday dinner invitations the way her family had when she was growing up. Standing in the parking lot after church while everyone else drove away, she would think, *Why didn't anyone invite me over for lunch?* Alone and in an unfamiliar place, a Sunday dinner would have gone a long way toward helping ease the loneliness she felt. Eventually, she stopped waiting and started inviting others over on her own, leading to a rich community of friends that provided the same loving companionship of her youth.

The early church provides a great blueprint for inviting others to share our faith and our food. Acts 2 describes how "believers devoted themselves to the apostles' teaching" (verse 42) and to prayer, but also to sharing in meals "with great joy and generosity" (verse 46). In this case, the philosophical tenets of our faith—sharing love and grace—have very practical applications. We can say we believe in God's love, but doing the work of living out that love in our community can feel daunting. Our lives feel too busy, our houses too messy, or our meals too simple—yet none of those reasons excuses us from the mandate to love our neighbors as we do ourselves. When we share our meals, we share our lives. And when we choose to extend a hand or an invitation in genuine friendship, we'll often find that the joy of companionship outweighs those other considerations.

Lord, thank you for the companionship we can have with one another. Help us to look for opportunities to invite others to experience the blessing of friendship. Amen.

-Kristin

One Good Step: Invite someone in need of companionship
to share a meal with you.

Influence

In the same way, let your light shine before others,
so that they may see your good works and give glory
to your Father who is in heaven.

MATTHEW 5:16, ESV

WE WERE SITTING OUTSIDE, visiting late one summer day. Sharing what God had been teaching us throughout the past year. As we went around the circle and each woman shared, I could see bits of my own story mirrored in the struggles of their own.

As we were almost to the end, one woman began to share that God was teaching her that sometimes he moves us out of or away from a group of people that we love because he has another space he wants us to influence. She told us how much she'd miss our group in this new season, but how God had been using her in a space she never asked to go but felt called to be in. And then she asked us, "Are you open to being used where God asks you to go?"

And I immediately felt convicted by her words. How often do I enjoy the comfort of where I am, unwilling or not wanting to see how God may have another place for me to occupy? I like my people. I like what's familiar to me. Sometimes a little too much. But my friend's words challenged me to remember that sometimes our greatest influence is in a new place God may lead us to, not where we currently are.

Often when we think of influence, it includes a large group of people or someone who is well known. But each of us has a measure of influence, in our homes, places of work, where we volunteer or anywhere else we find ourselves in community with others. Do we see the opportunities that are before us and take advantage of them to influence others in a positive way or do we miss it, thinking we would have too small an impact to really make a difference? We are each called to shine our light before others, in effect, influencing them so that they will see our good works and know they are from God.

Lord, help us to take advantage of the opportunity we have to influence the people we come across today. Amen.

-Kendra

One Good Step: Write down five places God has you right now. Pray about how you can intentionally influence others in each of those spaces.

Prune

He cuts off every branch of mine that doesn't produce fruit, and he prunes
the branches that do bear fruit so they will produce even more.

JOHN 15:2

"SEE THAT SUCKER growing between the stem and the branch—you have to pinch that off." Dad snapped off the sucker, despite the three small tomatoes already growing on it.

"But, wait . . ." I began as Dad pinched off another one, this one with flowers. "Dad!"

Pausing from his search for suckers among my beloved but admittedly unruly Brandywine tomatoes, Dad winked. "We prune the suckers so the plants stay healthy and you get earlier, larger tomatoes. Pruning forces the plants to focus on fruit production rather than growing foliage."

"I know. But I hate pruning the suckers that are already growing fruit." I sighed as I bent alongside him, helping search through my plants, pinching off suckers. "I guess we're pruning the good in order to get the best."

"Exactly, Tootsie. Now, get back to work."

I'll admit that pruning isn't my favorite garden task, especially when I'm cutting off lilac branches I know already have next year's buds or pinching the suckers off my tomatoes, but I've learned that the temporary disappointment in losing buds or potential tomatoes is far outweighed by the benefits both in the health of my plants and the ultimate harvest I collect.

God is the Master Gardener, and he prunes us and our lives for the same reasons Dad taught me to prune my tomatoes—health and harvest. Sometimes we've got unhealthy things festering that, if left to grow, will seriously stunt our spiritual growth. And other times, we have so many good things vying for our attention that if God didn't remove some of them, we'd never focus on the best things, the things that bring the biggest harvest to the Kingdom of God.

The question is whether we will trust him in the pruning, even when it hurts in the moment, or if we'll protest loudly, refusing to give up the things that are holding us back. God is trustworthy and good, and he can be trusted to see a far bigger picture than we ever will this side of heaven.

Lord, prune us. Remove the things holding us back from your best. Amen.

-Julie

One Good Step: What is God asking you to release? Make a plan,
and tell a friend who will gently hold you accountable.

Anticipate

I rise before dawn and cry for help; I wait for Your words. My eyes anticipate the night watches, so that I may meditate on Your word.

PSALM 119:147-148, NASB

MY FAMILY DIDN'T HAVE a lot of money when I was growing up. My sisters and I were always fed and clothed and loved, but we didn't always have a lot of extras. Whenever we had the rare treat of a Coca-Cola, we'd split the can three ways, and we were much more likely to shop at garage sales than the mall.

One experience we always anticipated, however, was back-to-school shopping. Each year, we would head to Kmart to find the jeans and shirts we liked and needed, and we'd put them on layaway. Then, we'd wait.

Layaway allows the purchaser to select their items and set them aside, gradually paying them off with a payment plan. At the end of the plan, you're allowed to bring your items home. But with the advent of technology that lets us make two clicks online to order an item that will show up on our doorstep in two days, waiting—and the joy it can bring—is something of a lost art.

Anticipation for something—whether it's items in layaway, a piece of chocolate at the end of a meal, a vacation you've spent months or years planning, or the prospect of curling up on the couch to watch a favorite program or read a much-anticipated novel at the end of the day—not only gives us something to look forward to, it's something our brains are hardwired to seek. Dopamine, the "feel good" chemical neurotransmitter that causes excitement and prevents pain, is released not just when we *experience* good things but also when we *expect* good things.

Anticipation can factor into our relationship with Jesus, as well. Whether we consider our time with him an event to look forward to or a chore to check off our list, our anticipation or lack thereof can influence our relationship with him. Our attitude reflects our mindset. When we live in the confident expectation that we can anticipate good things from a good Father, we will look forward to our time with him. As Christians, let's anticipate with hopeful expectation the goodness of the Lord by spending time with him. It's worth the wait.

Lord, help us to see the gift of anticipation in our lives and to cultivate it in our relationship with you. Amen.

-Kristin

One Good Step: Make a list of three things (big or small) you are currently anticipating.

Culture

[Jesus said,] "If any of you wants to be my follower, you must give up your own way, take up your cross daily, and follow me."

LUKE 9:23

"YOU MUST BE from the US." I'd barely said five words, but my accent had given me away. We were in Northern Ireland, Belfast to be precise, and had stopped on a whim at a chocolatier on our way back to our hotel.

"Good guess, yes." I laughed. "Is my accent that strong?" I pulled cash from my wallet, handing it across the counter.

"Oh, just a wee bit." He winked as he popped open the cash register.

Just as I tend to forget that I have an accent, I forget that I have a distinct culture with several subcultures, each of which significantly impacts how I engage with others, sometimes in hurtful, negative ways. Mine happens to be Midwestern/ Minnesotan, but it's the same for each of us. We have a culture—with good and bad elements—and it is often such an intimate part of our daily life that we don't see it until an outsider points it out to us.

It wasn't until I had several close friendships with women-not-from-here that I started to bump into the less desirable parts of my culture, parts that exclude and isolate outsiders rather than welcome them. Their experiences made me realize that because I belong to this place and to these people, I often don't see cultural impacts—just like I don't hear my own accent.

Oh, how I've regretted my blindness to the hard parts of my culture! I can embrace the best of my Midwestern, rural upbringing, but as a follower of Christ, it must no longer define me. My decision to follow Jesus brought with it a new, adopted culture, one that calls me to die to myself, living as a new creature according to his way. And that means I must recognize and actively work against subtle behaviors, language, and other cultural tools that make life harder for those who live and work within my culture but are not a part of it.

Lord, show us the hard parts of our culture, the parts that must die as we lay down the old and follow you. Amen.

-Julie

One Good Step: What do outsiders say about your culture? What negative parts of your culture do you need to actively work against?

Action

Faith by itself, if it is not accompanied by action, is dead.

JAMES 2:17, NIV

ALTHOUGH DIFFICULT TO OPENLY ADMIT, there have been many times in my life I have dismissed thoughts to help, encourage, or get involved because of five simple words: *Somebody else will do it.* As quickly as I'll think it, the motivation to step up or do something dissipates.

I'm released from feeling like I should act. Because really, with so many other Christians out there, surely God has someone else in mind who could do it. And that has alleviated me from guilt many a day. Too many days.

Until I saw a post by an adoption network I follow that told the story of a young man who had been in foster care his whole life. Moved from home to home, with no family, no permanency.

Until one Sunday morning, his social worker took him to a local church where he stood up during the service and asked for a family. As I read his story, tears began to fall. My heart broke.

The next morning I showed my husband the story. And together we talked. *What could we do? Surely, others have stepped up to help?*

"It doesn't matter if others have stepped up. *We* need to do something," I stated. And Kyle agreed.

Completely unsure what to say, I wrote an email to the foster agency overseeing the young man's case. I told them we were foster parents, and asked if there was anything we could do. And then I hit send. I didn't know what their response may be. All I knew was that I put away the reasoning, the excuse, that somebody else will do it. I decided, instead, that *I* needed to be that somebody.

Although at times the concerns of the world can be overwhelming, we as Christians should be at the forefront, leading the way on speaking up and taking action on these issues. Because haven't we all been rescued in some way? And although yes, there are times that there may be somebody better suited to step up, maybe, more often than not, *we* are that somebody. We are the ones who need to act.

Lord, help us to not just say we have faith, but be willing to act on it as well. Amen.

-Kendra

One Good Step: The next time you want to dismiss getting involved, choose instead to act.

JULY 17

Circumstances

Be thankful in all circumstances, for this is God's will
for you who belong to Christ Jesus.
1 THESSALONIANS 5:18

PHIL'S PARENTS DIVORCED just as he was getting ready to go to college. In the aftermath, he quickly realized there was no money available to pay for school. Disappointed, he realized that he would have to figure it out on his own.

Eventually, an uncle who worked at a bank helped him acquire a loan to pay the cost of his tuition. The loan involved a work-study program, so he was required to work a certain number of hours each week. At first, Phil was dismayed. Though he was a hard worker, his course load was challenging, and he hadn't planned on working quite as many hours as the work-study program required. But as the years passed and he approached graduation, he realized something he'd viewed as an obstacle—paying his own way through college—ended up being a blessing. The connections he made with others during his work-study years ended up forming lasting relationships that helped him get a job after graduation and continued through the course of his career.

Oftentimes, it's our most challenging circumstances—a diagnosis, a job loss, a troubled relationship—that teach us far more than our easy, unremarkable days. How we choose to approach difficult circumstances isn't simply a measure of how much or how little hardship we can withstand; it is a measure of the confident hope we have in Jesus based on what he has *already* overcome. When we look back and recognize God's handiwork in our lives or in the lives of those around us, choosing gratitude in every current circumstance is a recognition that our current trials are temporary, but our hope in Jesus is eternal. Our ability to endure the hardships life throws at us are oftentimes the catalyst for our conviction that God's love is real and will carry us through every circumstance we face, regardless of the outcome. That certainty is what gives us the courage to face our ever-changing circumstances with courage and hope.

Lord, help us to see the good in every circumstance, even those that feel over-whelming or insurmountable. Give us gratitude for every circumstance we face today. Amen.

-Kristin

One Good Step: What situation have you faced that felt like an obstacle in the moment but ended up teaching you something? How can recalling that experience influence your current circumstances?

Preference

I wish that all of you were [single] as I am. But each of you has your own gift
from God; one has this gift, another has that.

1 CORINTHIANS 7:7, NIV

ONE OF OUR KIDS has been adamant since she was young that she doesn't intend to marry or have children of her own. She would prefer to remain single. My husband and I have kept an open conversation with her, not wanting her to close off from us. We also understand that as she grows her opinions and life choices may change. Or they may not. Either way, we support her feelings.

What has been curious to us is others' responses to preferences on marriage and children when it comes up in broader conversation. People are usually quick to tell her that she will change her mind and make sweeping statements about how "everyone wants to get married and have kids." Quickly (and often unintentionally), they dismiss her opinion and feelings.

But this has caused our daughter to question herself. *Am I wrong to not want the things that everyone else seemingly does? To prefer singleness?* she asks my husband and me. And so, we turn to Scripture, as we so often do when looking for answers and find that Paul advocates strongly for people who feel so led to stay single. This is a valid life choice. We read several passages of Scripture to her, affirming her feelings, and she feels a bit relieved, feeling validated in her preference.

There are things in the church that are accepted as a best option or even a mandate, when in reality they may simply be a preference. Our culture can have an influence on our lives, including our faith and the way in which we read Scriptures. Sometimes we need to take a step back and ask ourselves, *Is this really required, or is this just a preference? Are there other options or opinions that are equally valid?* Understanding this truth can aid us in not only helping others navigate their lives and faith journey but also encouraging us to live out the way in which God would ask us to rather than according to the expectations or preferences of others.

Lord, give us wisdom to pursue the things you ask us to. Amen.

-Kendra

One Good Step: Write down five beliefs you have. Consider whether
those are mandates or simply preferences. Spend some time with God,
and seek his plan for your life, not just other people's preferences.

Include

Most important of all, continue to show deep love for each other,
for love covers a multitude of sins.

1 PETER 4:8

"HONEY, I INVITED THE NEIGHBORS to join us tonight for dinner on the patio."

In a perfect world, Aaron's statement would have been the prelude to a peaceful, lovely evening of quiet conversation and the melt-in-your-mouth steaks Aaron grills to perfection.

What Mark and Elizabeth received was a distracted, rowdy experience as Aaron and I simultaneously tried to engage in polite conversation while cajoling our toddler and preschooler to sit nice, chew with mouths closed, and *not* tell our neighbors about body parts and the proper anatomical names we'd been practicing.

It was pure chaos, and I regretted our invitation until Mark gave me a giant bear hug at the end of the evening, thanking me for including them with tears shining in his eyes. I suddenly realized that our boisterous dinner was a delightful change to their empty nest, and I resolved to include them in our family more often.

I adore my children, but I worry whether my childless friends want to be included in the zanier moments that are sometimes our real life. And so I tend to make the choice for them, excluding them from events I think they wouldn't want to attend.

The thing is, life with kids is chaotic and loud and exasperating and hilarious and poignant and sweet. If I exclude someone from giant parts of my life for fear that she will be uncomfortable or annoyed by it, then am I really her friend? And is she really mine?

What if, instead, I freely extended invitations and offered inclusion, allowing her to decide whether she wants to yell excitedly along soccer field sidelines and give standing ovations to middle school plays?

Intentional including goes far beyond the parent/nonparent issue. I'm continually surprised at how often people say an enthusiastic yes to an invitation to join Aaron's and my ordinary life. People, it seems, are just waiting to be invited, longing to be included. And, as followers of Jesus, we're the ones tasked with inclusion.

Lord, bring to mind those we have excluded because of differences in marital status, children/no children, age, wealth, culture, or religion. Help us focus on similarities, offering inclusion based on commonalities. Amen.

-Julie

One Good Step: Extend an invitation to someone in a different life stage than you.

Slow

The Lord isn't really being slow about his promise, as some people think.
No, he is being patient for your sake.

2 PETER 3:9

MY MOM IS A QUILTER. She created a quilt for my high school graduation using photos from my childhood printed on fabric and sewn together with care to display at my graduation party. She gave another one to Tim and me when we married, large enough to fit a queen-size bed. And she made personalized quilts for each of our daughters when they were born, complete with a fabric tag with their name and a Bible verse. Each time she shows me what she's currently working on, I always tease her that I'm happy to take more.

I love the artistry of quilting, but I'm afraid I don't have that kind of patience. As much as I tease my mom about giving me another quilt for Christmas, I know the hard work it involves. It takes hours upon hours to choose fabrics, measure correctly and cut pieces, then carefully sew them together. It's slow, painstaking work. If you consider the amount of time and money that goes into each quilt, it's a costly endeavor; any quilt from my mom is a priceless heirloom.

So many things in this life take time. In our fast-paced culture, we don't always value the power of slow. Patience is an underrated quality. Yet when you really consider it, the things we value are often slow to develop: character in people, proficiency in a career, quality handcrafted furniture or artwork. We appreciate the beauty and mastery required in each of these circumstances, but we don't often consider how it's only through slow, painstaking work that these ideals are accomplished.

Similarly, the work God is doing in and through us is often a slow process, one that we can't always appreciate in the moment. We wait impatiently for circumstances to change, dreams to come true, or goals to be reached without considering that God's timing is better than our own. The things we consider slow may instead be just the refining needed to create a beautiful masterpiece out of the patchwork pieces of our lives.

Lord, thank you for the gift of slow. Help us to appreciate it more. Amen.

-Kristin

One Good Step: What is something you've been working toward
or thinking about that seems slow in coming? Is it possible that the
slowness is beneficial rather than detrimental—why or why not?

Moment

Give us today our daily bread.

MATTHEW 6:11, NIV

"LOOK DEEP INTO the other person's eyes," the instructor stated. "Just stay in the moment, notice any thoughts you may have, look away if you need to, but then come back."

This was an exercise given at a training I attended on an early Monday morning, with very little coffee. As I stared awkwardly into the eyes of the stranger next to me, it was entirely too uncomfortable for this introverted girl.

After what felt like an hour, but was probably closer to five minutes, the trainer ended the torture, or exercise, and shared why she chose to have us do it. She explained how hard it is for individuals to stay "in the moment."

"Studies have shown that about 47 percent of Americans spend most of their time thinking about the future, whether that's tonight, tomorrow, or even next year," she said. "The other half of us spend most of our time thinking about the past."

She shared how challenging it is to just be in the moment; hence the incredibly awkward exercise of staring into a stranger's eyes. But what she said next got my attention: "People who spend all their time thinking only about the past suffer mostly from depression, and people who spend most of their time thinking only about the future suffer mostly from anxiety."

I was struck by how true these statements are. Depression makes sense if you're constantly thinking about the past, especially when you can't change or alter things that have happened. And anxiety seems logical if you're only ever thinking about the future, worrying about what is to come, wondering what is next.

But God offers us another option. Scripture tells us that we do not need to worry or be afraid about the future. And time and again God tells us that he loves us and will take care of us and provide for all our needs. That he also looks past all our old mistakes, forgives us, and offers us freedom from our being depressed over things we've done. We have freedom to really be where we are, confident that God is here too, offering us everything that we need for today. And mostly the freedom to be in this moment.

Lord, thank you for giving us all that we need for today. Amen.

-Kendra

One Good Step: Practice being in the moment today.

Self-control

The Holy Spirit produces this kind of fruit in our lives: love, joy,
peace, patience, kindness, goodness, faithfulness, gentleness,
and self-control. There is no law against these things!

GALATIANS 5:22-23

IT WAS AFTER a minor mother-daughter tussle that I found myself sitting in Grandpa Dan's fish house down by the lake. Lizzie has adopted the little shack, serving as a bunkhouse during the summer, as her own personal quiet spot when we visit the lake. Angry, she'd retreated there, and after waiting a few minutes for us both to reflect, I'd followed.

Having hashed out the "why" for the angry words, our conversation turned to the "how" of the argument, and the art of self-control. We're practicing what it means to fight fairly—to handle anger, disappointments, and misunderstandings in ways that resolve the conflict without giving our tongue free rein in our anger, leaving the other side eviscerated, emotionally raw, and wounded by attacks on their personhood.

Our differences resolved and peace restored, our conversation turned to self-control, and how important (but hard) self-control is when our blood is boiling and we are really angry.

"But, Mom, I see lots of Christians who don't practice self-control when they are mad, especially online. Sometimes, they are the meanest ones."

After a long beat of silence, I agreed. Her accusation is true. Sometimes, we *are* the ones with no self-control, spitting vitriol and poison at people we disagree with, people we momentarily forget are among those whom God loves, and for whom Jesus died.

As followers of Jesus, we are called to a higher standard. We are called to practice self-control, waging it over our bodies, our thoughts, and our wayward tongues. God does not tell us to practice self-control as long as the other side does too. No. God tells us to practice self-control without regard for what the other side does or does not do. The world is watching, and our lack of self-control damages his witness.

Lord, help us be women who control our tongues, our thoughts, our bodies. May we always remember that we are a dim reflection of you, and others are watching. Amen.

-Julie

One Good Step: Practice self-control over your tongue. When you are in a disagreement, keep to the topic at hand without name-calling or character smearing.

Fix

You will keep in perfect peace all who trust in you,
all whose thoughts are fixed on you!
ISAIAH 26:3

"WHY DO YOU SMELL LIKE DINNER?" Tim asked one night as I climbed into bed.

"That's not nice!" I said, laughing. "I'm having a problem with my hair. I'm trying to fix it with apple cider vinegar."

"Mmm," he replied noncommittally, sniffing a bit. Then, after a pause, he added, "Fish and chips sound really good right now."

"Stop it!" I said with a laugh, slugging him. "Thanks a lot."

It all started on vacation. The water in our cabin was so hard that, by week's end, my hair no longer felt clean. Instead, it felt sticky. Embarrassed, I returned home and tried every trick I could think of to fix it, including apple cider vinegar. But in the morning, the texture was the same. I had failed again.

A few days later while preparing for a visit from our heating and air-conditioning company, I decided to check the water softener. To my chagrin, it was empty. Not a single grain of salt remained. No wonder my hair wouldn't come clean. The water was too hard to clean my hair.

Afterward, salt level and hair texture restored to normal, I couldn't help but be struck by the significance. How often do we try to fix an external problem without dealing with our empty heart? All of our self-help remedies amount to nothing. We can't fix the things we encounter in this life without dealing with the root problem.

All too often I find myself wondering why I try so hard to rely on my own strength when I have a Father who is willing to take on my burdens. Why strive for what we already have been freely given? Why try to work out a salvation that's already been paid for? And why try to fix ourselves, even knowing that God would take the burden of our insecurities and give us nothing but freedom in return?

Thankfully, we don't need to waste time trying to fix ourselves without God's help. Instead, we can rely on promises he's given: His grace is sufficient. His power is made perfect in our weakness. And when we are weak, he is strong (see 2 Corinthians 12:9-10). Instead of trying to fix ourselves, let's turn to him.

Lord, thank you that we don't need to try to fix ourselves. Amen.

-Kristin

One Good Step: Think of a problem that feels too big for you to fix. Today, choose to surrender it to God and ask him to bear the burden.

Allegiance

*If you openly declare that Jesus is Lord and believe in your heart
that God raised him from the dead, you will be saved.*

ROMANS 10:9

MY HUSBAND AND I have been studying the New Testament lately in light of the culture of that day. We've learned so much about unspoken rules and cultural norms that don't translate as well two thousand years later when reading the same text. We've read books by authors much smarter than we are who have studied for years and graciously pass their knowledge on to us about the differences in culture that are important to keep in mind.

One topic that I have been ruminating on is the idea of allegiance and what it truly means from a biblical standpoint. I've been learning that for followers of Jesus in the New Testament, to say or proclaim that Jesus was Lord, was to deny your allegiance to Rome and Caesar. A dangerous undertaking, since saying anyone was Lord other than Caesar was grounds for treason, imprisonment, and even death. And yet, people would proclaim Jesus is Lord, knowing full well the implications of this statement. It completely changed their lives, and not always for the better.

People were willing to give up everything to offer their allegiance to Jesus. They would risk their social standing, family, and even freedom. And this challenges me today. I wonder, *Would I do the same?* Because although I appreciate growing up in a place where I can claim allegiance to Jesus without worry of imprisonment or death, I fear that we have lost some of the heaviness this statement implies.

And so, these are the questions I've been pondering: *Is Jesus really Lord of my life? Does allegiance to him supersede everything else?*

I'd like the answer to be a resounding yes, but if I'm honest, some days I don't know that I always put Jesus first, although I am trying. Because I'm learning that allegiance is not just words we speak, but a way of life that allows everyone around us to see that Jesus is Lord.

Lord, may my allegiance to you be above everything else in my life. And may the words and the actions of my life say, Jesus is Lord. Amen.

-Kendra

One Good Step: Write down the five most important things in your life that you love and then ask yourself, *Does my allegiance to Jesus exceed even these things?*

Middle

"For I know the plans I have for you," says the LORD. "They are plans for good
and not for disaster, to give you a future and a hope."
JEREMIAH 29:11

I PAUSED JUST INSIDE THE DOOR, momentarily taken aback at the sight of round tables and chairs for over four hundred businesswomen from my community. I was suddenly wondering why I was there, sharing a still-tender part of my story that did not yet have a Hollywood happy ending.

Taking a deep breath, I—once again—gave it back to Jesus and walked to my assigned seat, a pleasant smile masking the slight tremble in my limbs.

A mere eighteen months prior, I'd walked away from my legal career after a lifetime—since age twelve—of striving to be a lawyer, and I was very much still in the middle of the process—a jumbled up conundrum of varied emotions, uncertain about what God had next but knowing firmly that he was calling me to something new, despite not yet seeing it.

And that's the message I shared in a video interview—hope from the middle, certainty in God in the midst of an uncertain future, encouraging others who were contemplating their own countercultural career change. It was an excruciating day, watching that video play before all those businesswomen, and I left feeling scraped emotionally raw.

In the weeks, months, and years after that queasy day, I've had countless whispered conversations—lunches, emails, phone calls—women confessing to dreams requiring them to trade certainty for uncertainty, thanking me for sharing from the middle and for being an encouraging voice to take the Option B path and to trust God to see when they could not.

My obedience in sharing from the middle, while God was still working it out, while I was still waiting for the Hollywood ending had and continues to have ripple effects that are still rippling, still encouraging, still creating change.

Lord, may we have the courage to allow women to journey with us, allowing them to watch as your faithfulness unfolds around us, allowing them to bear witness to your goodness and your promises. Amen.

-Julie

One Good Step: Allow women to journey alongside you as you wait on God rather than waiting until you have the perfect "happily ever after" to share.

Friend

Love each other in the same way I have loved you.
There is no greater love than to lay down one's life for one's friends.
You are my friends if you do what I command.
JOHN 15:12-14

I WAS NERVOUS. My best friend from childhood had asked me to be her matron of honor, and although I was excited to share in her wedding day, I was dreading the speech I'd have to give at the reception. Public speaking is not my forte.

The outdoor ceremony was hot but beautiful, a cloudless July day with a lakeside view. From my vantage point at the front, I watched my friend offer a dazzling smile as she met her groom at the altar, and I listened with joy as she repeated her vows.

The outdoor ceremony was followed by an indoor reception. Despite the relief of cool air-conditioning, the guests quickly became aware that something was wrong: the bride and groom were missing. As the guests murmured among themselves and checked the time, it was increasingly clear that the guests of honor weren't going to appear. Exiting the room, I found out that my friend's anxiety had reached dizzying heights at the thought of being at the reception, and she simply couldn't enter.

With that realization, my own small fear of giving a speech seemed insignificant. I desperately wished I could offer a toast if it meant my friend could experience her reception. My friend is kind and funny and smart, and knowing her struggles has only made me love her more. Anxiety has been her daily companion for many years, and she had worked so hard to make her wedding day happen. I wished other people knew my friend the way I did. I hoped other people recognized how special she is.

Jesus, too, is that kind of friend to us. He sees us—our fears, our struggles, our humanity—and offers compassion and love. The secret struggles and quiet despairs we face don't make him turn away from us; rather, those moments are times when he hopes we'll lean in to him. Give him our burden. Follow him and find rest and a lightened life. Like any true friend, his love is unconditional.

Lord, thank you for the gift of your friendship. Help us recognize and experience the depth of true friendship in our relationship with you. Amen.

-Kristin

One Good Step: Are you friends with Jesus?
Spend time reflecting on what that means to you.

Response

Don't just listen to God's word. You must do what it says.
Otherwise, you are only fooling yourselves.

JAMES 1:22

NOT LONG AGO as I scrolled the internet, I came across a newspaper article about a house fire in a neighboring community where five of the seven children in the fire died. Their dad had tried to save all of them but was only successful at getting two out. As I read the details, I gasped, unaware that my young daughter had just come in the room.

Snuggling up next to me, she peered over my arm at my iPad. "Whatcha reading, Mom?"

Sighing, I looked at her, deciding whether or not to tell her. What *can* you say? Not wanting to scare her but wanting to be honest about the realities of this world, I tried to explain. "Sweetie, there was a fire the other night and some children died. Their dad tried to save them, but he couldn't get to all of them."

And all she could say was, "Oh."

"What do you think we should do?" I said, pulling her close. We talked about how we could send cards, get them things they might need. "But honey, what's the *first* thing we can always do to respond right now?"

And as we discussed how we can always start by praying, Jasmine and I clasped hands, bowed our heads, and prayed. Jasmine then offered to make a card for a dad whose heart was breaking. Her way of being the hands of Jesus. And later that morning I found out how to send it and some other practical things needed. My way of being the feet of Jesus.

Sometimes we can be overwhelmed by everything we read, all that we see. If we're not careful to filter the information constantly streamed our way, we can take in more than we can bear, more than we need to know. But even so, as Christians, we know that we need to stop, notice, and respond. To not always keep scrolling, but to pay attention to needs. To pray. And then to be proactive to do something in response to the needs around us.

Lord, help us to see the needs around us. To pray and then be willing to respond. Amen.

-Kendra

One Good Step: What or who is God asking you to pray for today? What is a practical action step you can take today in response to their needs?

Sharpen

As iron sharpens iron, so a friend sharpens a friend.
PROVERBS 27:17

"I MET STACY when she moved in next door. We both liked to walk, so we started walking together in the evenings. That was three years ago." Lisa paused to scan the water straight out from where our beach chairs were positioned, counting little heads before visibly relaxing. "Our friendship has been really good for me because we are so different. She is introverted, single, and career oriented, while I'm extroverted, a stay-at-home mom, and perhaps a little too laid back at times." She laughed at the self-assessment as we both watched the water, recounting—for the hundredth time—children as they splished and splashed.

"What has your friendship with Stacy taught you?" I silently offered Lisa a water bottle before I unscrewed the top of one for me.

"I've learned that my view of the world is just that: mine. I appreciate Stacy's perspective and her opinion precisely because we are so different from one another. Her friendship sharpens me, challenges me—in the best way—to rethink positions and to be better." Lisa paused to take a long drink. "Because of Stacy, I've realized that I need people in my life who think differently, who live differently than I do. I constantly need to be sharpened, to be honed to a better version of myself."

I, like Lisa, have grown to treasure my friendships with women who challenge me to do better, be better. It's risky to disagree, even politely, and having a friend who can and will express a different opinion or confront us when our actions don't line up with our professed faith takes courage. It is not easy to be the friend who provides the sharpening to our mindset, personality, or convictions, and yet, without that friend, we wouldn't be forced to examine ourselves, reconsidering our motives and whether we are living lives that point others back to God.

Lord, thank you for women who sharpen us, women who will gently remind us of who we are in you, especially when we are not acting like it. Amen.

-Julie

One Good Step: Call a friend who sharpens you, who makes you a better version of yourself, and thank her for playing that role in your life.

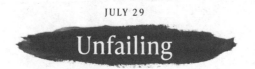

Unfailing

Let your unfailing love surround us, LORD,
for our hope is in you alone.

PSALM 33:22

TIM WAS HIS GRANDMOTHER'S ONLY GRANDCHILD, and Gram was devoted to him. When he was a newborn, she stayed with her daughter for two weeks. Each night, Gram would sleep with baby Tim's cradle placed next to the bed, waking to feed him his bottle at 2 a.m. In the morning, she'd return him to his mother while she went to work. They'd repeat the process every evening, and she cherished that time.

Over the years, her love and attention were unfailing. As a child, Tim spent a couple of summers at her home. She was strict but fair, and quick to pick up on any shenanigans. In the evening when she came in to say good night, she'd always check the temperature of the TV. If it was still warm, she'd know he hadn't shut it off when she asked, thereby losing the privilege of a TV in his room.

In high school, when she found out he was struggling in geography, she obtained an extra copy of the textbook and tutored him. On Sunday nights, he'd go to her home and work for a few hours on homework. She kept in close contact with his teacher to check on his progress.

In every circumstance, Gram demonstrated to Tim how loved, how worthy of time and effort, and how valued he was. Even when she gently scolded him for looking like a hippopotamus when he yawned without covering his mouth, she exuded love. Years later, he still talks about Gram and how much she invested in her relationship with him. He knew her love was unfailing because she proved it over and over and over again.

Similarly, our understanding of God's character—including his love—is what gives us confidence. It's what allows us to trust him. When something is unfailing, it's steadfast. Endless. Completely dependable. Those qualities don't rely on any merit of our own; they are inherent to the Creator of the universe. He never gets tired or weary, and his love is inexhaustible. What a miracle that level of grace and mercy is to us. What a source of hope we have in him.

Lord, help us to look beyond our circumstances and find our hope in your unfailing love. Amen.

-Kristin

One Good Step: Thank God for his unfailing love.

Understand

Live a life filled with love, following the example of Christ.

EPHESIANS 5:2

I'D SPENT A LONG WEEKEND AWAY with a group of friends. We left our families at home for some much-needed girl time. Our spirits were high the first night and next day as we ate out at a favorite restaurant, created a spa day in our hotel room, and spent hours catching up on work, kids, and life.

At the start of the second morning, we spent time walking around, window-shopping. As the hours passed, one friend got increasingly quieter. I noticed the change in her mood and gave her some space, wondering what could be wrong.

As we got back to the hotel after lunch, she pulled out her computer and sat on the bed. My initial thoughts swirled around whether I'd said or done something wrong. In the past, this would've caused me to avoid any interaction with the person, hoping the uncomfortable moment would just pass on its own.

But this time I pushed past the uncomfortable feeling and decided to address the situation head-on. I quietly entered the room and sat on the edge of the bed. "What's going on?" I whispered. "Is everything okay?"

She looked up from her computer and immediately burst into tears. She apologized, as the other women entered the room. Her mood shift had nothing to do with us and everything to do with the stress she was feeling at work. As the weekend was coming to an end, the overwhelming work she knew she'd be hit with on Monday loomed large, casting a shadow on the last part of our time together. We listened to her and affirmed her feelings. I left the conversation being reminded of how important it is to seek to understand another, not just assume.

Sometimes our own insecurities can get in the way of our simply just seeking to understand another person's thoughts and feelings. When we get too caught up in ourselves, we'll fail to really see or respond to another person's needs. As followers of Jesus, we want to live a life filled with love, and one of the ways that we do this is to stop, listen, and seek to understand what someone else may be going through.

Lord, help me to really listen and understand another person's struggle today. Amen.

-Kendra

One Good Step: Take time to listen and understand what someone else is going through today.

Gather

Where two or three gather together as my followers,
I am there among them.
MATTHEW 18:20

"WHAT DO YOU THINK? How should I respond?" I asked, reaching for a Kleenex to wipe a stray tear. A comfortable silence stretched as my Saturday morning Bible study pondered the situation, thinking carefully before offering advice. I knew these women, and I trusted they would give me godly counsel as I sought to respond gracefully to a hard situation.

I've belonged to small faith communities beyond my church family—formal and informal—continuously since my midtwenties. Bible studies, ministry groups, intimate circles of close friends, a collective of families committed to welcoming refugees into our community and homes, each of these faith communities have served a different role in my life, but all have had the common thread of Jesus woven throughout.

I thrive when I regularly gather (online or in person) with other people who love Jesus. I crave the collective wisdom, accountability, and companionship of those attempting to live similar lives, and I find their experiences and wise counsel gives me momentum to stay the course when my path looks particularly rocky and hard. And while I enjoy quietude before God, there is something deeply sacred about gathering around kitchen islands and firepits and over steaming cups of coffee with others as we wrestle with our faith and what it means to walk it out in our daily lives.

We were not meant to follow Jesus on our own. While it's possible, we were created to be in community, to be in familial relationship with other believers, a cobbled-together, adoptive family with Jesus in our midst whenever and wherever we have gathered. There are no preconditions to this promise, no requirements of time or location, no rituals to perform. We need simply to gather.

Lord, provide an adoptive, spiritual family for this season in my life, that I may be challenged, supported, and urged on as we grow deeper in our faith together. Amen.

-Julie

One Good Step: Be the inviter. Prayerfully invite a follower of Jesus you don't know well to coffee or out to lunch, or invite their family over for a meal.

August

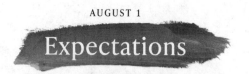

Expectations

I have learned how to be content with whatever I have.

PHILIPPIANS 4:11

IT HAPPENED FOR SEVERAL YEARS while my husband and I were raising our small children. I would look forward to a family vacation or weekend away with much anticipation, dreaming of all the fun we'd have and how much relaxation we needed, only to be frustrated by my kids' constant fighting, the dishes that still needed washing, and the food that still needed to be cooked.

Life felt very similar, only transported to a new location. Vacations weren't all that I had hoped for, and I would often end up disgruntled with my family and upset that things hadn't gone as I'd hoped.

After one disappointing vacation, even though I was embarrassed to admit it, I decided to tell a friend what had really happened. I was ashamed, especially because I didn't want to sound like I wasn't grateful for our time away. My friend listened to my frustration, saying that she understood but that I probably needed to learn to adjust my expectations. She explained that she had had a similar experience and once she'd changed her expectations, her whole mindset changed.

I thought about what she said and decided I needed to adjust my expectations. I have found that I get along much better with my husband and children during our times away. I no longer daydream of some picturesque view of my family not fighting or whining while they tell me they're bored. Now, I look forward to our times away as a family, knowing that we may have some rough moments but enjoying the memories we can make together.

Unrealistic expectations can come in so many ways, often when we don't even realize we're doing it. Our expectations, especially in relationships, can allow for disappointment when we don't see and love people, with all their lovely and not-so-lovely traits. As Christians we are encouraged to be content with what we have. Some expectations may turn out as we'd hoped, other expectations may never be met, and many may simply need to be adjusted so we are content.

Lord, show me any area of my life where I may be holding on to unrealistic expectations and help me change so that I can be content. Amen.

-Kendra

One Good Step: Think about an area of life you've been frustrated with and see if it's partially due to unrealistic expectations. What changes could be made so that you could be content?

Prosper

They are like trees planted along the riverbank, bearing fruit each season.
Their leaves never wither, and they prosper in all they do.
PSALM 1:3

THE BEST CLIMBING TREE in the neighborhood resides in my backyard. A basswood, its symmetrical branches stretch wide and low, creating perfect perches for those content with observing the world from seven feet high while simultaneously allowing the adventurous among us to climb high into the canopy until mothers gather underneath, demanding a return to earth.

And now, it is dying. When we first moved in, it appeared to be prospering, despite one strong root protruding slightly aboveground, wrapping back in on itself and around the tree. I pondered why a root would wrap around instead of reaching out and sinking deep into the earth, but thought nothing more when all else seemed to be well. I didn't know then that we had a girdling root, and that its stranglehold on our tree meant an early death.

It was last summer that a significant branch stretching high into the sky had died, and we've watched this spring as growth on one side of the tree started far thicker and greener than the growth on the side with the girdling root. And now, this fall, the dying has continued, more branches, more sections of my favorite tree withering away. As silly as it sounds, I'm heartbroken.

Trees with girdling roots will live for a time, but they do not prosper. Their roots are trained by their potting container to circle, unable to break the circling cycle to grow deep and wide. And, unable to do anything else but strangle, the trees die far before their life cycle naturally ends.

Humans are the same. When we focus too much on ourselves, spending our resources solely on us, we create our own girdling roots, strangling ourselves with our navel-gazing. It's when we stretch out, reach out, look out for those around us, seeing beyond ourselves to meet the needs of others that we prosper. Scripture is replete with imagery of rootedness, and it invokes depth and width and breadth because that is how we prosper. We live best when we are deeply connected with God and are actively living out our faith by engaging with those around us.

Lord, show us where we have girdling roots, ideas or preoccupations that are too narrowly focused, slowly strangling us. Amen.

-Julie

One Good Step: Perform a random act of kindness today, prayerfully asking God to put someone across your path.

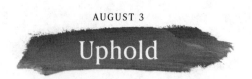

Uphold

Fear not, for I am with you. Do not be dismayed. I am your God. I will strengthen
you; I will help you; I will uphold you with my victorious right hand.

ISAIAH 41:10, TLB

OUR EIGHT-YEAR-OLD was in our bedroom again. I'd already tucked her in numerous
times, listened to a lengthy description of the main character in her book, and given
countless hugs. I held on to my thinning patience as she paused in the doorway
yet again.

"I'm having a hard time falling asleep," she admitted, like we hadn't noticed
her frequent visits.

I suggested a few things to help her relax, and she left. But when thunder rolled
in the distance, she returned within minutes. Sighing, I gave in. "You can sleep in
our room." Her grin was immediate, and she quickly left to go get blankets to make
up a little bed for herself. Snuggling into it, her eyes started to close.

"I feel better now," she said sleepily.

"I'm glad," I said, reaching down. She tucked my hand close to her chest and
squeezed. Within a couple of minutes, she was fast asleep.

Meanwhile, I tossed and turned. The flickering lightning looked like a camera
flash, illuminating the night sky over and over. Thunder crashed, and the winds
whipped through the trees. Restless, I tried to pray but found myself worrying
instead. While I couldn't seem to shut off my brain, my daughter had no such
problem. She knew she had nothing to fear. And that made all the difference in
her ability to sleep soundly.

Our own peace and rest not only comes from trusting in God but in knowing that he is always with us and for us, upholding us through every circumstance. God's upholding power means that he is able to keep us from sinking into
the depths of fear. His upholding power supports and lifts us, and—when we've
reached the end of our strength—he holds us within his hand. We can trust him.
Though we'll face storms in this life, he won't let us be overcome.

*Lord, remind us today of the way you uphold us in every circumstance. Thank you
for your constant, faithful presence we can trust in. Amen.*

-Kristin

One Good Step: List your fears. Spend time praying about giving them into God's care,
asking him to uphold you in every circumstance you're facing.

Generous

Tell them to use their money to do good. They should be rich in good works and generous to those in need, always being ready to share with others.

1 TIMOTHY 6:18

"MOM, HOW MUCH was on that check? She started crying when she opened it up!" Jonny asked, tumbling into the driver's side rear seat of the car.

"This is why we have a family giving fund." I deflected the question about specific amounts, focusing instead on the what and why. "Dad and I intentionally set aside money into a designated account, and we ask God to tell us how to spend it," I said, reaching for my seat belt and turning the car back on. "As soon as she told me about wishing she could help those families with back-to-school expenses, we were able to help. That money was already in the account, ready to give out. That's the thing about generosity—if we prepare ahead of time, we can immediately respond when God sends someone across our path. Isn't it fun to see how God uses his money?"

For some, *generosity* is a dirty word. We are constantly faced with requests to donate resources: time, talent, and treasure for all kinds of needs. It is tempting to grow weary and jaded, uncertain who will use the money wisest and wondering always if we are being hoaxed.

We've encountered a refreshingly rebooted generosity with our family giving fund. It's my job to obey God's nudge—giving *his* money cheerfully and immediately when asked. And while I do my best to be a good steward of his money, I leave it between God and the recipients as to how that money is spent. They are accountable to God for the money he places in their hands, not me. And while it sounds cliché to say that we can never outgive God, it is truth. God has repaid our generosity a thousandfold, plus more. My family has been provided for in ways that support us emotionally, spiritually, and monetarily that defy belief, even as we have provided for others.

Lord, may we set aside resources so that we can be used by you to meet needs around us. Amen.

-Julie

One Good Step: Establish a giving fund using your automatic payroll deduction into an account with God's name on it. Ask God how to use those funds, and be prepared to be blessed beyond measure in return.

Produce

The godly will flourish like palm trees and grow strong like the cedars of Lebanon. For they are transplanted to the LORD's own house. They flourish in the courts of our God. Even in old age they will still produce fruit; they will remain vital and green.

PSALM 92:12-14

I REMEMBER VERY DISTINCTLY the year my mom went back to college. I was in elementary school, and my younger sister had just started kindergarten. My mom wanted to work as a sign language interpreter and took classes while we were in school. I remember her studying and even shedding a few tears because it was so challenging and trying to cultivate a new skill was hard, but I also remember how proud we all were of her a couple of years later when her hard work produced a degree.

As an adult, I realize now even more the challenges my mom faced. She was one of the older students in her program, trying to train her brain to study again while also taking care of a growing family. It was hard but worthwhile, as she used that degree to help support our family for several years afterward.

I thought about this last year as I started to write my first fiction novel the month I turned forty. I wrote the first draft in a month and celebrated my fortieth birthday right in the middle of it. I told my family that this attempt at writing was a perfect reminder to me that you are never too old to produce good fruit and to try something new.

We can still produce good fruit at any age. There is never a point we pass in this life where we are unable to try something new. The only person who often holds us back is ourselves. It is a lie that we somehow reach a point of no return. Scripture reminds us that even in old age, we can remain vital and green. We can produce fruit. Fruit that is timely and needed and relevant and even vital. We simply have to be willing to try.

Lord, thank you that we can always produce new and good fruit at any time in our lives. Amen.

-Kendra

One Good Step: Think about something new you've wanted to try but haven't yet. What fruit might God be wanting to see produced from your life even now?

Sacrifice

Let each of you look not only to his own interests,
but also to the interests of others.

PHILIPPIANS 2:4, ESV

"I'M NORMALLY EARLY TO BED and early to rise, but my friend is a night owl, and I've learned that inviting her family over for dinner usually means a late night," Andrea confided as we sipped our coffee drinks. "Our conversation delves into the deep, harder stuff just about the time my eyes start to get heavy and my body longs to be in bed." Andrea paused as she reached for her scone. "Sacrificing sleep is a small price to pay for our friendship, but it sometimes feels hard in the moment."

Fiddling with my straw wrapper, I asked, "Do you think she would sacrifice her preferences for you?"

"Oh, yes! I know she hates sad movies, but she agreed to watch *Steel Magnolias* with me last month as long as I brought a box of tissues and Red Vines—*not Twizzlers*—as our snack. I know it wasn't her favorite, but I was having a rough week and wanted to watch it, so we did." Andrea picked off a bit of scone for another bite. "Now that I think about it, we sacrifice our preferences for one another on a regular basis. I guess that's what makes our friendship so strong."

Sacrifice often sounds like it requires grand gestures and life-altering consequences—and in extreme circumstances, it does. However, sacrifice also includes the small things such as setting aside our interests as we intentionally allow someone else's preference to take center stage.

Sacrifice—when done with love—reveals care and concern in a way words cannot, showing through our actions that we are willing to lay down our interests without grumbling or grudge-holding, elevating someone else in that moment. Loving sacrifice shows *agape*, brotherly love toward others—our coworkers, neighbors, friends, family—laying down self for another in a pale but important imitation of Christ's sacrifice for us.

Lord, nudge us when we have a choice between our way and another's way—that we might start recognizing opportunities for sacrifice.

-Julie

One Good Step: Start looking for ways to show affection, friendship, and love through sacrifice. Commit to one small sacrifice a day.

Think

And now, dear brothers and sisters, one final thing. Fix your thoughts on
what is true, and honorable, and right, and pure, and lovely, and admirable.
Think about things that are excellent and worthy of praise.

PHILIPPIANS 4:8

I WORKED AT A NEWSPAPER for several years. As a copyeditor, it was my job to read the paper from cover to cover and check for errors. While I enjoyed the camaraderie of the newsroom, over time, it became difficult to shrug off the heaviness of the stories. Though there were many heartwarming stories about people doing great things in the community, there were also detailed descriptions of wars, injustices, and deaths around the world.

Over time, I became wary of my surroundings when driving home late at night. When I headed to bed, gruesome details would return to my mind, making it hard to sleep. I even had a security system installed in our home since I was frequently alone. The lingering negativity resonated so much that I resorted to reading children's books in my free time, hoping their lightheartedness would provide an escape and boost my mood. Though I tried to think of what was pure and lovely, my mind was filled with some of the ugliest parts of humanity.

What we think about matters. That critical comment about us that lingers in our mind? That experience in our past that still haunts our present? Our desire to read the comments on an incendiary story? The impulse to let TV news or our social media feed be a low-level murmur in the background of our day? All of those play into something that researchers call negativity bias. Our brain reacts more strongly to negative stimuli than it does to positive stimuli. In fact, researchers have found that a five-to-one ratio is required for us to overcome negative stimuli. Every time we see, hear, or experience something negative, it takes five positive interactions in order to overcome the single negative.

Overcoming negativity bias requires intention, yet taking our thoughts captive is essential in helping us view the world with discernment. When we choose to fill our minds to overflowing with the truth of God's Word, the beauty of this world, and the love we have for others, we can counteract the negativity that impacts us.

Lord, help us think of the true, honorable, right, pure, lovely, and admirable things of this world. Amen.

-Kristin

One Good Step: Write down something negative that's bothering you.
Now, write down five positive ideas or experiences to counteract
the negative one. Intentionally choose to focus on the positives.

Cling

I cling to you; your strong right hand holds me securely.

PSALM 63:8

IT WAS A FREAK ACCIDENT that put my friend's teenage daughter in the emergency room, headed immediately into surgery for a severely broken arm. But it was complicated into something impossibly more difficult by circumstances outside of their control, resulting in a mother watching as her daughter was rapidly admitted and whisked away without her, without her dad, confused, in pain and left to navigate the healthcare system, making critically important decisions on her own.

And while there is a happy ending to the story, in the midst of the agonizing hours-that-felt-like-years while my friend waited outside the hospital, she did the only thing she could: cling.

She clung to Jesus, *knowing* that he loves her precious daughter, and that while she could not be there, God was there, his presence saturating the places she could not. She clung to Scripture, speaking truth in the form of verses whisper-recited every time her mind started to veer toward anxiety and fear. She clung to those who love her family, allowing their inner circle to rally around them, confiding what they were walking through, so that their community could encircle their daughter with prayer.

Clinging when the world tilts crazily to one side, threatening to overrun everything we know with turmoil and chaos is one thing, but what about when life is thrumming along, when routine is the norm, when we operate under the illusion of control? Do we cling then?

I don't cling often enough, I'll admit. I get lulled into a false sense of security, assuming I can manage well enough on my own, loving God but not clinging until the proverbial waters get choppy or my proverbial skies turn menacing, signaling a twister on the horizon. Then, I cling.

What if we practiced clinging as the default rather than as a spiritual storm shelter, used only in cases of dire emergency? What if we released our illusion of control, handing over the reins in the day-to-day rather than only in the midst of chaos?

Lord, take the reins of our day. We release our to-do lists, our obligations, our schedule and agendas, our control to you so that we might cling to the one who created and named the stars. Amen.

-Julie

One Good Step: Release every piece of today to Jesus, asking him to guide your every step and decision.

Courage

This is my command—be strong and courageous! Do not be afraid or discouraged. For the LORD your God is with you wherever you go.

JOSHUA 1:9

ONE MORNING as we were getting ready for a church service, my daughter came into our room and told me she had a song to sing for us. After she sang, she wondered if she could sing it at our church service.

As we walked into the sanctuary, she walked over to our pastor shyly, showed him her song, and asked if it'd be all right. Of course he agreed. As the worship portion of the service ended, Pastor Carl called Jasmine up on the stage, where she courageously shared the song she'd written and then felt led to share with others.

As we were driving home, I told her the thing I was most proud of was not how well she sang but that she had the courage to listen to what she believed God had asked her to do. I was proud that when God asked her to share her heart with others, she was obedient to do it, even though she was a little bit afraid. I finished by stating, "I'm not so concerned with how well you do, but that you're just willing to try."

Since then I've been thinking about my own life. How often have I said no because I was afraid? Because I was too scared to try? My daughter's courage reminded me of my own desire to want to always say yes to God, even when it comes to scary things, even hard things.

Maybe you, too, have struggled with saying yes to something because of fear or doubt or disbelief. Maybe you've given up on dreams you once had because it just seemed too big or too far out of reach. I wonder what would happen if we began to dream once again, began to say yes to things that once scared us—*what would happen in our lives?* And more importantly, *what would happen in our faith?* Maybe this is the time God would say to each of us: I'm not so concerned with how well you do, I just care that you're willing to try.

Lord, help us to have courage today to do the things you ask us to do. Amen.

-Kendra

One Good Step: What old or new dream is God asking you to courageously take one action step toward today?

Victory

They did not conquer the land with their swords; it was not their own strong arm that gave them victory. It was your right hand and strong arm and the blinding light from your face that helped them, for you loved them.

PSALM 44:3

"COME ON, you can do it!" my husband called out encouragingly. "Your sister would be so proud of you."

Walking behind him on the hiking trail, I shot a disgruntled look toward his back. "Are you kidding?" I scoffed. "My sister would think I was crazy. She and I would be at Starbucks right now."

Despite my husband's surprised look, it was true. My sister Katrina had a sense of adventure, but she wasn't a big hiker. Nevertheless, she would have loved how the foundation we created after her death raised money to help girls and women. Our biggest fundraiser was a charity mountain climb in Colorado.

As I continued to climb, I couldn't help but wonder what I'd gotten myself into. Even though I had the right equipment and had acclimated myself to the higher altitude, I was struggling. By the time I realized I wasn't going to reach the summit, I was discouraged. And after my knees locked up on the way down, I felt even worse, shuffling one painful step at a time as everyone else passed me by.

Eventually, we were the final pair. Knowing how much I was struggling, Tim asked if I wanted help in the final stretch. "Yes, please," I said with some relief, knowing my knees weren't going to improve. With a nod, he hoisted me on his strong back and trudged the rest of the way down. As we emerged from the trees, everyone cheered.

Even after all that disappointment, it felt like a victory.

I'm reminded of that experience every time I'm tempted to struggle alone on the mountains that rise up in my own life. When my faith is tested or life's circumstances press down, I recall the misery of trying to manage that mountain alone—and how the decision to accept help provided immediate relief. That's what God does for you and me. When we give our burdens to him, he gives us a hand and his strength—all because he loves us.

Our God hoists us high and carries us through. And instead of defeat, that power of working together feels only like victory.

Lord, thank you that your immense love gives us the strength we need. Amen.

-Kristin

One Good Step: What are some victories you have experienced in your own life, big and small?

Reconcile

Go and be reconciled to that person. Then come and offer your sacrifice to God.
MATTHEW 5:24

I TOSSED AND TURNED, unable to sleep as I repeatedly replayed my words, trying to determine whether I had offended her and to what extent, despite it being entirely unintentional. Staring wide-eyed at my ceiling, I prayed for wisdom, finally deciding to email an apology the next morning in an attempt to set things right, determined not to spend another night sleepless with regret.

As we gathered on a conference call later that afternoon, I followed my morning email with a quick verbal apology—understanding that my intent, even when it is good, doesn't prevent another's hurt.

"Oh, Julie. We're just fine. Today has been so busy that I didn't get a chance to respond to your email. I was not offended or upset, but I appreciate the apology nonetheless."

Exhaling a sigh of relief, I replied, "Well, my words were spoken carelessly, and I wanted to address it directly rather than pretend it didn't happen. I never want to cause you hurt, even unintentionally."

With the air cleared, we moved on through the meeting's agenda. Reconciliation brings me such a sense of relief as the tension—imagined or real—eases that I have become far more willing to face the hard moments of conflict necessary in order to arrive at peace. That has not always been the case, and I've let far too many situations slide past possible reconciliation into that awkward place of unspoken conflict avoidance than I'd care to admit.

For some of us it is hard to embrace conflict, talking honestly about hurts or frustrations, seeking reconciliation as we work through a misunderstanding or disagreement, especially when we caused, even unintentionally, the hurt. Reconciliation is countercultural in that it requires us to lay down our pride and listen carefully to someone else's perspective, prayerfully consider what role we played in the conflict, be accountable, and apologize when necessary rather than let things linger, unresolved.

But we are commanded to reconcile with others before we seek reconciliation with God, precisely because he knows the immense power in a unified church, in believers who know how to humble themselves in apology and stay in community with one another.

Lord, who do we need to reconcile with? Help us to practice the art of humble apology. Amen.

-Julie

One Good Step: Practice being quick to apologize, refusing to allow the sun to set without resolving conflicts whenever possible.

Follow

Your own ears will hear him. Right behind you a voice will say,
"This is the way you should go," whether to the right or to the left.
ISAIAH 30:21

I'D BEEN FEELING A NUDGE to be done for months but had been ignoring it. I'd been part of a ministry group of women for ten years and taught the leaders for the past five. I didn't want to leave the women I'd loved for so long and met with on a weekly basis. And yet I could hear God's gentle voice, telling me it was time to step away and allow for someone else to move into my position to teach. I was reminded of my own words, now coming back to haunt me. *This is never about me, my voice. I am happy to step away when God asks me to.* And this was that time.

As I prayed about how to approach the woman in charge, she emailed me wondering about my ability to teach for the coming year and then offered someone who could potentially colead with me. As I read her message, I knew. God had been speaking to her, too. The woman she suggested was an excellent teacher. I knew God was moving her into the spot I was about to vacate. I emailed her back, letting her know that I would be stepping down completely, and how much I thought of the new woman who would take my place. I was still a little sad to leave, but I was sure that I was being obedient to follow God's lead and listen to his voice.

Following the voice of God is a skill that comes with time and experience. And even when you've known Jesus for many years, you can still miss his leading at times. Following God's direction is not always just about avoiding sin, but it has much more to do with being sensitive to knowing when he wants you to go and when he asks you to stay. It's being able to follow his voice when he asks you to step away from something, or into a new place that may be yet unknown. Following God's leading is a skill we continue to hone over our lifetime.

Lord, today may I listen for your voice and follow where you lead me. Amen.

-Kendra

One Good Step: Where has God been leading you lately?
Today determine to take steps to follow where he leads.

Endurance

We can rejoice, too, when we run into problems and trials, for we know that they help us develop endurance. And endurance develops strength of character, and character strengthens our confident hope of salvation.

ROMANS 5:3-4

OUR FRIENDS RYAN AND MOLLY went on a backpacking trip in northern Minnesota for Ryan's fortieth birthday. Fittingly, the couple decided to hike forty miles over the course of a few days.

But a trip that was supposed to be a celebration didn't end up being all that celebratory. The death of Molly's dad shortly before their trip was a heavy weight on their hearts even as they prepared for the journey. Once there, the reality of hoisting a heavy backpack filled with all their belongings on their backs each day, then heading off to trudge miles along a difficult trail, didn't match their expectations of having some time to relax and enjoy the beautiful vistas. Despite the trail's location alongside Lake Superior, the water wasn't even visible much of the time as they were often immersed in trees. Walking often felt monotonous, but they had to stay on schedule in order to make it to the next campsite for the night. In the evenings, they never had the chance to enjoy a single sunset because they were too exhausted to do anything but fall into bed after setting up camp.

Yet whenever they would be tempted to regret the experience, they'd glimpse an incredible view. And over the course of the trip, they grew to rely on one another. They had hours of uninterrupted time to talk. Despite the monotony, those many quiet stretches gave Molly a sense of peace amid all that was going on after her dad's death. In the end, the couple felt achievement for their endurance through the challenging trail.

All too often, it can be easy to focus on the hardships we're facing and see them only for their negative qualities. Physically, emotionally, or mentally exhausted, we can't imagine trudging one more step. Yet our endurance often reveals facets of ourselves and of God: if we look back afterward, we're often able to see the fingerprints of his hope and light interwoven through the experience.

Lord, when hardships come, give us strength to endure and hope for tomorrow. Amen.

-Kristin

One Good Step: Reflect on an experience that required endurance. How was God's presence revealed during that time?

Known

Even children are known by the way they act,
whether their conduct is pure, and whether it is right.
PROVERBS 20:11

CLUTCHING A SOAKED TISSUE tightly in one fist, I sat in the reserved first pew, having lost the battle long ago against the tears silently leaking down my cheeks.

At the pastor's invitation, stories began to pour forth from the packed pews behind us, spanning the entirety of my father-in-law's life, some of which Aaron had never heard, never knew about his dad.

Bill, gentlehearted and unfailingly kind, built a lifetime of seeing others, of reaching out in moments of desperate need, of stepping into gaps. Coworkers from long-ago jobs, neighbors, and friends told stories that, despite their being strangers, shared the theme of Bill loving those around him well.

I've often thought of those stories, of the packed church, of the collective grief over a compassionate man who loved others well. He sought out those feeling slightly uncomfortable, intentionally easing their discomfort. He quietly met needs, setting aside his own time and preferences to care for someone else physically or emotionally. His actions over a lifetime revealed his character consistently, despite living in different places, having a variety of jobs, and engaging with untold numbers of individuals.

Known. Whether we cultivate it intentionally or not, we create a sense of being known, of being recognized by our consistent response to circumstances around us. And while all of us are flawed and imperfect, and prone to behaviors we don't want to ultimately be known for, it's something to think about.

Do strangers, neighbors, coworkers, friends, family know (mostly) the same version of me? As a follower of Christ, do I respond consistently across circumstances—especially stressful, hard circumstances? Do I, both in word and deed, point others back to God?

Those are the hard questions I ask myself when I wonder how I am known. And when I don't like the answer to the question, I ask God what I might need to change so that I'm known for something better.

Lord, reveal how we might be known for something better than what we are right now. Show us words or actions that are ungodly in character, that we might need to let go of or replace. Amen.

-Julie

One Good Word: Pick three people and list five words that describe each of them. Which of those words do you want to better emulate? Which words do you want to avoid being known for? Implement changes based on what you discovered.

Sweet

*My child, eat honey, for it is good, and the honeycomb is sweet to the taste.
In the same way, wisdom is sweet to your soul. If you find it, you will
have a bright future, and your hopes will not be cut short.*

PROVERBS 24:13-14

DURING MY ANNUAL FORTY-DAY SUGAR FAST, I usually hit my stride by about day ten and finish well. But one year, I was particularly stressed and happened to spot chocolates a friend had given me the day before. In a moment of weakness, I gobbled all four—even the raspberry crème one I'd normally find unpalatable. I ate them so quickly that, within a matter of minutes, I felt sick to my stomach. It was near the end of my fast and my body wasn't ready for the sugar deluge. That sweetness had a hidden cost.

Although the fast is physical, it often reveals the state of my heart. Forgoing sweets helps me recognize moments I'm tempted to reach for them. On days when a friendship feels strained or a work deadline looms heavily, I'll find myself sneaking into the pantry for a piece of chocolate. Though there's nothing wrong with the occasional treat, the fast reminds me that no matter how many sweets I eat, they will never truly satisfy. The fleeting comfort of cake or cookies can never replace our Comforter.

Many things in life appear sweet but only serve to make us sick or worse than when we started. Our attempts to satisfy through substitutions can come in many forms: overspending, an overly full calendar, bingeing TV shows or movies, numbing ourselves with an overabundance of food or drink, or too much time scrolling social media.

Thankfully, God's wisdom is freely given and always available. His wisdom is the sweetest thing this life has to offer, and the Bread and Living Water he provides are the only items that will never run out, never run dry, never cause regret, and never leave us dissatisfied. Instead, he will fill our hearts and our minds with things that are true, and noble, and lovely. Wisdom helps us foster the sweetness of friendships, the power of justice and mercy, and the wonder of his love. What a banquet to feast upon!

Lord, thank you that your wisdom provides true sweetness. Help us recognize the value in listening and following your Word. Amen.

-Kristin

One Good Word: Choose a piece of God's wisdom—
a verse or passage—and memorize it.

Finish

Finishing is better than starting.
Patience is better than pride.

ECCLESIASTES 7:8

THE EXCITEMENT HAD WORN OFF. We had moved a year and a half earlier, and the thrill over it had ended. I looked around, wondering what my next steps were—*Where should I go? Who can I meet? What should I be doing?*

And yet, in this season, God was constantly bringing me back to my home. To the people in my family. I knew that I was needed there. I knew that God brought us these kids, and their grief and trauma and attachment are all things I needed to deal with—but part of me wanted to run. As I dug my heels (figuratively) in the sand, I realized something about myself: I'm a good starter, but I'm not the best finisher.

I like the new thing—I have a hard time sticking with the old, especially when it becomes mundane or even drudgery. I've always had a tendency to be this way. I like the excitement of a new job. A new house. A new friend. But over time, when the work gets challenging, there's a part of me that looks for a way out. A new place or even relationship.

But sometimes God asks us to stay. To continue to love. To be still. When everything in us tells us to leave or walk away for no other reason than things have gotten a little too hard. So much of what we go through in life feels more like a marathon than a sprint. Things unfold and happen over time and usually not on the timeline we'd prefer. It can be easy to start something new, but it takes determination to finish, and to finish well.

There is a refinement that comes when we finish. A change that happens in our character, making us more Christlike. Developing the fruit of the Spirit in our lives—love, joy, peace, patience, kindness, goodness, faithfulness, gentleness, and self-control—in a way we may not otherwise grow if we walked away too soon. Allowing other people to see the stability we have as people who finish well.

Lord, help us to not only be people who start, but who finish. Amen.

-Kendra

One Good Step: What in your life is God currently asking you to finish? What is one step you can take to continue to stay in that place so you do finish well?

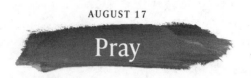

Pray

Bless those who curse you. Pray for those who hurt you.

LUKE 6:28

"I THINK I NEED to start praying for Haley."

My fingers involuntarily clenched the steering wheel, my eyes shooting her a quick glance before returning to watching the road. "Oh?"

"I know, I know." Brianna sighed as she played with a lock of hair, staring out the passenger window. "I'll maintain healthy boundaries."

"Oh, friend. I know you will." Pausing for a long moment, I admit, "And you are right, you should be praying for Haley, and honestly, I probably should too. I just don't want her to stir up any more drama for you at work. That was a rough six months."

I love Brianna, which means I get mad when someone treats her badly. She is quick to see beneath hurtful actions and words, looking for aching hearts and broken pieces in people who are unkind. She tries to see people as God sees them, which means she tends toward grace and mercy rather than offense or anger. It's one of her best qualities, and it challenges my angry response to those who hurt people I love. She's right, and I know it.

We pray good things for those we love, for those who have been good to us, but what, if anything, do we pray over those who have treated us ill? Do we pray for God's vengeance on the heads of our enemies, or do we pray for a Damascus-road encounter, a radical transformation that turns Sauls into Pauls? What is our responsibility in praying for our fellow fallen, hurting humans, even when they've been hateful? This is not for the faint of heart. It is countercultural and just plain hard to pray blessing over those who curse us, over those who are hurtful.

As we reconsider our response, a word of caution is in order. Let us not confuse sincere, ongoing intercessory prayer with allowing an unsafe person access to our hearts, bodies, or innermost thoughts. We are not doormats, and we can and should establish healthy, godly boundaries to keep us safe spiritually, emotionally, and physically.

Lord, give us the balance to see hard people as you see them, investing in prayer on their behalf while also maintaining safety for us and those we love. Amen.

-Julie

One Good Step: Pick one hard person in your life and pray for him or her every time you brush your teeth.

Goal

My goal is that they may be encouraged in heart and united in love,
so that they may have the full riches of complete understanding,
in order that they may know the mystery of God, namely, Christ.
COLOSSIANS 2:2, NIV

ONE BY ONE, small squares on the laptop screen lit up, filled with smiling faces from across the country and globe. Vicki's lilting Scottish voice resonated through the microphone.

"It's so good to see your faces," she said, amid a chorus of hellos.

It was evening here, but midday the following day for Aimee in New Zealand. It was close to bedtime for our East Coast friends, not yet dinner for those on the West Coast. The group of women gathered four times a year to discuss a quarterly magazine publication, and we would spend the next few hours discussing the various possibilities for the next issue. From poetry to seasonal DIY features to inspirational articles on Scripture, the topics—and our opinions on their merit for this particular issue—varied widely.

Yet woven through all the various viewpoints was the recognition that the collective goal was to find and feature articles that would inspire women, speaking truth into their hearts yet leaving them encouraged. The ones that spoke most strongly to us had the most vulnerability, the most insightful application. It was the heart of the stories the authors chose to tell that mattered, not the use of fancy language or long-winded descriptions.

Though we were separated by distance, our minds were in agreement. As Christians, this should always be our ultimate goal: to love God and love others, and to do so by sharing the Good News of Jesus with others. Though the way we choose to do so varies, our goal is the same—we are called to unity rather than uniformity. No matter our approach, the stories we choose to tell about Jesus and how he's changed our lives matter. Your story matters. That's always a goal worth having.

Lord, help us to strive for the goal of reaching out to others with your Good News. May we be united with others in our quest to follow you. Amen.

-Kristin

One Good Step: In what ways does your life reflect the Good News of Jesus?

Bridge

Jesus replied: "'Love the Lord your God with all your heart and with all your soul and with all your mind.' This is the first and greatest commandment. And the second is like it: 'Love your neighbor as yourself.' All the Law and the Prophets hang on these two commandments."

MATTHEW 22:37-40, NIV

IN THE PAST FEW YEARS, my husband and I have burned a few bridges. Not with people, but with ideas we'd held too tightly. Religious acts that we'd placed above simply loving people.

We've burned bridges to old ideology we couldn't support anymore after reading Scripture and actually trying to live it out. New conclusions were made, and growth happened.

And freedom has come. From expectations. From old ideas. From perspectives we'd turned into law and placed on others and ourselves, whether they believed the same things we did or not. And, although it's still not perfect, we are loving others in a way we haven't in the past. We're accepting those around us, giving with no strings attached, and finding ourselves comfortable among those who have differing ideas from us. It's not always been easy, but this new way of thinking and being has taught us more about God's love for us and for everyone around us.

We need to be willing to build bridges to people. Whether they are Christian or not. To love them no matter what they think or believe, understanding that love does not mean we approve of everything someone else says or does. We need to be sensitive to the Holy Spirit when he would ask us to build a bridge to people, even while burning a bridge to a former way of thinking that may not line up with the greatest commandment we were given by Jesus. Love God. Love people. It's the simplest and easiest way to start to build a bridge to those around us.

Lord, help us to love you and love others in a way that shows them who you are. Help us to be bridge builders to those around us. Amen.

-Kendra

One Good Step: What (if any) old ideologies have you burned bridges to that don't line up with Jesus' greatest commandment? Who can you build a bridge to by showing them the love of God?

Less

He must become greater and greater,
and I must become less and less.

JOHN 3:30

WE WERE OUT FOR DINNER with friends, chatting amiably about calendars and kids, when one of my friends asked about my volunteer work with a women's ministry organization.

"Oh, I love it," I gushed. "But a big part of it—for me—is working with Carol. She's the kind of leader you want to work with and learn from. She's a big part of the reason I've volunteered with them for so long."

I paused and looked at them expectantly as my friend offered a smile.

"Who is Carol?" he asked quizzically.

At first, I was taken aback. *How could he not know?* She's the director of an organization and has been running it for decades. Her events draw thousands. She has contacts and relationships all over the country; she's mentored countless people. And yet, he had no idea who she was.

But as I thought about it more, I realized how beautiful a testament it is to Carol's character that—unless they are intimately involved with the organization—people have no idea who she is. After all, she rarely steps on stage. She never seeks the spotlight, never talks about her own (lengthy) accomplishments. She's just as likely to be puttering around, lending a hand to clean up after an event as she is to be planning for the big moments.

In order to showcase more of Jesus, Carol has perfected the art of less. Becoming less doesn't mean denigrating ourselves, enrobing ourselves with a false humility, or pretending that our contributions don't matter. Rather, it shows where our priorities lie. In all things, it points others back to Jesus.

The funny thing is that, when you do know Carol, she seems larger than life. She's beloved by the people she works alongside. The way she reflects Jesus makes her shine even brighter to those around her.

It requires humility and trust to take all the things we're doing in the world—our work, our dreams, our plans—and place them squarely in the hands of Jesus. But when we recognize that he is in charge of all things, our priorities shift. Rather than being the rulers of our own lives, we know that we are ambassadors for him.

Lord, help us to reflect you in all we do. Amen.

-Kristin

One Good Step: In what ways do your words and actions point people back to Jesus?

Transform

The one sitting on the throne said,
"Look, I am making everything new!"
REVELATION 21:5

EVERY YEAR MY FAMILY GOES to Madeline Island on Lake Superior in Wisconsin. We rent a house on the lake and spend our days in the water and on the beach. For several hours we walk up and down the shores picking out our favorite rocks. Much to my husband's chagrin and warning that this year we won't be taking many home with us, we usually end up with a few bucketfuls of rocks. They're just so beautiful we can't part with them.

As I admire the rocks each year when we return home, I think about what God has taught me about transformation through our rock collecting. I've noticed that the ones that are the smoothest have been tossed in the waves. All their rough edges have been worn away by the constant friction. I've also realized that the submerged rocks are often the most beautiful. They are the ones that glisten and shine in the sun. They've been transformed by the constant friction—distinctly different from the rocks tucked further up on the shore that have never been tossed by the waves, never had anything to rub off their rough edges or submerge them at all. They are the ones that are dull and harsh, with no defining characteristics from any of the other rocks around them. They are the ones that get left on the shore.

As I think about the transformation of these rocks over time, I realize it's true for people as well.

God often uses the harder things we walk through in life to transform us. The grittier parts of life that rub off our rough edges. To change us from dull into something that is soft and beautiful. Others notice and are drawn to us. We can miss what God is doing because we hate the struggle, and often we don't see that his beauty is magnified in these places. But if we're willing to allow God to transform us, he will make us new.

Lord, thank you that you do not leave us the same but continue to transform us over time. Amen.

-Kendra

One Good Step: Think about one way God has used a life circumstance to transform you in the past. How can you remember that for the current transformation you are going through in your life?

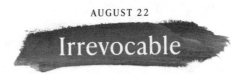
Irrevocable

The gifts and the calling of God are irrevocable.

ROMANS 11:29, ESV

IN THE EARLY MORNING LIGHT, we climbed aboard the tour bus in Paris and headed to Versailles, roaming the private apartments of Marie Antoinette and the opulent, glittering Hall of Mirrors. By the time we climbed back on the bus to Giverny, we were a bit tired, but the tour of Claude Monet's house and gardens perked us up immediately.

In the front of the house, fruit and ornamental trees coexisted with a central alley of iron arches. Across the street, the pond gardens—the site of Monet's famous water lily paintings—featured a Japanese bridge covered with wisterias, weeping willows, and nymphaeas that would bloom all summer long.

Monet spent years painting at this particular house. But in 1912 he faced a setback when he was diagnosed with cataracts in both eyes. As his vision deteriorated, the colors and tones in his paintings changed. Though discouraged by his failing eyesight, he continued to paint. In the end, Monet painted about 250 paintings featuring water lilies. Although each painting varies, there is beauty in each of them. Today, they can be found in museums all over the world.

The truth is that if Monet had given up, the world would never have witnessed his beautiful water lily paintings. Though I've never faced the challenge of failing eyesight, there are many days when I've questioned my own gifts or talents. I've wondered if the words I write or the actions I take each day really matter. But Scripture is clear that our giftings are irrevocable—they can't be undone. In Romans, Paul talks about how the Lord's favor on Israel and those grafted into his Kingdom is irrevocable. Though he is speaking specifically of a call to the Kingdom of God, it's also true of the gifts and call God has placed on each of us. Monet was already a famous painter by the time he moved to Giverny; he could have given up and stopped painting. Instead, his reaction was to persist. We, too, are called to love God and follow his irresistible, irrevocable call.

Lord, thank you for the irrevocable favor of your love. Give us the courage to persist even when challenges arise. Amen.

-Kristin

One Good Step: Encourage a friend with a message to remind them that their gifts and talents are irrevocable.

Lament

Be happy with those who are happy,
and weep with those who weep.
ROMANS 12:15

"MY BABY HAS NEVER KNOWN NORMAL. Some days it is hard to be surrounded by mothers of similar aged children whose biggest challenge is teething or not sleeping or being a picky eater. I don't want to be resentful, but sometimes I can't help it. Do you know how many MRIs my daughter has had in her first year of life? How many tests and procedures? And we still have more questions than answers, being asked to live in uncertainty. It's all so, so hard."

I listened helplessly as my friend's voice dissolved into tears, too many miles away to wrap her in a hug, helpless to do anything but clutch my phone and sit with her in her grief, both of us crying over what should have been, what is, and the unknowns, separately but together. It is possible to grieve deeply, hope wildly, love unconditionally, rage incoherently, and trust God explicitly, all at once.

God is not dishonored in our lament. We can bring our shattered hearts before God with no pretense. We can hurl an agonizing wail of "why" heavenward, shaking our fists as we rage at the unfairness of life without fear of punishment or retribution. And spent, we are invited to simply sit, surrounded by his presence, promised that he is near to the brokenhearted.

I am learning to honor lament, to be quietly supportive in the presence of another's tears or anger or however else her grief is manifesting in that moment without platitudes or clichés, offering a quiet hug, a coffee refill, and the gift of listening without fixing or soothing or diminishing. She controls the conversation, and sometimes a long, silent companionship fills our shared space, bringing a comfort that my words cannot.

Do not be afraid of lament, in yourself or those around you. We do not disappoint God in our wild grief. Jesus wept. He knows lament.

Lord, may we be women who are unafraid of sitting alongside those who are weeping. Amen.

-Julie

One Good Step: Do not avoid someone walking through grief. Check in with a phone call or a text, offering to bring a coffee and a listening ear.

Name

He counts the stars and calls them all by name.

PSALM 147:4

As a young adult I worked as a leader in the youth group at my church. I loved meeting the youth and spending time with them every week. There was one teen girl I got to know well over the years who came to church with her mom and siblings. I found out that her dad was not involved in her life at all, and even though she did not complain, I could tell this was a point of pain in her life. Especially when she was at church and surrounded by dads who were very involved in their kids' lives.

One year as her birthday approached, I decided to give her a Bible. She had mentioned that she liked the version I owned, and so I planned to give her a similar Bible. One Wednesday night as we prayed together at the end of the night, I felt impressed to tell her that God knew her name. That she was not forgotten. That even if her earthly father was not present, her heavenly Father was and he loved her. We both sat on the floor in tears as the truth of God's love flooded both of us.

Days later, as I wrote out a card and included a personal note in the Bible I planned to give her, I included the words of Psalm 147:4, a reminder once again that God knew her by name. When I gave her the Bible, both our eyes filled with tears once again. God's love was evident to her, even as she carried pain over the absence of her earthly father.

There are times in life where we can feel forgotten or left out by others. Relationships sometimes will leave us with unmet desires to be seen or heard. But not with God. He counts the stars and calls them by name. And how much more precious are we? Even if people on earth disregard us, God will not. He knows your name. You are precious to him. You are seen. You matter.

Lord, thank you for caring so much for each one of us and for knowing us all by name. Amen.

-Kendra

One Good Step: How has God shown you that he has not forgotten you? How can you show someone else today that they are seen and matter?

Best

Be sure to give to the LORD the best portions of the gifts given to you.
NUMBERS 18:29

"HERE'S THE THINGS that didn't sell at my garage sale," the woman said, handing my sister a grocery bag full of items. My sister thanked her and set it aside, but shot me a wry glance. It wasn't the first bag of leftovers we'd received.

Over the years, we've volunteered with local groups in a variety of settings. We've looked through items for our local homeless shelter. We've organized clothing giveaways for charity organizations. We've had furniture and household goods pass through our hands for refugees, pajamas and backpacks for foster families. And while some people give the best that they have—new clothing or goods they've purchased with intention, or well-maintained furniture or other items—many give their leftovers. Worse, they give without recognizing the inherent harm of giving the worst they have to offer. It says something to someone else when you only consider them worthy of your trash.

God asks us to give our best of all that's been given to us. We aren't asked to strive for someone else's best, but our own—the highest quality or excellence that we can provide out of the gifts God has lavished upon us. The intention matters as much as the action because the things we give to others assign value. For instance, if a friend has a birthday, we spend time thinking about the gift we will give to them. It will probably be something new or memorable. Maybe it would be something we baked or created by hand. Though it wouldn't necessarily cost a lot of money, it would be given with love and care. It would be our best.

As Christians, let us not only lead with love; let's lead with our very best. If we take to heart the truth that everything we do should be done as though we do it for the Lord, we will be more inclined to give the best of ourselves in every situation. Doing so will not only bless the recipient; it will reflect the love of the Father to those around us.

Lord, help us to give the best of ourselves, in every situation. Amen.

-Kristin

One Good Step: Share something that's the best part of yourself—a talent or skill, or even kind words—with someone else.

Freedom

The thief comes only to steal and kill and destroy;
I have come that they may have life, and have it to the full.
JOHN 10:10, NIV

"EVERY DAY I THINK ABOUT what I did," she said as tears ran down her cheeks, unchecked. "I think about the choices I made and wish I could go back and do something different. Each day I say how sorry I am, but I think God is punishing me." Her voice trailed off as she turned to watch our kids swimming together in the pool.

I sat a little stunned before reaching across our chairs for her hand. She turned back slowly, her gaze not quite reaching mine. "God doesn't do that," I whispered as I squeezed her hand. "He sees your pain, and he knows you're sorry. God forgives us; he doesn't continue to shame us. You've punished yourself enough for this." Her eyes slowly came to meet mine. "He grieves with you. He wouldn't saddle you with this guilt and shame. That is not who God is."

She let out a deep sigh as we continued to talk about God's grace and love—his character. I could tell she had a hard time believing. The lies of the enemy had wrapped tightly around her heart, weighing her spirit down with heaviness, and the process of cutting loose from those old beliefs would take time. Before we left, I prayed for my friend, for freedom from the things that had weighed her down.

The enemy will use whatever he can to keep us from knowing the truth of all that God would have for us, mainly the freedom that we can find in Jesus. When we hang on to guilt and shame over our past, we allow the enemy to put heavy loads of anxiety, depression, and self-defeating thoughts on us. But freedom is found when we realize that these things are not from God and that, in fact, Jesus wishes to set us free from the bondage of these lies. No matter what we have done, God's redemption and love are available to each one of us, right now. We don't have to wait for freedom—it's already here.

Lord, thank you for the freedom we can find in you. Amen.

-Kendra

One Good Step: Write down a lie you have been believing and ask God to help you combat the lie with the truth of his Word so that you can walk in freedom.

Release

Don't copy the behavior and customs of this world, but let God transform
you into a new person by changing the way you think.
ROMANS 12:2

AH, COFFEE. It is one of my favorite things. I love it all: the sound of it brewing,
the smell of it wafting through my house, the warmth on my hands as hot liquid
transfers through my beloved mug. And, of course, the jolt of energy the caffeine
provides.

But lately, I've found myself edgy and slightly anxious, fretting about circumstances beyond my control with far more frequency than is my norm. And when
those fretful thoughts began repeatedly creeping into my conversations, I realized
my thoughts were aligning with behaviors and customs of the world rather than
God's. But what to do? How could I stop the spiral, release the malaise that had
been slowly enveloping me of late?

When Kate mentioned that she'd quit caffeine, I had my answer. Her words
immediately resonated deep within me. And so I did too. I quit coffee—my almost
exclusive source of caffeine, cold turkey—not because that's the best way, but
because it felt like I was being asked to immediately release it, not wean off it. It
had become bad for me, especially these past few weeks and months.

There is nothing quite like releasing a crutch to make you realize how heavily
you'd leaned upon it. My temporary break from coffee is just that—a season in
which I release something I'd begun to cling to a bit too much, causing my already
slightly jittery thoughts to rev up rather than calm them down.

It's different for all of us. God may be asking us to release things that are always
bad for us, or things that are maybe just bad for us right now. He wants us transformed, not trapped. And if something is starting to trap us, he is going to ask us
to release it.

*Lord, help us discern what things might be trapping us, keeping us from the best
you have for us. Help us to release those things, trusting you have something better.
Amen.*

-Julie

One Good Step: What crutch might you need to release—whether it be
for a season or forever? Find an accountability partner and make
a plan for letting it go if quitting cold turkey isn't feasible.

Discover

Can you solve the mysteries of God? Can you discover everything about
the Almighty? Such knowledge is higher than the heavens.

JOB 11:7-8

MY MOM WAS IN FIFTH GRADE when she discovered her mother's gift. The family had recently moved to Mandan, North Dakota, and my grandma Donette was a neighborly sort of person. She'd often visit the neighbor ladies to have coffee and chat.

But one day, my mom ran over to ask a question, something that couldn't wait. Knowing her mother was inside the neighbor's house, she didn't bother knocking on the door, but instead let herself in. Hearing music, she headed toward the source. Standing on the edge of the living room, she hovered in the doorway as she watched Donette play a sweeping song on the neighbor's piano. She was spellbound. She'd had no idea that her mother played the piano at all, much less so beautifully.

As children, we see our parents only in relation to ourselves. In some ways, they are two-dimensional beings, not fully formed beyond the role that defines them to us. Their lives before us, their hopes and dreams, their more complex emotions—all of those are conversations that most parents don't have with young children. It's only later, as adults ourselves, that we can appreciate the fullness of who our parents are, in all of their complex, beautiful, imperfect humanity.

God, too, can sometimes seem unknowable. His ways are mysterious, his decisions unfathomable. And as his children, it can be easy to see him only in relation to ourselves—as a Father who loves us, yes, but one whom we'll never fully understand. Yet as we spend time reading God's Word and spending time in his presence, we'll often discover a fuller picture of him. His mercy. His grace. His justice. His love for truth. His forgiveness. His creativity. His unending love. Those discoveries can not only help us appreciate God, but they can give us a better understanding of our own purpose in this world.

Lord, help us to take the time to discover who you are. We long to know you more fully. Amen.

-Kristin

One Good Step: What's one surprising idea you've discovered about God recently? How does that change your understanding of him?

Communion

The Spirit of the LORD is upon me, for he has anointed me to bring Good News to the poor. He has sent me to proclaim that captives will be released, that the blind will see, that the oppressed will be set free, and that the time of the LORD's favor has come.

LUKE 4:18-19

YEARS AGO I HEARD the story of a young woman whose fiancé called off their wedding at the last minute. She was with her mother when she got the news and immediately fell to the floor in her grief. What has stuck with me was her mother's response. When asked what she did, her mother replied, "I got down on the floor with her." My eyes immediately welled with tears. This mother didn't ignore her daughter, or try to get her up off of the floor too quickly. She saw her child's pain and entered in. She got down on the floor and sat with her.

I remembered this the day we got the call that my daughter's birth mother had passed away. I immediately got down with my daughter and wept with her. She would not cry alone. I sat with her in her pain, unwilling to push past the moment too quickly.

And this is one of the reasons I love Jesus and the act of Communion so much. To me, Communion is the remembering that Jesus came, that he got down on the floor with us. That he carried every pain this world can afford, took it upon himself and offered his comfort and peace to us in the middle of our pain. He wept. He lamented. And we can move past this part too quickly. But Communion is one way we remember his sacrifice. His becoming one of us. His death. Resurrection and life. That offered hope. Good news to the poor. Release of captives. Freedom for the oppressed. And he still offers these today.

Lord, thank you that you came to earth to be with us. Thank you for entering into our pain and suffering and for offering us hope. Amen.

-Kendra

One Good Step: Read Matthew 26:26-29 and then spend some time with Jesus, remembering the ways that he has entered into your pain and communed with you.

Chase

A person who chases fantasies ends up in poverty.
PROVERBS 28:19

"YOUR HAIR IS GORGEOUS. It's so thick and long. And your curls. . . . Ugh! I wish I had hair like yours!"

Lizzie smiled politely as the sales associate waxed eloquently about Lizzie's curls.

Lizzie's hair *is* gorgeous, but it is also prone to matting, snarling, and frizzing in a matter of hours. Growing up with hair requiring extravagant hoop jumping and extra coddling has created a love/hate relationship with her curly locks.

As we walked out of the store, Lizzie sighed, "Why do we always want what we don't have? If they knew what my hair was like, they wouldn't want it."

"Oh, honey. We chase what we don't have. We see the end result and desire it, not recognizing the downsides, all the hard work and effort underpinning it. We're fickle creatures, aren't we?" Bumping her shoulder with mine affectionately as we strolled, I said, "This is a good reminder about chasing. We see someone else's life and want the bigger, fancier house, newer car, and beautiful wardrobe, but if we knew what was really going on in their life, we'd probably realize that we have it really good and not want to trade."

My daughter's thoughtful expression told me I'd scored a gentle point, and we moved on to more interesting topics. But I've circled back to the idea of chasing again and again. As an attorney, I've glimpsed the hardest parts of people's lives and have learned that no matter how perfect someone's life looks, they also hold hardship and hurt. No one is immune, and when we forget that, we risk chasing an illusion when we covet what they have.

Don't chase what another has, which is an empty fantasy. Instead, chase God. Chase the tasks God places before you, chase the Kingdom of God here on earth. It is there that you will find not only what you are looking for but something beyond what you had dared to dream.

Lord, help us discern when we are chasing fantasies and when we are chasing you. When we start to chase the wrong things, pull us back into alignment with you. Amen.

-Julie

One Good Step: What fantasies have you been chasing? Make a list. Then, make a list of three things of God to chase, instead.

Temporary

Our light and momentary troubles are achieving for us an eternal glory that
far outweighs them all. So we fix our eyes not on what is seen, but on what is
unseen, since what is seen is temporary, but what is unseen is eternal.

2 CORINTHIANS 4:17-18, NIV

FEELING SENTIMENTAL THE OTHER DAY, I read through old emails I sent Gram, my
husband's grandmother, more than a decade ago. She passed not long after meeting
our oldest daughter, but in the early years of our marriage she was a bright, steady
presence.

Scanning them, I was struck by the number of times I complained, usually
about work. In the first year of our marriage, my job was a frequent point of
contention. My husband was gone Sunday through Thursday, and I often worked
weekends, so it was difficult to find time to be together. Despite the scheduling
issues, I loved that job. But in my emails, I sounded like a leaky faucet. Bemoaning
a crummy schedule. *Drip.* Analyzing something a boss said. *Drip.* Expressing frustration (envy, more likely) about someone else's duties. *Drip.* Complaining about
a recent hire's better hours. *Drip.* They were mostly petty, but Gram treated each
grievance with kindness and wisdom.

My dad has often said the words "this too shall pass." While I rolled my eyes as
a teenager, age has made me more aware of the wisdom of that statement. Those
dirty diapers and endless nights of crying babies? Long gone. My husband's neck
problems and subsequent surgery? Thankfully, a thing of the past. The long hours
spent doing homework for grad school? Finished, as well. All of those circumstances
felt endless and challenging in the moment—and they were—but they were also
temporary. And in most cases, upon reconsideration, I can only recall the good
parts, the valuable lessons.

Recognizing that our troubles are most likely temporary doesn't diminish the
pain or stress they cause, but it does help us place them in context. When we can
see our current circumstances through the lens of eternity, we'll be empowered to
persevere. And maybe, someday, we'll even look back with gratitude.

*Lord, thank you that your eternal glory will always outweigh our temporary
troubles. Help us to hold on to that truth on the hard days. Amen.*

-Kristin

One Good Thing: Write a short list of challenges that you've experienced.
Thank God for the ways he worked in you and through you during those times.

September

Focus

The heartfelt counsel of a friend is as sweet as perfume and incense.
PROVERBS 27:9

FLIPPING THROUGH THE MAIL as I slowly walked back from the mailbox, I focused on the corner of Aunt Claire's beautiful stationery envelope barely peeking between the bills and random junk mail.

Tugging it out, I smiled at her familiar penmanship and the extra stickers she used as decoration. *I'll set this one aside to savor over my cup of tea, when I can give it my full attention,* I thought as I sorted through the rest, noting nothing else of joyful interest.

Aunt Claire tells the best stories. The only girl of five siblings and thirteen years older than my dad, she slips me unknown tidbits that are funny and heartwarming about grandparents I can barely remember, connecting me to my roots in new ways.

And as I write her back on my own beautiful stationery, hunted down when pages covertly ripped from Jon's spiral-bound notebooks no longer would do, I find myself slowing down, savoring, focusing on her, on the moment, on our friendship that has been steadily growing as we do this pen pal thing.

Social media and texting and emails are all lovely for staying in touch, but there is nothing quite like holding the same paper someone you love held, pausing to squint over a letter or a word to bring the present moment into focus as chaos fades.

I love these moments—the writing and reading of letters, the physically tangible connection when too many miles separate us. I appreciate the slowing down, the focus on this relationship, this time and place instead of living constantly in the future, anticipating the next task, the next event, the next everything. And I find myself wondering why I allow my focus to be constantly pulled forward into the future rather than pausing to simply be in this moment, present.

Lord, help us to focus on the people, places, and things in this present moment. May we be women who focus as much on the now as we do on the future. Amen.

-Julie

One Good Step: Who needs your attention right now? Practice focusing on the present moment rather than future events today.

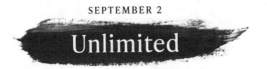

Unlimited

I pray that from his glorious, unlimited resources he will empower you
with inner strength through his Spirit.

EPHESIANS 3:16

BEEP. Beep. Beep. The alarm jarred me from sleep, and I tumbled out of bed to slap the off button on the clock. Sitting back on the edge of the bed, I rubbed the sleep from my eyes and tried to wake up. It was Saturday morning, and I'd need to leave shortly in order to make the 8 a.m. start time for our weekly women's Bible study. Shuffling down the stairs, I brewed coffee and grabbed a to-go cup on my way out the door.

Though I loved our Bible study, I had difficulty getting out of bed each Saturday morning. I've always been a night owl, but when Saturday mornings arrived, those late-night tendencies felt like a limitation. Although I firmly believe that Scripture is true in reminding us that we can do all things through Christ who gives us strength (see Philippians 4:13), my own limitations sometimes get in the way of truly believing and resting in God's unlimited power and authority.

A few years ago, I read a fascinating article. In it, the authors noted that scientists had discovered the gene that governs whether someone is an early riser or a night owl. I was thrilled—finally, I could stop feeling shame over my late-night tendencies. They were simply part of who I am. Though it seems small, the revelation sparked a question: What else spurs shame or insecurity? I'm sensitive, I'm shy, I like solitude. I accept those facets of myself, but sometimes struggle to embrace them. Yet aren't those characteristics just another kind of late-night gene?

Thankfully, God is not limited by what we see as our limitations. His power is unlimited, vast, infinite. Regardless of whether we see a part of ourselves as a blessing or a hardship, our ability to carry out God's work in the world is not constrained by our own limitations. For it is not us, but Christ who lives within us, whose unlimited strength and power we can access. Knowing that, we can be secure in his love and rest in his power.

Lord, thank you for the unlimited love you pour on us and the power of your strength at work within us. Help us to recognize and find our confidence in you. Amen.

-Kristin

One Good Step: Write down three traits or characteristics that feel limiting to you. Next, cross each of those items out and write down today's verse instead, reinforcing God's unlimited power.

Know

Be still, and know that I am God!
PSALM 46:10

I WENT TO COLLEGE as a postsecondary student my senior year of high school. Being so young, I had to wait to register for classes, and the choices were always somewhat limited. One of the only open options that fall was an ethics class.

One paper we had to write was about God and if he was real. An older gentleman in the class stated very early on in the class discussion that he was an atheist. As he explained why, the pain of his past experiences in the church was evident. As the conversation progressed, I shared that I had a belief in God. The gentleman came up to me after class and asked if he could read my paper. I agreed.

The rest of that week I pored over hardcover commentaries, searching Scriptures to base my belief of God on and all that I knew about him. I prayed as I wrote my paper, sharing why I believed in God and his goodness. When we received our papers back, my classmate and I sat outside as he read my words.

I waited for a few moments before he whispered, "Did you write this for me?" I was dumbfounded. I barely knew this man or his story.

I smiled at him and shrugged. "I just wrote what I know and believe to be true about God." He nodded and thanked me for letting him read my words as we said goodbye.

I never had another class with that man, but I often think of him and the journey he must have been on with God. I'm hoping my words were one of many small catalysts propelling him toward the love and knowledge of who God really is.

So many things can happen to us in life that are unfair or even evil that can skew the way that we see God. That's why knowing who God is, is so important. We must ask ourselves: *Do we know what we believe about God and his character?* Because these are the truths that will anchor us to our faith when the hard things in life come at us. If we settle what we believe about him, we will only need to be still and know that he is God.

Lord, help me to simply be still and know that you are God today. Amen.

-Kendra

One Good Step: Take time today reflecting on what you know to be true about God.

Glorify

May the God of endurance and encouragement grant you to live in such harmony
with one another, in accord with Christ Jesus, that together you may with
one voice glorify the God and Father of our Lord Jesus Christ.
ROMANS 15:5-6, ESV

I SPOTTED THE MAMMOTH CARDBOARD BOXES stacked on the steps of our front porch as soon as our car pulled into the driveway.

"What in the world are those?" I asked, turning a suspicious eye on my husband. "Did you order something online?"

He shrugged, looking confused, until his face cleared. "Oh, it must be the diapers my friends sent!"

Nonplussed, I continued to stare until he explained. "I told my buddies that we were bringing supplies down to Minneapolis, and they offered to help out by sending something for us to drop off."

Hearing his explanation, I couldn't help but pause and thank God for the way he is glorified when communities come together to serve one another. Recent unrest in Minneapolis and a pause in the city's bus service had left many neighborhoods stranded, their residents unable to reach stores in order to purchase groceries and other supplies. As a result, many churches and people from surrounding communities had banded together to provide food, diapers, and personal care items. Earlier in the week, a few of us had traveled to the area to spend the day at a local church, distributing necessities.

Despite the outpouring of support, the need was still great. On the phone the next day, Tim happened to mention what we were doing to a couple of coworkers who are also friends. Immediately, they offered to help.

Jesus demonstrated servant leadership by serving others during his ministry on earth, and I believe he is glorified whenever we come together to help one another. Though Tim's friends live thousands of miles away, they sent a collective 1,300 diapers to our home. Cluttering up the steps of my home, the result of their generosity was amazing to witness. But the heart behind their decision to help was equally encouraging. As members of the body of Christ, each of us has a part to play. When we work together in harmony, our collective voices—and the actions we take to serve one another—can glorify God.

Lord, thank you for the gift of friends who come alongside us. May our words and actions produce a sweet harmony that glorifies your name. Amen.

-Kristin

One Good Step: Glorify God by serving alongside someone today.

Give

You must each decide in your heart how much to give. And don't give reluctantly
or in response to pressure. "For God loves a person who gives cheerfully."

2 CORINTHIANS 9:7

"WHAT DO YOU THINK—how much should we give?" I glanced at Aaron's profile in
the driver's seat, broaching the subject of meeting a need we'd encountered the
night before.

One of the things I love most about my husband, Aaron, is his generosity. He
tends toward extravagant, often going above and beyond in his caretaking of those
around him. He picks up hard-to-find favorite desserts and beverages as a part of
his travel for work, delivering a beloved treat from a faraway place to a neighbor
or friend upon arriving home. He lends a hand moving, hauling, and building for
friends of friends. He mans the grill and refills the buffet line, happy to let others
visit during our backyard barbecues.

And while all of these things are good, it's his generosity with money that often
has me quietly thanking God that I married such a genuinely good man. When
encountering a financial need, I've learned to ask Aaron what he thinks and then
bite my tongue on my instinctive stingy response of "that's too much" at the number he suggests. He's almost always right, almost always tuned in to the number
Jesus would whisper also to me, if I only stopped and listened instead of wanting
to immediately raise a protest.

I've learned to follow Aaron's lead in generosity and have watched as—over and
over—God has provided even as we've taken care of others. While many Scriptures
discuss the technicalities of tithing, our heart condition matters as we give. Giving
while reluctant or grumpy is not what God wants. Everything we have has been
given to us by God, and he looks for people who'll hold his resources in open hands,
willing to partner with him when asked. We cannot outgive God, and when we give
without grumbling, he brings blessings back to us in exponential ways.

*Lord, unclench our fists from the resources you've provided and align our hearts
with yours, knowing that giving freely and cheerfully will be a blessing for others as
well as ourselves. Amen.*

-Julie

One Good Step: Meet a need with heart-stopping generosity this week,
and watch how God returns the blessing.

Settle

Is anyone thirsty? Come and drink—even if you have no money!
Come, take your choice of wine or milk—it's all free!
ISAIAH 55:1

IT WAS ABOUT FIVE WEEKS after I'd had my last baby that I finally decided it was time to clear the maternity clothes out of my closet. As I started to unpack my regular clothes once again, I began to see my things in a new light, noticing things I had overlooked before. Items that had small holes or were worn out, jeans with frayed bottoms, shirts from five years ago with the tags still on that just never quite fit.

In my moment of feeling empowered, I decided to get rid of everything in my closet that was mediocre, worn out, or never really fit well. And as I worked, I thought, *Why did I settle for these things?*

I began to realize that my closet mirrored the rest of my life. I recalled a number of times that I settled for something less than I could have.

The boyfriend after college who was a "great Christian guy," but would make offhand comments about how large my hips and thighs were, leading me to question my weight—I settled.

Being my own worst enemy by not trying new things because I was too afraid and simply wanted to play it safe—I settled.

And my closet was just another indication of a way that I had settled. *Maybe when I lose these last five pounds, these pants will fit just right.* So I settled.

As I continued to pack things up, I realized that God has so much more for me than the lies I'd settled for in the past.

Isn't this process something we all need to do? Whether it's our physical closet or just in the recesses of our minds and hearts, we can all look back on a time where we settled for less than God would give us. When the truth is, God would invite us to speak up for what we want. Go for goals that are wildly scary. And walk each day with confidence that he will give us what we need.

Lord, show us places in our lives where we've settled, and give us courage to move ahead with confidence that comes from you. Amen.

-Kendra

One Good Step: Pray and then take action from a place in your life where you feel like you settled.

Still

The LORD will fight for you; you need only to be still.

EXODUS 14:14, NIV

AN OFFHAND COMMENT from the night before was bothering me. As I lathered shampoo into my hair and dried it afterward, my stomach felt tied in knots. I thought of all the zippy rebuttals I could have said, argued with TV defense lawyer-level verve. Each time I replayed the encounter in my mind, I walked away feeling confident in my response.

I have pretty epic arguments that—thankfully for all involved—remain within the confines of my own head. I never think of those zingers in the moment, and that's probably a good thing. Because by the time I moved on to applying my makeup, I felt convicted to give my friend the benefit of the doubt. And instead of trying to sort the problem out immediately, I prayed. As I did, I felt a tug on my heart to simply wait and be still.

To my surprise, my friend messaged me a couple of days later. "I'm sorry I've been so scattered lately," she said. "I have felt so overwhelmed by life. I was thinking again about our conversation the other night, and I realized afterward you may have taken what I said the wrong way. *I'm sorry.*" As I read her message, I couldn't help but smile a little, glad I'd listened to God's nudge to be still and wait.

There's an assumption that stillness is simply inaction. But what if it isn't?

As the Egyptians pursued the Israelites into the desert after their flight from slavery, the Israelites began to think their destruction was inevitable (see Exodus 14). Even though God had faithfully helped them escape Egypt, they still didn't trust him. Freedom still felt like it was out of reach. Despondent, they asked Moses if he had brought them to the desert to die. He admonished them for their lack of trust in God and told them that the fight wasn't theirs, but God's. They needed only to be still.

When we pursue God's call on our life—as God had called the Israelites out of slavery into a new land—he is faithful. We don't need to fight for our own way. Our surrender to him isn't a sign of giving up; it's a sign of trust that he will do what he promised.

Lord, help us to recognize the areas of our lives where we need to trust you and be still. Amen.

-Kristin

One Good Step: What areas of your life are a struggle? What might happen if you chose to trust God fully and be still?

Steadfast

Oh give thanks to the LORD, for he is good,
for his steadfast love endures forever!
PSALM 107:1, ESV

I'VE KEPT A JOURNAL for as long as I can remember, documenting passages of Scripture that I'm reading and life events that arise. Some days I write more, others less. One morning as I spent my quiet time with the Lord, I looked back to the year before. It had been challenging, and I wanted to remember all that had happened. That year my journal had become a safe place for me to share my heart as I walked through a hard season, the hardest one of my life thus far. I reread words written through tears. Lament and angst covered the pages over situations and relationships that often felt, and in reality were, beyond my ability to control. But as I kept flipping through the pages toward the new year, I could see in ever so small ways how God's steadfast love consistently showed up for me throughout the year. Each day, he was there. And in the scope of the entire year, I saw progress that was undetectable when just looking at one or two days.

As I spent a few moments in prayer, I wrote this thanksgiving in my journal: "Lord, thank you for healing us in a million small ways that we didn't even see or notice. Thank you for your steadfast love that meets us every day." And my heart was immediately filled with gratitude in that moment for a God who is good, and whose love endures.

The steadfast love of God is easy to miss when we aren't necessarily looking for it. Life can be hard and good; we all experience seasons of rejoicing and times of pain. Through it all, Jesus remains the same, showing up in our joys and our sorrows. His steadfast love really does endure forever. We just have to have the eyes to see it.

Lord, thank you for your steadfast love that shows up continually, day in and day out, in each of our lives. May we lean into your love in every season of life. Amen.

-Kendra

One Good Step: Get a journal or notebook and begin to write down
a sentence or two of what God is teaching you each day
so that you can notice his steadfast love over time.

Refine

These have come so that the proven genuineness of your faith—of greater worth
than gold, which perishes even though refined by fire—may result in praise,
glory and honor when Jesus Christ is revealed.

1 PETER 1:7, NIV

IT HAD BEEN A MAD SCRAMBLE of a morning. Burnt waffles, lost homework, and then
the *coup de grâce*: my first grader stepped in a pile of dog poo, just as the school
bus rounded the corner, heading toward our stop. Frantically wiping poop off a
small left shoe (still attached to the child) with a nearby twig, I finally surrendered,
sighing resignedly as I waved the bus on, without my kid.

My evening ended with an email cheerily rejecting my submission. And the
stuff in between these two unpleasant events? Well. Let's just say that I'd spent the
day navigating especially difficult conflicts both as a lawyer and a parent almost
nonstop between the shoe incident and the rejection letter. In other words, I was
tired, cranky, and at the end of my string.

As I sat alone in the still of the night with the rest of my household tucked in
and sleeping sweetly, I pondered refinement and what God has to say about it at
work in our lives, wondering what would happen if we acted the most like Christ in
the moments when we want nothing more than to throw a tantrum like a toddler
in Target.

Ugh. That's hard to hear, especially in the midst of a bad day. But it's true. What
if we viewed frustrations and annoyances, hard moments and tough weeks as refining faith moments rather than allowing them to derail us into the ditch of emotional caterwauling? Is it easy? Of course not, but is it worth the effort? Certainly.

Just as gold and silver become purer and more valuable for having gone through
the refiner's fire, so do we. When we face challenges, turning to God rather than
running away, we emerge stronger spiritually, with faith roots having dug deeper
and wider, anchoring us, giving us a firmer foundation than before.

*Lord, help us to see the refinement, the value in hard moments, situations, and
experiences. May we emerge from those encounters with our faith not only intact, but
having grown stronger. Amen.*

-Julie

One Good Step: Shift your perspective on a hard situation, viewing it through the lens
of a refinement of your faith. How does that perspective shift change your response?

Marvel

You made all the delicate, inner parts of my body and knit me together in
my mother's womb. Thank you for making me so wonderfully complex!
Your workmanship is marvelous—how well I know it.

PSALM 139:13-14

BUMPING GENTLY up the side of the mountain in the gondola, I swung my gaze to
the side to gauge our current height, my stomach dropping as I registered how
small the parking lot appeared below. We were in Banff for a work conference, but
a break in the schedule meant that we had the day free to explore the countryside.

Arriving at the top of Sulphur Mountain, we walked outside to breathtaking
views. Fluffy clouds kissed the tops of mountains that surrounded us on all sides,
casting shadows on lush green forests and hillsides. Turquoise rivers wound through
the valleys below, while the city of Banff looked miniature in the distance. Taken
together, the view could have been a movie backdrop or maybe a painting, too
perfect to be real. But the relentless stiff breeze and hot sun warming my skin
reminded me that it was, in fact, real. As I inhaled a deep breath to take it in, all I
could do was marvel.

All too easily, we can get caught up in the mundane details of our lives. Wake,
eat breakfast, work, make dinner, watch TV, go to bed—the routine can seem an
endless *Groundhog Day* that leaves us feeling flat and restless. Caught up in our
humdrum habits, our focus turns inward, worrying about finances, appointments,
emails we need to return, and mounting responsibilities that suck our time and
energy. Unfortunately, the breathtaking, top-of-the-mountain moments can feel
few and far between. But what if we took the time to really look at the intricacy of
the big and small details of our lives each day? What if we took a closer look at the
way the sun-dappled light shines down through a cluster of trees, the shiny shell
of a ladybug wandering by, the way our breath moves effortlessly in and out of our
bodies? All of these are small miracles, marvels of the world created by our Father
God. Choosing to see the everyday marvels in our lives is the first step toward
appreciating them in a new way.

Lord, help us see the world around us with new eyes. Amen.

-Kristin

One Good Step: Find one thing in the world around you to marvel at.

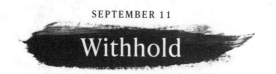

Withhold

The LORD will withhold no good thing from those who do what is right.

PSALM 84:11

I'D BEEN FEELING FRAZZLED and didn't want to admit it to anyone, not even myself. For several days I'd rushed around, feeling hurried and disgruntled. I snapped at my kids and husband as I tried to cross things off the mental list of things to do in my mind that never really went away. With deadlines looming, I was feeling the stress as I sat down for a chunk of time to write.

During the middle of my session, a message came through on my phone from a woman who is an acquaintance. "I have a playlist called His Presence on my Spotify," she wrote. "And I prayed for you and your book and cowriters this morning while listening to this. I wanted to send these four songs to you. Soak in his presence. He knows just what you need. He will not withhold from you."

As her words came across my screen, I stopped what I was doing, and tears came to my eyes. I took a deep breath as the truth of what she said resonated in my spirit. I turned on one of the songs she sent and sat quietly while I listened. The lies that'd been hiding just below the surface, telling me that I wasn't capable of completing the work, began to rise, and in the light of God's truth, were exposed for what they were. Just lies. Replaced with the reminder that God would not withhold from me. As peace began to replace the fear, I started to write, trusting that God would give me the wisdom that I needed.

So often we can find ourselves living with far less than God would desire for us, not seeing or asking for what we really need. But God is not going to withhold himself from us. When we need peace, love, or wisdom, he is there. We can live lives filled with the fruit of his Spirit—love, joy, peace, patience, and more—not because of what we can conjure up within ourselves, but because of the great abundance that God has to offer us.

Lord, thank you that you do not withhold from us. Help us to ask for what we need and believe that you will be there to offer it to us. Amen.

-Kendra

One Good Step: In what area of your life are you worried that God may be withholding something from you? How can you trust him to meet your needs today?

Cherish

A bowl of vegetables with someone you love is better
than steak with someone you hate.

PROVERBS 15:17

OUCH. I tried not to let my wince show as Frank stepped on my toes, again. *He is a terrible dancer, probably the worst I've ever danced with.* I groused mentally as we stumbled around the ballroom in fits and starts instead of gliding gracefully like everyone else.

My law school classmate and I were at a swing dance class put on by a community dance organization, and part of the lesson required us to rotate partners, learning to dance with a variety of people. My friend loved dancing, and she had talked me into tagging along because she didn't want to go alone.

"Sorry. I'm no good at this," Frank whisper-confessed, bringing my wandering thoughts back to the present as we executed a clumsy turn. "My wife really wanted to try dancing. I can't dance, and I have no rhythm, but I'm trying. Sorry I'm mangling your feet."

And with that revelation, my irritation melted away. I laughed off the pain, telling him that he was a sweetheart for making a valiant effort and steered the conversation toward questions about how he met his wife.

I've thought often of Frank over the years, especially when someone I love is asking me to do something I don't love, I'm not good at, and I simply don't want to do. Frank's efforts were an act of cherishing his wife. His willingness to support something she loved revealed his love for her in a way that was glaringly obvious to a random law student getting her toes smashed by his efforts.

How am I cherishing the people I love: my parents, siblings, husband, children, girlfriends? That's oftentimes a painful question, one I find myself falling short in when life goes on autopilot. Cherishing requires intentionality, time, and effort— all things in short supply when I'm stressed, when my attempt at work-life balance has swung too far off the centerline, when I see people primarily for what they can do for me rather than who they are to me and, more importantly, who they are to God.

Lord, as I pause for a long moment, bring three people to mind that need to be cherished. Show me exactly what cherishing looks like in each situation. Amen.

-Julie

One Good Step: Make intentional, specific plans to cherish
the three people God brought to mind.

Compassion

I was hungry, and you fed me. I was thirsty, and you gave me a drink.
I was a stranger, and you invited me into your home.

MATTHEW 25:35

"WHO DID YOU NOTICE TODAY that needed a friend?" we asked around the dinner table one evening.

My daughter quickly spoke up: "I asked someone to sit with me at lunch."

And then my son responded, "And I played with someone new during recess."

It seems like such a simple thing to do, but noticing others who may be left out, different than we are or in need of a friend, is the groundwork that teaches our kids compassion and care for others. It's the small daily act of noticing others and their needs that can easily get lost in all the busy activities of the day. Developing compassion is a habit I struggle to always be mindful of myself, and find I have to be intentional to continue to do it.

But we aren't the only ones who can easily forget. It's a reminder we find God offering the Israelites again and again throughout Scripture. In the Old Testament, God is often found telling his people—don't forget the poor, those who are new to your area or different in some way, those without family. And we need this reminder as much today as the Israelites did all those years ago.

This compassion for others wasn't just something God asked the Israelites to do; it was something Jesus reminded his followers of as well, but he takes it even one step further. He tells his followers, including us, that when we do these things—care for others, show compassion and love—it's as if we are doing them to Jesus himself. And when I think about my life and activities, I want to live in such a way that invites Jesus in—every day.

If we could see the compassion we offer as one way that we allow Jesus into our lives, we could change the world around us. It's easy to do, really. Begin by looking around at the places you already go and the people you already see. Notice who might need some extra attention—and start there.

Lord, give us eyes to see the needs of those around us and fill our hearts with compassion to act when necessary. Amen.

-Kendra

One Good Step: Show someone compassion today either in word or deed.

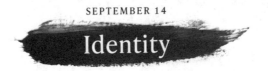

Identity

Once you had no identity as a people; now you are God's people. Once you
received no mercy; now you have received God's mercy.

1 PETER 2:10

A COUPLE OF YEARS AGO, friends of ours took their family to Sweden. On a visit to
Drottningholm Palace, my friend Samantha ran into trouble. Though she had pre-
purchased tickets for the castle on her phone, she couldn't connect to the internet
to download them.

Noticing two women descending the large staircase, she asked one of them if
she would mind helping with the tickets. Despite her attempts, the woman couldn't
get it to work either. She regretfully passed the phone back and continued on her
way. After some trial and error, the ticket issue was eventually resolved.

As they waited for their tickets to be scanned, Samantha noticed postcards, one
of which featured the lady they had just encountered.

"Excuse me, sir, can you tell me who this is?" she asked the staffer.

"Crown Princess Victoria," he replied.

Wide-eyed, my friend realized that she'd just asked a princess—a member of
the royal family of Sweden—for help, without even realizing it. On one hand, it
seemed like the worst sort of luck to overlook such an important detail. But on
the other hand, perhaps the princess didn't mind the mistaken identity. After all,
my friend had simply seen her and thought, *There's someone who looks like they can
help*. Don't we all want to move beyond the labels that normally define us and be
known as people who can help?

Our identity is formed by more than the roles that define us. We are more
than family members, friends, our occupation, our social class, or any other label.
Rather, the qualities and beliefs that distinguish us from someone else are what
forms our identity and, as Jesus-followers, our identity is ultimately found in him.
The words we speak, the actions we take, the way we move in this world—in all
of those details, our lives should reflect the ways of Jesus. Like the princess who
looked like someone who could help, let's let the love and grace of Jesus be what
forms our identity in this world.

*Lord, help us find our identity in you. Give us the wisdom to recognize what that
looks like in our daily lives. Amen.*

-Kristin

One Good Step: List some labels that you or others have used to identify yourself.
Reconsider them through the lens of Jesus and his example.

Near

But as for me, how good it is to be near God! I have made the Sovereign LORD
my shelter, and I will tell everyone about the wonderful things you do.
PSALM 73:28

As LIZZIE STOOD on the cusp of kindergarten, I was most nervous about the school bus.

My own childhood experience along winding country roads taught me what happens in the back of the bus. I remember the bus bully, the teasing, the language not appropriate for little ears. And, given my own experiences, I told my sweet daughter the cardinal rule of all bus riding: sit near the driver, as close as possible.

When the first day of school came, I wiped a stray tear or three, waved, and watched until the bus disappeared around the corner. As the week wore on, I watched her little head bobbing past window after window while she wove her way off the bus in the afternoons—obviously coming from a seat at the very back of the section she was allowed to sit in.

It was sometime that first weekend when she quietly confessed to trouble. A first-grade boy would sit next to her or nearby while chanting, "Kindergartner, kindergartner, kindergartner." Rather than get angry or say *I told you so*, I helped her brainstorm solutions, pondering what she might do differently Monday morning.

When the bus pulled to a stop that Monday afternoon, I smiled secretly as I saw two little girls seated immediately behind the bus driver. As my girl bounded off the bus, she exclaimed, "It worked! That naughty boy tried to tease me and the bus driver told him to leave us alone!"

I am no different than my daughter. I know life is best lived near to God. I know that we need to spend time in his presence, in the Bible, to pray first before reacting to difficult circumstances and situations—and yet I sometimes allow busyness and distractions to interfere, to drift me toward the proverbial back of the bus and away from the driver.

Lord, keep us near to you, drawing us back to your truth and your foundations when we are tempted by the empty allure found in the back of the bus. Amen.

-Julie

One Good Step: Pick one way to draw closer to God this week—
worship music in the morning, praying while in the shower,
listening to Scripture as you go for an evening walk.

Forgive

We praise God for the glorious grace he has poured out on us who belong to his dear Son. He is so rich in kindness and grace that he purchased our freedom with the blood of his Son and forgave our sins.

EPHESIANS 1:6-7

MY SISTER-IN-LAW MARLENE was startled and worried when an old coworker showed up at her office door. Her last meeting with the large man now looming in her doorway hadn't been pleasant.

Three years earlier, Marlene had been a department head, overseeing about six hundred employees. One of her least favorite aspects of the job was discipline. One day, she found out that an employee was stealing small tools and paper goods. In his defense, the man told her that he was giving them to his church, but she had no way of knowing if that was true. All she knew was that a lot of items were disappearing, and he needed to be terminated.

On the day he reappeared at her door, she was working for another governmental agency in a different town. Marlene's office was far away from the front counter, and when he arrived without announcing his presence, her initial thought was that he was there to get his revenge. But to her surprise, he wasn't there to do her any harm.

"I wanted to thank you for what you did," he said. Although he lost his children when he lost his job, the three years since being fired had been transformative. After hitting bottom, he was forced to look at the person he'd become, and asked God for forgiveness. He was proud of the person he now was and wanted Marlene to know that he was glad she had fired him. It had been the catalyst for lasting change.

Although we're asked to forgive others, sometimes the hardest person to forgive is ourselves. Guilt and shame are a heavy burden to bear. But when we recognize the kindness and mercy we have received through the gift of Jesus' sacrifice for our sins, and mirror his gift by forgiving ourselves, we can finally give ourselves permission to fully experience true freedom and hope for the future.

Lord, thank you for the gift of forgiveness. Help us to forgive ourselves. Amen.

-Kristin

One Good Step: Is there something for which you haven't forgiven yourself? Ask God to help you address any feelings of guilt or shame.

Support

Share each other's burdens, and in this way obey the law of Christ.

GALATIANS 6:2

I SAT QUIETLY as I listened to a dear friend engage in conversation with her parents one evening while we were all having dinner together. They were speaking of her younger sister, whose life was currently in chaos. Poor choices and unhealthy people were wreaking havoc in her life, as everyone who loved her watched with concern over her health and well-being.

My friend told her parents that they must be honest in their concern for her sister. They couldn't just continue to ignore her behavior and pretend like it wasn't happening. They didn't need to condemn her, but she needed to know that they knew what she was doing and that they loved and supported her through it all. Her parents nodded supposed understanding before her dad stated, "There's things about your past we still don't want to know about!"

My friend's shoulders shrugged as she made eye contact with me, and I tried to offer her an encouraging smile. "But, Dad," she responded, "how can you really support someone fully if you don't want to know what they've gone through? If you'd rather they just didn't tell you all the hard stuff?"

And I stared at my friend, tears in our eyes. I knew she was no longer thinking of her sister. She'd walked through her own trauma, a story I'd heard and cried tears with her through. I also knew that her parents did not know of her struggle, and her words resonated in my mind long after our evening ended. Her parents loved her, but they did not truly know all that she had been through and therefore hadn't supported her in ways that she truly needed.

Real support comes when we fully acknowledge all the good and hard parts of another person's story. When we can share fully and honestly everything that we have been through, and allow others to do the same with us, that's how we share each other's burdens. We weren't meant to carry burdens alone. We were meant to support one another.

Lord, thank you for the gift of community and support we can find in other believers. Help us to share our burdens and help us to carry others' burdens as well. Amen.

-Kendra

One Good Step: Who has been a good support to you? Who can you support by listening and carrying their burden with them today?

Empower

For God has not given us a spirit of fear and timidity,
but of power, love, and self-discipline.

2 TIMOTHY 1:7

"DAD!" A small, panicked voice echoed from the bedroom across the hall. As my husband rolled out of bed, the clock glowed with a time well past midnight.

Shadows. They'd become suddenly sinister in the eyes of our preschooler, causing terror night after night. We'd searched our memories, unable to pinpoint when and how and where fear first planted its seed, and what triggered the sudden onslaught.

I'd find myself whispering explanations and logic into little ears before bed each night, trying to empower him with knowledge and logic, trying to break the stranglehold fear had gained over my beloved child. Even as I prayed over the dreams and sleep of someone I love beyond words, my own silent, pleading prayer was banging around inside my head: *Lord, I do not want this for my child!* And the responsive thought that immediately flitted across my mind was this: "Daughter, I do not want this for *any* of my children."

Fear prevents us from becoming the greatest version of ourselves. It sneaks deep inside, twisting us up and holding us captive. Let me be clear: God does not want fear to hold us captive, but we are not shamed for being fearful. Instead, God empowers us to push back against fear, equipping us with spiritual truths to stand firm against it. And, because God is the Creator of all, including science and medicine, he has given us earthly tools in the form of godly therapists and pharmaceuticals to address trauma and rebalance hormones that can sometimes be the root of fear.

He empowers us to face our fears, to stand strong and with courage, but he never makes us stand alone. He promises in Joshua 1:9, Psalm 27:1, Isaiah 41:10, John 14:27, Philippians 4:6-7, and in so many other verses that he is with us in this battle, always. Always.

Lord, thank you for empowering us against fear while promising to stand with us as we face it. May the truth of your promise sink in deep into every crevice of our soul. Amen.

-Julie

One Good Step: Pick your favorite Scripture about fear and write it out, posting it on your bathroom mirror so you can read it and see yourself at the same time.

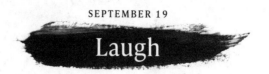

Laugh

She is clothed with strength and dignity, and she laughs without fear of the future.
PROVERBS 31:25

MY FRIEND SANDY has the most infectious laugh I've ever heard. It's unmistakable. Unforgettable. It's the kind of laugh that, when you hear it loud and clear from across the room, it automatically brings a smile to your own face. Somehow it makes you feel like you're in on the joke too.

There's power in laughter. It relaxes your body, decreases stress hormones, increases infection-fighting antibodies, triggers the release of feel-good endorphins, increases blood flow (good for the heart), and may even help you live longer—one Norwegian study found that individuals with a strong sense of humor outlived those who didn't laugh as much.

I met Sandy a few years ago through a women's ministry organization. The more I've gotten to know her, the more I appreciate and value her laugh. Her ability to laugh isn't because her life has been easy but because she continues to trust God. Three of her five children have had learning challenges, including autism, attention deficit disorder, a reading disability, epilepsy, and depression. Early on, she and her husband were told that one of their children might never speak. One of their children is currently estranged from the family. And Sandy herself has struggled at times with mental health challenges. Yet she is authentically joyful—in all circumstances.

Recently, her husband died unexpectedly. A post I saw on social media the other day immediately brought a smile to my face: Sandy and her granddaughter, eating apples and peanut butter on the porch. *Live life while you mourn a life*, part of her caption read. Sandy told me once that laughter in the midst of storms is good for others' souls too. Sandy is able to smile, and laugh, and have joy because she continues to trust God. He's strong enough to carry her in every circumstance. The child they were told might never speak? He's now a college graduate with a family of his own. The challenges we face reveal who we are and what we truly believe about God. Sandy trusts God and, because of it, she's able to laugh.

Lord, thank you for the gift of laughter. Amen.

-Kristin

One Good Step: Watch or read something that makes you laugh.

Community

What then shall we say, brothers and sisters? When you come together, each of you has a hymn, or a word of instruction, a revelation, a tongue or an interpretation. Everything must be done so that the church may be built up.

1 CORINTHIANS 14:26, NIV

EVERY SUNDAY NIGHT a small group of believers meet together in homes to study the Scriptures and life of Jesus. We are a collective of married and single people, with different faith backgrounds and ethnicities. Everyone is given the opportunity to share their thoughts on the Scripture that is shared. Each person's voice brings a richness to the conversation from their perspective and life experience. I often leave pondering questions or new things about Scripture that I hadn't previously known or given much thought to beforehand.

Since we started meeting and discussing, I've started to see Scripture in such a new light. How often the text is written to "we" and not just "me." I'm taking a step back to better understand that the New Testament was written to the body of believers as a whole, and not just in a way that always applies only to my individual life. This has led me to acknowledge how needed community is within the context of our faith.

Our Christian life was meant to be lived within a community of believers who can come alongside us, encourage us, challenge us, and help us to grow in our understanding of Jesus. When we come together, everything must be done so that the church, the people of God, is built up in our faith, understanding and love so that we can go out and live the ways of Jesus in our everyday lives. If we don't have community with other believers, in whatever format works for us, we won't have all that we need to live a godly life. We'll miss the richness that comes from listening to others and learning from their varied life experiences. We need each other. We need community.

Lord, thank you for the community of people you place in our lives that can challenge us and build us up so that we are able to go out and love people as you did. Amen.

-Kendra

One Good Step: Are you currently a part of a community of believers that uplifts and challenges you? If not, spend some time today asking God how you could go about finding the right place for you to be.

Align

Obey my commands and live! Guard my instructions as you guard your own eyes.
PROVERBS 7:2

"Oh, Kate. I think I'm broken." My answer came out as a chuckle ending in a groan in response to her cheery greeting asking how I was that morning. A misaligned rib was jabbing at what felt like my lung as I shifted on her adjusting table, trying to find a comfortable spot.

One of my dearest friends is a chiropractor, and her wisdom and skill have been invaluable, helping me sort out pregnancy-induced sciatica as well as some otherwise mysterious health issues with a family member. This time, I'd been tossed off a ski tube in dramatic fashion, and she clucked over me as she realigned what must have been every rib along the right side of my body.

One of the many things Kate has taught me is that our bodies are amazing, miraculous creations, especially when our vertebrae are aligned and our nervous systems are functioning as God intended. It's amazing how twisted up nerves can cause problems in every area of our body, creating weaknesses for disease to infiltrate that wouldn't otherwise exist and, in turn, providing better than usual immunity when we untwist them, allowing them to send and receive signals, uninhibited.

The more I learn about how our bodies work when our spines are aligned, the more I am reminded of the critical importance of cultivating spiritual health. We need to stay aligned with God to function at our very best. Aligning ourselves spiritually means we listen and obey, repent and seek forgiveness, growing deeper in our faith rather than staying in one spot for too long, becoming stagnant. We are called to an active, living faith that coexists alongside every part of our day, even in the mundane ordinary.

Just as I carve out time to see Kate to make sure my nervous system is aligned, I need to examine what I'm doing well (or not) from time to time with God, correcting my spiritual course. Alignment requires intentionality and work, but the reward is priceless.

Lord, show us where we need to realign ourselves with you, getting back on track so that we might be the best version of ourselves and the best examples of you that we can be. Amen.

-Julie

One Good Step: Consider where you need to be better aligned with God in your thoughts, words, or actions. Make one change today.

Enjoy

*I decided there is nothing better than to enjoy food and drink and to find satisfaction
in work. Then I realized that these pleasures are from the hand of God.*
ECCLESIASTES 2:24

THE MORNING WE LEFT Northern California, there was a red flag warning, meaning
that conditions were right for fires to start and spread rapidly. We'd spent a beautiful weekend with friends and my husband's brother, Phil, and our sister-in-law,
Marlene. The weather had been perfect. But as we taxied down the runway, I could
tell the wind had picked up significantly.

That night, just as Phil dropped into bed, he got a call. A wildfire was spreading and he needed to evacuate. Grabbing his wallet and a few items, he jumped in
his car and left. Marlene had left the area that afternoon for a visit to another part
of the state, so Phil waited alone in the Costco parking lot as the sun rose. By that
afternoon—little more than twenty-four hours after our plane took flight—their
home in a residential area of Santa Rosa had burned to the ground.

The loss felt shocking. Everyone was safe, and that was the most important
consideration. But it still hurt to think of their cherished items gone. As a couple,
Phil and Marlene spent a lot of time traveling around the world, and their home
reflected those special memories.

After our first visit to see them more than ten years ago, we started collecting our own wine. But we'd rarely drink the best and oldest wine. After Phil and
Marlene's house and its contents burned—including rare wine that was decades old
from around the world—we began to see it differently.

Drink the good wine. That's the message we received from their experience.
Don't wait, because the opportunity could be gone. God wants us to enjoy the food
he's supplied us, the satisfaction of a hard day's work, and life's simple pleasures.

Not everyone enjoys wine, but I've squandered other opportunities to use special items, waiting for a certain day that never arrived. I've had unique spices go
stale, fancy lotions and bath salts dry up, and sweet treats expire—all because I was
saving them for a "special" day that never came.

Thankfully, Phil and Marlene have been able to rebuild, and their new home is
just as lovely as their previous one. But the lesson remains: today is special. We are
alive, awake, breathing. Those are gifts we shouldn't squander.

Lord, open our eyes to seeing each day as the miracle it is and enjoying it. Amen.
-Kristin

One Good Step: Choose to use an item you've been saving for a "special" day.

Mourn

The LORD is close to the brokenhearted; he rescues those whose spirits are crushed.

PSALM 34:18

I GOT A TATTOO. I wanted to do something to commemorate my kids and decided on a group of birds. My oldest suggested that I get a bird to represent the baby we'd lost through miscarriage. I agreed to add it.

The day I got my tattoo I came home with mixed emotions. I didn't love it like I thought I would. In fact, I hated it. I found myself looking up ways to get rid of tattoos and sat in my closet crying. "Lord," I whispered, "why do I feel such angst about this?"

Immediately a memory of sitting in my closet after my sister died of cancer and weeping in a similar fashion came to mind. I looked again at my arm where my tattoo was only partially covered. I didn't mind it so much. Only when I could see the full picture, with the bird meant to remind me of our miscarriage, did I not like it.

And it struck me. *This feels like mourning.* Years earlier when I'd miscarried, our lives were hectic. We had small children and foster kids. I didn't have time to grieve. Or so I thought. But ignoring pain never really makes it go away.

I wept when I realized what was behind my angst. For months afterward, I mourned for that baby like I'd never done before. And the pain felt new and fresh, like it was happening again, and in a sense it was. Grief would hit me like a wave and I'd whisper, "God, help me." And he'd be right there. Offering his peace, right alongside the pain.

As I realized the truth that we often avoid mourning in our culture, I came to understand that my grief wasn't holding me back. Instead, it was there to walk me through my sadness, and this time, I treated it like an old friend. Slowly, I began to feel peace as I allowed myself to mourn.

The most important lesson I learned was that God was there, right in the middle of my mourning. He is so close to us when we are heartbroken. We can trust that he'll bring us through our mourning.

Lord, thank you for binding up our broken hearts and for being near in our grief. Amen.

-Kendra

One Good Step: Don't be afraid to mourn, whether it's the loss of someone, or something, such as a job, a dream, or a possession. God is there with you.

Calling

I press on to reach the end of the race and receive the heavenly prize
for which God, through Christ Jesus, is calling us.

PHILIPPIANS 3:14

"WHAT DID IMPETUOUS PETER DO NEXT?" Leaning toward my young audience, I held
the page of the children's Bible open for all of them to see.

"He cut off the bad guy's ear with his sword!" a little boy exclaimed, perhaps
with a bit too much enthusiasm for the grisly turn of events.

"Oh, Impetuous Peter." I shook my head sorrowfully, seven little heads shaking
along with mine. "Was that what Jesus wanted him to do?"

"NOOOOOO!" a cacophony of voices called back.

Simon Peter, one of the twelve disciples, the rock of the early church, has been
forever nicknamed Impetuous Peter in my house because of his early tendency to
be, well, impetuous. He is a favorite of mine, a beautiful example of how God uses
us, despite our rough edges. And Peter is not the only imperfect person called by
God to accomplish his will.

Rahab, a prostitute in Jericho, pledged allegiance to God, hiding Joshua's spies.
She is one of five women identified by name in the lineage of Christ and is listed
among the great cloud of witnesses in Hebrews 11.

Ruth the Moabitess—a widowed refugee from a despised people group—fled
famine with her mother-in-law, married Boaz and became great-grandmother to
King David and ancestress to Jesus. She is one of two women with a book of the
Bible bearing her name.

Saul the Pharisee was zealous in his relentless persecution of early believers
until he encountered Jesus on the road to Damascus. Saul became Paul, authoring
thirteen (maybe fourteen) books in the New Testament.

God calls us. And our origin story, our past, our mistakes, our character flaws
do not negate that calling. God uses imperfect people throughout Scripture so that
he gets the glory and so we cannot deny our own calling, claiming that Peter, Paul,
Ruth, Rahab, and all the others were an anomaly, somehow slightly more perfect
than the rest of us. It was not them; it was God through them.

Lord, clear away all the disqualifications we hide behind in an effort to deny our
calling. Amen.

-Julie

One Good Step: To whom is God calling you? Ask him to show you the neighbor,
coworker, the coffee shop barista he would send you to, if you let him.

Purpose

The LORD will fulfill his purpose for me; your steadfast love, O LORD, endures forever. Do not forsake the work of your hands.

PSALM 138:8, ESV

I WAS DISCOURAGED. My parents had asked me to vacuum my bedroom, but when I proudly displayed the finished floor, the smile tugging at the side of my mom's mouth clued me in to the fact that something was off. Surveying the scrupulously neat lines crisscrossing the emerald green carpet, I couldn't understand what had gone wrong.

"That was a great start," she said tactfully. "But you need to make sure that the vacuum picks up all the dirt on the floor."

Looking closer, I saw what she meant. Dust bunnies peeked from under the edges of my bed, and I could see unidentifiable specks on the floor and along the edges of my sunflower-themed room.

"Ohhhh," I said. "So, not like a lawn mower." She shook her head no. Plugging the vacuum back in, I started over, concentrating less on creating perfect lines and more on making sure the floor came clean. My mistake—understandable for a ten-year-old—was in misunderstanding the vacuum's purpose. It wasn't meant to simply make the room look pretty; it was meant for practicality.

A recent study concluded that having a sense of purpose in life is associated with a lower risk of death. But what constitutes a purpose? Stanford psychologists William Damon, Jenni Menon, and Kendall Cotton Bronk define it as "a stable and generalized intention to accomplish something that is at once meaningful to the self and of consequence to the world beyond the self."[2]

Yet in the same way that Moses once told God he didn't have the leadership skills to liberate the Israelites from Egypt's oppression, many of us struggle to identify our purpose. Perhaps we tell ourselves we aren't smart enough, good-looking enough, or educated enough to help further God's Kingdom. But God's plan is simple: he asks us to love him and to love our neighbors. Apart from that, there is freedom in how we accomplish those goals. Each of us has our own part to play, which God has equipped us to accomplish (see Hebrews 13:21).

Lord, thank you that you have a plan and purpose for each of us. Help give us your confidence in accomplishing your work. Amen.

-Kristin

One Good Step: What is your purpose? If you don't have a ready answer, try reframing the question this way: What can I do with my time that is important?

---

[2] William Damon, Jenni Menon, and Kendall Cotton Bronk, "The Development of Purpose during Adolescence," *Applied Developmental Science* 7, no. 3 (2003): 119–28, https://www.tandfonline.com/doi/pdf/10.1207/S1532480XADS0703_2?needAccess=true.

Accountable

I tell you this, you must give an account on judgment day for every idle word
you speak. The words you say will either acquit you or condemn you.
MATTHEW 12:36-37

"I WANT YOU TO HOLD ME ACCOUNTABLE in the way that I speak about others," I told
a friend not long ago. I'd been careless with my words and knew that I needed to
change some of my words and the thoughts that were behind those words. I told
a dear friend who knows me well of my struggle. She knows the good and the bad
and loves me anyway. I knew that she would be able to hold me accountable in a
loving way.

Every so often she'd check in with me, just to see how I was doing. She'd ask
hard questions and chuckle when I got annoyed by her reminders to watch the way
that I spoke about others. But the truth was, when I stepped back and looked at the
big picture, I appreciated her honesty and ability to speak in a way that challenged
me, while still fully loving me. Her accountability helped me change a behavior that
was unhealthy and allowed me to develop a new, healthier way to be.

Accountability is hard. We live in a culture that often wants to put the blame
on others. We try desperately not to be at fault. And even as Christians it can be
hard to take accountability for our thoughts and actions. Sometimes it's easier to
hide parts of ourselves we'd rather others didn't know about or see. That's why it's
important that we have a community of people in our lives who love us enough to
hold us accountable, while still encouraging us, knowing the good and the not so
good about us—much in the same way that God treats us. We'll give an account for
everything we speak. This should be enough of an encouragement (and a warning)
for us to want to hold ourselves accountable now.

*Lord, help us to be courageous enough to hold ourselves and those around us
accountable for our words and actions. Amen.*

-Kendra

One Good Step: In what area of your life do you need some accountability?
What good friend could be an accountability partner for you? Be sure
to pick someone who will love and encourage you.

Fathom

Can you fathom the mysteries of God? Can you probe the limits of the
Almighty? They are higher than the heavens above—what can you do?
They are deeper than the depths below—what can you know? Their
measure is longer than the earth and wider than the sea.

JOB 11:7-9, NIV

I SAT MESMERIZED on a broad swatch of blue-black basalt, a once-upon-a-time red-hot
lava flow, arms wrapped around my knees, watching the pounding waves of Lake
Superior crashing along my rocky ledge.

We'd returned to my favorite spot, and I was content with sitting in quietude,
allowing the rhythmic noise to wash over me as every to-do list item faded to black
and I simply existed in the present. Resetting. Recalibrating. Refreshing.

There is something about rocky beaches and wild waves of Lake Superior along
Minnesota's North Shore that calls to me. Its dangerous beauty reminds me of the
fathomlessness of God in a way little else does. It's my sacred place, a place that
snaps everything back into the right perspective when I've started to put God into
a box that is a hundred thousand times too small.

And I do. Put God in a box, I mean. I have a tendency to get our relationship
mixed up and backward, with me pretending I'm in control until chaos descends
and I quickly hand the proverbial wheel to Jesus. I save my prayers for the really
big, worthwhile things rather than taking all of it to him in prayer. I make plans and
ask God to bless them, rather than asking God what the plan is. This is a perennial
mistake for me, something I am continually readjusting, relearning. I need constant
reminders that God is God and I am . . . me.

Maybe you do this too? Have you made God a box and tucked him inside,
forgetting that he is fathomless, beyond knowing, at least while we are on earth? Do
you forget to wait for his lead, trying to navigate life on your own until suddenly
you're in over your head and you've—finally—hit your knees in prayer?

*Lord, we acknowledge your sovereignty, your godship, your fathomlessness. Forgive
us our tendency to put you in a box, our determination to operate under the illusion
of control. Restore us to a right relationship with you. Amen.*

-Julie

One Good Step: Meditate on Job 11:7-9, asking God
where you need to cede control back to him.

Faithful

"For the mountains may move and the hills disappear, but even then my faithful love for you will remain. My covenant of blessing will never be broken," says the LORD.

ISAIAH 54:10

JENNY AND HER YOUTH PASTOR HUSBAND, Carl, had just returned home from a weekend leadership conference. Flushed with excitement about their mission and plans to move forward with the youth they worked with at a local church, they eagerly anticipated incorporating their new ideas. But that night, they got an unexpected call from the senior pastor. The next morning, he broke the news to Carl: he was being let go. Moreover, the church wanted him to tell others he was leaving voluntarily.

The couple—with a mortgage and two young sons to consider—felt overwhelmed at the suddenness of the decision and their lack of recourse. Should they look for a new job in the ministry or leave it entirely? Should Carl return to school for a new career? Should they stay in Arizona or move away? Despite their uncertainty, they decided to trust God. He'd been faithful to them in the past, and they knew he would remain faithful as they moved forward.

The couple decided to move in with Jenny's family in Minnesota while they sorted things out. Within the span of a week, they went from living in a comfortable home to sleeping on a blow-up mattress. Carl enrolled in a local university and eventually got a new job as a youth pastor.

But just a few short weeks after their move to Minnesota, Jenny's father became sick, spiraling into a decline that continued until his death three years later. Though Jenny felt bitterness about the reason behind the move, she was grateful for the extra time she had with her dad. If Carl hadn't lost his job, they would never have moved home and had those years with her dad. Faithfully following God's call gave them extra time with him before his death.

When circumstances change or challenge us, it can be a temptation to feel bitterness or anger over a lost dream or situation outside of our control. Yet when we choose to trust God—despite our circumstances—he is always faithful in his promises. Though life may take unexpected turns, his faithfulness is an ever-present source of immovable comfort. Oftentimes, he is working in ways we'll only realize later on.

Lord, thank you for your faithfulness. Help us to remain true to you in the twists and turns of life. Amen.

-Kristin

One Good Step: Spend time praying and thanking God for his faithfulness to you.

Different

Jesus Christ is the same yesterday, today, and forever.
HEBREWS 13:8

UNCLE JIM AND AUNT TINA didn't always have it easy, but they loved one another deeply. They both loved to dance, and it was something they did together, even when things were hard. They danced in the kitchen, at the local watering hole, outside under the stars—it didn't matter where they danced, it mattered only that they still danced.

And then Jim got sick. It was a rare condition, one that slowly stole his ability to move even as his mind remained alert and aware until his death several years ago. Aunt Tina showed me a picture of her and Jim on the dance floor, him in a wheelchair, her arms wrapped around him from behind, swaying them both to the music. "We never stopped dancing. We just danced different after he got sick."

We just danced different. Her words have stayed with me. As our circumstances change, as the path we thought we were on suddenly veers to the left, we are faced with different—different choices than the ones we thought we had, different circumstances than we planned, different outcomes than we'd expected. What do we do when we are faced with *different?* Especially when that different is incredibly hard? How do we find a new way forward?

We stand firm on the bedrock, foundational truth of our faith: Jesus Christ is the same from everlasting to everlasting, unchanging, unshifting, certain. He is the firm foundation our faith must be built upon or it will crumble and fall when the storms of life rage. He is present in the different, and he provides us a safe shelter when what we face feels like it is more than we can handle. When we have a firm faith foundation, we can still dance, still do the things we love, even if they look different than before.

Lord, help us to build a deep and abiding faith foundation on your truth, that we will find ourselves firmly rooted, even when life is far different than what we'd expected. Amen.

-Julie

One Good Step: How are you continuing to build your faith foundation? Invest time weekly in strengthening your foundation, that you may stand firm on its truth, always.

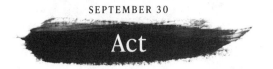

Act

Learn to do good. Seek justice. Help the oppressed.
Defend the cause of orphans. Fight for the rights of widows.

ISAIAH 1:17

MY DAUGHTER JASMINE AND I were running errands around town when she asked me about human trafficking. Concerned over several posts she'd seen on social media, she wanted to know more about it. I started to tell her the things I had learned, statistics I'd read and organizations I knew were helping. Jasmine listened intently, and then I stopped midsentence, as a new thought crossed my mind.

"You know," I said, "I could keep telling you what I know, but I have a better idea. When we get home, why don't you look up some facts about human trafficking and then find organizations who are helping? You could share with the rest of the family at supper. It's been a while since we've offered assistance to an organization. Let's decide as a family a place we could support." Jasmine agreed.

When we got home, she took my computer and spent time researching statistics and finding a couple of organizations that are helping those being trafficked. That night at dinner, she explained to the rest of the family what she had learned, and together we decided to donate to an organization that is fighting human trafficking in this country and abroad. Jasmine ended our time by praying for all those affected by trafficking. I was proud of her for taking the initiative to learn about a problem and then act to do something about it.

As Christians, we aren't just called to show concern for what is happening in the world, but to also act. Sometimes the problems seem so large that we can become paralyzed by fear or worry that whatever we would do wouldn't really make that much of a difference anyway. But God is clear: We are to do good and seek justice. We are to help the oppressed, defend the orphan, and fight for widows. In short, we are to act. Don't worry about the size of the action. If we all do something, it'll add up quickly.

Lord, may we be people of prayer, with our hearts turned toward the concerns of the world, and may we be moved to act by what we see. Amen.

-Kendra

One Good Step: What is a cause that you have a passion for? Find an organization that is working in that area, and then take an action step to partner with them.

October

Apologize

If you are offering your gift at the altar and there remember that your brother
or sister has something against you, leave your gift there in front of the altar.
First go and be reconciled to them; then come and offer your gift.

MATTHEW 5:23-24, NIV

"I'M SORRY," my husband stated with a pained look on his face, arms stretched out
as if he had nothing to hide. "I don't have any excuse to give. I was wrong, and I'm
sorry." He finished as tears welled in my eyes and then slid down my cheeks. Even
though his actions pained my heart, I knew that he meant his apology.

As he went on to explain what had happened, he never once made excuses or
downplayed his behavior. He owned what had transpired and promised that his
actions would change to show that he was truly sorry. I was grateful for his apology,
and together we worked to fix what had transpired between us.

My husband and I have not always been so quick to apologize. For years, I
would get mad and give Kyle the silent treatment until my anger would dissipate.
Often apologies would never be mentioned, and we'd just move on. Kyle in turn
would sometimes keep things from me, not wanting to hurt me or cause strife
between us.

But over the years, we've both learned how important being honest, apologizing, and owning our words or actions are to the long-term health of our relationship. It hasn't always been easy, but we are both now quick to apologize to one
another, without excuses, attempting as quickly as possible to right our relationship.
Even though it's hard, we know it's the best way to keep our marriage strong.

Scripture speaks often of forgiveness and forgiving those who've hurt us, but
what of apologizing when we've done something wrong? We are told that if someone has an offense against us, we should first go and be reconciled to the other person before coming to God. This implies that our relationship with God is affected
by our relationship with one another. If we aren't willing to apologize when we need
to and live at peace with others, our relationships with God will be affected as well.
Let's be people who are quick to forgive and quick to apologize.

Lord, give us the courage to apologize when we need to. Amen.

-Kendra

One Good Word: Apologize to someone that you have hurt or offended.

Longing

He satisfies the longing soul, and the hungry soul he fills with good things.

PSALM 107:9, ESV

PERUSING THE MENU, I glanced up to look down the length of the noisy, laughing group of college students. Seated at one end of our table, smiling indulgently, was a couple roughly the age of my parents. An hour earlier, they'd shown up on our doorstep to visit their son, a friend of mine. They had made the stopover in Oxford while on a trip to London and offered to take our group of friends out for dinner. Eating out was infrequent and special, so we gladly agreed.

As we sat visiting and discussing our studies with our friend's parents at a delicious Lebanese restaurant, I felt a sudden pang of homesickness. Their demeanor was casual and comfortable, and I couldn't help but wish it was my own family visiting. Though I loved my friends and my studies, I longed for the comfort of home.

But as the night wore on, I felt cheered by the couple's presence. Though it wasn't my parents at the end of the table, and the other people my age were friends rather than siblings, it felt like a family dinner. The couple probably didn't give the evening a second thought. But to someone who had never lived farther than forty-five minutes from home and felt untethered, a little lost, and a little lonely, their generosity felt meaningful. Though an ocean separated me from my own family, my longing for home was satisfied. And as the night ended, I went back to my quiet dorm feeling nothing but gratitude.

Years later, I still remember the longing and loneliness of my far-from-home heart. We know that God puts the lonely in families, and he satisfies those longings for home that we feel. Yet we can partner with him in doing so—in our generous invitations, in our heartfelt conversations, and in the way we simply notice those who are overlooked or ignored or feeling out of place. Let's resolve to be that safe place, that shelter for someone else. Let's give someone else the warmth and comfort of home, even when they're far from those they love, either by chance or circumstance. When we do, our actions point others back to a loving God who can satisfy every longing.

Lord, thank you that you satisfy the longings of our hearts. Amen.

-Kristin

One Good Step: Invite someone who may be longing for connection to share dinner with you.

Continue

They encouraged them to continue in the faith, reminding them that
we must suffer many hardships to enter the Kingdom of God.
ACTS 14:22

MY BROTHER JUSTIN is an efficiency expert. An industrial engineer by training, he finds the choke points, the slowest parts in any process, and then reimagines and reworks that small piece until it is efficient and productive before moving on to the next slowest part, and then the next. His work on improving factory assembly lines leaks into all areas of his and—by extension—our lives, with his ability to identify and problem solve the weak points in a plan a wonderful tool that has resulted in great advice over the years.

When asked for advice recently about a potential project that had me frustrated, he suggested I needed to continue forward rather than stopping every time I encountered an obstacle. His actual words to me were to stop stopping and start starting, the catchy phrase gleaned somewhere along the way in the myriad of books he reads and the obstacles he encounters on a routine basis. It's often the stops and pauses that cause breakdowns and inefficiency in systems and processes, and finding ways to continue pressing forward by eliminating the stops and restarts brings success faster than more elaborate, difficult-to-implement solutions.

Honestly, his words weren't what I wanted to hear. I was longing for permission to quit proactively because continuing was too hard, or at least pause with the hope that perhaps I need not restart for an indefinite amount of time—a quit by default, if you will. But his words are true, and I was finding a million reasons to stop and keep stopping, none of which got me closer to the finish line.

God will use us as his hands and feet, but we have to be willing to stay the course, to continue, even when the way forward is more challenging than we anticipated. Saying yes to God is always an adventure worth taking, but we'll get nowhere if we balk every time we encounter an obstacle. In fact, it's often in the hardships that we finally give up the illusion of control and rely entirely upon God, developing a deeply rooted faith because we continued, because we watched God show up in circumstances beyond our own abilities.

Lord, make us doers of your Word, women who continue to stay the course, even when obstacles are harder than we'd imagined. Amen.

-Julie

One Good Step: Stop stopping and start starting. Take an actionable step forward to continue something you've been wanting to quit because it was hard.

Acknowledge

Put on then, as God's chosen ones, holy and beloved, compassionate hearts,
kindness, humility, meekness, and patience.
COLOSSIANS 3:12, ESV

I WAS WAITING IN LINE to check out at the grocery store. I hadn't seen the young man at the register before, so I knew he must be fairly new. He studied my shirt for a moment with his lips pursed. It simply had the words "Foster, Adoptive, Biological. Mom" printed on it.

"I really love your shirt," he said. "Are you a foster mom?"

"Yes," I replied. "I was. I have three adopted kids from foster care."

He nodded. "I was in foster care as a kid myself." He didn't look more than twenty-one years old, still very much a kid himself.

"Oh?" I responded. I've learned to wait for more, keeping my eyes on him as I paused to acknowledge him.

He took this as his cue to continue: "I was in twelve foster homes as a kid. I wasn't bad; it just never worked out for my sister and me. It was really tough. My mom was a drug dealer, my dad was in prison. I knew I didn't want to be like them." I nodded, waiting for more. "I was finally adopted, my sister and I. We're in a good family now," he said with a smile.

"I'm happy for you," I responded. "You're really brave."

He grinned. "I knew I wanted to be better; that's why I work here."

"You're doing a great job," I stated.

As we finished bagging my groceries, I could see the man in line behind me give the young man an encouraging smile as well—he'd heard our conversation. I wished him well as I left.

It takes a few moments of our day to pause, listen, and acknowledge another person. I found out this young man's story in just a matter of minutes, and sharing something this personal changed the atmosphere in our little checkout line. Suddenly, we were connected and seeing, really noticing another person. Listening to and acknowledging another's story—even their pain—and in turn showing compassion and kindness in the middle of an ordinary experience is one of the greatest gifts we can give someone.

Lord, help us to listen and acknowledge someone and offer compassion, kindness, and love as we do. Amen.

-Kendra

One Good Step: When was the last time someone stopped, listened, and acknowledged you? How can you pass that experience on to another?

Thirst

Those who drink the water I give will never be thirsty again. It becomes a fresh,
bubbling spring within them, giving them eternal life.

JOHN 4:14

BARELY PAUSING FOR BREATH, I finished gulping the water in my glass. Four tall glasses already, and the morning was only halfway gone. I refilled the glass, water swirling as it settled.

A few days earlier, I'd stopped eating sugar. But a strange side effect was a constant, inexhaustible thirst. It took a while before the realization set in: this thirst wasn't new. My body had been thirsty for a very long time. I had simply ignored or overlooked it, instead eating a small snack or a bite of chocolate. I'd mistaken my body's cues for water, temporarily fixing the problem with food instead.

Misreading our need for water isn't uncommon. In Jesus' encounter with the Samaritan woman at the well—in which he reveals that he knows everything about her yet loves her anyway—he tells her about living water only he can provide. Though they are surveying a well filled with physical water, it's a spiritual filling he's concerned about.

Wells are filled in one of two ways: either they are a reservoir that simply holds water, or they contain spring water. While a reservoir is a still pool of water, a spring is like a fountain that bubbles up, the motion coming from within rather than without. *Barnes' Notes on the Bible* describes this ever-living fountain as remarkably resilient: "[It] flows at all seasons of the year, in heat and cold, and in all external circumstances of weather, whether foul or fair, wet or dry. So religion always lives; and, amid all changes of external circumstances—in heat and cold, hunger and thirst, prosperity and adversity, life, persecution, contempt, or death—it still lives on, and refreshes and cheers the soul."

This new life—this endless living water we gain through the power of Christ's sacrifice—springs up like an endless, effortless fountain that is always in motion, joyful, and free. When we embrace it, it becomes an inner source that never runs dry. It's both immediate and eternal, and its inexhaustible supply satisfies our thirsty souls in a way nothing else can.

Lord, thank you that your living water satisfies our thirst. May we always seek to be filled. Amen.

-Kristin

One Good Word: Drink half your body weight in ounces of water throughout the day. Consider how the living water Jesus provides refreshes your soul.

Surrender

Whatever were gains to me I now consider loss for the sake of Christ.
What is more, I consider everything a loss because of the surpassing worth
of knowing Christ Jesus my Lord, for whose sake I have lost all things.
I consider them garbage, that I may gain Christ.

PHILIPPIANS 3:7-8, NIV

THE IDEA OF SURRENDERING EVERYTHING to Jesus was something my husband and I had been wrestling with for a while. At the same time, we had talked about moving, buying a larger home, a place with some land. We looked for months but couldn't find anything we really liked. Nothing was perfect. As we considered what it meant to surrender everything, I started to wonder if we were looking in the wrong place for a home.

So instead of looking outside of town, we started looking more in the heart of our city. We wanted to be in a more diverse neighborhood, and instead of looking at homes first, we just started driving around and praying, *Lord, where do you want us?* The first time we walked into our current house we knew it was the place, after only entering the front porch.

But as we started to tell other people about our upcoming move, their responses were mixed. Some were happy for us, but others, many well-meaning Christians, asked us if it was safe where we were moving to. *Were we sure this was good for our family?* A curious question to me, especially after we'd explained how strongly we felt God leading us to this new place.

A few weeks after being in our new home, as I was feeling very grateful for God's leading in our lives, he impressed on my heart that the safest place to be was always surrendered to his will. I knew that it was true. Not because it was easy, but because it was where he had called us.

Surrendering our will to follow God does not mean our lives will be safe, at least not by the world's standards, or easy. And sometimes people may question our decisions. But surrendering to God brings other assurances, like peace and joy, even when external circumstances look otherwise. It's not always the easiest path, but it is worth it to gain all that God has for us.

Lord, help me surrender everything to you. Amen.

-Kendra

One Good Step: What is one area of your life that you need to surrender to God?

Grit

Be on guard. Stand firm in the faith. Be courageous. Be strong.
1 CORINTHIANS 16:13

"Go Lizzie!" I cheered loudly as she crossed the finish line. Her first season of cross-country had been a doozy. With all junior high races canceled, her coach trained his junior high runners all season so they could run varsity races, double the junior high distance. The last race of the season had been her first.

Wrapping her in a tight hug, I whispered, "I'm so proud of you!"

"Mom, I was *last*." Her whisper brought clarity as I realized, yet again, that my daughter and I are far more alike than different.

"Lizzie, you're measuring yourself against the wrong standard." I pulled back to look her in the eyes. "This is your first attempt, and you showed grit. It's not fair to compare yourself to girls who have years of experience."

"I know," she sighed.

"It doesn't matter whether you came in first or last; you did something you were nervous about doing. You reached deep and didn't quit. You had grit. Come on, let's go find Dad and Grandma. They want to hug you too."

Grit. How often do we measure ourselves against the wrong standard, assuming there is only first and last place? How often do we measure our success by looking around us instead of looking to God, comparing ourselves to women who are further along than we are? How often do we quit preemptively, not wanting to fail and so stopping the moment it looks like we might?

God isn't looking for winners; he is looking for women who dig deep when things are challenging, unpredictable, and uncomfortable. How do we get grit? It's like a muscle. We have to exercise it in order to develop and keep it. We learn from failure, reconsidering and trying again rather than giving up. We embrace small beginnings, refusing to compare our little thing to another woman's bigger, more successful thing, understanding that she, too, had a small start. And we count grit as an accomplishment, celebrating it in its own right, regardless of whether we crossed the finish line first, last, or somewhere in between.

Lord, thank you for the plans you have for our lives. Help us to be gritty, willing to dig in when others would pull away. Amen.

-Julie

One Good Step: Where is God asking you to be gritty? Tell a friend so she can be an accountability partner and cheerleader when you want to quit.

Fruit

Just as you can identify a tree by its fruit,
so you can identify people by their actions.
MATTHEW 7:20

DRIVING DOWN THE DUSTY LANE, we passed a pole barn and continued on until we could see the trees. Friends of ours owned a landscaping company and had graciously offered to let us pick apples on their property, free of charge. Apple-picking is a favorite fall pastime, and I immediately envisioned the batches of applesauce that would soon be cooling in my kitchen.

But as we pulled up to the grove and climbed out, my breath caught at the sheer volume of apples—only to stutter as I neared the trees. I've been to other orchards in the past. They're carefully maintained, the trees picturesque. But this orchard wasn't meant for tourists. Swaths of the ground were unmowed, and I dodged a few literal pits where trees had been uprooted to be planted elsewhere. Bees buzzed, and the air was redolent with a vinegary aroma from the fallen fruit that littered the ground. Though the trees were in neat rows, a few had spots on the leaves, and some apples had been munched on by insects.

But as I sidestepped areas of overgrown grass and waved off yet another swarm of tiny gnats, I couldn't help but marvel at God's creation. Though the setting was imperfect, many apples were glossy and beautiful. Some branches hung low, heavily laden with fruit. As I began to fill my bag, I praised God quietly for the gift of the fruit and for our friends' provision.

The trees were producing fruit, regardless of whether or not anyone noticed. Their circumstances were imperfect. Some of the fruit had gone to waste. And yet they continued to faithfully produce fruit, doing what they were meant to do.

How often can the same be said for us? When trials come or we're hard-pressed by circumstances, do we continue to produce good fruit? When no one notices our sweat and tears, no one praises us for a job well done, no one recognizes our hard work—do we still continue to produce good fruit? Even if God is the only one who sees the fruit of our labor, it's worth it. As Galatians 6:9 tells us, our faithfulness still produces a harvest—if we don't give up.

Lord, may the fruit of our lives reveal the work of your glory. Amen.

-Kristin

One Good Step: What kind of fruit is your life currently cultivating?

Indulge

And now, dear brothers and sisters, one final thing. Fix your thoughts on
what is true, and honorable, and right, and pure, and lovely, and admirable.
Think about things that are excellent and worthy of praise.

PHILIPPIANS 4:8

WALKING BRISKLY INTO HOME DEPOT, I was on a mission to get in and get out and on
with my errand list until my eyes snagged on the display of tulip bulbs ready for
planting this fall. My footsteps slowed as I struggled internally with whether to stay
on task or allow myself to detour—for just a moment—to the bulbs.

Giving up, I detoured, examining varieties and vibrant color combinations,
spending a few indulgent moments lost in thought imagining what my front flower
bed might look like if I planted it with shades of orange tulips this spring instead
of purples. Giving in, I picked up two bags of bulbs and continued on my original
mission, already planning when and where I'd plant them.

Midwinter in the Midwest is the low point in the year climate-wise, at least for
me. Because I know how long those days tend to feel, I plan for them, beginning
in the fall. I plant tulips in October so that I can have the earliest possible color
along my front walk, and I stash a small bag of hyacinth bulbs in my garage fridge
so I can force them on my windowsill in January. These small, green luxuries keep
my spirits up when winter feels long and have proven themselves good for me
emotionally, spiritually, and even physically.

Indulging need not be decadent or prohibitively expensive. I have friends who
love a fancy candle, a luxurious bath, or a nibble from their favorite dark chocolate
hidden on the top shelf in the linen closet. It's finding small, joyful things and stash-
ing them away for moments when we need an indulgence, something lovely and
true and pure to wash away the ugly of this world. God is the Master Creator—the
author of all recipes, the original gardener, the first to use color in breathtaking
ways, the establisher of the Sabbath—and he invites us to spend time resting, creating, enjoying the best his creation has to offer.

Lord, thank you for the gift of indulgences. Help us embrace them as they were
meant to be: an opportunity to refresh and recharge. Amen.

-Julie

One Good Step: Indulge yourself in a favorite way today.

Advocate

If anyone does sin, we have an advocate who pleads our case before the Father.
He is Jesus Christ, the one who is truly righteous. He himself is the sacrifice
that atones for our sins—and not only our sins but the sins of all the world.

1 JOHN 2:1-2

OVER A SIX-YEAR PERIOD OF TIME, my husband and I were foster parents for the county that we live in. We took in around twenty children during those years. We worked with many county workers, judges, specialists, therapists, doctors, and other community support persons on a regular basis. Although fostering was challenging at times, we were also encouraged to see how many different people and professionals would come alongside these kids to advocate for them and try to offer them the best chance at life.

One role that I appreciated most was that of the guardian ad litem. This person was hired by the county but did not work for the county. They were solely there to advocate for the best interest of the child, apart from the parents, judges, or even social services. Their sole goal was to offer a recommendation based only on what they believed to be best for the child and the child's future. I loved how the guardian ad litem would join with the child, seeing only what was best for them. The guardian ad litem was often a voice for a child who had yet to really have one for themselves. Guardians ad litem became some of my favorite people over those years, and even now, I appreciate how they loved the kids in our home.

When I think about the many ways that Jesus comes to our rescue, one of my favorites is that of our Advocate. Just like the guardian ad litem, Jesus pleads our case, advocating the best for us. What a gift! He gives voice to us, even when we cannot speak for ourselves. He is the best Advocate we could ever have. And even when we sin, even when we mess up, he still remains on our side, ready to stand in the gap for us. His sacrifice on the Cross atones for all of our missteps. He is always a ready Advocate for us.

Lord, thank you that you are the perfect Advocate for each one of us, regardless of what we've done. Thank you for your sacrifice. Amen.

-Kendra

One Good Step: How has Jesus been an Advocate for you? Spend some time today thanking him for how he's shown his care for you.

Work

May the favor of the LORD our God rest on us; establish the work
of our hands for us—yes, establish the work of our hands.

PSALM 90:17, NIV

"OKAY, ASHLYN, what do you want to be when you grow up?" Fingers poised over the keyboard, I glanced up to see my five-year-old daughter's face screwed up in concentration. School was starting later in the week, and I'd created signs for each child that commemorated the occasion. Along with their grade level, favorite book, and things they loved, I'd added the category of what they wanted to be in the future.

"I want to be the person you see at Target," she said.

"Which person?"

"The one who helps you buy stuff," she said helpfully.

"A cashier?" I sought clarification.

"Yes!" she said, beaming.

"Okay," I said, turning to Noelle. "What about you?"

"Ooh, I want to be the person who fixes doll hair. You know, like the people we saw at the American Girl store."

"Me too!" Elise called from the other room.

I couldn't help but smile at their answers, because even though we've talked about a vast range of vocations—scientists like Marie Curie, world changers like Rosa Parks, and pilots like Amelia Earhart are among their favorite people to read about—it's the individuals they see on a daily basis who have made the most impact. I asked for an occupation, but they responded with attributes. The occupations they mentioned are filled by people they've seen at our local stores on a consistent basis, people who smile and say hello, people who offer to help. And when my daughters look at the world, they want to be the same thing: a person who helps, a person who cares for others. They want to be someone who fixes problems, makes changes, and finds solutions.

No matter our title, we can be known by who and what we represent. When we give the work of our hands over to God's care, everything we do is equally worthy and worthwhile. Though our jobs may vary, we have the opportunity to influence others every day.

Lord, thank you for the work of our hands. May our efforts glorify you. Amen.

-Kristin

One Good Step: What are some ways you can use your daily work to influence others?

Seasons

Give thanks in everything; for this is God's will for you in Christ Jesus.
1 THESSALONIANS 5:18, CSB

NOT LONG AGO, as I made my way through my local grocery store buying all the things necessary for that week, I found myself daydreaming about when my husband and I were first married. How meal planning then took little effort, if any, and how sometimes, I secretly long for those supposedly easier days once again.

During that shopping trip, I got a text from a younger woman who is struggling with some things in her career—she told me she longs for another season in life, one that will be "easier" than her current situation.

As I drove home, I was convicted about how easy it can be to remember the good parts of our lives and dismiss the hard. And although some seasons are more demanding than others, we all have things that are good and things that challenge us during each phase of life—and being grateful for the season I am in is a choice I get to make.

As I began to put my things away at home, I quietly thanked God for the gift of my family, for food to eat, health, and a home to make meals and memories in. By the time I was done putting everything away, my heart was bursting with gratitude for what I currently have. It's not a perfect season, that's for sure, but it is still one worth being grateful for today.

It's often easy to focus on what is hard about the current season we're in and not notice the good. Sometimes, we can look at others' lives and think they are in an easier season (which may or may not be true) and long for something different. But there is always good and hard, working together in all seasons of life. They may be different struggles, but one is no less valid than another. Remembering to give thanks will remind us of the goodness of our current season.

Lord, thank you that no matter what season we find ourselves in, we can find things that we are thankful for. May you direct us, each day, to notice and appreciate all that you have given us. Amen.

-Kendra

One Good Step: Write out five things you are thankful for in your current season and place the list somewhere you will see it throughout your day.

Neighbor

Love your neighbor as yourself.
LUKE 10:27

"I SENT CHRISTY MONEY," Sarah said, grabbing her car keys as she turned toward the front door.

"Oh? Isn't she the neighbor who said those awful things about you to her friend who you work with?" Snagging my purse, I followed her to the car.

"The very one. She is on round two of a dozen chemo treatments." Sarah paused, looking at me as she started the car. "The Holy Spirit told me to give her $300 out of my emergency stash, so I did. I put a little care package together, tucked the money into the card, and left it on her doorstep."

"How do you feel about that?" I asked after a long pause, knowing the whole story, the deep hurt, and the complicated feelings Sarah had about Christy.

"I'm conflicted. I want to support her family, but I also didn't want to do it because I was afraid of her response. What if she misunderstands the intent behind my care package and says something nasty about me to her friend and that person passes it on to my other coworkers? I don't want to go through that again." Sarah sighed, throwing her arm over the back of the passenger seat as we backed down her driveway, "But I just keep giving Christy to God. If he asked me to do it, I have to trust that he'll work it out."

"Oh, friend. You are loving your neighbor. God will honor that."

When Jesus commanded us to love our neighbors as ourselves, a Pharisee asked Jesus to define the label "neighbor." Jesus responded with the story of the Good Samaritan, a story so ubiquitously famous that many people don't realize it origi-nated in Scripture. Despite its familiarity, we've lost a key fact through culture and time: the Samaritan was the despised, hated enemy of the man lying unconscious and injured. In other words, the Samaritan was the villain, not the hero, of the story. It was the enemy who stopped to help. And when Jesus told us to love our neighbor, he intentionally includes our enemy in that command. We are to love our enemies (and everyone else) as ourselves.

Lord, help us be women who honor your command to love our neighbors. Amen.

-Julie

One Good Step: Ask God for an outreach assignment, and then, like Sarah, be responsive to the assignment, even if you are left trusting the results to God.

Abound

You, Lord, are forgiving and good, abounding in love
to all who call to you.
PSALM 86:5, NIV

WE WALKED ALONGSIDE STREAMS of people as they passed through the hallways of the Saint Paul RiverCentre, traveled down escalators, and converged on a massive hall. It was Love Somalia's meal packing event, and people from the Twin Cities and beyond had banded together to support the effort. In the cavernous warehouse-style space, food-packing areas were stationed at regular intervals. I marveled at the sheer volume of people and supplies present, the reminder of how God abounds in grace and good works. After a quick orientation, we washed our hands, stretched blue hair nets over our hair, and got to work measuring and dumping rice and other staples into bags.

Our small group of families chatted as we worked, pulling up boxes to use as steps to lift smaller kids to the height of the table, all working toward the goal of six million meals for Somalia, a country on the brink of famine. At the time, Somalia was experiencing intense drought. In the hardest-hit areas, the lack of water wiped out crops and livestock, and communities were forced to sell assets and borrow food and money to survive. Over 6.2 million people needed assistance.

The meal packing event was massive in scale. In some ways, the process felt akin to ant life, as we worked busily in the vast room. Steadily, we filled meal after meal, box after box. By the end of our shift, the people in the room had collectively packed 2,998 boxes that would provide 647,568 meals, feeding 1,774 kids for an entire year.

In the mundane moments of our everyday lives, we can forget about the boundless nature of God, but the immense scale of the meal-packing endeavor was a small reminder of how big he is. He abounds in love, mercy, grace, justice—but he also abounds in resources. We can't outgive God. But as Christians, we can partner with him to share our own resources with those in need. The abundant life we are promised in John 10:10 isn't one of hoarding; it's one of extravagant generosity, our partnership with Jesus an echo of the extravagant grace we ourselves have received.

Lord, thank you that you abound in grace, mercy, and love. Help us to realize how vast your reach is and to find our own small ways to help your work in the world. Amen.

-Kristin

One Good Step: What is a skill, quality, or resource that you abound in? Today, endeavor to share it with someone.

Generations

One generation shall commend your works to another, and shall
declare your mighty acts. On the glorious splendor of your majesty,
and on your wondrous works, I will meditate. They shall speak of the
might of your awesome deeds, and I will declare your greatness.

PSALM 145:4-6, ESV

ONE MORNING as I was getting ready to write, I spent time thinking about all the authors whose words have made a difference in my life. I'd been reading devotionals written by other women for years before I ever wrote a word of my own. It started in my early twenties, when I created a habit of getting up each day, reading my Bible and a short devotional or Bible study. Women a generation ahead of me like Beth Moore, Kay Warren, Joyce Meyer, and Lysa TerKeurst would meet me every morning with a little bit of encouragement and conviction.

Now, in my early forties, I get to continue a legacy that they began years ago. My writing is not completely my own; it's been shaped and built on the words and inspiration of the women who've come before me. Women who were faithful to write consistently, just as I would consistently read their words. And now, I get to offer this same encouragement to other women from the generation behind me. I find myself grateful, for those who came before, and for the women who'll come up behind me, continuing the generational legacy of faith.

Our faith is not created or lived out in a vacuum. We are all shaped, not only by reading the Bible, but by the words spoken, sung, and written by people of faith. Some we may know personally, and others we may know simply from a distance. One generation will tell the next of the awesome deeds of God, sharing all that he has done in their lives. Offering encouragement for those who'll come up after them, the next generation, so that they, too, will know that our God is faithful. Our God is good. Our lives become a testimony to those who'll come after us of the greatness of our God.

Lord, thank you for the generations of faithful followers who've come before us. May we learn from their words and example. And help us to do the same with the generation who'll come after us. May we commend your works to them through our words and our actions. Amen.

-Kendra

One Good Step: Thank someone who has influenced your life and faith.

Nevertheless

Nevertheless, that time of darkness and despair will not go on forever.

ISAIAH 9:1

"I'M GOING TO QUIT."

Mom's eyes bulged at my whispered words.

In my anxiety-induced panic, I'd driven one hour and twenty-six minutes to arrive unannounced at my mom's office door. As her door swung shut behind me, I verbally vomited all the ways in which I couldn't handle law school and needed to quit—one week before my first semester finals—before dissolving into a heaving, sobbing mess.

I've often thought of that young woman desperate to escape the pressure, the hard work, the stress, the perceived looming failure, wanting her mom to give her permission to quit. If I could, I'd promise her the degree would help others, and that there was a cute classmate named Aaron who was going to notice her the next semester and ask her out. If she quit, she wouldn't meet the love of her life.

Today's word is a promise that our hard circumstances are momentary. Chapters 7 and 8 of Isaiah are a warning to the nation of Israel that the Assyrians would overrun and carry the Israelites off into captivity. But chapter 9 begins with the word *nevertheless*—an assurance that their despair and destruction is temporary, that the Messiah's Kingdom is on the horizon, that there is hope.

Nevertheless. I have breathed this word over my life so many times since ambushing my mom at her office almost two decades ago. I have walked through far more challenging seasons than that first finals week—some in which I had no choice and some in which I did—but the lesson has remained the same: this hard thing is not forever. God does not leave our story stuck in destruction and despair. He moves us through and beyond to new life, oftentimes using parts of that difficult circumstance later for his glory (see Romans 8:28). When I find myself in untenable circumstances, I no longer turn immediately to thoughts of escape. I pray, I do not lose hope, and I whisper *nevertheless* as I wait.

Lord, what circumstances are we seeking to quit when you'd tell us to stay with a nevertheless, a prayer, and hope? Amen.

-Julie

One Good Step: Confess your temptation to escape a tough situation to a faith mentor—a pastor or a godly friend—who will give you trusted, biblical advice and come up with a plan for sticking it out.

Radiant

I saw the glory of the God of Israel coming from the east. His voice was like
the roar of rushing waters, and the land was radiant with his glory.

EZEKIEL 43:2, NIV

I BOUGHT A HAPPY LIGHT RECENTLY. Though it was still warm and sunny outside, I
was thinking ahead to the darkest part of winter, with its short days and gloomy
weather. Though I love the cozy warmth of my home, I miss the radiant sunlight
of the summer months. Happy lights, also known as light therapy lamps, give the
user exposure to light when there's less sun in the fall and winter months. Sitting
near a light therapy box that gives off bright light that mimics natural, outdoor
light is believed to increase energy levels and boost your mood.

So in the mornings, after I pour a cup of coffee and swirl in caramel pecan
cream, I sink into my floral orange chair and immediately turn on the light. It's best
to use it in the morning, as it affects brain chemicals linked to mood and sleep. As I
sit and read the news or a devotional, the light illuminates the entire room. In fact,
the radiance of it fills the room with such a bright glow that my husband can see it
outside the house when he returns from exercising. It's searing to the eyes (and not
recommended) to look directly at it, so it's best to be adjacent to it.

How often our physical world echoes the spiritual world. Because isn't Jesus
the radiant light of the world? And aren't we meant to be positioned next to him,
basking in his glory that radiates for all the world to see? Like my happy light, it's
important for us to start the day in the radiance of the Son. I find that the more
I focus on him, the more my perspective shifts, and I'm energized by his love and
care. Only then can I go about the course of my day. As we seek to follow him, the
radiance of his love will reflect off of us for all to see.

*Lord, thank you for the radiant light of your love. Help us to begin each day with
you. Amen.*

-Kristin

One Good Step: Consider your morning routine. How might you
incorporate the radiance of God's presence into your day?

Humility

Always be humble and gentle. Be patient with each other, making allowance for each other's faults because of your love.

EPHESIANS 4:2

UGH. UGH. UGH. My inner critic was on a roll. *You are terrible with details—the worst! How could you forget to confirm the meeting with Angela after getting dates from Kendra and Kristin?!*

We were supposed to have a business meeting in the morning, had had the meeting on our calendars for weeks, and yet I'd never confirmed with Angela. And so I did what I should—humbly apologized to Angela, taking full ownership of the mistake without excuses, and then apologized to my business partners for failing to follow through, letting them know the steps I was taking to make it right.

They were well within their rights to be irritated with me, and I awaited their response a bit anxiously, knowing I deserved their ire for throwing a wrench into our week's tasks.

What I received was grace—from all involved. Angela sent a kind response suggesting a new date, and as I sent that new date to Kendra and Kristin, they cheerfully agreed, good-naturedly teasing me about whether I had confirmed our new meeting even as they admitted to mistakes and the need for grace.

Their gentle, humble response to my error is not the norm in society, and I know it. I've worked in places and alongside people who use mistakes to showcase smug superiority, an opportunity to wield the error as a weapon against the offender in a vicious game of workplace politics. And I know people who deflect, hide, or blame others for their mistake, too proud or too scared to admit they are fallible and human. Neither response is godly, and both lead to distrust and dysfunction when left unchecked and unaddressed. Toxic environments—work, volunteer or otherwise—exist, in part, because of a lack of humility.

As followers of Jesus, we are called to better. Jesus' style of leadership is always from a position of humility, not pride. He modeled humility in leading others, in cultivating relationships, in interacting with those who hated him, and he told us to do the same.

Lord, thank you for establishing the standard. Help us to humbly own our mistakes and quickly extend grace for the mistakes of others. Amen.

-Julie

One Good Step: Practice acknowledging your mistakes without excuse or shifting the blame, and offer unqualified grace when others do the same.

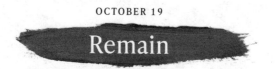

Remain

Remain in me, as I also remain in you. No branch can bear fruit by itself;
it must remain in the vine.

JOHN 15:4, NIV

IT WAS MORNING, and I was rushing to get kids out the door for school when my phone rang: *It's Dad.* We shared a little small talk before he casually asked, "You remember last week when I went to the VA for a biopsy of my prostate?"

"Yes," I cautiously replied.

"Well, they called me this morning, and the tests came back positive."

Cancer.

I asked more questions, wanting more details. Things I could reason, assess. I wanted hope to hang on to. He did his best to answer. I knew I should pray for him before we hung up, but I just couldn't do it. I was too afraid I'd burst into tears.

The conversation ended, and I listlessly went through the motions. Getting everything on my to-do list checked off, all the while the words swirling around in my brain: *Dad has cancer.*

I know people like to tell stories looking back, in hindsight. And although that can be so encouraging to hear how someone survived, or made it through, what of the times when you're still waiting? Wondering what the end result will be?

As I sat in my living room after a too-busy morning, I finally had a chance to open my Bible. *Lord, you know I need to hear from you today.*

I read John 15:4. The words soaked into my mind: *Remain in me. Remain in my love.*

Remain. But what does that mean? To abide. Cling. Persist. Reside. So simple and yet easy to overlook if I'm not careful, unaware. That day my senses were heightened, waiting for a word of hope. But I was given the word I could cling to, if just for one day: *remain.*

Most days we live in some sort of uncertainty in one area of life or another. It may not always be in large or profound ways, but there is still a lot of unknown in life. Every day we can choose to remain in Christ. To cling to him. Remain.

Lord, may we choose to ignore the voices of doubt, fear, and worry that try to invade our thoughts. May we instead turn to you and remain in you. Amen.

-Kendra

One Good Step: What area of life feels uncertain right now?
What would it look like to remain in Jesus in this season?

Celebrate

Yes, the LORD has done amazing things for us! What joy!

PSALM 126:3

COOKIE DOUGH, *Neapolitan, and brownie batter ice creams. Maraschino cherries, whipped cream, chocolate sauce. Oh, and sprinkles.* Skimming down my list, I penciled in the items I needed to purchase, tapping my pen as I tried to recall anything I needed to add. *Can't forget the marshmallow creme.*

Our family was in a bit of a rut. We had been working and doing school from home for a few weeks and were already restless. Each day felt a bit like a broken record, the same routines repeated over and over. So I had decided that the following weekend we were going to start a new tradition: Sunday Sundaes. Each Sunday evening, I planned to pull out ice cream and all the fixings and turn it into a celebration. Months have passed since that first sundae celebration, and it's now a tradition we rarely miss.

Celebrations are dotted throughout Scripture: in Nehemiah, as the Israelites dedicated a wall; in the Year of Jubilee every fiftieth year; in the Passover, as a remembrance of God's faithfulness to his people. Celebrations help define our calendars and provide a rhythm to our lives. We're good at celebrating big moments like birthdays and holidays with fireworks and food, presents, and gatherings. But what about smaller, everyday celebrations?

Life is full of opportunities to celebrate—if only we'll choose to see them. We can celebrate the dishes being done with an impromptu dance party. We can celebrate the end of a successful working day with a relaxing bath or a sunny day with a walk outside to enjoy the fresh air. These small celebrations, woven into the fabric of our lives, make ordinary moments feel extraordinary. When we find small moments to celebrate, we honor God's work in our lives—they are a testament to his love for us. The same God who mourns when a sparrow falls is surely pleased when we stop to notice the beauty of a sunrise, the spicy flavors of a good stew, or the warmth of someone's hand in ours. When we choose to find reasons to celebrate, we remind ourselves of God's goodness and thank him for all he's done and is doing.

Lord, thank you that we can celebrate this life in big and small ways. Help us to find opportunities to do so each day. Amen.

-Kristin

One Good Step: Find something to celebrate, then do it.

Accomplishment

Jesus replied, "'You must love the LORD your God with all your heart, all your soul, and all your mind.' This is the first and greatest commandment. A second is equally important: 'Love your neighbor as yourself.'"

MATTHEW 22:37-39

SMILING, I PULLED MY OLD JOURNAL out of the box, pausing in my sorting and purging mission to read what nineteen-year-old me had to say. She was feisty in her dogged determination to be a lawyer, measuring decisions—and all of life—through the narrow focus of obtaining her law degree. Her journal was full of quotes from famous people about success and reaching goals, mantras based on proving worth.

I love that girl, despite her understanding of accomplishment being all mixed up and wrong. She didn't know what she didn't know, and as I reread her words wrestling with faith and God and how he might fit into her plans, my heart ached for her and the years she'd spend trying to find purpose and accomplishment the wrong ways before she got it right.

If life is about collecting degrees or whether we have an office with a door rather than a cubicle, then we are living too small and too narrow a life. If we measure accomplishment by the model year of the car in our driveway, or the size of our waist, then we are using the wrong standard.

God may send us to law school or put us in a corner office, but it's never to rack up prestige points against colleagues and neighbors. Being accomplished in God's eyes is far simpler—although certainly not easier. As women who love and follow Jesus, our command for living is clear: we are to love God with our whole heart, soul, and mind, and love others as ourselves. These two commandments are the bedrock principles of our faith, the foundation upon which all else is built.

When we understand that Matthew 22:37-38 is our life's mission, we measure accomplishment by God's standard—by investing in people and relationships in our homes, our neighborhoods, our communities. We become world changers right where God has planted us, living ordinary, extraordinary lives.

Lord, may we trade the world's definition of accomplishment for yours. Show us where we are mixing up the world's standard with yours. Amen.

-Julie

One Good Step: What's your definition of accomplishment? What might you need to change as you meditate on Matthew 22:37-38?

Assistance

Two people are better off than one, for they can help each other
succeed. If one person falls, the other can reach out and
help. But someone who falls alone is in real trouble.
ECCLESIASTES 4:9-10

I TOSSED AND TURNED all night long. We'd had to make a pretty heavy parenting decision, and already I was afraid I'd made the wrong choice. I couldn't sleep, convinced
I was going to mess up my kids and they'd never recover.

My husband finally rolled over and looked at me. "Honey," he said, "we will
figure this out together. You are not alone. We're in this together." And tears fell as
his words hit to the heart of my mom guilt. I was feeling like I had to make these
big decisions alone. With no input or assistance from others or even from God. I
hugged Kyle as I tried to remind myself, once again, that the weight of these decisions did not rest solely on me. There were others around me who could help carry
the burden with me.

But as I thought about my response the next day, I wondered, *When did I start
to believe that I had to manage or take care of everything alone without any assistance
from others?* And to be honest, I'm still not sure of the answer, but I am trying to
change the way I think and behave to allow others to help me when I need it.

Many of us have grown up in a society where independence is highly valued.
And although in many ways this is not a bad thing, sometimes we can be too
independent. We can carry burdens alone, not wanting to ask for assistance or
bother others. We forget to pray and ask God for help. But the reality is, we need
wisdom from God and support from other people. It's too hard when we feel
completely alone. We were made to accept assistance at times from others, and
to offer it when we see someone else struggling. We are so much more successful
when we mutually support one another.

*Lord, help me to ask for assistance from others when I need it, and help me to
offer assistance to those I see who are struggling. Amen.*

-Kendra

One Good Step: What area of your life have you been trying
to manage alone? Who could you ask for assistance?

Honor

We ask God to give you . . . spiritual wisdom and understanding.
Then the way you live will always honor and please the Lord,
and your lives will produce every kind of good fruit.
COLOSSIANS 1:9-10

THE CHURCH SANCTUARY WAS FULL, but still people streamed inside. From my vantage point near the front, I could see additional folding chairs being set up, crowding the back wall. By the time the service began, the seats were filled, and people had begun to collect at the edges and spill over into the hallway and front foyer.

It was my sister's funeral, and I'd never seen our church so full.

At twenty-eight, Katrina's death felt premature and—though she'd been battling breast cancer for five years—shocking in its suddenness. The day of her funeral, many spoke of her character, her warmth, and the way she could draw people into her sphere so easily.

In the few decades she'd spent on this earth, Katrina had lived with a fullness and joy that enveloped those around her. She was part of the leadership of her local MOPS, worked with her church's women's ministry, and sang on the worship team. Even as her body weakened, she consciously chose to live in a God-honoring way. And the fruit of her life was evident from the crowd that strained the confines of the church to honor her memory.

The word *honor* sounds like something old-fashioned, part of court proceedings or a page from the medieval past. Today, the Medal of Honor is the United States' most prestigious award given to military service members who have distinguished themselves through acts of valor.

But in the Old Testament, honor is often used to talk about showing reverence to God. It's both a characteristic, a description, and an action. When we honor God, we reflect his name. Our words make him known. We worship, respect, and elevate his name. And we do so by loving God and loving others. When our actions demonstrate that we aren't doing things for our own glory, he is the one who is honored, and the evidence is in the fruit we produce: "love, joy, peace, patience, kindness, goodness, faithfulness, gentleness, and self-control" (Galatians 5:22-23).

Lord, help us to honor your name in all we say and do. Amen.

-Kristin

One Good Step: Consider whether or not your daily choices honor God. In what ways do you reflect his name to others? What kind of fruit does your life produce?

Provision

The LORD is my shepherd; I have all that I need.

PSALM 23:1

I FIRST MET my friend Sarah when we both wrote for a website specifically for moms. Since then, I've followed her journey as she and her husband listened to God's call to become full-time missionaries in Honduras. I asked her to share what God has been teaching her, and this was her response:

Last night we sat the third empty bottle of water by the door. The water truck hasn't been by, so we are running low. We have one more bottle with water in it. Two months ago I would have panicked and made plans to disobey the curfew to go get water. Well, I would have sent Jason out to get water. I would have stressed, worried, and probably stayed up for hours in my bed until 2 a.m. thinking, "How will we get water!?" Instead, this time of isolation has taught me again and again that God will provide. Psalm 23 is true. We will never lack. Usually the water trucks come on Tuesday (today is Monday). So I'm excited to see how God will provide what we need. The water truck will be by today. How do I know this? Because we need water and God provides what we need. This resting in God's provision is a lesson I didn't know I needed to learn. Oh the Kindness of God to teach me of His provision during this pandemic. What a good, good Father.

And as I read about her daily life now, I wonder if I would have the same reaction, the same understanding of God's provision. Sarah's attitude is commendable, but she would shrug off any compliments, knowing it is God working in her mind and heart to trust his provision.

Maybe you've never been a missionary like my friend Sarah, but there are times in all of our lives when we need to trust for God's provision beyond what we can currently see with our physical eyes. Sometimes provision comes in ways we expect, and other times God grows our faith and trust in him and his provision in ways we would not even imagine.

Lord, thank you for being such a good Father and for providing all that we need. Amen.

-Kendra

One Good Step: What is one thing you are trusting in God's provision to meet in your life right now? Write it down, and see how God provides.

Relinquish

For who can know the LORD's thoughts?
Who knows enough to give him advice?

ROMANS 11:34

"AND, I'M PRAYING THAT the mattresses we need will be donated for *free*."

The moment I made the bold request, I knew I was in trouble. I was doing a short presentation for a group of fifty employees at a local nonprofit, having been introduced as helping lead their Christmas program in which local families are adopted by community members. Small needs like toys and clothes are met as well as the sometimes-bigger needs of furniture, household goods, and mattresses. There is a perennial, desperate need for mattresses, and while my audacious prayer was for something inherently good, I'd publicly put God on the spot without hearing from him first and without pausing to ask whether this was his will. It was *my* plan, and I was asking God to do *my* will, publicly.

Just because we are well intentioned doesn't mean we can hijack God's sovereignty, demanding he do things our way, in our timing. And I'd forgotten that for a moment, running ahead of God because people needed mattresses and I knew God could do it. What I failed to ask God is *if* he would do it, and in the manner in which I'd just so boldly declared.

Oh, how I came to regret my hasty words. No mattresses, free or otherwise, materialized that Christmas season, despite my best efforts. And while the myriad of other needs were met, finding a partner for mattresses crashed and burned. And, faced with repentance, I tearfully relinquished control back to God, where it always should have been in the first place.

Don't get me wrong, God is *good* and he absolutely answers prayers. But I'd arrogantly put his name on the line with my public declaration centering attention on me, without prayerfully seeking his plan. As someone who has a gift for problem-solving, it was a powerful, humbling lesson in relinquishing control, remembering that God is sovereign, and his way is always better, even if it doesn't always make sense in the moment.

Lord, forgive us our attempts to control you and your plan. Help us to relinquish control, prayerfully asking you to show us the next steps to take. Amen.

-Julie

One Good Step: Make a list of the things you are attempting to control in your life. In what ways is God asking you to relinquish control in each situation?

Direction

The LORD directs the steps of the godly. He delights in every detail of their lives. Though they stumble, they will never fall, for the LORD holds them by the hand.

PSALM 37:23-24

I SURVEYED the dining room table with trepidation. Tiny cars with pegs in them littered the surface of the game board while messy stacks of pretend money and career cards lined the edges. The cover had been tossed haphazardly to the edge of the table, the directions abandoned next to it.

The Game of Life had been lying on my kitchen table for three days. When we first began, it seemed straightforward: collect a job, money, and a family before retiring. But I had forgotten how much the twists and turns of the game quickly became just as complex and confusing as the real life the game mimics. We ran out of time to finish the game that evening, so the kids had made us promise to leave it out. Days later, it was still sprawled across the table, making eating meals a challenge. In my mind, it was less than ideal.

My husband shrugged when I complained over morning coffee.

"That's pretty true to life, honestly," he said. "It takes more than a few days to build a life."

That was too philosophical to dissect at 6:30 a.m. But later I kept returning to the idea: *What happens when our own life seems to mimic that board game?* Sometimes life can seem messy and directionless, and what seems straightforward on the surface is actually much more complicated.

The truth is that one of the hardest parts of the Christian walk is being patient when things don't happen as quickly as we'd like or in the way we expect. Which direction should we go? What should we do next? It's easy to become discouraged or impatient because we can't envision the larger story God is writing. Yet even though we can't see how the disparate threads are being woven together, God can—in fact, he delights in the details.

As Christians, let's encourage one another to continue to seek God's direction. Though things may not happen as quickly as we hope or in quite the way we expect, he has not forgotten us. In our momentary frustration, may we never lose sight of that living hope.

Lord, thank you that we can look to you for direction. Amen.

-Kristin

One Good Step: Spend time praying about an area of life in which you need direction.

Pause

Fools have no interest in understanding;
they only want to air their own opinions.

PROVERBS 18:2

"HAVE YOU READ THIS? What is going on?" Her early morning text linked to an online post declaring outlandish behavior by a government agency.

Digging a bit further, I realized the policy at issue had been around for a long time and was being taken out of context. My friend was being intentionally emotionally baited, provoked into an outsize response.

"Jess, that article is trying to provoke you to outrage," I texted back, explaining why. I ended with, "Pause. Take a deep breath, and don't take the bait, friend. It's exhausting and anxiety producing, and we don't need any more of either in our lives."

We live in a culture that thrives on outrage. I see it everywhere, not just in politics, but both sides of the political spectrum are especially adept at revving their base up with distorted headlines and stories spun for maximum outrage.

There *are* situations in which we must be gravely concerned and moved to action, but failing to pause, asking God which issues legitimately require our energy and which are red herrings, meant to distract and provoke us unnecessarily, is a waste of our precious energy and creates undue anxiety.

I've learned to consume news with a critical eye, pausing to prayerfully consider motives and special interests before investing emotionally. And I read extensively—from a wide array of sources considered left, right, and central—no longer content to rely solely upon any source with dogmatic loyalty.

My loyalty is to Jesus, always. Political parties and love of country must be a distant second to my faith, or I risk making them idols in my life. Pausing for a long moment when faced with an inflammatory claim—no matter the source—helps me stay Christ centered, and reminds me to pray before jumping on bandwagons that Jesus may not be asking me to join.

Lord, remind us to prayerfully pause when invited to be outraged, especially by political parties or those with an agenda. Give us discernment, remembering to be centered in Christ. Amen.

-Julie

One Good Step: Practice pausing to pray for discernment and wisdom after you consume headlines, articles, and news programming, asking God to give insight into motives and hidden agendas—for all sources.

Written

When the LORD finished speaking with Moses on Mount Sinai,
he gave him the two stone tablets inscribed with the terms
of the covenant, written by the finger of God.

EXODUS 31:18

ENTERING THE LONG HALL, I looked around with amazement. On both sides of the room, benches ran parallel to the walls, the vertical windows above them reaching high toward a classic Gothic vaulted ceiling. Jostled by the crowd, my attention was drawn from the elaborate architecture to the object of my visit: a rare Gutenberg Bible.

Gutenberg's Bible was produced in the 1450s as the first substantial book produced in the West using movable metal type, an advancement akin to the internet in terms of its impact. Before movable type, scribes had to write each word of a book. Most Christians didn't have the opportunity to read the Bible for themselves. Many couldn't read Latin and didn't have access to the written word anyway. The advent of a printing press made books, including the Bible, more accessible to ordinary people. This new technology motivated and transformed literacy and education all across the world.

Because of Gutenberg's innovative printing press, the Word of God—and many other texts—became much more accessible to the common man. Rather than locked away in a monastery, ideas could be freely shared. As more and more people had access to God's Word, they were able to learn the truth of his love and grace and mercy for themselves. What a legacy! The Bible is now the world's bestselling printed book, available in more than 636 languages, with at least 1,142 languages that have access to the New Testament.[3]

Written words have power because of what they signify; it's the meaning behind them that gives them the ability to move us, anger us, and fill our hearts with hope or disdain, fury or purpose. Like Gutenberg's Bible and the technology that powered it, the words we read and write have the power to change the world. What a great privilege it is for us to partner with God in sharing his Word with others.

Lord, thank you for the gift of your written Word. Help us to recognize its value. Amen.

-Kristin

One Good Step: Write out your favorite verse.
Send it to a friend along with a note of encouragement.

---

3 Joseph Hartropp, "Johann Gutenberg, Printer: 3 Ways He Revolutionised Christianity," *Christian Today*, February 3, 2017, https://www.christiantoday.com/article/johann-gutenberg-printer-3-ways-he-revolutionised-christianity/104388.htm.

Intercede

I urge you, first of all, to pray for all people. Ask God to help them;
intercede on their behalf, and give thanks for them.
1 TIMOTHY 2:1

MY FINGERS HOVERING over my phone's keyboard, I paused. I wanted to know how
my friend's sister was doing, knowing she'd been rushed to the hospital the evening
before, but I found myself hesitating. *Do I really need that information? Can't I pray
over her, over their family without asking that question? What is the best way I can
support my friend in this moment?*

Instead of asking for updates, I texted her a prayer, asking God for the words,
for what specifically to pray for as I typed. And as I typed, the words came to me
unbidden, gushing forth as I poured my heart out on my friend's behalf. Sending it
off with an emoji heart and a note that she need not respond. There wasn't anything
I could do for my friend physically, but I interceded for her spiritually, praying both
for her sister and for her.

Intercession is one of my favorite things about being in a faith community. The
incredible story of Peter's imprisonment and subsequent middle-of-the-night rescue
at the hands of an angel detailed in Acts 12 is preceded by the simple statement
that the church was praying earnestly, fervently, unceasingly upon learning of his
imprisonment (see Acts 12:5). Intercessory prayer is a habit woven throughout
both the Old and New Testaments, with Jesus' prayer in the garden of Gethsemane
(recorded in John 17) being especially poignant as he prayed over not only his disciples but also over all future believers.

Life sometimes feels impossibly hard, and attempting to go it alone leaves us
vulnerable spiritually. It's those moments when we need women who notice and
respond, women who firmly and lovingly stand alongside us, women who intercede
on our behalf, praying the prayers we are too tired or too discouraged to pray. And
while we are often good at meeting a friend's physical needs with a meal dropped
off or assistance in other ways, we might forget that prayerful intercession is perhaps
the most valuable gift we can give another.

*Lord, give us eyes and ears to notice the people around us desperately in need of
intercession. Amen.*

-Julie

One Good Step: Text someone a prayer.

Joy

Always be joyful.

1 THESSALONIANS 5:16

SITTING CROSS-LEGGED ON THE FLOOR, I paused when I saw the journals. My sister Katrina had died several months earlier after a battle with breast cancer, and my mom, my sister Kendra, and I were helping my brother-in-law sort through books in their office to decide what to keep or donate. The three of us ranged around the room, sorting through piles, stopping every once in a while to ask about a title. On both sides of me, books were piled high. Each of them was special for one reason or another. But what I held in my hands was different.

Glancing over her beautiful script, I couldn't help but remember how stunned we were when she was first diagnosed at age twenty-three. She exuded health. But as the years passed and the cancer returned, stealing her hair and vitality, it was harder to hope. When she died, a part of us did too.

The journal felt like a gift, and between what she had written there and in old emails she'd sent over the years, her words were a treasure uncovered. In one message, she detailed her current challenges but ended with these words: "So, how am I emotionally? Well, I choose to have peace. I choose to have joy. And you know what? You can have what you choose. My life is filled with joy, peace, love and usually, patience. He is faithful. My God is faithful." In the midst of her pain and confusion over God's purpose, Katrina chose joy.

Paul told the early church more than once to be joyful; in fact, he repeated it even after he himself languished in prison. I've heard it said that the Christian who cannot be joyful refuses to trust God in some way, because joy is not simply a result of our present circumstances but our hope for the future. On hard days, that truth can remind us that the decision to choose joy is inextricably linked to our hope for the future, no matter what it may hold. We are forgiven and will spend eternity with Jesus, and that is always a reason to be joyful.

Lord, thank you for the gift of joy. Help us to choose to always be joyful. Amen.

-Kristin

One Good Step: What circumstances do you need to claim joy in?

Reclaim

You are the light of the world. A town built
on a hill cannot be hidden.

MATTHEW 5:14, NIV

AS CHILDREN we did not celebrate Halloween in our home. We would typically attend a fall-themed event at our church. I never felt like I was missing out on much, because we still got lots of candy and played games in the basement of the church while sipping hot apple cider, surrounded by our church family.

As parents, we wondered what we should do with our own kids on Halloween. At the same time, we were reading books about living among people and what it looks like to engage in culture in a way that shines a light. Our pastor asked us, "Is Halloween redeemable for the Kingdom?"

We believed that it was and began to pray about how we could reclaim the holiday. We decided to bring our firepit out to our driveway, bought full-size candy bars to pass out, and made hot chocolate for chilly hands walking through our neighborhood. We allowed our kids to dress up in costumes that were fun and never scary, and we went around, greeting neighbors and inviting others to warm themselves by our fire. It was just another way for us to get to know and build relationships with those around us, and it has become a favorite tradition in our home.

As Christians, we can discern and decide what from our culture should get reclaimed and what needs to be let go of. For us, we found Halloween to be a great way for us to connect with those around us, and we'll take any opportunity to build relationships with the people in our neighborhood. We get to shine the light of Jesus on what can be a particularly dark night. We need to remember that we are the light on the hill and that when we shine, others will be drawn into God's love.

Lord, help us to be wise as we engage our culture. Give us discernment to know what can be reclaimed for your glory. May we each be a light to the world, so that others will know your love. Amen.

-Kendra

One Good Step: What is something in our culture that you can reclaim, and how can you use it to be a light to those around you?

November

Gospel

The LORD has anointed me to bring good news to the poor.
He has sent me to comfort the brokenhearted and to proclaim
that captives will be released and prisoners will be freed.

ISAIAH 61:1

RUBBING MY FOREHEAD, I stifled a sigh. Though I tried to hide my dismay, my reaction must have given me away. Tim glanced over at me. "What's wrong?"

"Nothing," I said. "I just had to snooze someone on social media. She's so nice in person and her kids are adorable, but I can't handle the negative articles she keeps posting. It's influencing the way that I see her as a person, and I hate feeling that way."

His expression turned a little sheepish. "I've hidden a lot of people lately too."

The older I get, the more I realize how powerful our words are—even, and perhaps especially, the ones that we *don't* say face-to-face. I have to admit that I'm sometimes discouraged at the way people choose to wield their words. All too often on social media, the posts are incendiary or the words divisive. Part of me can't help but wonder: *Is this what you want to be known for?*

Instead of getting pulled into the news of the day, let's choose to share the best news of all—the gospel of Jesus. According to *Easton's Bible Dictionary*, *gospel* is a rendering of the Greek *evangelion*, "good message." This good message includes "the gospel of the grace of God" (Acts 20:24), "the gospel of the kingdom" (Matthew 4:23), "the gospel of Christ" (Romans 1:16), "the gospel of peace" (Ephesians 6:15), "the glorious gospel," "the everlasting gospel," and "the gospel of salvation" (Ephesians 1:13). What a wonderful list describing the gospel: grace, peace, everlasting, glorious, salvation—truly Good News! One of my favorite Scriptures, Isaiah 61:1 reminds us that we are anointed with a wonderful task: we have good news of great joy for *all* people. What a radical perspective. What a lifelong mission.

Let's be people who refuse to give up our long-term influence with someone just to prove a point. Perspectives shift and people change, but we have the opportunity to reflect and demonstrate with loving words the sovereign, saving grace of our Jesus. Let's choose to speak the gospel, sharing the Good News of Jesus with all we encounter.

Lord, thank you for the gospel and our opportunity to partner with you in sharing the Good News. Amen.

-Kristin

One Good Step: If you have social media, scan through previous posts on your page. Are your words and actions speaking the Good News of Jesus? Why or why not?

Thanksgiving

Enter his gates with thanksgiving; go into his courts with praise.
Give thanks to him and praise his name.
PSALM 100:4

ONE FALL to help our family focus on all that we were grateful for, we made a thankfulness chain out of paper leading up to Thanksgiving. For each day during November, we would take a strip of paper, write something we were thankful for on it, and then add it to our paper chain. The only rule was that you could not list the same thing twice. At first it was hard to think of new things, but once we started looking each day for something we were thankful for, it became easier to notice.

We started to notice things like the clean water that poured so effortlessly from our faucets, the heat coming out of our vents, and the food in our fridge. We found ourselves thankful for a call from a grandparent or a message from a friend. As we read through the paper-chain list of things we were grateful for on Thanksgiving morning, we noticed how many times a day we could be thankful. And we realized they were all blessings that are easy to overlook when you're not paying attention. Looking for things to be thankful for each day started a habit that continued long after Thanksgiving came and went.

Being thankful is a skill that we can develop when we choose to focus on what we are grateful for each day. Even in a hard season, there are things I can thank God for—even if it's just his love and mercy toward me. We are to praise God in all things. This doesn't mean we have to be grateful for difficult circumstances or that we should deny a challenging season we are in. But it does mean we can find something to praise, something to be thankful for, even as we acknowledge our struggles. No matter what is happening, in good times and bad, we can choose to offer up thanksgiving to God.

Lord, give us eyes to see the goodness of you around us, and teach our hearts to be thankful, in good and hard times. Amen.

-Kendra

One Good Step: Each day leading up to Thanksgiving, write down one thing you are thankful for each day.

Boundaries

Guard your heart above all else, for it determines the course of your life.

PROVERBS 4:23

"BECAUSE WE'RE ALL WORKING FROM HOME, the guardrail crash test demonstration was completed over video conference. Several of us had our kids watch the 4-door Dodge pickup slam into the guardrail at fifty-five miles per hour. Jed and Nora loved it. The guardrail did its job."

My brother Jacob, a guardrail expert for his state's department of transportation, enjoys telling me about his latest work projects. I've learned some interesting things about mountain cliffs and road safety over the years, but this notion of guardrails has been especially intriguing as I've wrestled with erecting appropriate boundaries in my life around relationships, time commitments, and what I invite into my life via social media.

Guardrails are sturdy and strong, erected on safe ground several feet (when possible) back from the danger they are guarding against. They are a visual and physical boundary, warning of danger sometimes before the danger itself is evident.

We sometimes erect boundaries too close to the proverbial cliff—allowing ourselves to get too close and thereby risk getting pulled off or pulled in by the very thing we were trying to avoid. What if, instead, we envisioned our boundaries based on a guardrail, establishing firm lines we don't cross, well back from the edge of temptation, bad influences, harmful choices, and things we know aren't ultimately good for us?

Just as guardrails are designed specifically for a particular location and installed before the moment they're needed, we need to do the same. My boundaries set around things dangerous for me may be designed and installed differently than your boundaries. While there are things that are inherently dangerous to all of us physically or spiritually, there may be things that draw me too close to sin and dangerous choices that don't tempt you at all. God knows our perennial weak spots, and he will help us each erect the boundaries necessary for thriving, if we allow him.

Lord, show us where our boundaries are faulty and will not hold up to a crash test. Help us shore up our weak spots with strongly built guardrails. Amen.

-Julie

One Good Step: Sit down with pen and paper and list five things you need to avoid, establishing guardrails (or revising preexisting ones) to protect yourself.

Wanted

May you have the power to understand, as all God's people should,
how wide, how long, how high, and how deep his love is.

EPHESIANS 3:18

MY DAUGHTER WAS FOUR YEARS OLD when she first asked me about her birth family. She knew she was adopted, but she was trying to figure out what that actually meant. We talked about her birth mom, and then after a moment of quiet, a question came, one we'd never discussed before.

"Why didn't my other mommy want me?" she whispered.

I paused, unsure how to begin, but knowing that what I said next would matter. I could see my little girl's fragile heart in that moment. I prayed and then explained how young her mom was, how she loved Jasmine so much she wanted to make sure she had parents who could care for her long term. And my words seemed to fall a little flat, even to my own ears. With my daughter's eyes still on me, I sighed and whispered to her, "You have always been wanted." She smiled. And then I held her, wondering if she'd ever fully know the depth of our love for her.

And even now, years later, she struggles at times with truly knowing that she is wanted. As she's grown, we've been able to explain to her so much more about family history and trauma, addiction, and mental illness. We affirm that her life has purpose, that she is wanted by God. How much he loves her. This is the truth we are hoping will settle deep in her heart. She is wanted.

So many things can happen to us in life that can make us wonder if we are wanted. We can all experience times when our hearts cry out, *Lord, am I wanted? Am I loved?* And it's in those moments that he gently reminds us that he does love us. Apart from where we came from, what we do, who we are, what titles we have or hats we wear. He wants us. Just as we are.

Dear Lord, I pray for those of us who have wondered if we were wanted. May we believe and experience your love for us in the depths of our hearts. Amen.

-Kendra

One Good Step: How has God shown you that you are wanted by him?

Overflow

I pray that God, the source of hope, will fill you completely with joy
and peace because you trust in him. Then you will overflow with
confident hope through the power of the Holy Spirit.
ROMANS 15:13

MY MOM HAD JUST STARTED running a bath upstairs when the phone trilled. The phone was located on the first floor in our 1920s house, so she dashed downstairs to catch it. Her sister was on the line, and as the two started chatting, my mom forgot about her bath.

Suddenly, a great whooshing, dripping sound could be heard on the main floor. Noticing the odd noise, my sisters and I raced into the kitchen to see water streaming through the ceiling, through the light fixture, onto the table and floor underneath. The lights were on in the chandelier, and we watched in horror as parts of the fixture began to fill. Someone ran up to shut off the water upstairs while my dad painstakingly flipped the light switch. It was a memorable mess, to say the least.

That mental picture comes to mind every time I think of God's overflowing love. When something overflows, it's not a gentle trickle—it's a veritable deluge. That bathwater touched everything in its path, found its way through all barriers, sought every crevice. Nothing could stop it—until the source was shut off.

We, too, are called to overflow with the love and hope of Christ. Our connection to the source—the Holy Spirit—is what allows us to spill over into the lives of others. It's only when we are cut off from our source that those qualities stop flowing.

The word *overflow* is used throughout Scripture to describe qualities of God (redemption, compassion) or of us, his followers (joy, grace, love, hope) that only happen when we abide in him. As Christians, our ability to overflow with good things is directly tied to the power of the Holy Spirit at work within us. Our firm footing with Christ gives us the confidence we need and facilitates the wonderful things that spill over into each area of our lives.

Lord, thank you that—through your power—we can overflow with love, joy, hope, and grace. Help us to demonstrate those qualities to everyone we meet, pointing back to the Source who fuels us. Amen.

-Kristin

One Good Step: What qualities or characteristics has your life overflowed with lately? How does that tie to your connection to the Holy Spirit?

Observe

Do to others whatever you would like them to do to you.
This is the essence of all that is taught in the law and the prophets.
MATTHEW 7:12

EVEN AS I STOMPED AWAY, my angry words lingering in the air, I wondered why such a small thing had evoked such an oversize reaction. *Mom didn't deserve that. She isn't who I'm mad at. Why are my emotions out of control? Why did I do that? What's wrong with me?*

I can still remember the confusion, tension, and general angst that would sometimes overwhelm my teenage self, resulting in an outburst over something trivial and pointless. My mom bore the brunt of my raging hormones because I knew she was safe. She remained calm in the midst of my storms, was unwavering in her love, and firm in her boundaries. She would pause to observe the situation before she reacted, knowing when to push back and when to simply wrap me in a loving hug as I melted into a puddle of tears.

My mom has a gift for seeing through the facade to the heart of a situation or person, responding with calm compassion to the root cause instead of engaging the swirl of hot emotions. It's a trait I work to emulate, because it dissolves unnecessary potential conflict and shows the other person that I see *them* and not simply the issue they are presenting.

Taking a moment to observe the entirety of the situation, considering root causes and what lies unspoken in the face of someone's emotional tempest, is not for the faint of heart. Our natural instinct is to get defensive, fighting back rather than taking a breath and considering what else might be happening. But observing is the wiser choice, asking God to reveal how we can defuse the emotion so we address the underlying issue in the moments before we engage.

Heavenly Father, give us eyes to see and ears to hear past facades and camouflage to the heart of the matter. May we be observant as we encounter those you love. Amen.

-Julie

One Good Step: Practice taking a deep breath and a long pause before you respond to someone's angry words or actions. As you pause, ask God to show you what else might be going on.

Selah

The LORD your God is in your midst, a mighty one who will save;
he will rejoice over you with gladness; he will quiet you
by his love; he will exult over you with loud singing.

ZEPHANIAH 3:17, ESV

I KNEW THAT FALL was going to be a busy one for me and my family. After having released a book and planning for several speaking engagements, I purposely left time and space in my schedule to be home and have downtime. But as the first several weeks of the fall chugged along, I found myself frustrated that I was still feeling tired and exhausted mentally, even with all the "down" time in my schedule.

I wondered how it could be, that although I had planned to rest physically, my mind was often still unsettled and racing, thinking of all the things that needed to be done each day. As I took my frustration to God in prayer, I realized that while I had planned for time to physically rest, I needed to also find a way to rest my mind and soul. Selah, a pause and a time to reflect on who God is and all he has done for my spirit. I determined a couple of times a week to put my phone on silent and lie down to rest my brain in the afternoon. Even if it was just for twenty minutes. I found that when I did this I felt more peace and less anxiety as I went throughout my days. My mind began to calm and not race quite as often. Although it wasn't perfect and I still had my frantic moments, creating a rhythm of selah allowed me to actually get more accomplished with less stress and strain.

Rest is not something only our bodies need, but our minds and spirits as well, and if we ignore any area of our well-being, we'll find ourselves worn out and frustrated. Remembering to rest our minds and spirits in the truth of God's Word is just as important as resting our physical bodies. Selah is a rhythm of life that is regularly overlooked in our busy culture, but not by our God. He knows what we need, better than we often know ourselves.

Lord, thank you for quieting us with your love. May we take time to pause and allow you to refresh our souls. Amen.

-Kendra

One Good Step: How can you start to incorporate a selah rhythm into your life? What may you need to give up or add to do this?

History

Those who are wise will take all this to heart; they will see
in our history the faithful love of the LORD.
PSALM 107:43

WE HAD A GENEALOGIST RESEARCH our family last year. I already knew bits and pieces of lore passed down from grandparents and aunts but was eager to have a professional find out more.

One of the most interesting stories the genealogist uncovered was about an ancestor, John M., who came over during the Revolutionary War from Brandenburg, Prussia, as a mercenary soldier for the British Army. Once he reached these shores, John defected to the Patriots and served in the 10th Regiment of Virginia. His pension application named lots of officers of the Revolutionary War, including Generals Francis Marion (famously known as the Swamp Fox) and Horatio Gates, who received 17,500 acres of military bounty land. John even lived on General Gates's land for four years before moving to Pennsylvania, where he married a Native American woman and had nine children. Although unconfirmed, there is a tantalizing rumor that during the war she served as a spy.

While I found that piece of family history fascinating, it caused me to wonder what others will say about my own life someday. Stories are important—not just because they are part of history in general but because they are part of *our* history. The stories we believe about ourselves shape the way we interact with the world and those around us. When we hear stories repeated again and again, we believe they are true, and they become part of us.

Years from now when we reflect back on our own life, will the story our life tells be part of the history of Jesus, reflecting his grace and mercy? As children of God, let's mirror our spiritual heritage by being people who rise and end each day singing God's praises and telling the story of how he has loved us so well. May our lives become one more small story in the history of God's faithfulness.

Lord, thank you for the history of your faithful love that's been passed on to us. Help us to recognize it and reflect it in our own lives. Amen.

-Kristin

One Good Step: What stories do you tell others that will one day
contribute to the history of faith? Spend time considering
what you convey through your actions and words.

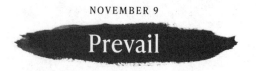

Prevail

You can make many plans, but the LORD's purpose will prevail.
PROVERBS 19:21

"OFTEN, WE PRAY prayers for comfort—for God to remove us from difficult circumstances—rather than for his will to prevail in the midst of the storm. We beg to get out rather than get through. And because we are seeking to escape, we don't stop to ask what bigger thing God might be doing in us and through us." Aaron's paraphrase of Mark Batterson's words in *Draw the Circle* as he maneuvered our vehicle through rush hour traffic had my heart seizing as I processed what he was saying.

Have I done that, Lord? I thought. *Have I been more concerned with my comfort than that your will prevail? Have I been so busy plotting an escape that I've completely missed what you were doing, trying to do? Is comfort an idol in my life?*

Oh boy. Those are convicting, hard questions, aren't they? I admit I've desperately begged for escape, unwilling to ask God to use me in a hard place. And when I think of godly, incredible women around me, I realize that some of their best work—books they've written, sermons they've preached, ministries they've started—is rooted in dark, hard experiences they'd not wish on their worst enemy. God uses impossibly hard things to accomplish his will, oftentimes with more impact than the easy-peasy life of comfort we desperately pray for.

What does it mean for God's will to prevail? He promises that he will cause all things—the good and the bad—to work together for his glory and for the good of those who love and are called by God (see Romans 8:28). God promises to not leave or forsake us in the midst of crisis and chaos, but he did not promise to remove the storm or that we will understand "why" this side of heaven. Just as Jesus asked to be rescued even as he prayed for God's will to prevail in the garden of Gethsemane, our ultimate prayer should be for God's will, not our comfort.

Lord, may we tear down our idols around comfort, praying that your will prevails in the midst of all things, the good and the bad. Amen.

-Julie

One Good Step: Start asking for God's will to prevail in every prayer you pray. And ask God what circumstances you have tried to blindly escape rather than seeking his will in the midst.

NOVEMBER 10

Generosity

> But who am I, and who are my people, that we should be able
> to give as generously as this? Everything comes from you,
> and we have given you only what comes from your hand.
>
> 1 CHRONICLES 29:14, NIV

ONE DAY I CAME HOME and noticed two people sitting outside on our sidewalk. All around them were their belongings, suitcases, boxes, and bags. I thought it odd, but went inside without commenting.

As my family and I observed them from our kitchen window, wondering what we should do, my six-year-old offered her suggestion. "Mom," she started, "you need to go and talk to them. You could tell them they could live in our basement. We have an empty room, and no one is using it. Tell them they could live there." I looked at her for a moment, realizing that she'd made the connection, that these individuals, with all their belongings strewn around them, probably didn't have a place to live. Her solution was to offer our home, knowing we had more space than we needed.

"Okay, honey," I responded, "I'll go and talk to them." I went out and greeted them. They explained that they did have a place to live across town but they just needed a ride. We offered to help, and my husband loaded up their belongings in our truck to bring to their home.

Later on, I thought about my daughter's quick response to offer them a place to live. She has heard so often in our house that a main tenet of our faith is to be generous to those around us, including strangers, so it naturally came out of her when faced with someone's need.

When we understand generosity as simply giving out of what God has so generously given to us, we'll be happy to share with those around us. Knowing that everything is from him frees us from thinking we've simply earned what we have, spending it only on ourselves. Christians will be known for their love, and one of the ways that we show our love is by generously sharing what we have when we see the needs of others.

Lord, may we see all that we have as your generosity toward us, and may we share it generously with others. Amen.

-Kendra

One Good Step: Who around you has a need? How can you be generous to help meet their needs?

Choice

"If you refuse to serve the LORD, then choose today whom you will serve. . . . But as for me and my family, we will serve the Lord."

JOSHUA 24:15

BACK IN COLLEGE, a boyfriend unexpectedly ended our relationship. It was clear that he wasn't over his ex-girlfriend, and they were getting back together. At the time, I was blindsided and hurt. As time went on, the sting faded, but a niggling voice in my brain still mourned the loss.

A few years later, he was visiting town and asked to meet for dinner at a restaurant. I had just started dating Tim, but I already knew he was important. I had the sense that if I went to the dinner, I would know—either there were unresolved feelings I had to figure out before moving forward with Tim, or this would provide needed closure.

Dinner that night was fun. His personality was still funny and warm, and we had a great conversation. But when he invited me to continue talking after dinner, I declined. Though he was the same person, I wasn't. I had made my choice. On the way home, I called Tim and explained what had happened, ending with my relief. I no longer needed to worry about a pesky "what if" arising in the future. When Tim asked me to marry him, I said yes without reservation.

I'm grateful for that encounter because I think the opportunity is rare. Yes, sometimes we're asked to make a big choice and we understand the gravity. But all too often, our life is made up of small choices that add up to the sum of a larger choice. It would be a mistake for me to think that my single decision to close the door on a former relationship was the only time I would choose my now-husband: as most people would tell you, love is a daily choice. So it is in our relationship with Jesus, as well. Though we begin by making the larger choice of salvation, we must follow it up with smaller decisions to love and serve him—because choosing Jesus daily determines the trajectory for our life.

Lord, give us your wisdom as we face choices. Help us choose paths that honor you. Amen.

-Kristin

One Good Step: Write a list of five small decisions that have added up to larger choices in your life. How does knowing the contents of that list influence your decisions today?

Diversity

[Jesus said,] "And I, when I am lifted up from the earth,
will draw all people to myself."
JOHN 12:32, ESV

ONE MORNING as we had family devotions with our kids, we talked about the Day of Pentecost and how when the Holy Spirit came, the believers who were there began to speak in all the different languages of people that could be found throughout the city.

"How amazed the people were to hear about the hope of Christ *in their native language*," I said. "It showed God's design that all men, of every background, would be drawn to him."

We then discussed our recent move to our new neighborhood, in the heart of our city, and how we felt God was asking us to go to a place where diversity among the people living there was paramount.

My husband explained, "As believers in Jesus we are unified in our faith, but we are not uniform. God is calling all people to himself regardless of age, race, social class, or language."

And I've realized over time that this moving to a new space has been nothing less than a blessing. Many of our new neighbors are different from us in many ways, but they are also kind and interesting, engaging and unique. Living here and getting to interact with the diverse people around us has given us nothing short of *joy*.

There are times being a Christian is seen as a downfall, a negative—sometimes justifiably, but we've decided we'd rather be a family that is known more for what we are *for* than what we are against. We believe, without question, that God is *for* every person—no matter who they are or where they are from.

The body of Christ, the church, is much more diverse than people who look like, act like, or even think just like me. And because this is true, we get to be a people who celebrate our diversity, rather than being afraid or opposed to it. Let's be individuals who exemplify God's love extravagantly, to all people. We are called to be unified in our love of Christ, but not uniform.

Lord, may we each grasp a vision of your Kingdom that includes people from every nation and tongue. May we celebrate our diversity while being unified in our love of Jesus. Amen.

-Kendra

One Good Step: Spend time getting to know someone who, on the surface, appears different from yourself.

Fun

I recommend having fun, because there is nothing better for people in this world than to eat, drink, and enjoy life. That way they will experience some happiness along with all the hard work God gives them under the sun.

ECCLESIASTES 8:15

"DID YOU JUST SNORT?" I asked, taking a sip of my favorite tea, glancing at Aaron over the cup rim. The house was quiet, and we were relaxing for a few minutes before we, too, trundled off to bed.

"Maybe" came out as a croak as Aaron dissolved into giggles, wiping tears as he fought for control over the laughter that finally won, bubbling up and out, rendering him speechless as the giggles turned into guffaws that left him crying and gasping for breath.

My husband rarely loses control emotionally, and I found myself staring at him in bewilderment before I also succumbed. Laughter—the real kind—is contagious, and soon I, too, was gasping for breath.

It had been a rough couple of months, and a friend's social media post asking for memes had gathered over one thousand silly/funny/groan-worthy responses. I'd been quietly chuckling over the thread for days before pulling it up and handing the phone to Aaron.

And that silly thread is what had Aaron and me laughing like loons in the midst of hard times and hard things. As we worked to get ourselves finally back under control, I realized how desperately we'd needed those few minutes of uncontrollable, stomach-clenching laughter.

It's so easy to fall into a rhythm of unrelenting responsibility to the point that having fun feels immature and frivolous, a waste of time when more pressing needs await. And while we are called to be reliable and responsible, laughter—the gut-clenching, tears-streaming kind—is refreshing and life-giving for our souls. We need fun to counteract all the hard, and God knows this. He tells us to have fun, to enjoy food and life as a counterbalance to our work.

Lord, invite us into something fun today, whether it be laughter or an activity that brings us pure, unadulterated joy. Amen.

-Julie

One Good Step: Pull a harmless prank, find a great joke to tell, or otherwise act like the twelve-year-old trapped in your adult body. Intentionally seek out something funny or do something fun today.

Silence

For God alone, O my soul, wait in silence, for my hope is from him.

PSALM 62:5, ESV

MY AUNT LIVES ON a dusty gravel road that curves gently through woods and farmland. As a child, I loved jumping on hay bales in the fall, hearing the jingling of bells as my uncle readied his big Belgians for a winter sleigh ride, or packing into the hot backseat of a car to go for a swim at the lake. The country had a quiet beauty. Even though the wind whispered through the trees and crickets sang outside, with no traffic for miles, the air held a silent stillness.

Looking back, that silence is just as memorable as the sleigh rides and hay bales. While noise can affect our stress levels by raising adrenaline and cortisol, silence can relieve tension in just two minutes. Silence lowers our blood pressure and increases blood flow to the brain, and periods of silence throughout the day have been found to help decrease insomnia.

Silence is essential, yet many of us seem uncomfortable with it. Several years ago, researchers conducted a study in which they left the participant alone in a sparse room for no more than fifteen minutes. During that time, the person had nothing to do, but they could push a button and shock themselves if they wanted to. An astonishing 67 percent of men and 25 percent of women chose to push the button and shock themselves rather than sit quietly.[4] As people used to the constant hum of modern society, we have become uneasy with silence.

Silence is not only important for our health, it's a gift from God. Silence gives us the opportunity to meditate on God and his work in our lives. It helps provide mental clarity to face our problems and the space we need to pray. Silence is an opportunity for us to practice stillness and to listen to God's voice. Rather than an empty space, it's a direct pathway to intimacy with God, who meets us there. When we choose silence, it can become a holy hush—filled with awe—that focuses on our gracious God.

Lord, thank you for silence. Help us to see it as a positive opportunity to meet with you. Amen.

-Kristin

One Good Step: Find a time to be silent. Turn off or set aside all distractions, and find a quiet spot to simply sit for at least five minutes.

---

4 Timothy D. Wilson et al., "Just Think: The Challenges of the Disengaged Mind," *Science* 345, no. 6192 (July 4, 2014): 75–77, https://science.sciencemag.org/content/345/6192/75.

Strength

When I am weak, then I am strong.

2 CORINTHIANS 12:10

"I JUST DON'T THINK I can do it anymore," I whispered to my husband Kyle over our kitchen sink as my hands scrubbed supper dishes left too long in a dirty sink.

We'd been foster parents for our local county for almost six years. Most of the time I enjoyed what we did, and although there were moments of hard, overall I felt a sense of accomplishment from helping kids through traumatic circumstances.

But this fall felt different. I was tired. Too often at the end of what I knew I could handle. I knew I was at a breaking point when we'd agreed to take another sibling group into our home and that night I tossed and turned, unable to sleep, as tears slipped down my cheeks.

The next morning, my husband looked at me, concern in his eyes and said, "I'm calling the social worker. We can't do this right now." I nodded in agreement. Too ashamed to give words to the moment, engulfed with the feelings of shame that I'd somehow failed.

The next week, after many discussions, we made the painful decision to stop being foster parents for our county. And although I knew I needed to stop, I still felt a bit like a failure. Like I quit because I just couldn't quite handle it. And the lie that I was weak whispered across my soul.

But as life continued to go by, and the days turned to months and now years, my view of that experience has shifted over time. My ability to accept that I am human and have limits is freeing me from a once perfectionistic, I-can-do-anything-without-little-help attitude.

I am finally coming to fully understand and embrace the idea that I don't need to be superhuman, and neither do you. We don't have to be ashamed of our perceived weaknesses, because God is there to fill in every gaping hole for us. And because of it, we have the freedom to readily acknowledge our own weaknesses and limitations, realizing it's often in the middle of them that we find our strength in our Savior.

Lord, thank you that when we feel weak, you are our strength. Amen.

-Kendra

One Good Step: Think of one area of your life you have felt weak in. How has God shown you his strength through your weakness?

Foreigner

The LORD protects the foreigners among us. He cares for the orphans and widows,
but he frustrates the plans of the wicked.

PSALM 146:9

"WHAT ARE YOU MAKING for Dinner Buddies?" I sent the WeChat message to my friend Li Zhang.

"I'm bringing one of my favorite dishes. I don't know . . . you might not be able to handle the heat."

"What? Bring the heat! I can handle it." Snickering softly to myself, I knew my bold proclamation had my friend laughing. We both knew her palate was accustomed to far hotter foods than my Midwestern taste buds, and she loved to bring various spicy dishes to test just how much heat I could handle before conceding that something was simply too hot to eat.

We fell into the Dinner Buddies idea quite by accident during my friendship with Li, and the roughly weekly tradition has continued for years, involving a succession of visiting Chinese interns, scholars, and teachers as they come for a year or two as part of our school's immersion program before returning home. We take turns making food we consider "traditional" to our cultures and then enjoy dinner together, building the bonds of friendship, exploring one another's cultures through food and conversation, finding a safe place to ask hard questions of one another.

My friendships with people-not-from-here through our immersion program but also through our increasingly diverse community are some of my most precious friendships. As my friends quietly confess stories of verbal abuse because of their accents, clothing, skin tone, or cultural practices, my heart breaks. When my friends are treated abominably because they are refugees, having fled a home filled with bloodshed and trauma that I cannot fathom, by people who proclaim to love and follow Christ, I wonder how the church has gotten it so wrong. Joseph fled with Mary and baby Jesus to Egypt—refugees seeking protection, before they were called back home. There are countless times in Scripture and in the history of the church in which the Israelites and, later we as Christ-followers, were and are the foreigners, the ones seeking refuge in a different land. God is for the foreigner. God is for the refugee. And he calls us to be welcoming, generous, and kind to those far from home. We will find ourselves blessed by the richness of those friendships.

Lord, help us to be intentionally welcoming to those who are far from their original home. Amen.

-Julie

One Good Step: If you live near a college or university, contact the school about hosting a visiting student for an American holiday.

Counsel

Come and listen to my counsel. I'll share my heart
with you and make you wise.

PROVERBS 1:23

GRABBING A TISSUE, I wiped an errant tear and exhaled a shaky breath. Looking up, I tried to smile at the counselor who sat quietly across from me. She waited, without judgment, until I felt composed enough to continue. A short while later, our time ended. As I closed her door, a mix of heaviness and relief lingered.

Growing up, I always thought counseling was something other people did. Not because I didn't think it was valuable, but because my life felt too ordinary. I came from a stable home and had parents who loved me. Though I struggled at times, part of me believed my problems weren't problematic enough. In some ways, I undervalued myself, feeling unworthy of the cost and time of professional help.

When I finally did seek help, I realized I wasn't alone. Far from it, in fact: a 2017 study revealed that 42 percent of Americans have seen a counselor at some point.[5] Of course, counseling is not a magical elixir. But for those who are struggling, it can be a lifesaver. Our discussions made me feel less alone, like I'd been through the fire and emerged on the other side.

Of course, counsel can come in many forms. As friends, we can speak truth and love into one another's lives. We can seek professional help, as I did. And we can always turn to Jesus, our Wonderful Counselor (see Isaiah 9:6). In the Old Testament, counselors were often portrayed as wise kings like Solomon, providing advice to the people. But in Jesus, we find a counselor who is fully man and fully God, understanding us in our humanity in a way no one else does. Jesus knows everything about us—all our secrets, fears, and foibles—yet loves us anyway. What's more, he knows what we should do (see Hebrews 4:15-16). As our Counselor, he asks us to bring all of our worries and cares to him. Though we may be distressed, with Jesus, we are never alone. We can always seek his counsel.

Lord, thank you for the wise counsel that friends, counselors, and you provide. May we be unafraid to seek help when we need it. Amen.

-Kristin

One Good Step: Seek counsel in a problem you're facing—whether it's in the form of a trusted friend, a professional counselor, or with Jesus.

---

[5] Barna Group, "Americans Feel Good about Counseling," Barna, February 27, 2018, https://www.barna.com/research/americans-feel-good-counseling/.

Persevere

I have told you all this so that you may have peace in me. Here on earth you will have many trials and sorrows. But take heart, because I have overcome the world.

JOHN 16:33

HER HUSBAND GONE, she found herself suddenly navigating a life she'd never imagined. Single parent to three, a mortgage she could no longer afford, a million details tied up in a web of uncertainty and chaos preventing her from moving forward as she waited on events beyond her control.

In the midst of the overwhelming sorrow and hurt and the temptation to curl up in a ball and do nothing, she persevered. Scripture filled her house, handwritten on small pieces of white paper and taped everywhere—on kitchen cabinets, mirrors, and doorframes—reminding her constantly of God's goodness and his promises.

And God moved—in small and big ways—in the midst of all the hard. Her family, friends, and church family rallied around her. And then, after she spent years waiting in uncertainty but continuing to trust in God, he provided her a lovely new house she could afford, and her old house sold in less than a day. Rather than dispersing the storm, God met her in her perseverance, in the middle of the uncertainty and chaos. He reminded her, in a thousand ways, that he is the Overcomer and that the sorrows and hurts of this world are no match for his sovereignty.

Because she clung to God, persevering in what she knew to be true despite how dire the circumstances looked, her faith developed the kind of deep, wide roots that come from heartbreak and hard times, not understanding but finding God in the midst of suffering nonetheless.

That's the thing about perseverance: it will take us into an intimacy with God we often don't search out when life is smooth sailing. We often see God the clearest when we are at our most desperate, when all of the meaningless distractions of ordinary life are suddenly stripped away. When life is hardest, press into God. He will stand alongside you in the middle of the storm, even if he doesn't stop it.

Lord, when our worlds turn upside down and inside out, help us persevere, clinging to your promises, knowing that you have overcome this world. Amen.

-Julie

One Good Step: Pick three verses that encourage you when life is hard, verses that help you persevere, and post them where they will catch your eye.

Hospitality

Cheerfully share your home with those
who need a meal or a place to stay.
1 PETER 4:9

WHEN MY HUSBAND AND I were first engaged, our extended families decided to host Thanksgiving together. It made sense since we all lived in the same community, and it made the holiday so much easier for my husband and I without having to rush from one gathering to the next. It became a tradition that has continued on every year since.

But what started as just our two families coming together has evolved into something so much more inviting. Since this started a new tradition for our families, it opened the door to inviting others in as well. Now, anytime someone doesn't have a place to go on Thanksgiving, they're invited to our little gathering. We've welcomed single people, college students away from their families, neighbors, and anyone else who needed a place to go. Keeping our circles open on Thanksgiving has made it one of my very favorite holidays.

Hospitality is defined not only as inviting in friends, but also strangers. When I think of how we truly started to be more hospitable to those around us, it began on Thanksgiving. You never knew who you could be sitting next to, it might have been someone who was a complete stranger to you, and yet, this opening of our family's door on Thanksgiving opened up the possibility of doing it more often on the ordinary days of our lives.

We are told often in Scripture to be hospitable. To be willing to open our homes and our lives to those around us. For some of us, this is easy, since we grew up in homes that shared their tables with others regularly. But for some of us (myself included), this is a new way to live. And it can be scary. But hospitality doesn't have to be elaborate or expensive. It simply means offering a space for others to gather, to get to know one another and build relationships.

Lord, give each one of us a heart's desire to be hospitable toward those we come in contact with, inviting them into our spaces cheerfully and sharing your love with them. Amen.

-Kendra

One Good Step: Invite someone to have a meal or a cup of coffee with you.

Behold

And we all, with unveiled face, beholding the glory of the Lord, are
being transformed into the same image from one degree of glory
to another. For this comes from the Lord who is the Spirit.

2 CORINTHIANS 3:18, ESV

ONE OF MY CHILDREN'S FAVORITE PLACES to visit is the Science Museum of Minnesota.
With more than 370,000 square feet at its location on the banks of the Mississippi
River, it includes a giant 60-foot astronaut, a ship, a triceratops, a mummy, fantas-
tic LEGO creations, and much more. More than a million people experience the
museum or its traveling exhibitions each year. It's a sight to behold!

One of the exhibits we always wander through is the Human Body Gallery
and an area called "Wonder Years" that details early human development in babies
and kids ages zero to five. One of the exhibits includes oversize pairs of glasses
that—when placed on your face—allow you to visualize how much and how far
infants can see when they are newborn, one month old, and three months old. It's
fun to peer through the thick glasses and gaze with fuzzy vision around the room,
imagining how little they can see.

Newborns, for instance, can only focus on objects that are eight to ten inches
from their face. Though that small distance might seem problematic, in reality it's
the perfect distance for them to be able to focus on their caregiver when being held.
Nothing matters beyond beholding that person's face.

As God's children, we too have the ability to see him face-to-face. The word
behold is used in the Bible to draw the reader's attention ("Look!"). But in 2
Corinthians 3:18, the Greek word for behold, *katoptrizó*, means to reflect as a mirror. When an infant looks at its caregiver, it finds its identity in that gaze. Similarly,
when we behold Jesus, we find ourselves reflected—with love—in his gaze. As we
behold God's glory, we are able to reflect him more and more. And when we do, we
become more like him, able to extend that same grace and love to others.

*Lord, help us to behold—and reflect—your glory. As we seek to follow you, may
beholding your glory help transform us into your image. Amen.*

-Kristin

One Good Step: In what ways does beholding God and his nature
help us to become more like him?

Taste

Whatever is good and perfect is a gift coming down to us from God our Father, who created all the lights in the heavens. He never changes or casts a shifting shadow.

JAMES 1:17

"MOM, WHAT DO YOU THINK heaven looks like, is like?" We were driving home, and Jonny's question was one I've often wondered myself. I am not an expert on heaven, and while Scripture contains a few descriptive glimpses, I didn't have a definitive answer for my inquisitive son.

"Well . . ." I paused a long moment, trying to gather my words. "I once heard a sermon describing the earth as little tastes of heaven and little tastes of hell, all rolled together over our lifetime." Glancing in the rearview mirror, I asked, "What do you think? Might we be experiencing little pieces of what heaven is like here on earth?"

"If that's true, then dessert last night was a little taste of heaven!"

Laughing, I agreed. And with that conversation, a new tradition began. When we see something breathtakingly beautiful, when a food explodes in delightful flavors across our tongues, when we snuggle into an extra warm blanket on a cool evening, when we hear something that makes our souls sing, we categorize it as a little taste of heaven. Our declarations are an expression of gratitude, a simple acknowledgment that all good things are gifts from God, regardless of whether they are actually in heaven or not.

It's remarkable how such a simple statement has changed my perspective. I am less prone to take small luxuries for granted when I identify them as heavenly, and it helps make me intentional about noticing the good things—even the smallest of them—as I go about my day. It's hard to stay grumpy when savoring a sip of a decadent coffee or lingering on the sight of giant snowflakes floating gently to earth. Pausing to identify tastes of heaven jolts us out of racing mindlessly through our days, forcing us to stop momentarily to remember the King we serve, the universe's Creator who named the stars and yet also numbers the hairs on our heads.

Lord, thank you for tastes of heaven on earth. May we pause to savor them, reminding ourselves and those around us that you are the giver of every good gift. Amen.

-Julie

One Good Step: Practice pausing momentarily over small joys in your day, identifying them and thanking God for them.

Yet

Though the fig tree does not bud and there are no grapes on the vines,
though the olive crop fails and the fields produce no food, though
there are no sheep in the pen and no cattle in the stalls, yet I
will rejoice in the LORD, I will be joyful in God my Savior.

HABAKKUK 3:17-18, NIV

"I DON'T UNDERSTAND why God won't answer my prayer," a dear friend whispered one night as we sat on my front porch. "I've prayed for this relationship to be repaired for years, but nothing seems to change," she confided as she wiped tears from her eyes.

"I'm sorry, friend," I responded as I sat with her in her pain. I shared with her some of my own unspoken prayers, yet to be answered. She nodded, a shared understanding of the pain we both knew. As we ended the night, we prayed for one another.

"Thank you," she said as we hugged and she put her coat on to leave.

"Of course," I responded. "Anytime—this is what friends are for."

The next morning she sent me Habakkuk 3:17-18, a reminder to rejoice, even as we wait. And this verse continued to challenge me the rest of the week. *How do I hold on to hope in all of the unknowns of life? All of the unanswered prayers?*

The more I ponder Habakkuk's words, the more I believe the answer lies in our "yet." Yet will I rejoice. Yet will I remember God is my Savior. Yet will I have hope.

Our yet doesn't deny our pain or diminish our troubles. Just as we see in this passage of Scripture, we can and should acknowledge all that is hard. This isn't a denial of all we are going through. This is simply reminding ourselves of who God is in the middle of hard circumstances or seasons. Yet we will remember who God is.

Lord, we pray for those of us who are in a hard spot, hanging onto our yet. May you encourage us today, as we cling to our hope in you. Amen.

-Kendra

One Good Step: Write down a prayer you have been waiting for God
to answer, maybe even something you gave up on long ago.
How can you hang on to your yet, even as you wait?

Time

He has made everything beautiful in its time. He has also set eternity in the human
heart; yet no one can fathom what God has done from beginning to end.

ECCLESIASTES 3:11, NIV

AS THE CLOCK TICKED DOWN, my heart rate ticked up. The room was tense, the silence broken only by the occasional cough or scratching of pencils. It was Saturday morning, but it seemed like another school day. With just a few hours for us to complete hundreds of questions, the ACT test felt like a marathon. By the end, we were exhilarated and exhausted.

During those few hours of the ACT test, time sprinted by. Yet when we're waiting our turn at the doctor's office, time can pass agonizingly slowly. Though each of us has the same amount of time each day, we often think and talk about it the way we do money—how we spend it, how we don't have enough. Time feels slippery.

Time is complex, and it's also a little confusing. Did you know that, if someone is flying high in the air, and another person is on the ground, time passes more quickly for the person on the plane? Though the time difference is measured in less than a second, clocks run more quickly at higher altitudes because they experience a weaker gravitational force than clocks on the earth's surface. Time is relative.

Like our understanding of time, our understanding of God is complex. After all, he is at once present with us and yet completely outside time's boundaries. For him, one day is as a thousand years, and a thousand years is as one day (see 2 Peter 3:8). The concept seems paradoxical, but God is timeless.

Even though we may understand the temporary nature of today, there is still part of us that longs for the eternal. This spark is part of a larger story God has designed in which there is no beginning and no end, something—like God himself—that is beyond the boundaries of our present understanding. Though time often feels inconstant, God himself is eternal, everlasting, and infinite. Knowing that, we can take comfort in his presence no matter what.

Lord, thank you that though our time is finite, we serve an infinite God. Help us to see time the way you do. Amen.

-Kristin

One Good Step: How does your understanding of time influence the way you see God? How does it shape your view of eternity?

Audacious

Keep on asking, and you will receive what you ask for.
LUKE 11:9

AARON'S INCOMING CALL was initially surprising but not alarming. Sitting in the uncomfortable spectator chairs, watching my children attempt roundhouse kicks in their starched white uniforms, my dismay grew as Aaron explained that he was stranded on the side of the interstate two hundred miles away at 7:00 p.m. on a school night. He didn't know what was wrong, only that his engine had suddenly seized and died.

As I hung up the phone, I turned to God. We were two weeks away from hosting our large annual women's conference, and the leadership team has grown accustomed to unbelievable, chaotic *distractions* arising just before the conference. Unexplainable illnesses, sudden financial problems, challenges in relationships— the array of bewildering events over the years would fill a book and give meaning to the saying "Truth is stranger than fiction." The pattern is clear, and we've learned to collectively hit our knees in prayer over these events, running to God immediately, asking for his divine intervention as we focus on final details for a conference that changes lives for eternity.

And this time was no different. Even as I called a friend to ask for help retrieving my husband, I prayed a desperately audacious prayer, telling God that I needed a new engine, and could I please have it for free. Even as I prayed for something that felt a bit extreme, my mind whirled with the momentarily tight spot we were in and the already chaotic schedule these next two months held. We didn't have the time or money for a blown engine, and my heart squeezed at the thought of adding this to the pile. Praying an audacious prayer resulted in an audacious answer: it's a rather long, slightly complicated story, but three weeks after the conference we had a brand new engine installed for a total cost of forty dollars.

I don't normally pray so audaciously, but I shouldn't be afraid to privately ask big things of God—none of us should. We are invited—encouraged—to pray prayers allowing God to be big, bigger in situations than we'd normally dare ask or believe. God doesn't mind audacious prayers prayed with a humble heart and right motives, and there is no prayer we can pray that is too big or too much for God.

Lord, thank you for hearing our audacious prayers. May we never put you or your abilities into a too-small box. Amen.

-Julie

One Good Step: Don't be afraid of audacious prayers, bringing your request before God persistently.

Confidence

Let us then approach God's throne of grace with confidence, so that we
may receive mercy and find grace to help us in our time of need.

HEBREWS 4:16, NIV

AT FIRST, I felt stodgy next to her grace and poise, awkward beside her larger-than-life persona. Her confidence magnified my own insecurities. I knew it was my problem to fix and resolved to focus on getting to know her. I quickly realized she was truly lovely, inside and out.

Just a few years later, I saw the same woman at an event and was happy to be reacquainted. To my surprise, her once bright light had dimmed; she seemed anxious and uncomfortable in her own skin. As I flashed back to our meeting years earlier, I was saddened at the change. I wondered what had altered in her life to make her confidence falter.

According to Strong's concordance, the word *confidence* that Hebrews 4:16 tells us to approach God's throne with is from the Greek *parrésia* and means freedom of speech and/or confidence. Its origin is a combination of *pas* ("all" or "every") and *rhésis* ("speech"). Rereading the verse, I realized I've been misreading it all along. I thought that confidence was an external attitude we project toward others—but it's not. Confidence isn't just certainty in our own abilities, it's equally tied to the word *confidential*. When someone holds our confidence, it's with the understanding that our words will be kept private.

Holy confidence, then, is found at the feet of Jesus. When we come to the throne of grace, his strength can uphold us, his love can comfort us. When we are willing to "speak everything" to him, our unrestrained outpouring helps us leave behind shame or embarrassment, knowing we can trust him. As our champion, he intercedes on our behalf.

This confidential unburdening of ourselves often leads to the other kind of confidence, as well—one that isn't found in the changing nature of our circumstances, but in the unchanging nature of a holy God. He alone gives us the confidence to look at the world around us, appreciating it for the way it is but holding it loosely in our hands—knowing heaven is our true home.

Lord, thank you that we can trust you with the intimate details of our lives, giving us the freedom to live with a newfound confidence. Amen.

-Kristin

One Good Step: What does "holy confidence" look like to you?
How might you experience that in your own life?

Workmanship

We are his workmanship, created in Christ Jesus for good works,
which God prepared beforehand, that we should walk in them.

EPHESIANS 2:10, ESV

SOMETIMES SOCIAL MEDIA IS TIRING. People can be rude and even cruel in the way that they talk to one another. The way we think of others changes when we are only willing to engage them in an online platform. We lose our ability to see the person fully, easily forgetting they are the workmanship of God.

It reminds me of years earlier when I worked as a therapist at a Veterans Affairs hospital in my community in their chemical dependency and mental health program. At first when I was assigned a new case, I would pull up the veteran's chart and go over their history. Often I would see pages of a life lived in chaos and unhealthy patterns. I would make assumptions about the person in my mind, based solely on their record.

And then I would meet the veteran in person to go over their history and reasons for wanting therapy. My perspective of them would often change once we were face-to-face. Because people are more than just a list of diagnoses in a chart. They are more than the history they have, the mistakes they've made. In front of me would be a person who was funny or kind, passionate or hardworking. They were more than what I'd simply read on the screen. After a while, I stopped reading their chart prior to meeting them. I knew I would only have a complete picture of the person after seeing them face-to-face.

The same is true of social media. We are not seeing the whole person and make judgments based only on certain aspects of the person. But this shouldn't be. We are all created by God. We are his workmanship. Made in his image. And although it can be easily dismissed through a screen, when we're face-to-face, it's not so easy. We are so much more than the mistakes we've made. The missteps we've had. And it's time we stepped back and remembered to see the fullness of another person, the workmanship of God in their life.

Lord, may we see others in their entirety and acknowledge the workmanship you are doing in their lives. Amen.

-Kendra

One Good Step: Who is someone you have judged unfairly? How can you begin to see the workmanship of God in their life?

Free

You have been called to live in freedom, my brothers and sisters.
But don't use your freedom to satisfy your sinful nature. Instead,
use your freedom to serve one another in love.

GALATIANS 5:13

"COURTNEY, please come downstairs."

Courtney recognized her mom's tone of voice. *Oh boy. Mom saw my grades.* "Yes, Mom?" she called as she started down the steps, wondering whether she might wriggle free of the looming consequences.

"Court, when we agreed you could attend your distance-learning classes at the desk in your bedroom, being free to work at your own pace, it was dependent upon you getting your work turned in on time and keeping your grades up. You aren't handling that well, so you'll be doing school at the kitchen table next to me this week."

It was after the dust had settled and the school day was complete that my friend—Courtney's mom—made her daughter popcorn and hot cocoa and had a quiet conversation around the idea of being free and the flip side of that coin—accountability, and discipline.

Like Courtney, we love the concept of being free—we crave it even. The ability to make our own decisions, to control our own destiny, to accomplish tasks at a pace we set sounds *amazing.* But being free does not mean living without consequence, and, without accountability and discipline, freedom can spiral us into situations of our own making that put us into bondage, leaving us panicked and facing undesirable consequences.

Jesus died so that we might be *free.* His sacrifice on the Cross freed us from death, absolving our sins, and making us right with God. He gave us the opportunity to choose a new life by believing in him and the freedom to choose what we might do with it. Jesus invites and beckons rather than forcing or dictating, and we are free to respond, or not.

That hard-won freedom offered by Jesus' crucifixion does not give us a license for doing whatever we want, whenever we want to. Without discipline and accountability, freedom can lead to ruin, ensnaring us in sin. But, when we lay down our freedom, willingly subjecting ourselves to discipline and accountability, offering our lives to God and abiding by Jesus' teachings, we will find abundant life.

Lord, may we use the freedom you offer wisely, making choices that align with your Word. Amen.

-Julie

One Good Step: Pick one area where you've been abusing freedom, making unhealthy decisions in some way. What boundary are you going to establish, starting today?

Benediction

The LORD bless you and keep you; the LORD make his face shine on you and be gracious to you; the LORD turn his face toward you and give you peace.
NUMBERS 6:24-26, NIV

AT THE END of every Sunday morning service at the small, red-sided First Baptist Church, the pastor would raise his hand and pronounce a benediction. Though I loved the singing and always appreciated the message in the sermon, the benediction was often my favorite part of the service. The words were usually Ephesians 3:20-21: "Now to him who is able to do immeasurably more than all we ask or imagine, according to his power that is at work within us, to him be glory in the church and in Christ Jesus throughout all generations, for ever and ever! Amen" (NIV). Those phrases were familiar and comforting, and I loved the word *immeasurably*. As a child, I could imagine quite a few good things, so the fact that God could do far more than we could ever ask or imagine sounded pretty impressive.

The word *benediction* comes from the Latin *bene* ("good") and *dicere* ("to say"). In other words, benedictions are "good words" from God, a joyful and unifying call for his people. From the priests in the Old Testament (see Numbers 6:24-26) to the final words of some of the New Testament letters, benedictions are short statements that petition God on our behalf or assure the church of his promises. Benedictions convey blessings; even more, they signal unity and purpose in the church body.

In some ways, they remind me of the way family members call out, "Love you!" as they leave home. Though they hope to see one another again soon, there's always the recognition that—should it be the final time they hear a dear one's voice—they want the last words that ring in their ears to be words of love.

As members of the body of Christ working together in this world, let's choose to speak a good word into the lives of those around us. Let's intentionally speak blessings into the lives of those we encounter. Let's remind one another: *You are loved. Your life has purpose and meaning. And the God who can do immeasurably more than we can ever ask or imagine? He can do the same in your life too.*

Lord, thank you for the benedictions you've spoken into and over our lives. Help us to do the same for others. Amen.

-Kristin

One Good Step: Choose to speak words of encouragement to someone, whether it's in person or through a message.

Stay

Wait patiently for the LORD. Be brave and courageous.
Yes, wait patiently for the LORD.
PSALM 27:14

MY DAD WAS the public works director for our small town when I was growing up. When snow was in the evening forecast, it was his job to stay awake, watching the weather and deciding when to call his plow crew and head out. They'd plow through the night, clearing the way for school buses and commuters long before the sun rose. Sometimes, they'd plow through the night and long into the following day, continuously circling their routes, trying to stay enough ahead of the storm to keep everyone safe and the roads open.

Watching the world from the front seat of his snowplow gave my dad knowledge and perspective. He knew which cars slid off icy roads in higher percentages than others and steered me clear of those makes and models as I grew into adulthood. But most importantly, he learned the wisdom in staying. Long retired, he still tells me to stay home and stay put anytime we get a particularly nasty blend of rain/snow, reminding me that anything I had planned—no matter how pressing it feels in the moment—is not worth the risk of taking to the streets too early, before the plows have had a chance to sand slippery streets, melting the ice and making it safe.

My dad tells me to stay put when the roads are icy because he knows what's happening behind the scenes and inside the plow trucks. He knows that the salt needs time to melt the ice and an hour or two will make the difference between a treacherous intersection and safe, wet roads.

God is no different. He often works behind the scenes, asking us to stay put, to wait, to trust that he sees, he knows, and he is at work. Sometimes, staying is the hard, brave, smart thing to do.

Heavenly Father, give us wisdom to know when you are telling us to go and when you are asking us to stay put. May we know when to wait, refusing to run ahead of you, knowing you are at work behind the scenes on our behalf. Amen.

-Julie

One Good Step: Ask someone with a deeply rooted faith (a mentor, a pastor) how they distinguish when God is asking them to wait and when he is telling them to go.

Adopted

God decided in advance to adopt us into his own family by bringing us to himself through Jesus Christ. This is what he wanted to do, and it gave him great pleasure.

EPHESIANS 1:5

"I NEEDED TO TELL YOU because I wanted you to be able to make this decision, fully informed," my very sweet friend, who also happens to be an attorney, stated one day over the phone.

"Okay," I responded, waiting for her to continue.

"When you adopt a child, you are placing them firmly in your family. They now have the same standing as any of your biological children would have. They have the same access to any rights or privileges being in your family would provide and any inheritance upon your death. According to the law there is no difference between biological or adopted children."

"I understand," I said with a smile. "That is exactly what we want."

"I figured you did," she responded. "But I just wanted you to have all the information."

I smiled as I hung up the phone. My friend loves me and is always looking out for me, and I appreciate her wisdom. As the days passed by, I thought more about her words and how they do not just relate to adoption among people, but adoption with God as well.

I love that God decided to adopt us, giving us the same standing as all of his children. There is no longer Jew or Gentile, slave or free, male or female according to Galatians 3:28. We all have the same rights and privileges as God's children. We are fully a part of his family. Entitled to all of the inheritance he has for us. And the best news? He didn't do it because he had to; he did it because he wanted to. It gave him great pleasure to welcome us in. God is pleased that you have been adopted into his family.

Lord, thank you for loving us so much and adopting us all as your children, offering us each the same rights, privileges, and inheritance. Amen.

-Kendra

One Good Step: How have you experienced being included in the family of God? Who do you know that needs to be a part of a family? How could you invite them into your life (and family)?

December

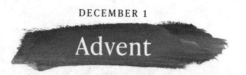

Advent

Dear children, let's not merely say that we love each other;
let us show the truth by our actions.

1 JOHN 3:18

IT WAS YEARS AGO that Kendra, Kristin, and I sat—as young moms with young children—on a Sunday afternoon, sipping coffee at a local coffee shop, lamenting the impending holiday season. The rushing, the overwhelm, and the attitudes of young children with mile-long wish lists; it all felt a bit too much for our already exhausted souls.

On a whim, we pondered what it might look like if we adopted acts of kindness as our Advent celebration, weaving Jesus intentionally throughout our days with acts of kindness and generosity toward others, bringing our faith into tangible clarity for our children as well as ourselves. We wanted to reclaim the Christmas season for our faith, and meeting the needs of others seemed both countercultural and refreshing.

We jettisoned traditions that consumed time and energy while bringing us no joy (I now buy my Christmas cookies from the store and am far happier for it), making room for a new tradition that is fast approaching a decade of adventures. We've encountered groan-worthy, belly-flopping failures and overwhelming, tear-inducing successes, finding Jesus in the midst of it all.

Advent—for those who did not grow up with the tradition—is a liturgical season on the Christian calendar, a time of preparation and expectant waiting for the celebration of the birth of Christ as well as his second coming. There is no biblical mandate for Advent, and our adoption of kindness throughout Advent is simply our way of preparing our hearts for the wonder of Christmas morning. It has turned the days stretching between December 1 and Christmas Day from a slightly dreaded, overbusy season into some of our favorite days and weeks of the year. What we do and how often we do it is infinitely customizable; the point is to pause the Tilt-A-Whirl of holiday frenzy, rediscovering our Savior while we serve as his hands and feet to the world around us. Join us this year—you won't regret it.

Lord, as we celebrate Advent, who might we extend physical and emotional generosity toward? Send us. Amen.

-Julie

One Good Step: Make intentional plans for one kind act each week
of Advent, always leaving room for God to change the plan.

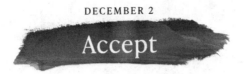

Accept

Accept each other just as Christ has accepted you
so that God will be given glory.

ROMANS 15:7

MY PARENTS MET while they were in college. The first fall they were together my dad asked my mom to come home with him to meet his parents. Before they arrived, my dad explained to his parents that my mom's mother was deceased and her dad had recently remarried. He went on to expound that my mom's family tradition growing up had always been to open presents on Christmas morning, and he wondered if they would be willing to make a change to their plans to help my mom feel at home.

My grandparents' own tradition had always been to open up presents on Christmas Eve, but they quietly changed their custom, accepting and accommodating what my mother had known as a child to make her feel welcome.

It wasn't until after they were married and years later that my mom found out the truth about their family traditions. She was shocked that my grandparents would so easily shift their own desires to accept hers as their own, even without knowing her yet.

I love hearing my parents recount this story and the valuable lesson of being willing to accept and even change something we hold dear for another person. My grandparents had the wisdom to see how important the tradition would be for my mom and decided to accept it without any fuss about what they had previously done.

It takes maturity to accept different ways of doing things, especially when it goes against our own personal preferences. It takes a willingness to set aside what I may want or think of as important in order to accept what someone else may want or desire. As believers, we are called to be the ones who are gracious, understanding that Christ has accepted each one of us. In turn, we should be willing to accept one another. Because when we do, we will look different from the rest of the world and God will get the glory.

Lord, thank you for accepting each one of us. Help us to extend that acceptance to those around us. Amen.

-Kendra

One Good Step: Think of one way you can accept someone else today, putting their preferences above your own.

Volunteer

Feed the hungry, and help those in trouble. Then your light will shine out from the darkness, and the darkness around you will be as bright as noon.

ISAIAH 58:10

"WHO'S OPEN?" the volunteer in charge called out, looking around the busy room. Raising my hand, I waved a little. She spotted me and herded her charge my way.

"This is Isaiah," she said, handing me his list and a lumpy bag full of items hidden from view. Trusting brown eyes peeked at me out of a small face.

"Hi, Isaiah!" I said cheerfully. "I'm Kristin. How old are you?"

"Five," he said shyly, looking away.

I smiled. "I bet you picked some great presents for your family. Which one should we start with first?"

As Isaiah helped me choose the gift and the paper to wrap each in, I kept him busy looking for tags and bows while deftly cutting the paper and wrapping the items. Lotion and fuzzy socks for his mom, a tool set for his dad. A Barbie for his little sister, an unwieldy basketball for his big brother, a mug and kitchen gadgets for his grandma.

Kids Hope Shop is an event put on annually by our local homeless shelter. It allows at-risk kids in the community to "shop" for Christmas gifts for their family members for free. Their items are wrapped by volunteers and they're served a meal while at the facility. Though I'm always exhausted at the end of my gift-wrapping shift, it's one of my favorite days of the year.

We are the hands and feet of Jesus in the world, and we have the great privilege of using our bodies and minds to serve others by volunteering. When we recall the unselfish way in which Jesus washed the feet of his disciples or provided bread and fish for a hungry crowd, it becomes easier to look beyond our own circumstances and problems to see the needs of others. Though volunteering benefits others, the truth is that it always benefits us as well. No matter where we serve, we can always walk away grateful for the reminder of the servant leadership of our Jesus.

Lord, help us to approach volunteering with the same heart for service that you have. Amen.

-Kristin

One Good Step: Schedule a time to volunteer somewhere within the next month.

Grace

God saved you by his grace when you believed. And you can't take credit for this;
it is a gift from God. Salvation is not a reward for the good things
we have done, so none of us can boast about it.

EPHESIANS 2:8-9

RECENTLY I WAS READING A BOOK that explained what the words *grace* and *faith* would have meant to a first-century Christian as these words were commonly used to describe a relationship between two people. The idea of grace was in reference to a gift that a patron might bestow on someone, and in return, the person receiving the gift would respond with faithfulness and allegiance. There were strings attached, relationally, between the two parties involved. Now, if the patron had a request, the receiver was beholden to fulfill it. The two were tied in relationship to one another because of the gift that had been exchanged.

And so, as Paul explains to his readers what Jesus has done for us, he uses a scenario that would have been very relatable to the people reading his letters. They would have known how this system of grace and faithfulness worked. They would have understood the free gift of grace, but also the faithfulness that was then expected in return from the receiver. They would have known that gifts had strings, relationally, between the gift giver and receiver and after they accepted a gift, their faithfulness would have been required back to the giver.

As I've thought more about grace and what it would have meant to the early-church believers, I realized that often I may have missed the faithfulness that is required from me for accepting God's grace. Is grace a free gift, available to everyone? Yes, absolutely. But once we've accepted his gift of grace, there is an expectation that we would faithfully turn around and give that grace out to others around us. The gift of grace is not just meant for me to hold tightly to, with no expectations from God in regards to my faithfulness back to him. We have been given grace, freely, and in turn, freely must give it out to others.

Lord, thank you for the gift of grace you've given to us. May we respond in faithfulness and extend that same grace out toward others. Amen.

-Kendra

One Good Step: What is one way you can extend the gift of grace that you have received toward someone else today?

Peacemaking

I want to see a mighty flood of justice, an endless river of righteous living.
AMOS 5:24

"TURN OFF THE NEWS. Take a break from it. You'll feel refreshed after some time away." My words were good intentioned as I listened to a best friend tell me how utterly exhausting it has been to be a person of color living in our culture.

"Julie, I wish I could, but I can't. What we are seeing on the news is a desperate need for justice, for change that has been too long in coming. My son inherited my brown skin. I can't take a break from this, no matter how exhausting it is."

My friend and I are spiritual sisters, and her loving but firm rebuke was deserved. The problem is, I *can* turn off the news. I don't have the same stake in seeking justice as my BIPOC (Black, Indigenous, People of Color) brothers and sisters do because my day-to-day life isn't impacted. I can be tempted to spout Scripture about loving one another and peace because angry protests and demands for justice make me uncomfortable.

But I cannot abandon my friend. I love her. I love her son. I cannot unhear her words, her stories. I cannot ignore her tears as she worries about her brown-skinned son. I cannot smooth over the hurt and anger in the name of surface-level peacekeeping when what she needs are people who will come alongside to do the hard work of peacemaking.

Peacemaking requires humility and intentionality. It requires us to be quiet, listening carefully to concerns and stories that may not be anything like our experiences without dismissing or diminishing another's words. It requires us to ask questions, offering to come alongside on actionable steps forward as someone else leads, rather than assuming we know the solution and can fix it. Peacemaking often requires apology and repentance, asking God to show us where we've been hard-hearted and wrong and then doing better. I spent far too many years thinking peacemaking required smoothing over conflict, leaving hard things unresolved and unaddressed when doing so required difficult conversations and uncomfortable feelings. Peacemaking seeks justice, and justice oftentimes requires us to speak up, to stand up, to step outside of our comfort zones.

Lord, show us where we have been peacekeepers, maintaining a surface level comfort when you've called us to peacemaking, standing against injustice and oppression. Amen.

-Julie

One Good Step: Diversify your social media feeds. Listen to voices from different races, genders, and perspectives, asking God to reveal where you can be a peacemaker.

Breath

Because he bends down to listen, I will pray as long as I have breath!
PSALM 116:2

EYES CLOSED, I sat in the cozy orange chair in my living room while I inhaled deeply, held my breath, then exhaled slowly. After repeating the action for a few minutes, I reopened my eyes and returned to my tasks feeling both calm and energized.

Several months earlier, I had noticed that practicing simple breath exercises helped calm the anxiety that tugged at my brain. I'm not alone: studies have found that a breathing practice is effective in fighting anxiety, depression, and stress, and even incorporating a single breathing practice can significantly reduce blood pressure. Our breathing pattern (how quickly or slowly we breathe) can also influence the emotion we experience. That's astounding, considering that the average person takes 17,000 breaths every day. We can go about three weeks without food and three days without water, but only about three minutes without air. After just a few minutes without oxygen, our cells begin to die.

Breath is essential to life, but it's also a gift from God. Consider the words of Genesis 2:7: "The LORD God formed the man from the dust of the ground. He breathed the breath of life into the man's nostrils, and the man became a living person." Through breath, God created life. We breathe in oxygen, which our bodies need to survive. But it's also true that our breath is a metaphor, a way for us to remember how the spiritual corresponds with the physical: when we breathe in God's truths, we can exhale the lies the world tries to feed us. When we inhale peace, calm, and rest, we can exhale turmoil. In this way, the spiritual air we breathe in throughout the course of the day has a direct impact on the state of our heart and mind. Let's take those 17,000 breaths as opportunities to intentionally breathe in the truth and love of God.

Lord, thank you that you breathed life into us. Help us to slow down and breathe in your presence. Amen.

-Kristin

One Good Step: Find a cozy spot to sit and take a few minutes to breathe deeply. As you do, inhale God's truths and peace and exhale any lies or turmoil you feel.

Redemption

O Israel, hope in the LORD; for with the LORD there is unfailing love.
His redemption overflows.

PSALM 130:7

WE WERE ON OUR WAY to our daughter Jasmine's birth mother's funeral, and I was angry. Just a month earlier she had planned to come visit us for the first time. And all my dreams of Jasmine knowing her birth mom had played out in my mind.

But the meeting hadn't happened, and instead we got a call a few weeks later that she had died unexpectedly. As we drove to the funeral, I was angry with God. *It was a very good plan, God. Why couldn't you have just allowed it to happen? I wanted you to redeem this situation.*

Toward the end of the funeral and luncheon afterward, I had a quiet moment with one of Jasmine's aunts who smiled as she watched Jasmine playing with her son. "I'm amazed at the way that God has redeemed my sister's story," she said.

And I stared at her blankly. *I'm sorry—what?!* I thought. I stuttered agreement as she explained.

"Jasmine," she said. "Just look at her. God is redeeming my sister's story through her life." And she smiled as she said it, saying how grateful and encouraged she felt that God was affirming to her that her sister's life had meaning and purpose, even amid all the pain.

I felt ashamed. Here we were, two women seeing the same situation but having a completely different response. She was seeing the Father's heart, and I, in that moment, had forgotten. She could see the redemption of God, and I couldn't. I wasn't looking for it. I was angry that things didn't turn out how *I* had planned, and I was questioning the goodness of God. I quickly asked God to forgive me and to give me eyes to see his redemption.

We've all experienced things in life that we wish had a different outcome. And we also have a choice of whether we will be angry with God or choose to look for his redemption in the midst of all our unmet expectations. Sometimes, it just takes a shift in our perspective.

Lord, thank you that even when things do not go as planned, your redemption, your goodness is still working behind the scenes. Amen.

-Kendra

One Good Step: Write down a situation where you have unmet expectations and ask God to show you his redemption, even in the midst of what is hard.

Leverage

"You must love the LORD your God with all your heart, all your soul, all your mind, and all your strength." The second is equally important: "Love your neighbor as yourself." No other commandment is greater than these.

MARK 12:30-31

"How can I help you, and how can I pray for you?" Tara leaned in slightly from across our table, waiting to hear what I might request, ready to leverage her connections to help me and sincere in her offer of prayer.

Tara and I meet over lunch roughly twice a year. Similar in age and motivation, we share a love for Jesus and have been cheerleading one another's adventures in work and ministry for a long time. She ends our meeting the same way every time, asking whether I need an introduction to anyone, asking whether I have any roadblocks that she or someone she knows might know how to solve. She generously offers to leverage her resources to assist me in reaching my goals. And I do the same in return. It's admittedly a fun process—brainstorming one another's needs, asking whether she knows so-and-so does such and such and offering to connect her. Leveraging connections and knowledge works out well for both of us, and we leave our lunch with new ideas, new potential connections, and perhaps a new perspective on something we've been struggling with.

And while it's easy to think of leverage mostly in business terms, assuming we don't have anything of value to offer, that's not true. Leverage is simply responding to the needs of another, offering assistance with our time, skill sets, connections, and resources. We leverage our skills when we make an extra big batch for dinner so that we can take a meal to a friend recovering from surgery. We leverage our time when we sit quietly, listening to someone's story, being intentionally present when life is hard. We leverage our faith when we pray for someone else, standing alongside her spiritually, asking God to provide exactly what she needs. The truth is, when we leverage what God has entrusted us with to help those around us, we are loving our neighbors as ourselves, just as God commanded.

Lord, show us the resources, the skill sets, the networks we can leverage for those around us. May we be generous toward others, just as you've been generous toward us. Amen.

-Julie

One Good Step: Who will you leverage your time, skill sets, or resources for today?

Keep

A time to keep, and a time to cast away.
ECCLESIASTES 3:6, ESV

MY SISTER KATRINA died at the end of October, the day after her son turned four. She practically breathed creativity, and hospitality was innate to who she was. She was the kind of person who threw a party when she moved into the neighborhood rather than waiting for someone else to do it; the kind of person who baked cookies with her daughter while wearing matching aprons. Holidays, then, were very much something she enjoyed.

When she died, the idea of celebrating Thanksgiving and Christmas the way we always had while grieving such a great loss seemed untenable. As we moved from burnished leaves to frozen ponds, those once-cherished holiday traditions—usually anticipated—suddenly felt hollow. Once-joyful tasks like baking and gift giving now felt heavy, weighed down with sorrow and remembrance. As the holidays approached, none of us seemed all that certain about keeping traditions that only made us remember what we'd lost.

So our family did something new: we rented a house for a few days in December, all together. We looked out over the icy, snow-crusted lake, curled up by the warmth of the fire, and simply spent time together. And though the ache of missing Katrina still clung heavily to us, there was a comfort in doing something new together. We decided to keep our time together while forging a new tradition.

Whether it's within the holiday season or outside of it, grieving or not, perhaps it's time to reevaluate the things we keep doing simply because that's the way we've always done it. Love a holiday cookie exchange? Keep it. Loathe cooking? Get takeout. Feel obligated to travel but don't enjoy it? Host a gathering at your house instead. Our lives are made up of seasons of growth and change, but sometimes we get stuck in patterns—keeping a tradition, even though it no longer serves us—and forget to reevaluate.

What do you need to keep or let go of? I'm reminded of Mary and Martha: Martha, industriously cooking and cleaning while Mary sat at the feet of Jesus (see Luke 10:38-42). Martha did what was expected of a gracious host. But Mary did what she longed to do. Like Mary, let's keep what nurtures our souls. Let's keep what matters most—loving God and loving others—and hold loosely to the rest.

Lord, help us to keep what matters and rethink the rest. Amen.

-Kristin

One Good Step: Reevaluate your habits and traditions. What do you want to keep? What might you choose to do differently?

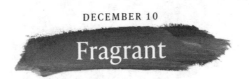

Fragrant

Thank God! He has made us his captives and continues to lead us along in Christ's triumphal procession. Now he uses us to spread the knowledge of Christ everywhere, like a sweet perfume. Our lives are a Christ-like fragrance rising up to God. But this fragrance is perceived differently by those who are being saved and by those who are perishing.

2 CORINTHIANS 2:14-15

AS A YOUNG GIRL, I would walk into my house after a sleepover or a long day away and pause to draw in a deep breath, finding comfort in the smell of my house, of my family. It wasn't that my house smelled of anything in particular; it simply smelled like home. My best friend's house and other houses I visited had their own fragrance—not bad, just different from mine.

My ability to distinguish between my home and others based on an intangible but identifiable familial scent has long since faded away, but the feelings evoked as I walked through my childhood front door has remained etched into my memories. I didn't know it then, but fragrance is powerful. A whiff of a long-gone loved one's perfume or the odor of stringent cleaners lingering in hospital hallways can evoke powerful responses of grief or joy. It's incredible how something seemingly intangible can impact us so deeply, and that's why Scripture uses fragrance to describe our lives.

Comparing our lives to a Christlike fragrance means how we live is important, and what we do matters. If we are a living representative of Christ—and we are— then our life becomes an intangible, subtle fragrance pointing others toward God. Or not. It's our choice.

What creates a fragrant life? The fruit of the Holy Spirit found in Galatians 5:22-23: love, joy, peace, patience, kindness, goodness, faithfulness, gentleness, and self-control. The question is how well we live our faith out loud, how well we embody these character traits in the big and the small, when life is easy and when it feels impossibly hard. When we strive to practice these traits in the good and the bad, even imperfectly, we'll be that Christlike fragrance wafting to heaven, to God himself.

Lord, may our lives, taken as a whole, be a sweet, Christlike fragrance to those around us. May we always point people toward you. Amen.

-Julie

One Good Step: Spend time in prayer asking God for one way to live a more Christ-fragrant life.

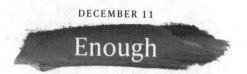

Enough

My God will meet all your needs according to
the riches of his glory in Christ Jesus.
PHILIPPIANS 4:19, NIV

MY SISTER KATRINA died at twenty-eight, after a long, five-year battle with cancer. Fifteen years later and as a mom myself, I talked with my mother about what would be my own worst fear, the death of a child that she saw realized.

When I asked her what that experience was like, she paused for a moment and then said, "You're not going to really know until you experience it. As hard as it is, God's presence is so real, so close, it's a sweetness that is not there in everyday life. It just carries you."

I swallowed hard as I thought of my sister and the pain, but also the peace we felt following her death. My mom continued, "I remember thinking a while after Kate died, 'Oh no, I have a feeling I'm not going to have this closeness forever.' I realized he's sufficient for whatever you go through. He is enough. It's very individual how God meets you in the way that you need. There were so many people praying. There is a comfort, even now, that he's always enough."

My mom's words tapered off as she smiled at me and wiped her own eyes. "I often wonder, *What if I was alone?*" She finished as she shook her head. "I know the Lord is sufficient," she said with the conviction of someone who has walked through a hard time and seen God be faithful.

My mom's experience gives me hope. No matter what we face in life, what hard times we are bound to walk through, our faith can hold fast. Because Jesus is enough. All the lessons and stories we've read are true. When life is difficult, and we wonder if what we've been told is true, we will find that God remains faithful to meet all of our needs. He holds us. He remains, now and forever, all that we need. He is enough.

Lord, thank you for the assurance that you are enough no matter what we face in life and for giving us all that we need. Amen.

-Kendra

One Good Step: When has God shown up in a hard season and revealed that he is all that you need? Who needs to hear that encouragement today in something they're facing? Let them know that God is enough.

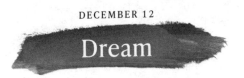

Dream

Hope deferred makes the heart sick, but a dream fulfilled is a tree of life.
PROVERBS 13:12

ONE OF THE THINGS I remember most about my wedding day is a cheeseburger. Much of the day is a blur—the last-minute preparations, endless posed photos, the two of us smiling through tears as we said our vows, hugging family and friends, the laughing at the reception—all of those memories are broad, sweeping strokes in my mind. By the time we left our late-morning wedding, we were exhausted but exhilarated. After checking in to our hotel in preparation for an early flight the following day, we collapsed on the bed, unmoving, for a while.

Then we ordered the best cheeseburger I've ever eaten. As we sat cross-legged on the bed, inhaling room service fries, we opened cards from our wedding guests. We smiled at the messages and notes written by loved ones. And on the cusp of our new life together, we dreamed. We dreamed of our home together, of lazy days watching movies and eating takeout, of babies we'd welcome into our home (sleepless nights and snuggles and all), of vacations, of career goals, of growing old together. Life stretched before us, full of promise.

We didn't think of the hardships: career difficulties, conflict with one another, parenting woes, despair over hurt feelings, and worry over finances. We didn't stop to reflect on the challenges we might face or the way they'd fray the edges of our relationship. No, as we dreamed of our life together, we thought only of the good things.

And while that might not be the most practical, it demonstrates the power of our dreams. The Bible describes the fulfillment of a dream as a tree of life, yet it's not just the attainment but the process that's a promise: "But when the desire comes, it is a tree of life" (Proverbs 13:12, NKJV). It's not just the dream itself—it's the hope of the dream. That's what sustains us, putting roots in the ground, growing with us through the challenges and hardships we face. Much like the way we abide in Christ—he is the vine, we are the branches—choosing to dwell within a dream can provide life-giving hope and joy.

Lord, thank you for the dreams you've given us. Give us the courage to pursue them even when hardships arise. Amen.

-Kristin

One Good Step: List your dreams. How does seeing them as fulfilled—
even if they have yet to be achieved—change your perspective?

Lovely

Dear brothers and sisters, one final thing. Fix your thoughts on what is true,
and honorable, and right, and pure, and lovely, and admirable. Think
about things that are excellent and worthy of praise.

PHILIPPIANS 4:8

"SLUG BUG! No backs!" Lizzie crowed, leaning over from her spot in the front passenger seat to gently punch me in the arm.

"What? No! Where?" Bewildered, I searched the intersection we sat at. "Oh. The canary-yellow one? It's lovely—that's a good color for a Beetle."

"It's cute. Also, I said 'No backs.' So you can't hit me back." Her grin was infectious as she celebrated winning this round of her game.

I'm not interested in vehicles beyond their ability to safely transport me across town, and the makes and models of most cars is utterly wasted on me. Lizzie usually wins our slug bug game because I rarely notice even the distinctive VW Beetles. My gaze slips right past them, my brain never registering what is right before my eyes. It's only when Lizzie is sitting alongside me that I attempt to scan the roads, noticing how many rainbow-hued little cars share the roads with us, giving the first of us to spy one the opportunity to "slug" the other one.

We see what we look for. Isn't that an interesting revelation? If we are looking for what is lovely—surroundings or traits in people that are beautiful, hope-filled, and encouraging—our attention will be drawn to those characteristics and circumstances first. We'll notice the good in the people and places around us. If we're expecting to be disappointed, disgusted, or dismayed, we'll find it, our attention skipping over the lovely to focus on the things that fit those criteria.

The question is what are we training our eyes to see? Looking for lovely doesn't mean we ignore ugly things, naive or blind to reality. It simply means we are searching out God in every person and every circumstance, looking for him at work in the world around us. If we're looking, we'll find him.

Lord, thank you for sunsets and rainstorms, for laughter and quiet conversations with dear friends, for favorite foods, scents, and sounds. Help us notice the lovely things around us each day.

-Julie

One Good Step: Make a list of five lovely things you encounter
in the people and places you go today.

Gift

There are different kinds of spiritual gifts, but the same Spirit is the source of them all. There are different kinds of service, but we serve the same Lord. God works in different ways, but it is the same God who does the work in all of us. A spiritual gift is given to each of us so we can help each other.

1 CORINTHIANS 12:4-7

"MAKE SURE YOU CHECK all the pockets!"

It was Christmas morning, and my sister had just opened a gift from my aunt and uncle: a beautiful new purse. While my grandma Jo was known for her gorgeous shoe collection, her daughter—my aunt Bernnetta—loved purses. Because she had all sons, rather than daughters, she frequently sent them to us for holidays and birthdays.

We'd learned, however, that she often placed other small items in the wrapping paper or tucked them into one of the side pockets. On at least one occasion, we overlooked the small surprise or accidentally threw it away with the paper. Now we knew better.

My aunt's gifts were always a delight to receive, not only because they were thoughtfully given but because we never knew what to expect. We had to look beyond the surface in order to discover the full gift.

In the same way, God has given each of us spiritual gifts. Sometimes they are obvious, like someone with a desire to teach others or a heart for hospitality. But many times they may be a skill we've overlooked, a hidden talent or aptitude that we shrug off as not holy enough or helpful enough for the Kingdom of God. Yet each of us has been given spiritual gifts, not so that they can remain hidden or go unused, but so that we can help each other. As members of the body of Christ, we are called and equipped to work together for the Kingdom of God. No one is immune or excluded or left out. Everyone's in. Everyone's included. And everyone has a gift.

Lord, thank you for the gifts you have given us. Help us to be faithful to use them. Amen.

-Kristin

One Good Step: List some of the gifts God has given you. What talents or aptitudes have you overlooked or not considered worthy of using for him?

Sacrifice

Don't forget to do good and to share with those in need.
These are the sacrifices that please God.
HEBREWS 13:16

WHEN OUR CHILDREN WERE YOUNG, we realized how absorbed they were by all of the gifts that they wanted for Christmas. They would begin making their lists months earlier—sometimes more than a page long, marking down everything that they wanted to receive. Their thoughts were consumed by all the potential gifts, and we realized we needed to make a change to shift their thinking.

We decided that each year our kids would receive three gifts, along with their stockings, but one gift would be something that they would pick out for someone else. We explained to our children that part of sacrifice is sharing with those in need. We ordered catalogs from Christian organizations that shared needs from around the world and offered us ways to help by buying farm animals for families, drilling wells for clean drinking water in communities, or helping kids receive health care services.

The first year we started this new tradition of sacrificing our wants to share with someone else, and every year since, my kids will spend hours scouring the magazines, reading about the needs of others and ways to help. Each of our kids picks their three top needs that they feel are important and then their final choice. After dinner one December evening, we sit and listen to everyone's top choices and why they picked their final choice. Once they've chosen their gifts to give to someone else, we pray over the people who will receive them, asking God to bless our small gift. It has become a favorite tradition, one my kids look forward to each year and has helped them to remain others focused, even while still asking for things that they want.

Often we can think that sacrifice has to be huge or involve suffering in some way, and although sometimes sacrifice is these things, more often than not sacrifice is done in daily, small or simple ways. Anytime we share with those who are in need, anytime we remember the poor and share out of what we've been given, that is also a sacrifice. And any sacrifice, big or small, pleases God when we are careful to focus on the needs of others.

Lord, thank you for sacrificing for us. Help us to follow your example and offer up sacrifices, both big and small, by meeting the needs of others. Amen.

-Kendra

One Good Step: Offer a sacrifice to God by meeting the needs of someone else.

Crave

Like newborn babies, you must crave pure spiritual milk so that you will
grow into a full experience of salvation. Cry out for this nourishment,
now that you have had a taste of the Lord's kindness.

1 PETER 2:2-3

FLIPPING MY BOOK UPSIDE DOWN, I placed it on the bed and vaulted to the floor. It was
midnight, and after doing hours of homework, there was only one thing I craved:
the salty, crunchy, chewy delight of chips and cheese. I'd been living in England for
a couple of months and quickly fell in love with the local snack.

At least a couple of times each week, my friends and I would walk to one of
the stands that dotted Oxford at night. Stores and most delis closed by 6 p.m., so
a late-night run to the closest chips-and-cheese stand provided the perfect study
break. Our favorite places were Toussain's, by the main bus stop, and Chef's Corner
in Bonn Square—privately and fondly referred to as "No nonsense," due to the
severe disposition of the proprietor's stalwart wife. Their flashing lights proclaiming
kebabs and—*be still, my heart*—chips and cheese. Chips are actually french fries,
and the cheese is grated, not nacho. Ketchup, mayonnaise, mustard, oil, vinegar,
and salt can also be added, although I preferred the original version.

My friends and I would quickly eat them up, but within a night or two I'd be
back. Cravings are funny things. We crave cheese because it contains L-tryptophan,
which improves mood and promotes relaxation. We crave chips because our body
is low on healthy fats. Or we crave something because we're trying to self-medicate
or overcompensate: one study showed that when people increase the number of
hours they sleep, they decrease their sugar intake.[6] Cravings are signals from our
body of something we lack.

Yet, as people, we are more than just bodies; we are also made of spirit. When
our spirit craves more time spent with Jesus, we can fulfill the longings of our soul
by reading his Word. But unlike the temporary comfort from fulfilling our body's
cravings, the satisfaction we find in his presence is long lasting.

Lord, help us to crave more of you. Amen.

-Kristin

One Good Step: Craving God's Word takes practice. Grab a three-by-five card
and write out a verse you'd like to focus on. Keep it in your pocket,
and take it out throughout the day to work on memorizing it.

---

6 King's College London, "Sleeping for Longer Leads to a Healthier Diet," EurekAlert! news release, January 9, 2018,
https://www.eurekalert.org/pub_releases/2018-01/kcl-sfl010818.php.

Befriend

A new commandment I give to you, that you love one another: just as I have loved you, you also are to love one another. By this all people will know that you are my disciples, if you have love for one another.
JOHN 13:34-35, ESV

WHAT AM I DOING HERE? I really only know Vanessa, so maybe I can make an excuse about work needing me and leave early. Kat's thoughts swirled uncomfortably as she watched the other women along on the birthday getaway weekend race back to their hotel rooms to grab sweaters. Walking toward the lobby, she spotted Terri sitting in one of the cozy chairs, ready to go. Gingerly sitting in the chair across from Terri, Kat panicked silently. She knew of and respected Terri but didn't know her personally and wasn't sure how to break the awkward silence.

Leaning forward, Terri did it for her by quietly asking, "What are you afraid of?"

"You!" Kat exclaimed, laughing nervously, hoping it came off as a joke, despite the truth in her voice.

Terri, a marriage and family therapist by training, nodded solemnly before walking over and giving Kat a hug, whispering, "You belong" in her ear , and then returning to her chair just as the others began rejoining them, chatting happily.

Terri is a befriender, a woman who actively puts the women around her at ease. She looks for the girl on the fringes, pulling her in and including her. She loves others well, with the divine insight and wisdom that comes straight from the Holy Spirit.

When God calls us to love one another, he is asking us to be befrienders—women who notice when someone feels uncomfortable and actively seek to bring her into the group, letting her know that she belongs. Befriending requires bravery, risking the rejection inherent in reaching out. It requires a willingness to engage in the slightly uncomfortable, slightly awkward conversations that come with getting to know a new person. It requires effort, an investment of time and energy not usually necessary with our oldest, deepest friendships. But the result of befriending is that the world will see who we belong to and want to join the family of God.

Lord, may we practice the art of befriending today. Amen.

-Julie

One Good Step: Practice striking up conversations as you wait in line, as you ride public transportation, as you go about your daily life.

Nudge

Come to me with your ears wide open.
Listen, and you will find life.

ISAIAH 55:3

I HAD PLANNED A PARTY where women could come and shop for products, and I hadn't invited Julie. I knew her well enough to know that she doesn't particularly like those kinds of parties and would rather not attend. We're good enough friends that she can be honest about it. It's one of the things I love about our relationship.

But as the week of the party approached, I felt a nudge to invite Julie. *That's silly,* I thought. *Julie doesn't even like these parties.* More than once the thought came to me to invite her, but I brushed it off.

The night of the party one woman, a mutual friend of Julie's and mine, showed up looking sad. She was going through a hard season and just needed to talk. I listened and offered encouragement, but as the night ended, I thought, *I wish Julie would have been here to offer a listening ear as well.*

The next morning I called Julie and told her about the party. "I would have come!" she said.

"Of course you would have, friend," I replied. "Why didn't I listen to that nudge earlier in the week? I guess I just thought it was silly and probably wouldn't have mattered. I should have told you to just stop by."

Because if there's one thing I know about Julie, she loves people and will take any opportunity to come alongside and love women in her life well. And I missed the nudge to invite her. We made a pact that day that we would listen to a nudge, even if it seemed futile, even if nothing came of it. We determined we would rather err on the side of listening than miss an opportunity from the Holy Spirit.

Learning to listen to the Holy Spirit takes time and intention. Sometimes we do well; other times life can get so busy, it drowns out his still, small voice. But God is continually gracious to us. He continues to speak to us, nudging us, each day. If only we'll open our ears to hear.

Lord, help us to listen to the nudge of the Holy Spirit today. Amen.

-Kendra

One Good Step: Listen for a nudge from the Holy Spirit and then take a step to act on what he tells you to do.

Approval

Am I now seeking the approval of man, or of God? Or am I trying to please man?
If I were still trying to please man, I would not be a servant of Christ.

GALATIANS 1:10, ESV

THE DAY I CHECKED the "inactive status" box on my law license renewal form, putting my law license into a category that allows me to keep it but prohibits me from giving advice or stepping into a courtroom, I wept. Accustomed to deeply satisfying, challenging work and the subtle authority introducing myself as an attorney brought, I was suddenly suffering from an acute identity crisis I'd arrogantly thought I'd already hashed out and left behind.

I was addicted to the approval of people, and the withdrawals were far more painful than I'd thought possible. What would colleagues think of me for quitting—was I a failed lawyer in their eyes? Would former clients and fellow businesswomen think I was yet another woman who opted out instead of leaning in, thereby failing my daughter's and granddaughter's generations?

I did what I could to avoid spaces and places filled with business connections that first year, not wanting to see disappointment or gleeful disdain in acquaintances' eyes, not wanting to explain that I didn't have a fabulous backup plan but had simply trusted God when he showed me that for me, it was my career or my family—not both. Several years later, I can honestly say that I have no regrets. God's way was far better, and he has given me new outlets for my skill sets.

Letting go of man's approval is a slow, painful process, one that I will likely wrestle with until my dying breath. Trusting God requires being okay with man's disapproval. God often asks things of us that are countercultural, a laying down of our prestige and power and wealth in unusual ways, a setting aside of our culture's indicia of success, a realigning of our lives with the red words of Jesus. But it's worth it.

Lord, show us where we are addicted to man's approval instead of seeking yours. What changes are you asking us to make? Help us seek your approval in those changes rather than man's. Amen.

-Julie

One Good Step: Sit in silence before God, asking him to show you where you are placing the approval of man over his. Make a change, today.

Renew

Those who hope in the LORD will renew their strength. They will soar on wings like eagles; they will run and not grow weary, they will walk and not be faint.

ISAIAH 40:31, NIV

WALKING DOWN THE ROWS, I ran my finger over the spines of books and breathed in the earthy, dusty smell of their pages. Thousands of books lay waiting in the quiet hush of the library, ready to be picked up and read. From fairy tales to science fiction, recipe books to graphic novels, the library is a place that fosters imagination, creativity, and knowledge.

Perhaps that's why visiting the library has always felt a little luxurious to me. All of those books, movies, and resources available at my fingertips—at no cost! Each time I walk out the door, bag straining with the weight, I feel lucky. Though I've had many library cards in my name—including the Bodleian Library at Oxford, a process that involved me giving an oath to the senior librarian that I would not deface the books or start anything on fire—each card I possess feels like a cross between a treasure map and a passport.

It's not simply checking books out and reading them that I like; it's also the process of renewing books that seems equally luxurious. After all, I never seem to have enough time, and being able to renew a book is a relief as much as it is a reminder.

When we renew a library book, we extend our hold on it. It serves as both a notification and permission to continue the course. But what does it mean to Christians to know that we, ourselves, should seek renewal? Why is it that hope is what renews us? Isaiah 40:31 tells us to renew our strength. The Hebrew word used for *renew* in that verse is *chalaph*, which means to pass on or away; elsewhere it means to change or replace. In this way, hope is a requirement for the constant renewal of our faith. It's what gives us permission and the push we need to continue seeking God and his will in our life, making us more effective and restoring our faith.

Lord, thank you that hope is the catalyst that renews our faith. Help us to constantly seek to renew our faith, hope, and trust in you. Amen.

-Kristin

One Good Step: In what ways has your faith been challenged lately? Meditate on Isaiah 40:31 and spend time praying for hope that leads to renewal.

Family

Now you Gentiles are no longer strangers and foreigners. You are citizens
along with all of God's holy people. You are members of God's family.

EPHESIANS 2:19

"FAMILIES DON'T HAVE TO MATCH."

It's a statement on a shirt I bought from a small organization raising funds for
foster care. As a foster and adoptive parent myself, I am always on the lookout for
others who are raising awareness and try as often as I can to partner with them.

This shirt in particular always gets a lot of curious questions as I'll explain my
family to strangers and acquaintances alike. Their responses are varied: some offer
us praise, others have follow-up questions about safety or birth families, but one
man's response in particular has stuck with me. He simply asked, "Why would you
do it?"

At first, I thought it was an obvious answer, but as I've continued to consider
his question, the real answer goes so much deeper than the surface things I could
say like, "it's the right thing to do," "we just love kids," or "it was modeled to us by
others." All of these answers would be true, but they don't really get to the heart
of why.

The truth is that Kyle and I have always had an overwhelming sense that we
have been brought into the family of God. That we are loved and accepted. And
we want nothing more than for others to experience that same sense of family, of
belonging. That's the real reason why we've brought kids in, adopting them into
our family as our own. We want to give out of what we've been so graciously given:
a family.

Families don't have to match. This is the whole truth surrounding the family of
God. There are no longer strangers or outsiders or foreigners. Everyone is welcome.
We are all members! And shouldn't our earthly families simply mirror our heavenly
one? If we are children of God, the answer is a resounding yes. There are no more
strangers or foreigners among us, only family.

*Lord, may we welcome others into our families, just as you have welcomed us
into yours. Amen.*

-Kendra

One Good Step: Who is someone around you that needs a family?
How could you invite them into yours?

Believe

Though you have not seen him, you love him. Though you do not now see him,
you believe in him and rejoice with joy that is inexpressible and filled with
glory, obtaining the outcome of your faith, the salvation of your souls.

1 PETER 1:8-9, ESV

"MOM, THE TOOTH FAIRY forgot to come last night," my daughter said, a hitch in her
tone. She was clearly devastated but trying to put on a brave face.

My eyes widened behind her back as I shot a dismayed look at my husband.

"Gosh, I'm sorry," I said soothingly. "Let me check with her and get back to
you, okay?"

"Okay," she said.

"Nice job, tooth fairy," my husband teased after she left the room. In our home,
I'm the tooth fairy, and normally I have no problems remembering to stash a dollar
on the dresser. Luckily for me, our particular tooth fairy has an email address, and
she sent my daughter a message later that day to apologize for being a little under
the weather and needing to reschedule.

On one hand it seems naive that kids would believe in a magical creature that
collects teeth. But in some ways, I envy children. As we grow into adulthood, it
becomes harder to believe. Disappointments happen. The world reveals its cruelty
and evil. And we struggle to hold on to the truth and the miracle of our belief in
Jesus and his love for the world.

I wonder if what we often lose when we shift to adulthood is the gift of imagination: the gift to see endless possibilities. And yet I've seen Jesus at work in my own
life and in the lives of others. I've experienced his comfort, his grace, his mercy.
And my experience combined with my decision to believe is what gives me faith.

Let's recover some of what we've lost. We can't see Jesus—and yet we wait. We
can't always understand what's going on—yet we trust his plan. We can't always
feel his presence—yet we love him. This belief requires us to look forward, focusing
ever and always on the inheritance in heaven that is "imperishable, undefiled, and
unfading" (1 Peter 1:4, ESV). That's a belief worth holding on to.

*Lord, thank you for your Son. Help us to hold tightly to the truth of what we
believe. Amen.*

-Kristin

One Good Step: In what ways have your beliefs changed over time?
What's the best way to hold on to the unshakable truth of Jesus?

Glory

Glory to God in the highest heaven, and on earth peace
to those on whom his favor rests.

LUKE 2:14, NIV

WHY THE SHEPHERDS? The question popped into my head as I read the Nativity story in Luke for the thousandth time. *What was God doing when he sent angels to the shepherds to declare Jesus' birth?*

My curiosity sparked research resulting in an entirely new understanding of the depth of meaning behind the Nativity story. It began a new, tender love for the shepherds, characters who previously seemed a bit of an afterthought as I placed their wooden figurines firmly off to the side of the holy family on my mantel every Christmas.

Culturally speaking, shepherds were nobodies. They held the lowest of positions in society, legally prohibited from testifying in court because their testimony was worthless and deemed unreliable. And yet a heavenly host appeared to them, filling the heavens with song as they declared the birth of the Messiah—arguably the second-best news (the first being Jesus' resurrection) the world has ever received. Why would God entrust such an important announcement made in so spectacular a fashion to societal outcasts whose word could not be trusted?

And, on the other end of Jesus' life, an angel announced to a woman—another people group prohibited from testifying in court—Jesus' resurrection, sending Mary as the sole witness back to the disciples (see John 20:1-2).

God intentionally announced the Messiah's birth and his resurrection from death to people without influence, position, or power. God is God, and he does not share his glory.

God sees the nobody, the outcast, the one deemed unacceptable and he *loves* them; he loves us. And he frequently uses nobodies to accomplish his will, because we don't take the glory for what we know was not possible under our own strength and ability. We give God glory when we point others always back to God, humbly acknowledging God's hand in our ministries and work.

Lord, thank you for choosing shepherds and women for your most important declarations. Thank you for using nobodies to accomplish your will. We linger before you this Christmas in reverent awe, acknowledging your glory. Amen.

-Julie

One Good Step: Share the story of the shepherds—how God sent a heavenly host to fill the heavens with song to a group of nobodies—with someone you love.

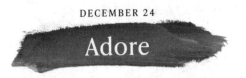

Adore

To us a child is born, to us a son is given, and the government will
be on his shoulders. And he will be called Wonderful Counselor,
Mighty God, Everlasting Father, Prince of Peace.

ISAIAH 9:6, NIV

CHRISTMAS WAS MY FAVORITE time of year as a child. I loved everything about the season, especially attending Christmas Eve services at our church. We would come to the church late at night, bundled up against the cold outside, the sanctuary dimly lit. We'd quietly enter and be handed a candle. Finding a pew, we'd sit and wait while the room slowly brightened as one candle was lit off another around the room, finally reaching our row. The piano would begin to softly play as some would stand and others sat. We would sing songs and carols and then take time to pray communally, remembering with gratitude the birth of Jesus. It was such a peaceful moment in our little community: I remember feeling completely safe and loved as we'd sing songs of adoration to Jesus.

Finally, we would finish the service with the chorus, "O come let us adore Him, Christ the Lord!" My heart always bursting with love and adoration for Jesus. Even today, I'll find myself humming this tune as I pull out Christmas decor and string lights. Taking time to truly adore Jesus with a grateful heart for coming to earth as a human being is my favorite part of the Christmas season.

He is to be adored. Not just for what he has done, but for simply who he is. Wonderful Counselor. Mighty God. Everlasting Father. Prince of Peace. These are just a few of his names that we remember, especially this time of year. And as I ponder who he is, I wonder, *Is there any better news than Jesus coming to earth? Than all that he offers to us?* The reconciliation and peace he ushers in is enough to adore him all year long, not just at Christmastime.

Lord, thank you for coming to earth. For offering us redemption. For being all that we need and all that we could ever hope for. We love you. We adore you. Amen.

-Kendra

One Good Step: Write down some of the names of Jesus that mean
the most to you, then spend a few moments adoring him.

Immanuel

While they were there, the time came for the baby to be born, and she gave
birth to her firstborn, a son. She wrapped him in cloths and placed him
in a manger, because there was no guest room available for them.

LUKE 2:6-7, NIV

I SPENT MUCH OF MY TIME as a child at my aunt and uncle's farm, the barn being a favorite place to play. My family had many animals that lived in the barn, and it was loud, stinky, and messy most of the time. The feeding troughs were rough, splintered pieces of wood nailed tightly and lined up in a row, filled with hay for the animals to eat. We loved to jump in them and play, but always left dirty with more than a few splinters.

When I ponder Jesus' birth, how he was born in a stable and placed in a manger, I remember my family's farm. I think about what that would be like—now as a mother—to birth a child in that sort of a space and then place my child in the manger. I don't know if I could do it. And yet, that is where God chose to make his arrival, to enter in as Immanuel—"God with us"—in the most humble of places (Matthew 1:23).

As I've thought about the Christmas story, I realize how much more it means that God would choose to come to us this way—by way of a stable and not a palace. I don't know that I could relate to someone who grew up in a palace. My growing years were good, but not anything fancy or regal. The fact that God would come to us this way reminds me that he is willing to meet us right where we are at—right in the middle of the mess of this life.

As we celebrate his birth, let's remember that Jesus came to earth in such a way that we could understand him. Let's not forget that he could empathize with us. Today and every day, let's remember that we can bring our messy moments to him, because he understands us and he meets us in the dark, splintery places of our lives with his love and mercy. He is with us.

Lord, thank you for being Immanuel, God with us. Amen.

-Kendra

One Good Step: How is God showing up as Immanuel in your life right now?

Harmony

Above all, clothe yourselves with love, which binds us
all together in perfect harmony.

COLOSSIANS 3:14

"WHAT COLOR IS THE SKY in your world? Do you always wear rose-colored glasses?" Her snappish remark, made in a moment of frustration, stung momentarily before I shrugged it off.

"Usually. I try, at least." I smiled wryly, refusing to take the bait with a snippy reply of my own, knowing her remark stemmed from deep frustration that had nothing to do with me. The tense moment defused, I turned the conversation back to the dilemma before us.

I try to live in harmony with others, assuming the best of people. And that can be an unpopular stance to take, especially in the midst of conflict. Everyone wants you on their side, agreeing wholeheartedly that the other side is ridiculous, malicious, or worse.

Assuming the best does not mean minimizing or excusing bad behavior, but it does require pausing to consider motivation and intentions, reflecting momentarily on why they are acting this way, considering what might be the real issue, and praying about how it can be resolved without allowing hurt feelings and offense to make things worse.

Attempting to live harmoniously requires us to be intentional about how we might live peacefully alongside another, despite differences of opinion and person-alities that tend to rub a little raw, especially with fellow believers. It does not mean we ignore shortcomings or turn a blind eye to issues that must be addressed. It does not require us to be doormats, allowing someone to run all over us. We can have healthy, harmonious boundaries.

Remember: God loves the people we don't particularly like and, perhaps, even long to loathe. People who irritate us are created in his image. They are loved by our Savior, no matter their flaws, and it would be wise of us to remember it lest we become the one guilty of sowing disharmony and discord, doing untold damage to the family of God in the eyes of a watching world.

Lord, may our default response to others be loving. Help us to live in harmony with fellow believers and those around us. Amen.

-Julie

One Good Step: Practice not taking the bait when someone else
does or says something inflammatory, praying silently how
you might defuse and redirect the situation instead.

Forever

The LORD is good. His unfailing love continues forever,
and his faithfulness continues to each generation.
PSALM 100:5

NOTHING SEEMS TO LAST FOREVER these days. A week after we moved into our house, the dishwasher went out. One week. Within a year, we'd replaced our other kitchen appliances, along with reinforcing the foundation we didn't know was crumbling. And it's not just things that break. Jobs and careers can shift and change over time. Relationships we think will be there forever don't always last.

It seems the more I try to cling to the things of the world, the easier they can slip through my fingers. And if I'm not careful, I can too easily put my hope in things that are fleeting, leading to disappointment and discouragement. But I am learning to look to the things that will last forever and let go of those that just won't. I'm starting to cling to things like God's love and forgiveness, mercy and grace. His presence and peace that will be with us always. These are the things that I can cling to, that won't slip through my fingers. God and his promises are what I can firmly place my trust and hope in each day.

We have all at times put our hope in things that didn't last. How many of us have suffered heartache or pain from people or circumstances that were fleeting? I'm sure every one of us. We are all in need of hope in something that will last forever, and we've found it in Jesus. He is what will last. His love. His grace. His peace. How amazing that no matter what we face in life, God is good and he is with us. His faithfulness is not just for us, but continues to each generation. His promise to be faithful is what will last forever. Of this we can be sure.

Lord, thank you for being good. We give you praise for your unfailing love for us that continues forever, lasting from generation to generation. Amen.

-Kendra

One Good Step: What have you tried to cling to lately that you know isn't going to last forever? How can you turn that person or situation over to God and rely on his promises that will hold true for eternity?

Faith

Faith is confidence in what we hope for
and assurance about what we do not see.

HEBREWS 11:1, NIV

MY FRIEND CEENA AND I have a pact. When God seemingly goes silent and life feels especially uncertain and chaotic for one of us, the other becomes the recounter of God's past faithfulness and the vocal reassurance of his current involvement.

The best way to see God's fingerprints is often in hindsight, and she and I are one another's faith historians. We gently remind one another of the times and ways in which God showed up in previous circumstances, recounting in detail how he provided exactly what we needed at exactly the right time, cleared an impossible path, or intervened in a way that was beyond our wildest hope. Because Ceena and I have objectivity, we can look for the fingerprints of God on a situation the other person cannot, and we actively point it out, standing in the gap with prayer and faith when the other's faith feels a bit tremulous.

And while I pray you find yourself a friend as loyal and loving as Ceena, you can be your own faith historian, collecting stories of God's faithfulness in your life, in the lives of your friends, neighbors, church members, storing up all the ways in which you witnessed God proving himself faithful and then recounting those stories to yourself—sometimes on repeat—in the midst of your current need. If you do not yet have your own stories or stories from those you know and trust, Scripture is replete with accounts of God's faithfulness in times of heartache and uncertainty. Ruth, Naomi, Rahab, Esther—some of my favorite women in Scripture—were met by God in the most incredible ways, despite their backstories. Faith grows when we feed it, and the best fuel I've found is reminding ourselves and others of God's past faithfulness when we feel utterly helpless and alone.

Lord, make us faith historians, storing up memories of other times and other places in which you've divinely intervened on our behalf or on behalf of someone close to us. Amen.

-Julie

One Good Step: Find a safe place to write down one-sentence reminders of times God has been faithful, adding to your list as you see God move. Meditate on these memories the next time your faith feels a bit shaky.

Experience

I want to know Christ and experience the mighty power that raised him from
the dead. I want to suffer with him, sharing in his death, so that one way
or another I will experience the resurrection from the dead!

PHILIPPIANS 3:10-11

As an undergraduate in England, I loved exploring Oxford. Our senior tutor constantly reminded us that we were in the land of *Alice in Wonderland*, and the fact that he carried a very large round clock with him everywhere made that whimsical idea seem like a logical comparison.

Though we share a language and a history, England is very different from the US. Ketchup is sweeter, and peanut butter is hard to find. "Digestives" have nothing to do with health; they're actually cookies. "Pudding" means dessert, mailboxes are "pigeonholes," and trucks are "lorries." There are double-decker buses zooming around, bells ring out from churches every fifteen minutes, and street performers often play the Scottish anthem on bagpipes. Not to mention the fact that the local Pizza Express has seventeenth-century paintings decorating their walls.

Though someone could have explained the differences, experiencing them was what made them real. If someone had mentioned ketchup, for instance, I would have assumed I understood what it was. But in reality, I would have missed the unique nature of the British item. Most of the time, experience is what gives us a more intimate understanding of the truth. We can understand the facts intellectually, but it's experience that influences us. Yet how can this translate to Christianity? We are told that we must take up our cross and follow Jesus in order to live a Christian life—but how is that possible?

Let's begin by loving the people Jesus loved (that's everyone) and serving the people Jesus served. Let's allow our hearts to be broken by the situations that pained him. Because it's only when we truly *live* like Jesus, seeking always to be transformed into his likeness, that we can begin to *experience* the truth of the parables he taught. When our book knowledge becomes heart knowledge—courtesy of a life lived in pursuit of Jesus—our understanding is deepened through experience. In this way, we can be united with him in both our suffering and our joy.

Lord, help us to seek experiences that honor you and help us to more fully understand you. Amen.

-Kristin

One Good Step: What is the difference between knowledge
and experience when it comes to your Christian walk?

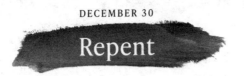

Repent

Prove by the way you live that you have repented of your sins and turned to God.

MATTHEW 3:8

"DAD, I'M SORRY I snuck the chocolate chips you were saving for cookies." Giving her dad a sad, puppy eye look, Sam tried to look repentant.

"This isn't the first or even the tenth time we're having a conversation about sneaking chocolate chips." Gently pulling her into a hug, he said, "Saying you are sorry without changing your behavior means that you are sorry you got caught. An apology in this situation isn't enough. I need to see changed behavior, repentance. You're grounded."

"Dad." Groaning, Sam handed him her phone. "Why do you have to be so strict? It's just chocolate chips."

"Oh, honey. This isn't about the chocolate chips; this is about apology without repentance."

As Sam's dad—my friend—told me about how a parenting tussle over chocolate chips had turned into a life lesson on repentance, I tucked several thoughts away for the long drive home.

Unrepentance, the willful and continued engaging in something sinful, something God has set a boundary around for our own health and well-being, is an uncomfortable place to pitch one's proverbial tent—I know from past experience. Choosing to live continually outside of the boundaries God sets for those who love and follow him puts us at increased risk of undesirable consequences and pulls us away from intimacy with God. In the story of the Prodigal Son, we are the wayward child, and God is the father, waiting, hoping, ready to throw a feast upon our return home, to him.

Friend, there is nothing, *nothing*, that is so dark, so awful, so sinful that you cannot get back to God. God redeemed Saul—a Pharisee who stood by approvingly as Stephen was martyred, a man who zealously hunted down Christians—into the beloved Paul, author of at least thirteen books in the New Testament. God offers second chances, fresh starts, clean slates, and redemption, but the price is repentance—both an apology and changed behavior.

Lord, remind us of our unrepentant sins, the dangerous things you've set protective boundaries around that we insist upon dabbling in. Invite us into repentance and a renewed intimacy with you. Amen.

-Julie

One Good Step: What do you need to repent from? If it requires a significant life change, make an implementation plan and recruit an accountability partner as you repent.

End

Before the Passover celebration, Jesus knew that his hour had come
to leave this world and return to his Father. He had loved his disciples
during his ministry on earth, and now he loved them to the very end.

JOHN 13:1

I'M ALWAYS A LITTLE CONFLICTED about New Year's Eve. On one hand, it's great to have
an excuse to celebrate with friends and family. But as I get older, I'm equally likely
to be fast asleep by the time the glittering ball drops in Times Square. I'd much
rather see midnight arrive on a quiet breath than with a loud bang.

The day itself is always a mix of emotions too. There's nostalgia over the end of
another year, mixed with the heady promise of expectations for the one to come.
The final day of the year is an end, a time to reflect on a change that has happened
in the past year, a shift in perspective we've experienced, or a loved one we've lost.
It's bittersweet.

Yet we know that beginnings and endings are inseparable. Scripture talks about
how, just before Passover, Jesus knew that his time on earth was coming to an end.
Perhaps it was a little bittersweet for him, too. Because instead of blithely passing
over the moment—focusing on his return to the Father or the work his disciples
would accomplish after his death and resurrection—he paused. He didn't simply
reflect on the end or the beginning that would follow. Instead, he concentrated on
what remained constant; he focused on love. By now, his disciples were not simply
companions but friends. Jesus had loved them during his ministry, and in this in-
between moment, he continued to love them.

If we're honest, there are times when we can feel unlovable—days when doors
close or dreams end, when new beginnings seem out of reach. But even as Jesus left
this world and his earthly ministry, his disciples—and us, by extension—were not
forgotten. We were always loved, always wanted. Our Jesus is the same yesterday,
today, and forever. His love transcends all endings and beginnings, years past and
years to come.

We were loved—to the end. What a humbling, marvelous truth.

*Lord, thank you that you have loved us always, in every circumstance. Help us to
remember that every end is also a beginning, and that your love covers us through it
all. Amen.*

-Kristin

One Good Step: What endings have you experienced this year?
What beginnings are you anticipating?

About the Authors

After a fifteen-year career as a lawyer, JULIE FISK decided to follow her childhood dream of becoming an author. She shifted her storytelling from courtrooms and boardrooms to dinner tables and backyard barbecues, where she uncovers truth about faith, kindness, and friendship. Together with her cofounders of The Ruth Experience, Julie connects with thousands of women online through real, raw stories of living out faith. When she's not writing or speaking, you can find Julie with her husband and their two kids filling their home and backyard with friends.

Do it afraid. KENDRA ROEHL has sought to live out that advice as a social worker, foster parent, mother of five, and public speaker. She has a master's degree in social work and has naturally become a defender of those in need, serving others in hospice, low-income housing, and veterans' affairs programs. Kendra and her husband are well-known advocates for foster care, taking in more than twenty children in six years and adopting three of them. As a cofounder of The Ruth Experience, she continues to care for others as a frequent speaker and an author of several books.

A career in journalism set KRISTIN DEMERY up to one day publish her own stories of living this wild, precious life. She is now an author of several books and part of a trio of writers collectively known as The Ruth Experience. Kristin served as a newspaper and magazine editor, and her work has been featured in a variety of publications, including *USA Today*. She still works behind the scenes as an editor for others while writing her own series on kindness, friendship, and living with intention. An adventurer at heart, she loves checking items off the family bucket list with her husband and three daughters.

Visit them online at TheRuthExperience.com.

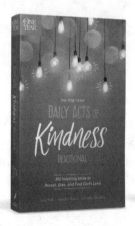